T0299079

The Political Economy of Trade Policy

Theory, Evidence and Applications

World Scientific Studies in International Economics
(ISSN: 1793-3641)

The complete list of the published volumes in the series can be found at
http://www.worldscientific.com/series/wssie

51 World Scientific
Studies in
International
Economics

The Political Economy of Trade Policy

Theory, Evidence and Applications

Devashish Mitra

Syracuse University, USA

World Scientific

Published by

World Scientific Publishing Co. Pte. Ltd.

5 Toh Tuck Link, Singapore 596224

USA office: 27 Warren Street, Suite 401-402, Hackensack, NJ 07601

UK office: 57 Shelton Street, Covent Garden, London WC2H 9HE

Library of Congress Cataloging-in-Publication Data
Names: Mitra, Devashish, author.
Title: The political economy of trade policy : theory, evidence and applications /
    by Devashish Mitra (Syracuse University, USA).
Description: 1 Edition. | Hackensack, NJ : World Scientific, 2016. | Series:
    World scientific studies in international economics |
    Includes bibliographical references and index.
Identifiers: LCCN 2015040491 (print) | ISBN 9789814569149 (hardcover) |
    ISBN 9814569143 (hardcover)
Subjects: LCSH: Commercial policy. | International trade.
Classification: LCC HF1411 .M5548 2016 (print) | DDC 382/.3--dc23
LC record available at http://lccn.loc.gov/2015040491

British Library Cataloguing-in-Publication Data
A catalogue record for this book is available from the British Library.

In-house Editor: Alisha Nguyen

Typeset by Stallion Press
Email: enquiries@stallionpress.com

Printed in Singapore

About the Author

Devashish Mitra is Professor of Economics and Cramer Professor of Global Affairs at the Maxwell School of Citizenship & Public Affairs, Syracuse University. He was the Chair of the Economics Department at Syracuse University from 2006 to 2010. He is coeditor of *Economics and Politics* (2006–present) and *Indian Growth and Development Review* (2014–present). In addition, he is/has been associate editor of the *European Economic Review* (2012–2015), *Journal of Development Economics* (2010–present), *Journal of International Economics* (2006–2015), *International Journal of Business and Economics* (2004–present) and *International Review of Economics and Finance* (2004–present) and an editorial board member of other journals including the *Review of International Economics* (2009–present). Professor Mitra is also a member of the trade program of the International Growth Centre, UK based at the LSE and Oxford, a fellow of the CESifo network, a research professor at the Ifo Institute, Munich and a research fellow at the IZA, Bonn.

Professor Mitra's research and teaching interests are in International Trade, Political Economy and Development Economics. More specifically, he has worked on the role of politics in the determination of trade policy and on the impact of trade on productivity and labor market outcomes. He is currently working on the impact of trade on employment, labor shares and unionization. His work has been published in well-known journals like *American Economic Review, Review of Economics & Statistics, Economic Journal, Journal of International Economics* and *Journal of Development Economics*. He holds a Ph.D. in Economics from Columbia University.

Contents

**Part III. Political Contributions Approach
         to Endogenous Trade Policy: Empirics   161**

**Part IV. Endogenous Choice of Policy
         Instruments: Theory and Empirics   199**

Preface

This volume is a collection of my coauthored as well as solo-authored papers on the political economy of trade policy, written over more than a decade. On this broad topic I have had long and very fruitful collaborations with my coauthors, Pushan Dutt (INSEAD), Pravin Krishna (SAIS, Johns Hopkins University), Dimitrios D. Thomakos (University of Peloponese) and Mehmet A. Ulubasoglu (Deakin University). Without these interactions, these papers would not have been possible. I thank my coauthors as well as the original publishers of these papers for giving me permission to reprint them in this volume.

My work on the political economy of trade policy started during my doctoral dissertation days at Columbia University. In fact, the title of my PhD dissertation was *Essays in the Political Economy of Trade Policy*. I owe my interest in the field of international trade to my three teachers and advisors at Columbia, namely Jagdish Bhagwati, Ronald Findlay and Dani Rodrik. I was lucky to have been a student of these three giants of the field. I thank all of them for their very helpful guidance when I was a doctoral student and Dani in particular for getting me started on this topic of political economy.

My research agenda in the political economy of trade policy, that started at Columbia, continued when I became a faculty member at Florida International University and then at Syracuse University. I am indebted to all three institutions for their support and for providing me with the right intellectual environment for my research.

The publishers, who presently have the copyrights for the published articles reprinted in this volume, have granted permission to include them in this volume. In alphabetical order, they are the American Economic Association (Chapter 1), Elsevier (Chapters 2, 3, 4, 6 and 8), MIT Press

(Chapters 5 and 9), John Wiley & Sons (Chapters 10, 11 and 12), Palgrave Macmillan (Chapter 13) and Emerald Group Publishing (Chapter 15).

Finally, I would like to thank the late Bob Stern, who invited me to put together this volume. I consider this invitation a great honor.

Devashish Mitra
Syracuse, New York, USA
July, 2015

Political Economy of Trade Policy:
An Introduction

We are all familiar with the gains from trade, arising from exchange and specialization, greater variety of goods consumed or used as inputs into production and greater market competition. Since we understand well the benefits of free trade, we need to explain departures from it in the real world. The last three decades have seen the emergence of the political economy models in international trade that try to explain the existence and the extent of the anti-trade bias in trade policy. Some of these models also try to explain why more efficient policy instruments have not been used. While this literature started out as primarily theoretical, the last decade and a half has seen an explosion of empirical work in this area, which has been able to uncover industry-specific and country-specific determinants of protection.

Part I. Endogenous Lobby Formation: Implications for Endogenous Trade Policy

I started working in this area more than a couple of decades ago as a doctoral student at Columbia University. My interest in this line of research began after reading an initial draft of a handbook chapter by Dani Rodrik on this topic. Dani, who was then a professor at Columbia, brought to my attention a major weakness of the existing literature: who gets to lobby the government was predetermined in all political economy models of trade policy. He suggested that addressing this issue could be an important contribution, and I immediately started working on this idea. In other words, I worked on a model of endogenous trade policy where lobby formation was also endogenous, i.e., whether a sector is politically organized or not is endogenously determined. The subject of this idea is Chapter 1 in this collection of my solo-authored and coauthored papers.

The initial version of Chapter 1, which was part of my doctoral dissertation, only had the case with symmetric sectors. This meant that while nothing could be said about the specific distinguishing characteristics of a sector that would make it more likely to be politically organized than another sector, the model did throw light on the equilibrium proportion of sectors that would be politically organized or would form lobbies as a function of country-level characteristics such as the government's responsiveness to political lobbies and the degree of asset inequality in a country. This would also be an additional channel through which these country characteristics would determine the overall nature of trade policy. My dissertation version of this paper used a very simple political support function framework, where the government maximized a weighted sum of welfare levels of the various factor owners, with the politically organized ones getting higher weights.

The final version of this paper, which was published in the *American Economic Review*, is what is included in this collection (Chapter 1). It is different from the initial version in two main respects. It incorporates the Grossman and Helpman (1994) "Protection for Sale" framework (with menu auctions) more explicitly. Thus, with the government's objective function being a weighted sum political contributions and aggregate welfare, political contributions now get factored into the lobby formation decision. At the same time, it has a section that is devoted to an extension to asymmetric industries. Through this asymmetry I am able to shed some light on which type of industries get politically organized in equilibrium.

The main results of this study are (1) free trade can not only be a consequence of aggregate welfare maximization but also of aggregate political contributions maximization by the government; (2) greater asset inequality leads to an increase in the formation of lobbies and at the same time greater trade protection; and (3) industries facing relatively inelastic demand, with high levels of capital stock, with fewer capitalists and that are geographically less dispersed, are the ones more likely to get politically organized in equilibrium.

The next two chapters look at the theoretical applications of this idea of lobby formation or political organization. Chapter 2 applies this idea to trade agreements, while Chapter 3 (coauthored with Pravin Krishna) shows how unilateral trade liberalization by one country can induce reciprocity by its trading partner. In Chapter 2, there is an import-competing sector whose capitalists decide whether they should incur the costs of political organization. If they do decide to incur these costs then they are represented by a lobby that bargains with the government over an import tariff and political contributions. In this bargaining, the contributions will at the very least compensate the government for the welfare loss arising out of the tariff. In many cases they will not cover the costs associated with resources lost during the process of political organization. Thus, prior to the political organization decision the government might have an incentive to commit to a free trade agreement. Whether the government will want to sign such an agreement or not will depend on the size of the political organization costs, the bargaining power of the government relative to the import-competing lobby and the government's weight on aggregate welfare relative political contributions.

The idea is similar to that of Maggi and Rodriguez-Clare (1997) in that in both models there is a cost incurred prior to the lobbying taking place. In their model, capitalists decide which sector (import-competing or export) to put their capital in. This investment is made by factoring in the possibility of protection to the import-competing sector down the road. This leads to a distortion in resource allocation and has welfare costs for which the lobby does not compensate the government during their bargaining as those costs are sunk in that they already have been incurred prior to the bargaining. In my model, there is no capital mobility. In fact, capital is used only in the import-competing sector. Similar to the Maggi and Rodriguez-Clare framework there are costs (those in political organization) in my model that are incurred prior to lobbying.

Chapter 3 (which is coauthored with Pravin Krishna) looks at the question of "reciprocated unilateralism," once again using the idea of lobby formation. There is a pre-existing import-competing lobby in the foreign country, but the specific factor owners in the export sector there are not politically organized to begin with. When the home country liberalizes its trade policy (reduces the tariff on its imports) it increases demand for the foreign country's exports. This expands the potential market for the foreign country's exports. This leads to the formation of an export lobby in the foreign country that neutralizes the import-competing lobby there and brings about trade liberalization in the foreign country. Therefore, if we take into account possible lobby formation or political organization effects we can see that trade liberalization in one country, by creating export lobbies in its trading partners, will lead to the reciprocation of that liberalization, i.e., there will also be trade liberalization in the foreign country.

Part II. Majority Voting and Ideology: Implications for Endogenous Trade Policy

There are two main approaches used to the modeling of endogenous trade policy. One is the lobbying approach that we discussed above. The other uses the median-voter approach. Let's say voters differ from each other (are heterogeneous) along one dimension (a single individual characteristic). Let's also assume that an individual's most preferred trade policy is an increasing function of the variable describing this characteristic. If we rank individuals in increasing or decreasing order of this characteristic, then the median individual's most preferred policy, say the level of import protection that maximizes the welfare of this median individual, cannot be beaten by any other level of protection under majority voting. This also would be the trade policy in a Nash equilibrium under political competition between two parties, whose sole objective is to win elections. This approach was used within a two-sector, two-factor Heckscher-Ohlin framework by Mayer (1984). In this framework, if the two factors of production are labor and capital, both fully mobile between the two sectors, then trade or trade protection benefits one factor and hurts the other. While protection benefits the scarce factor and hurts the abundant factor, trade openness benefits the abundant factor and hurts the scare factor. This comes straight from the well-known Stolper-Samuelson theorem. Thus trade protection benefits labor in capital-abundant (rich) countries, while it hurts labor in labor-abundant countries.

In all countries, the majority are mainly owners of their labor, so most of their income is labor income. This means that there is inequality in every country. As a result, with the application of the median-voter approach in the presence of inequality, we should see positive import protection in equilibrium in rich countries but negative import protection in poor or labor-abundant countries. While this prediction of the model is consistent with what we observe in rich countries, it is not consistent with what we observe in labor abundant countries. In that case, is the median-voter approach totally useless? Or is the Heckscher-Ohlin framework, with its assumption of perfect mobility of factors between sector, not capturing important aspects of the real world?

There are many possible and plausible reasons for a positive level of protection seen everywhere. One of them arises from terms-of-trade effects, which has recently been captured within a median-voter, Heckscher-Ohlin framework by Dhingra (2014). In Chapter 4 (coauthored with

Pushan Dutt), we take the view that while the exact level and orientation of trade protection might not be predicted by Mayer's median-voter, Heckscher-Ohlin model, it might be able to explain variations in trade policies across countries and over time. Greater asset inequality would lead to a greater demand for redistribution towards labor as the median voter derives most of her income from her labor. This means that greater inequality should lead to higher protection in capital-abundant countries and lower protection in capital-scarce countries. This is the hypothesis we test in Chapter 4 (with Pushan Dutt) using cross-country data and find considerable evidence in support of it.

While a prolabor redistribution comes from majority voting since asset inequality is unequal in all countries, it can also come from a left-wing government in power. A right-wing government, on the other hand, would redistribute less towards labor. Thus, trade policy will depend on the ideological orientation or the political valence of the party in power. This arises either because who the constituents of a political party are depends on its ideology or the ideology itself determines where the trade-off between equity and efficiency needs to be resolved. Marrying the Stolper-Samuelson theorem with this idea of ideology, moving left in the political ideology spectrum of the government in power should lead to an increase in trade protection in capital-abundant countries while it is expected to lead to a reduction in trade protection in capital-scarce countries. This is what we empirically study in Chapter 5 (coauthored with Pushan Dutt) using cross-country data and find considerable support for our hypothesis.

In Chapter 6 (also with Pushan Dutt), we look at a model that encompasses both the above ideology hypothesis as well as the inequality (median-voter) hypothesis. Using cross-national data, we find that both ideology of the government as well as the degree of inequality are important determinants of trade policy.

In Chapter 7 (again coauthored with Pushan Dutt), we extend our ideology and inequality hypotheses to agricultural protection, adding to them the possibility of sector specificity of factors of production, lobbying and public finance considerations. Once again both ideology and inequality turn out to be important. However, here we find support for the sector-specificity of labor. Interestingly, while lobbying is found to be more important in developed countries, the public finance consideration of raising revenues turns out to be more important in the case developing countries.

The final chapter (coauthored with Pravin Krishna) in this section, Chapter 8, is a different application of the majority voting approach.

It is a completely theoretical paper that once again looks at the issue of "reciprocated unilateralism," studied in Chapter 3, through a completely different lens. In this paper we show that a unilateral trade reform in a partner country, by shifting the terms of trade in favor of the home country, creates a higher relative wage in favor of the export sector at home, leading to an expansion of that sector. As a result, the popular support for reform at home increases. In a two-country framework, we also find the possibility of multiple majority voting equilibria — protection in both countries or free trade in both countries. Thus unilateral trade liberalization by one country can move the equilibrium to the one with free trade in both countries.

Part III. Political Contributions Approach to Endogenous Trade Policy: Empirics

There are two chapters in this section, Chapters 9 and 10 that are both coauthored with Dimitrios Thomakos and Mehmet Ulubasoglu. They are both on the empirical investigation of the Grossman and Helpman (1994) "Protection for Sale" model, which takes the political contributions approach to modeling trade policy. The government maximizes a weighted average of aggregate welfare and political contributions, while each lobby maximizes its own welfare net of its contributions. The lobbies first present their respective contribution schedules, each of which is a function of the tariff vector. In the next stage, taking these contribution schedules as given, the government maximizes its objective function. The political equilibrium tariff on the imports of a good is inversely related to its import demand elasticity and the import penetration ratio in the case of a politically organized sector. Other things equal, a politically organized sector gets greater import protection (import tariff) than an unorganized sector. Also, the import protection given to a politically organized sector decreases with the proportion of the country's population that is politically organized and the weight the government attaches to aggregate welfare in its objective function. The above results (with respect to industry characteristics and country characteristics) for unorganized sectors go in the opposite direction. We test these predictions in Chapter 9 using three-digit industry-level data for Turkey for multiple years spanning democratic and dictatorial regimes. Note here that Turkey is truly a small open economy, an assumption of the Grossman-Helpman model.

As found in the case of the US, the estimated weight on aggregate welfare is many times the weight on contributions. In our case, it is

60–100 times depending on the specification and year. Also, the weight attached to aggregate welfare turns out to be higher in the democratic regime relative to the dictatorial regime. Another result, that is similar to the result for the US, is that a very large proportion, in the range of around 60–90 percent, of the overall population is politically organized.

The extremely high weight on welfare and the high proportion of the population politically organized do not seem plausible and are mutually inconsistent as the first result means there is limited incentive for lobby formation. Chapter 10 deals exactly with this issue for both US and Turkey. Several changes to specification, such as treating all sectors as organized, restricting focus to net importing sectors, making adjustment to the import-demand elasticity measures, etc., are carried out. These modifications give us possible estimated parameter combinations that look much more plausible than what was there in the earlier empirical literature. It is important to note here that our tests favor treating all sectors as organized.

Part IV. Endogenous Choice of Policy Instruments: Theory and Empirics

Chapters 11 (solo-authored) and 12 (coauthored with Dimitrios Thomakos and Mehmet Ulubasoglu) deal with the issue of the choice of policy instruments. If the government redistributes income to its favored groups, then why does it use trade policy to do so? There are other policies, such as direct subsidies, which are much more efficient in that they can result in a given amount of redistribution causing a smaller loss in aggregate welfare. Rodrik (1986) showed that this welfare ranking can be reversed when we compare endogenous tariffs with endogenous subsidies, since there is a free rider problem associated with lobbying for tariffs as it protects all firms in a particular import-competing industry. Subsidies, on the other hand, can, in principle, be firm specific. In Chapter 11, I argue that even the capitalists in an import-competing industry might prefer tariffs to subsidies. Since subsidies come from a common pool of government revenues (and there are costs to raising additional revenues), lobbying for a firm-specific subsidy by one firm leads to negative, congestion externality on other firms. Thus there is too much lobbying and a higher than optimal level of subsidies overall for the capitalists as a group. In the case of lobbying for a tariff its general nature (as opposed to the firm-specific nature of the subsidy) creates a positive externality in lobbying when lobbying is done by individual firms (rather than through an industry lobby). In addition, there is still the possibility of a congestion externality because the cost to the government of providing these concessions is increasing and convex in aggregate concessions provided. Given that these are offsetting externalities, lobbying for tariff might lead to an optimal amount of protection for capitalists in the industry as a group. Thus, the capitalists might prefer tariffs to subsidies due to several reasons. Even when there is an industry association, it is possible to coordinate lobbying for a tariff but in the case of a subsidy additional lobbying on the side (for which there turn out to be incentives) by individual firms cannot be prevented by the industry association.

From theory in Chapter 11 we move to the empirics of the choice of instruments in Chapter 12 (coauthored with Dimitrios Thomakos and Mehmet Ulubasoglu). Our empirical investigation about the mix of protection (import tariff) and promotion (production subsidy) is guided by the theoretical literature on this question. As in the case of our investigation of the Grossman and Helpman (1994) "Protection for Sale" model, we again use Turkish three-digit industry-level data from 1983 to 1990. The ratio of protection to promotion is inversely related to the ratio of import-demand elasticity to the output supply elasticity and to the import penetration ratio and positively related to the degree of concentration within an industry. This means the ratio of protection to promotion is inversely related to the ratio of their respective marginal welfare costs and to the degree of free rider problem in lobbying. The more concentrated an industry is, the less severe is the free-rider problem in lobbying expected to be.

Part V. Political Economy of Trade Policy: Surveys of the Literature with Applications

Chapters 13 and 14 are literature surveys. While Chapter 13 is solo-authored, Chapter 14 is coauthored with Pravin Krishna. Chapter 13 was an entry for the second edition of the _New Palgrave Dictionary of Economics_. It surveys the two main approaches to the political economy of trade policy, namely the median-voter approach and the special-interest approach. The applications of these two approaches to policy issues such as trade agreements, unilateralism versus reciprocity, regionalism versus unilateralism, hysteresis in trade policy, choice of policy instruments, etc., are discussed. The empirical literature is discussed, with an emphasis on the new "structural" approach.

Finally, Chapter 14 (coauthored with Pravin Krishna) surveys the various alternative political-economy approaches to unilateralism in trade policy. The focus is on the possible causal connections between unilateralism and reciprocity in trade policy, i.e., whether unilateral trade liberalization by one country can lead to reciprocal liberalization by its partner in the absence of bilateral negotiations.

Part VI. Conclusions

The collection of papers in this volume are on a broad range of topics falling in the area of the political economy of trade policy. I hope putting all these papers in one place will create a handy resource for researchers and students.

References

Dhingra, Swati (2014). "Reconciling Observed Tariffs and the Median Voter Model," *Economics and Politics* 26(3), 483–504.

Grossman, Gene M and Elhanan Helpman (1994). "Protection for Sale," *American Economic Review* 84(4), 833–50.

Maggi, Giovanni and Andres Rodriguez-Clare (1998). "The Value of Trade Agreements in the Presence of Political Pressures," *Journal of Political Economy* 106(3), 574–601.

Mayer, Wolfgang (1984). "Endogenous Tariff Formation," *American Economic Review* 74(5), 970–985.

Rodrik, Dani (1986). "Tariffs, Subsidies, and Welfare with Endogenous Policy," *Journal of International Economics* 21(3–4), 285–299.

Part I

Endogenous Lobby Formation:
Implications for Endogenous Trade Policy

Chapter 1

Endogenous Lobby Formation and Endogenous Protection: A Long-Run Model of Trade Policy Determination

By Devashish Mitra*

This paper provides a theory of lobby formation within a framework in which trade policy is determined through political contributions. Under certain conditions, free trade turns out to be an equilibrium outcome either when the government has a high affinity for political contributions or when it cares a great deal about social welfare. Moreover, greater inequality in asset distribution results in a greater number of lobbies and, in most cases, more protection for each of these lobbies. Furthermore, industries with higher levels of capital stock, fewer capitalists, more inelastic demand, and smaller geographical dispersion are the ones that get organized. (JEL F10, F13)

The idea that government policy is determined through the interaction between organized interest groups and politicians is not new in the economics literature. In fact, there is an entire body of literature called the "New Political Economy" which uses such a framework to analyze economic policy determination. According to Ronald Findlay (1991), "this framework portrays the state as passive and emphasizes the efforts of interest groups through the intermediation of political parties whose only concern is electoral success." Pressure-group models originate from economic theories of regulation which show how the political process favors organized groups or industries over unorganized ones. In the

* Department of Economics, Florida International University, Miami, FL 33199 (e-mail: mitrad@fiu.edu). I am indebted to Dani Rodrik, my dissertation sponsor at Columbia University, for very helpful comments, suggestions, guidance, and encouragement. I am also grateful to Jagdish Bhagwati and Ronald Findlay for helpful discussions and encouragement throughout this project. I would also like to thank Arnab Basu, Alessandra Casella, Shubham Chaudhuri, Pravin Krishna, Philip Lane, Steve Matusz, John McLaren, Paul Pecorino, Costas Syropoulos, Daniel Trefler, and seminar participants at Baruch College, Columbia University, Florida International University, the University of Toronto, the Midwest International Economics Conference (Fall 1996), and the Southeastern International Trade Conference (Fall 1996) for useful comments and discussions. Finally, special thanks are due to two anonymous referees and Cem Karayalcin for detailed comments on earlier drafts of this paper. The standard disclaimer applies.

classic George Stigler (1971) paper, members of a pressure group decide on resources devoted to lobbying in order to maximize their total income net of lobbying expenditure and the legislators supply protection or regulation to maximize votes. At the margin, the votes gained through political contributions are balanced by those lost from supplying protection. Sam Peltzman (1976) formalizes the Stigler model and investigates the determinants of the supply of regulation. He argues that the size of the benefits to organized interest groups is limited by the fact that the government is also to a certain extent concerned about the interests of the rest of the population. Similarly, Gary Becker (1983) argues that the deadweight loss that a policy generates imposes a natural limit to the gains that interest groups can extract.

In the last two decades, the "New Political Economy" framework has been applied extensively to issues of trade policy formulation. The pioneering model in this literature is Findlay and Stanislaw Wellisz (1982). It is a two-sector model in which production in each sector is carried out using a factor of production specific to that sector and an economywide general factor, namely, labor. Both types of specific factor owners are fully organized and they lobby against each other. This simple model makes the strong point that there exists an equilibrium tariff determined through the Nash interaction between these two opposing groups.

Another important contribution to the endogenous trade policy literature is the political support function approach pioneered by Arye L. Hillman (1989). Under such an approach, the government's objective function (also called the political support function) incorporates its preferential treatment of an organized industry as well as the cost of protecting this industry given by the excess burden to society.[1]

The political economy literature on trade policy has evolved from the simple Findlay-Wellisz model to the state-of-the-art Gene M. Grossman and Elhanan Helpman (1994) model.[2] The latter is pathbreaking for several reasons. Firstly, its framework is multisectoral. Secondly, it provides microfoundations to the behavior of organized lobbies and politicians. Moreover, the level of protection for each industry is derived as a function of industry characteristics and other political and economic factors. In the Grossman-Helpman model, organized lobbies make political contributions to get trade policies in their favor and against the unorganized population.[3]

The above-mentioned models provide a description of policy that emerges in the presence of organized interest groups. The next natural questions to ask are how these organized lobbies come into existence and what determines their equilibrium number. In this paper, I try to address this important issue and study the interaction between lobby formation and economic policy determination. The tradition in the formal economics literature has been to focus on one kind of policy at a time. Following this tradition, I focus only on one specific type of policy, namely, trade policy. Treating the existing political economy literature as the second

stage, I add a first stage in which agents with common interests decide whether or not to incur the costs of getting organized. In doing so, they take into account the benefits from organization they can obtain in the second stage and the losses they would incur by remaining unorganized. The framework used for the second stage is borrowed from Grossman and Helpman (1994).

Endogenizing lobby formation provides quite a few surprising, new insights.[4] Besides improving our understanding of trade policy formulation, these new insights emphasize the need for extending the modeling of lobby formation to aspects of the political economy literature other than trade policy.

The most surprising result I obtain is that the equilibrium trade subsidy (import tariff in the case of an importable and export subsidy for an exportable) for an organized group is no longer always positively related to the government's affinity for political contributions. In certain cases, the level of ad valorem trade subsidy for each organized group turns out to be decreasing in this affinity for political contributions.[5] Moreover, when everyone in the population owns a specific factor, free trade is an equilibrium outcome either when the government is highly responsive to political contributions or when decision-making is highly social welfare oriented. A high affinity on the part of the government for political contributions leads to the formation of a large number of opposing lobbies which cancel each other out. Though surprising, these results are entirely consistent with what is observed in the United States where the government's decision-making can be considered to be highly responsive to special

---

[1] Hillman and Heinrick W. Ursprung (1988), Hillman (1990, 1991), and Hillman and Peter Moser (1996) are interesting applications of the political support function approach to issues of international industry regulation, the relationship between market structure and equilibrium protection, bilateral exchange of trade concessions, and the relationship between domestic politics and foreign interests.

[2] Applications of this prevailing framework to issues of trade negotiations and free-trade areas are Grossman and Helpman (1995a, b).

[3] See Dani Rodrik (1995) for a detailed and insightful survey of the literature on the political economy of trade policy. For an in-depth comparison of the different approaches within a unified framework, see Helpman (1995).

[4] The theory of lobby formation used here is derived from models of endogenous market structure in industrial organization theory. (Oligopoly models with a given number firms are the ones with exogenous market structure, while those with fixed costs of entry for firms are the endogenous market structure models. In the latter, the number of firms is endogenously determined.) Moreover, the microfoundations of lobby formation have been worked out in this paper using communication based refinements of the Nash equilibrium.

[5] This result is in sharp contrast to the Grossman-Helpman result where taking the existence of organized groups as given, the trade subsidy for each organized group is monotonically increasing in the government's affinity for political contributions.

interests and political contributions.[6] This kind of decision-making has led to the formation of a large number of political action committees.[7] On the other hand, the trade regime in the United States can be considered to be close to free trade.

The paper also looks at the implications of changes in the distribution of asset ownership for trade taxes and subsidies, which again is a much-neglected aspect of the current literature.[8] A greater degree of inequality of asset distribution (brought about by a higher level of asset deprivation) results in the formation of a larger number of lobbies, each of which gets a higher trade subsidy (except in the homogeneous fixed-costs case where the trade subsidy on each

---

[6] Sharyn O'Halloran (1994) argues that the U.S. legislature has always been more powerful in the area of trade policy than the executive. When the president has been from the majority party in the Congress, the legislature on its own has delegated the function of trade policy formulation to the executive in order to resolve the conflicting forces (i.e., cancel the net opposing forces) of different organized interest groups and at the same time avoid responsibility towards them. In other words, in the United States, through the pressures of opposing lobbies on it, it is ultimately the legislature that directly or indirectly determines trade policy. Since legislators are more accessible than the president and care more about narrow constituency issues and less about broader distributional consequences of policies as compared to the president, they can be influenced by small coalitions more easily. Therefore, government's decision-making in the United States can be considered to be highly responsive to special interests.

[7] The number of business political action committees (PACs) increased from 89 in 1974 to 776 in 1978 (Graham K. Wilson, 1981). Between the end of 1974 and the end of 1984, the number of trade association PACs increased by 120 percent and the number of corporate PACs by an astonishing 1,780 percent (Allan J. Cigler and Burdett A. Loomis, 1986). The number of registered lobbyists in Washington had grown from 3,400 in 1975 to 7,200 in 1985, the number of business corporations operating offices in Washington from 50 in 1961 to 545 in 1982, and the proportion of U.S. trade and professional associations headquartered in and around Washington from 19 percent in 1971 to 30 percent in 1982 (Robert H. Salisbury, 1992).

[8] The only exceptions are Wolfgang Mayer (1984) and Rodrik (1986). In the former, the level of tariff gets affected by asset distribution through the preferences of the median voter, while in the latter it is through the free-rider problem in lobbying.

organized group remains the same). This result is consistent with the smaller number of lobbies and less protectionist trade regimes in East Asian countries as compared to Latin America, where asset distribution is more unequal and asset deprivation is higher.[9] An analogy can be drawn with the work on inequality and growth by Alberto Alesina and Rodrik (1994) and Rodrik (1994), who argue that higher asset inequality leads to greater distributional conflicts that are detrimental to economic growth and, hence, are able to explain the difference in the growth performances of East Asia and Latin America.

Finally, I also look at the industry characteristics that determine whether an industry is organized or not. Industries that have large capital stocks, face inelastic demand functions, have very few capital owners, and are geographically less dispersed are the ones that get organized in equilibrium.

In Section I, I present the formal model along with the results from some comparative static exercises. In Section II, I look at the consequences of relaxing the homogeneity assumptions. Section III concludes the paper.

I. The Model

Consider a small open economy. Individuals are assumed to have identical preferences. Each individual possesses labor and, at most, one kind of specific factor of production. There are N nonnumeraire goods, each requiring a different kind of factor of production specific to that good and labor. In addition, there is a numeraire good which is produced under constant returns to scale using only labor.

---

[9] Gustav Ranis (1990) provides figures for land Gini coefficients in 1950 in the following countries: Taiwan (0.4), Korea (0.5), Colombia (0.8), and Mexico (0.8). World Bank (1991) and United Nations Development Programme (UNDP) (1993, 1994) provide figures on percentage of population below the poverty line as follows: Korea (5 percent), Singapore (10 percent), Argentina (16 percent), Brazil (47 percent), Colombia (42 percent), and Mexico (30 percent). These figures show higher levels of poverty and thus higher levels of asset deprivation in Latin America than in East Asia. Jeffrey D. Sachs (1985, 1986) discusses the large number of inefficient sectors in Latin America that received a large amount of trade protection. Mancur Olson (1982) talks about fewer coalitions and relatively liberal trade policies in Hong Kong, Taiwan, and Singapore.

Each consumer chooses c_Z and c_{X_i} to solve the following optimization problem:

$$(1) \quad \text{Max } U = c_Z + \sum_{i=1}^{N} u(c_{X_i}) \quad \text{subject to}$$

$$\sum_i p_i c_{X_i} + c_Z = E$$

where c_Z is consumption of the numeraire good Z, c_{X_i} is consumption of good X_i, and E is total income. $u' > 0$ and $u'' < 0$.[10]

Each good X_i is assumed to have p^* as the exogenous world price. p_i is the domestic price. There are other strong symmetry assumptions made below to simplify the analysis. In Section II, I look at the consequences of relaxing these symmetry assumptions. A few additional results are generated, but the qualitative results under the symmetry assumptions go through even when asymmetries are introduced.

From the first-order conditions,

$$(2) \qquad c_{X_i} = d(p_i)$$

where $d(\cdot)$ is the inverse of $u'(\cdot)$. The demand for the numeraire good is given by

$$(3) \qquad c_Z = E - \sum_i p_i d(p_i).$$

The indirect utility function is given by

$$(4) \qquad v(\mathbf{p}, E) = E + \sigma(\mathbf{p})$$

where $\mathbf{p} = (p_1, p_2 \cdots p_N)$ is the vector of domestic prices of the nonnumeraire goods and

$$(5) \quad \sigma(\mathbf{p}) = \sum_i u(d(p_i)) - \sum_i p_i d(p_i)$$

is consumer surplus.

Good Z is manufactured using labor alone under constant returns to scale and an input-output coefficient equal to one by choice of units (i.e., $Z = L_Z$), so that the wage rate $w = 1$ in a competitive equilibrium.

The output of each nonnumeraire good is given by the following production function

$$(6) \qquad X_i = F(K_i, L_i)$$

where $K_i = \bar{K}$ for all i. K_i is the sector specific factor in the ith good and L_i is the amount of labor used in the ith good. Notice that the total amount of each sector-specific capital stock is the same, the only difference being that each can be used in the production of only a specific product. $F(\cdot)$ is assumed to be constant returns to scale and $F_1 > 0$, $F_2 > 0$, $F_{11} < 0$, and $F_{22} < 0$.

The quantity of each good supplied domestically is given by

$$(7) \qquad X_i = X(p_i) = \pi'(p_i)$$

where $\pi(p_i)$ is the profit function and gives the total reward to K_i. It can be shown that $\pi''(p_i) > 0$, i.e., the profit function is convex with respect to price.

I assume that the only policy instruments available to politicians are trade taxes and subsidies.[11] The net revenue from taxes and subsidies, expressed on a per capita basis is given by

$$(8) \quad \tau(\mathbf{p}) = \sum_i (p_i - p^*)[d(p_i) - (1/M)X(p_i)]$$

where M is the total population. By assumption, the government redistributes revenue uniformly to all the citizens.

---

[10] A utility function of this kind greatly simplifies the analysis. Besides, its use is now standard in the political economy literature on trade policy. Paul R. Krugman (1992) argues in favor of using this kind of a utility function for analyzing political economy issues in a multisectoral general-equilibrium framework. The essence of his argument is that in such a framework our partial-equilibrium intuition goes through and since general-equilibrium concerns are not uppermost in the minds of politicians or lobbyists, this might be a better framework for analyzing such issues.

[11] The implications of the presence of other policy instruments such as consumption and production taxes and subsidies at the disposal of the government in the presence of exogenously given lobbies are worked out in Avinash K. Dixit (1996).

Let l^h represent individual h's endowment of labor and s_i^h her share of the ith specific factor. Therefore, income of the hth individual is given by

$$(9) \qquad E^h = l^h + \sum_i s_i^h \pi(p_i) + \tau(\mathbf{p})$$

$$h = 1, 2 \cdots M.$$

The indirect utility function of an individual is given by

$$(10) \quad w^h(\mathbf{p}) = l^h + \sum_i s_i^h \pi(p_i) + \tau(\mathbf{p}) + \sigma(\mathbf{p}).$$

I assume that each individual owns at most one type of specific factor.

Let H_i denote the set of individuals who own the ith specific factor. Also, let each of the sets have m members [i.e., $\#(H_i) = m$ for all i] who own equal amounts of the specific factor. The assumption that members within a group own equal amounts of the specific factor is not necessary for the general analysis in this model, but it greatly simplifies the analysis of the Nash interaction among the asset owners.

Let $\theta = mN/M$. Therefore, θ is the proportion of population that owns some factor of production besides labor. It is also a measure of the degree of equality of the ownership of specific factors. From (10) and the assumption that each individual owns at most one type of specific factor, the total welfare of the set of individuals owning the ith specific factor is given by

$$(11) \quad \Omega_i(\mathbf{p}) = \sum_{h \in H_i} l^h + \pi(p_i)$$

$$+ (\theta M/N)[\tau(\mathbf{p}) + \sigma(\mathbf{p})].$$

From now on, for notational simplicity, let us assume that each individual in the economy is endowed with exactly l units of labor.

In some or even all sectors, the specific factor owners with similar economic interests will organize themselves into lobby groups that coordinate their lobbying activity. The lobbying activity in this model is the exercise of political influence over govern-

ment's economic decision-making through contributions.

Until this point, the framework has been identical to Grossman-Helpman (1994), except for the different symmetry assumptions. At this point, a departure is made from their framework. The number of lobbies "n" will be endogenously determined.

The model has two stages:

First Stage.—In the first stage of the game, owners of each kind of specific factor decide whether to contribute to the financing of the fixed and sunk costs (defined in labor terms) of forming an organized lobby. This fixed cost consists of the costs of forming an organization, establishing links with politicians, hiring professional lobbyists, building a communications network among members, designing a scheme of punishments for defaulting members, etc. Forming a lobby can also be one way of getting closer to the government, so that political influence can be exercised on government's decision-making. A lobby can be considered to be an organizational set up to reduce transactions costs in lobbying activity, coordinate campaign-giving decisions, and communicate political "offers" to the politicians. In sectors without lobbies, the individual owners consider themselves small to communicate their offers or persuade the government to formulate economic policy one way or the other, since the transactions costs for these to be done at the level of the individual may be very high.[12]

---

[12] Terry M. Moe (1980) looks at forming a lobby as a sunk investment. According to him, an organized lobby requires an administrative structure, a mechanism for communication between members and avenues for member participation to facilitate division of labor and specialization. For large groups, Moe argues that a political entrepreneur or a leader has to undertake this investment. However, it can be argued that a leader or a political entrepreneur will not be necessary for business lobbies. Olson (1965) writes:

> The high degree of organization of business interests, must be due in large part to the fact that the business community is divided into a series of (generally oligopolistic) "industries," each of which contains only a small number of firms. Because the number of firms in each industry is often no more than would comprise a "privileged" group, and seldom more than would comprise an "intermediate"

Second Stage.—In the second stage, as in Grossman and Helpman (1994), the government sets trade policy to maximize a weighted sum of political contributions and overall social welfare. Lobbies provide the government with their contribution schedules that truthfully reveal their preferences taking into account the government's objective function. Each lobby takes the contribution schedules of other lobbies as given.

The problem is solved by working backwards, i.e., by starting from the second stage. An equilibrium in this game is the number of lobbies formed n^0 and a domestic price vector p^0.

In the second stage, the government can be influenced by the lobbies and so the problem of the government is as follows:

$$(12) \quad \text{Max}_{p \in P} \Omega_G(p) = [\sum_{j \in \Lambda} C_j(p) + a\Omega_A(p)]$$

where Λ is the set of organized interest groups (lobbies), $\Omega_G(p)$ is the objective function of the government, $\Omega_A(p)$ is aggregate social welfare, $C_j(p)$ is the contribution schedule of the jth lobby, and P is the set of domestic price vectors from which the government may choose. The set P is bounded such that each domestic price lies between some minimum p_{min} and some maximum p_{max}. Following Grossman and Helpman (1994), attention in this paper will be restricted to equilibria that lie in the interior of P.

The parameter a in (12) is the weight the government attaches to aggregate social welfare relative to political contributions. The higher is a, the lower is the government's affinity for political contributions and the higher is its concern for social welfare.

The truthful contribution schedule of each lobby $i \in \Lambda$ is given by

$$(13) \quad C_i(p) = \text{Max}(0, \Omega_i(p) - b_i)$$

where the scalars b_is (the net welfare anchors for the different lobby groups) are determined in equilibrium. As in Grossman and Helpman, I

focus on equilibria where lobbies make positive contributions. In other words, in the neighborhood of the equilibrium

$$(14) \quad C_i(p) = \Omega_i(p) - b_i.$$

Substituting (14) into (12), we have

$$(15) \quad \text{Max}_{p \in P} \Omega_G(p) = [\sum_{j \in \Lambda} (\Omega_j(p) - b_j)$$
$$+ a\Omega_A(p)] \Rightarrow \text{Max}_{p \in P} [\sum_{j \in \Lambda} \Omega_j(p)$$
$$+ a\Omega_A(p)].$$

It is important to note that the government's maximand in (15) is an additively separable form of the more general Hillman (1989) political support function, i.e., the Grossman and Helpman (1994) political contributions approach provides microfoundations for models that use the political support function approach. With the number of lobbies given, (15) yields the following expressions for the ad valorem trade subsidy (import tariff or export subsidy) t_O^0 for organized groups and the ad valorem trade tax (import subsidy or export tax) t_u^0 for unorganized groups respectively:

$$(16) \quad \frac{t_O^0}{1 + t_O^0} = \frac{(N/\theta) - n}{(Na/\theta) + n} \cdot \frac{1}{\mu_O^0 e_O^0}$$

$$(17) \quad \frac{t_u^0}{1 + t_u^0} = \frac{-n}{(Na/\theta) + n} \cdot \frac{1}{\mu_u^0 e_u^0}$$

where μ is the ratio of imports or exports to domestic output and e is the price elasticity of import demand or export supply. t_u^0 is always a negative number, so that a higher tax means a higher absolute value. The above equations can be translated into the following proposition which is the Grossman-Helpman "modified Ramsey rule":

PROPOSITION 1 (*Grossman-Helpman Result*): *When the number of lobbies is fixed, the equilibrium ad valorem trade subsidy (import tariff or export subsidy) for an organized group and the magnitude of the equilibrium ad valorem trade tax (import subsidy or export tax) on an unorganized group are inversely related to the price elasticity*

---

group, it follows that that these industries will normally be able to organize voluntarily to provide themselves with an active lobby—with the political power that "naturally and necessarily" flows to those that control the business and property of the country.

*of import demand or export supply, the import-
(or export-) domestic output ratio, and the government's weight on social welfare. The trade
subsidy is inversely related to the number of existing lobby groups, while the magnitude of the
trade tax is directly related to it.*

Since each organized group gains from a higher
price for its own product and lower prices for
products produced by other industries, the tariff or
export subsidy declines as the number of organized groups increases. For the same reason, the
tax on the unorganized groups keeps increasing.
Therefore, we have $(dt_O^0/dn) < 0$ and $(dt_u^0/dn) < 0$
(proof in Appendix A).

Going back to the first stage, let the fixed
labor cost of lobby formation for the ith group
of specific factors be F_i. Fixed costs here are
heterogeneous because groups differ in their
organizational abilities. Moreover, groups that
have formed associations for other purposes
(e.g., sharing technical know-how, etc.) may
find it cheaper to get politically organized than
other groups; or some groups may be geographically more concentrated than others. Besides,
this is the easiest type of heterogeneity to introduce in this framework. In the next section, I
will consider other kinds of heterogeneities.

Let $\tilde{\Omega}_O(n)$ and $\tilde{\Omega}_u(n)$ respectively denote the
equilibrium gross welfare of an organized group
and that of an unorganized group when there are n
lobbies. Also, let $\tilde{C}(n)$ be the equilibrium contribution by a representative organized group.

Taking $i - 1$ groups as organized, let the
members of another group decide whether to
form a lobby or remain unorganized. Nash interaction among group members is assumed in
their contribution decisions towards the provision of the fixed cost of lobby formation.[13]
However, once the lobby is formed, the lobby
machinery can enforce perfect coordination

among the members of that group in the collection of political contributions. There are three
possibilities:

Case (a): Contributing to the full financing of
the fixed cost F_i is the only Nash equilibrium
outcome among the group members when

$$(\tilde{\Omega}_O(i) - \tilde{\Omega}_u(i - 1) - \tilde{C}(i))/m > F_i.$$

This is the "privileged group" case in Olson
(1965), where the benefit from the public good
to at least one person exceeds the total cost of
providing it.

Case (b): Under the following condition

$$\tilde{\Omega}_O(i) - \tilde{\Omega}_u(i - 1) - \tilde{C}(i) > F_i$$

$$> (\tilde{\Omega}_O(i) - \tilde{\Omega}_u(i - 1) - \tilde{C}(i))/m$$

there are two possible Nash equilibrium outcomes—either there is no contribution to the provision of the lobby or the fixed cost is fully
financed by the members. Olson argues that business groups are never larger than what constitutes
an intermediate group, i.e., they are smaller than
the minimum size that precludes group coordination for public good provision. In a group of this
size, one could assume that preplay communication can take place. For example, when capitalists
in an industry feel that they are going to benefit
from forming a lobby, they start communicating
with each other—write letters, make phone calls,
etc. Hence, one can use some popular communication based refinements here. The better equilibrium for the group (i.e., the lobby is formed)
satisfies the conditions for the three popular communication-based refinements—coalition-proof
Nash, strong Nash, and the Pareto-dominance refinement and, hence, group coordination becomes
the likely equilibrium outcome.[14]

---

[13] An equivalent exercise is $\text{Max}_{f_{ji}} h_{ji}(f_{ji}, f_{(-ji)}, f_{(-i)}) =$
$\text{Max}_{f_{ji}} h_{ji}(f_{ji}, f_{(-ji)}, n')$ where $h_{ji}(\cdot)$ is the payoff function
for individual j in the ith group, f_{ji} is the contribution to the
financing of the fixed cost of lobby formation by the jth
member of the ith group, $f_{(-ji)}$ is the contribution vector of
all the other members in that group towards lobby formation, $f_{(-i)}$ is the vector of such contributions in all the other
groups, and n' is the number of organized lobbies in the rest
of the economy. This shows that the analysis in the model
will be equivalent to the Nash interaction among all the
asset owners in the economy.

[14] B. Douglas Bernheim et al. (1987) look at an important
class of "noncooperative" environments where players can
freely discuss their strategies, but cannot make binding commitments. They introduce a refinement of the Nash set, the
concept of coalition-proof Nash equilibrium. An agreement is
coalition-proof if and only if it is Pareto efficient within the
class of self-enforcing agreements. In turn an agreement is
self-enforcing if and only if no proper subset (coalition) of
players, taking the actions of its complement as fixed, *can
agree to deviate* in a way that makes all its members better off.

Case (c): The Nash equilibrium outcome is obviously "not providing the lobby" if the total benefit is less than the total fixed costs, i.e.,

$$\tilde{\Omega}_O(i) - \tilde{\Omega}_u(i - 1) - \tilde{C}(i) < F_i.$$

From the analysis of the above three cases, the conclusion that emerges is that a lobby is formed under the following condition:

$$\tilde{\Omega}_O(i) - \tilde{\Omega}_u(i - 1) - \tilde{C}(i) > F_i.$$

Let groups be ranked and indexed in ascending order of their fixed costs (i.e., subscripts are in ascending order of their fixed costs), such that

$$F_{min} \leq F_1 < F_2 \cdots < F_{n-1} < F_n$$

$$< F_{n+1} \cdots < F_N \leq F_{max}.$$

In the case of a continuum of lobbies, the above ordering means that $F'(n) > 0$. Let n^0 be the equilibrium number of lobbies when the number of lobbies is endogenized, such that an interior solution exists.

There are two cases:

(a) Discrete Number of Lobbies.—With discrete number of lobbies, it can be shown that the following is a Nash equilibrium (among other possible Nash equilibria): $\tilde{\Omega}_O(n^0) - \tilde{\Omega}_u(n^0 - 1) - \tilde{C}(n^0) \geq F_{n^0}$ and $\tilde{\Omega}_O(n^0 + 1) - \tilde{\Omega}_u(n^0) - \tilde{C}(n^0 + 1) < F_{n^0+1}$ (i.e., all groups with fixed cost less than or equal to F_{n^0} are organized).

(b) Continuum of Lobbies.—When n is continuous and so $F(n)$ also continuous in n,[15] it can be shown that if $\tilde{\Omega}'_O(n) - \tilde{\Omega}'_u(n) - \tilde{C}'(n) < F'(n)$, there exists a unique Nash equilibrium and [if it is an interior one, i.e., $n^0 \in (0, N)$] it is the one that satisfies the

condition $\tilde{\Omega}_O(n^0) - \tilde{\Omega}_u(n^0) - \tilde{C}(n^0) = F(n^0)$ [i.e., all groups with fixed cost less than or equal to $F(n^0)$ are organized].[16]

From now on, I assume that there is a continuum of nonnumeraire goods and the total measure or the mass of nonnumeraire goods is normalized to unity, so that $n \in [0, 1]$.

Let NB represent net benefit from lobby formation. NB is net of political contributions, but gross of fixed costs. This net benefit is given by

$$(18) \quad NB(n) = \tilde{\Omega}_O(n) - \tilde{\Omega}_u(n) - \tilde{C}(n).$$

Gross benefit is gross of both political contributions and fixed costs and therefore is given by

$$(19) \quad GB(n) = \tilde{\Omega}_O(n) - \tilde{\Omega}_u(n)$$
$$= \tilde{\pi}_O(n) - \tilde{\pi}_u(n)$$

since the other terms are the same in both $\tilde{\Omega}_O(n)$ and $\tilde{\Omega}_u(n)$. From (18) and (19), we have

$$(20) \quad NB(n) = GB(n) - \tilde{C}(n).$$

Differentiating (19) with respect to n yields

$$(21) \quad GB'(n) = \pi'(t_O^0)\frac{dt_O^0}{dn} - \pi'(t_u^0)\frac{dt_u^0}{dn} < 0.$$

$[\pi'(t_O^0) > \pi'(t_u^0) > 0$ since $t_O^0 > t_u^0$ and $\pi'' > 0$. Also $(dt_O^0/dn) < (dt_u^0/dn) < 0$ (proof in Appendix A).] This comes from the convexity of the profit function and the larger

---

A more demanding refinement is the strong Nash refinement which requires that no coalition (including the whole set), taking the actions of its complement as given, *can cooperatively deviate* in a way that benefits all of its members. The Pareto-dominance refinement requires that the Nash equilibrium is Pareto efficient among all possible Nash equilibria.

[15] This is a good approximation when there are a large number of groups.

[16] The uniqueness of this equilibrium can be proved as follows. Suppose we have groups indexed in ascending order of fixed costs as before. Let $n \in [0, N]$ and $F_n \in [F_{min}, F_{max}]$. Suppose in an equilibrium, an infinitesimal mass of groups of size ε_1 around k is organized and another infinitesimal mass of groups of size ε_2 around l is not organized and $k > l$. Let equilibrium net benefit of a unit group from organizing be NB^0. The cost to this unorganized mass around l of getting organized is $F_l\varepsilon_2$, while its net benefit is $NB^0\varepsilon_2$. This mass has an incentive to get organized since $NB^0\varepsilon_2 > F_l\varepsilon_2$ (because, for the mass around k to be organized in equilibrium, it is necessary that $NB^0 \geq F_k$ and we know that $F_k > F_l$). This is a contradiction, since then the original state is not an equilibrium. Hence, if an infinitesimal mass around k is organized, then masses with a lower fixed cost should also be organized.

reduction in the domestic price of the organized groups as a result of an increase in n.

With truthful contributions, the equilibrium contribution level by an organized group when there are n organized groups is given by

$$(22) \quad \tilde{C}_O(n) = \tilde{\Omega}_O(n) - \tilde{b}_O(n)$$

where $\tilde{b}_O(n) = \tilde{\Omega}_O(n) - \tilde{C}_O(n)$ is the net (of contributions) welfare or payoff anchor (determined in equilibrium) of the contribution schedule of an organized group. This is different from the net benefit (gross of fixed costs) NB from lobby formation which is the difference between the net payoff of an organized group $\tilde{b}_O(n) = \tilde{\Omega}_O(n) - \tilde{C}_O(n)$ and that of an unorganized group $\tilde{\Omega}_u(n)$.

In order to calculate the equilibrium contribution by an organized sector, I ask the question what will happen if a small number of sectors, of measure Δn, decide to defect. Then the policy maker will obtain welfare

$$(23)$$

$$\tilde{\Omega}_G^D(n) = (n - \Delta n)[\tilde{\Omega}_O(n - \Delta n) - \tilde{b}_O(n)]$$

$$+ a\tilde{\Omega}_A(n - \Delta n).$$

(In the case of discrete sectors $\Delta n = 1$.) The first term represents contributions, while the second represents aggregate welfare weighted by a. In equilibrium, the policy maker's welfare is given by

$$(24) \quad \tilde{\Omega}_G(n) = n[\tilde{\Omega}_O(n) - \tilde{b}_O(n)] + a\tilde{\Omega}_A(n).$$

(23) and (24) have to be equal for Δn small enough.[17] Writing the equality and taking the limit $\Delta n \to 0$ gives us

$$(25) \quad \tilde{b}_O(n) = \tilde{\Omega}_O(n) + [n\tilde{\Omega}'_O(n) + a\tilde{\Omega}'_A(n)].$$

From (22) and (25), we have

$$(26) \quad \tilde{C}(n) = -[n\tilde{\Omega}'_O(n) + a\tilde{\Omega}'_A(n)].$$

The above expression means that the equilibrium

contribution level by an organized sector compensates for the reduction in the gross welfare of the other existing organized groups and the reduction in the overall social welfare brought about by the formation of that organized group.

(26) can also be written as

$$(27) \quad \tilde{C}(n) = \tilde{\Omega}_O(n) - \tilde{V}'(n)$$

where $\tilde{V}(n) = n\tilde{\Omega}_O(n) + a\tilde{\Omega}_A(n) = V(p_O^0(n), p_u^0(n), n) = \text{Max}_{p_O, p_u}[n\Omega_O(p_O, p_u, n) + a\Omega_A(p_O, p_u, n)]$, p_O and p_u being the organized and unorganized nonnumeraire sector prices. Using the envelope theorem, $\tilde{V}'(n) = \Omega_O(p_O^0, p_u^0, n) + [n\Omega_{O3}(p_O^0, p_u^0, n) + a\Omega_{A3}(p_O^0, p_u^0, n)]$ where the subscript "3" stands for the partial derivative with respect to the third argument. This expression when plugged into (27), yields

$$(28) \quad \tilde{C}(n) = -[n\Omega_{O3}(p_O^0, p_u^0, n)$$

$$+ a\Omega_{A3}(p_O^0, p_u^0, n)].$$

Given the additive separability and quasi-linearity of the utility function, we have $\Omega_{O3}(p_O^0, p_u^0, n) = \theta(CT_O - CT_u)$ where $CT_O = W_O - \tilde{\pi}_O$ and $CT_u = W_u - \tilde{\pi}_u$ are the consumer surplus plus tariff revenue generated by an organized sector and that generated by an unorganized sector respectively, while W_O and W_u denote welfare (the sum of consumer surplus, producer surplus, and tariff revenue) generated by them. We also have $\Omega_{A3}(p_O^0, p_u^0, n) = W_O - W_u$. Let W^* be the welfare generated by a nonnumeraire sector under free trade. $D_O(n) = W^* - W_O(n)$ and $D_u(n) = W^* - W_u(n)$ are the deadweight losses created by an organized and an unorganized sector respectively as functions of n. Plugging all these expressions into (28), we get

$$(29) \quad \tilde{C}(n) = -n\theta(CT_O - CT_u)$$

$$- a(W_O - W_u) \Leftrightarrow \tilde{C}(n)$$

$$= n\theta(GB(n) + \Delta D(n))$$

$$+ a\Delta D(n)$$

where $\Delta D(n) = D_O(n) - D_u(n)$. A fraction $n\theta$ of the reduction in consumer surplus plus tariff revenue is borne by the existing organized

---

[17] For a more detailed discussion of truthful contributions, the interested reader should refer to Grossman and Helpman (1994).

population as one more group converts itself from unorganized to organized and an organized lobby compensates for it through its contribution as shown by the first right-hand-side term of (29). The second term shows the compensation for the additional deadweight loss brought about by its entry.

I now turn to changes in the contribution level by an organized group as the number of organized groups increases. This is given by

$$(30) \quad \tilde{C}'(n) = \underbrace{\theta(GB(n) + \Delta D(n))}_{+}$$
$$+ \underbrace{n\theta(GB'(n) + \Delta D'(n))}_{-} + \underbrace{a\Delta D'(n)}_{-}.$$

There are three effects. The first term is positive, showing that as n increases, a greater number of organized groups have to be compensated for the loss in their consumer surplus and tariff revenue. The second and third terms are negative, since the reduction in the consumer surplus plus the net revenue accruing to each existing group and the reduction in overall welfare (increase in deadweight loss) through the entry of another lobby gets smaller and smaller as n increases.

Plugging (29) into (20) and differentiating with respect to n, we have

$$(31) \quad NB'(n) = \underbrace{(1 - n\theta)GB'(n)}_{-}$$
$$\underbrace{- \theta(GB(n) + \Delta D(n))}_{-} \quad \underbrace{- (a + n\theta)\Delta D'(n)}_{+}.$$

Thus, the first two terms in the above equation are negative and the third term is positive. It can be shown that the first two terms dominate the third for all a, n, and θ (proof in Appendix B). This is intuitive. $\Delta D(n)$ is the difference between an organized sector's Harberger triangles (from the trade subsidy) and an unorganized sector's Harberger triangles (from the trade tax). $\Delta D'(n)$ shows how this difference between Harberger triangles changes as n changes

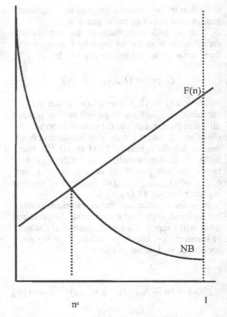

FIGURE 1. UNIQUE EQUILIBRIUM

and therefore, can be considered to be small. Therefore, we have

$$NB'(n) < 0.$$

The intuition behind the above derivative is that as n increases, there are more lobbies working against each other and a smaller unorganized population to exploit. Therefore, the net benefit from forming a lobby keeps diminishing.

Since $NB'(n) < 0$ and $F(n)$ is increasing in n, there is a unique equilibrium where $NB(n^0) = F(n^0)$ and the equilibrium number of organized groups n^0 is determined endogenously (see Figure 1). [$F(n)$ is increasing in n, since groups have been arranged in ascending order of their fixed costs, which is the appropriate way of determining the equilibrium.] To the left of the point of intersection, the net benefit of organizing to a marginal group exceeds the

1126   THE AMERICAN ECONOMIC REVIEW   DECEMBER 1999

fixed cost and hence an additional mass of groups will benefit from forming lobbies. To the right of the intersection, the opposite is the case and some of the groups are better off not organizing.

Comparative Statics

(1) *Change in* θ *(Distribution of Factor Ownership).*—θ refers to the level of equality of asset ownership because of the assumption that within each sector, individual asset owners possess equal amounts of the asset. Even when this assumption of perfect intrasectoral asset equality is relaxed, θ can represent the degree of equality in overall asset distribution if changes in θ are made keeping intrasectoral asset distribution constant. Otherwise, θ can be considered to be a measure of "asset deprivation" (similar to the measure of poverty given by the proportion of population below the poverty line), with a higher θ implying lower asset deprivation. The level of income inequality and the proportion of population in absolute poverty are highly positively correlated.[18] Given that there is a strong relationship between assets held (including human capital) and incomes earned, there will also be a strong positive correlation between asset inequality and asset deprivation. Changes in θ are made holding constant the total number of nonnumeraire goods.

PROPOSITION 2: *(a) A reduction in* θ *leads to an increase in the equilibrium number of lobbies.*

(b) The entry effect exactly equals the direct effect when fixed costs are homogeneous, so that the magnitudes of the equilibrium ad valorem trade subsidies and taxes remain unchanged. The direct "θ" effect dominates when fixed costs are heterogeneous.

Since NB is a function of $n\theta$, $NB_\theta = ndNB/d(n\theta)$ and $NB_n = \theta dNB/d(n\theta)$ which together yield

---

[18] The correlation between these two variables using figures from the UNDP (1993) turns out to be 0.55.

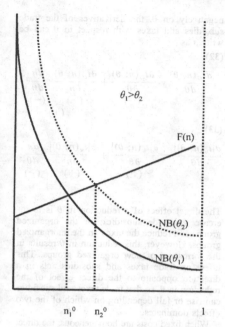

FIGURE 2. CHANGE IN θ

$$NB_\theta = \frac{n}{\theta} NB_n < 0.$$

The intuition behind the above derivative is that as θ increases for a given n, there is a smaller unorganized population to exploit. Therefore, the net benefit from forming a lobby is decreasing in θ.

(a) A reduction in θ leads to a shift in the NB curve to the right and, therefore, to an increase in the equilibrium number of lobbies (see Figure 2). Normally, one would expect the equilibrium number of lobbies to be lower when specific factors are more equally distributed, because fixed costs of lobby formation would rise when a larger number of people needs to be in each lobby. However, this result is obtained here even without letting fixed costs vary with θ.

(b) Since the endogenous level of n depends

negatively on θ, the derivatives of the trade subsidies and taxes with respect to θ can be written as

(32)

$$\frac{dt_o(n;\ \theta)}{d\theta} = \underset{(-)}{\frac{\partial t_o(n;\ \theta)}{\partial\theta}} + \underset{\underset{(+)}{(-)}}{\frac{\partial t_o(n;\ \theta)}{\partial n}} \cdot \underset{(-)}{\frac{dn}{d\theta}}$$

(33)

$$\frac{d|t_u(n;\ \theta)|}{d\theta} = \underset{(+)}{\frac{\partial|t_u(n;\ \theta)|}{\partial\theta}} + \underset{\underset{(-)}{(+)}}{\frac{\partial|t_u(n;\ \theta)|}{\partial n}} \cdot \underset{(-)}{\frac{dn}{d\theta}}.$$

The direct effect of a reduction in θ is to increase the trade subsidies for the organized groups and reduce the taxes on the unorganized groups. However, this reduction in θ results in the formation of new organized groups. This effect on trade taxes and subsidies acts in a direction opposite to the direct effect of the reduction in θ, so that trade taxes and subsidies can rise or fall depending on which of the two effects dominates.

When fixed costs are homogeneous, the direct effect can be shown to be exactly equal in magnitude to the indirect effect, so that trade taxes and subsidies are unchanged. This is so, since both the trade subsidy and the trade tax and also NB are all monotonic functions of $n\theta$, i.e., of the proportion of the population organized. NB is monotonically decreasing in $n\theta$. Hence, with constant fixed costs, $n\theta$ does not change and so there is no change in the trade subsidy for an organized group or the trade tax on an unorganized group. With heterogeneous fixed costs, the direct effect dominates (since entry is less than in the case with homogeneous fixed costs), so that the trade subsidies rise and trade taxes fall as a result of a fall in θ.[19] The magnitude of the trade tax on an unorganized group falls.

(2) *Changes in a.*—A lower a means a higher affinity on the part of the government for political contributions.

PROPOSITION 3: *(i) A reduction in a leads to*

(a) *an increase in the equilibrium number of lobbies;*
(b) *an increase or decrease in the magnitude of the equilibrium ad valorem trade subsidy for organized groups, depending on the extent of entry of lobbies induced [the ad valorem trade subsidy for organized groups decreases if the entry effect dominates; the strength of the entry effect is inversely related to the degree of heterogeneity of fixed costs];*
(c) *an increase in the magnitude of ad valorem trade taxes on unorganized groups, greater than in the case with an exogenous number of lobbies.*
(ii) *Free trade can be an equilibrium outcome when $\theta = 1$ (i.e., everybody possesses a specific factor) for (a) very high values of a (nobody is organized) or (b) very low values of a (everybody is organized).[20]*

$NB_a < 0$ (proof in Appendix C). Hence, for a constant n, NB increases as a decreases. As a decreases, the government's affinity for contributions from lobbies increases and, therefore, in order to obtain higher contributions, it provides organized groups with higher concessions and is willing to exploit the unorganized population more for the benefit of the organized groups. This leads to an increase in NB.

(i) (a) In Figure 3, a reduction in a results in a shift of the NB curve to the right. This results in an increase in the equilibrium number of lobbies from n_1^0 to n_2^0, i.e., entry of new lobbies.

(b),(c) The following derivatives show us

---

[19] The reason here is NB is a decreasing function of $n\theta$, and so $n\theta$ should fall with heterogeneous (rising) fixed costs as NB shifts to the right and since trade subsidy for an organized group is decreasing in $n\theta$, it will rise as θ falls.

[20] In this model $\theta = 1$ implies perfect equality of asset distribution because of the perfect intrasectoral asset equality assumption. However, if this assumption is relaxed, $\theta = 1$ and overall asset inequality are consistent and therefore, the observation on the United States made earlier becomes relevant.

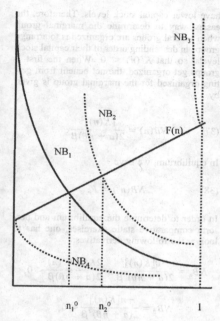

FIGURE 3. CHANGE IN a

the effect of a change in a on t_O and t_u when n is endogenized:

(34)

$$\frac{dt_O(n; a)}{da} = \underset{(-)}{\frac{\partial t_O(n; a)}{\partial a}} + \underset{(-)}{\frac{\partial t_O(n; a)}{\partial n}} \cdot \underset{(-)}{\frac{dn}{da}}$$
$$(+)$$

(35)

$$\frac{d|t_u(n; a)|}{da} = \underset{(-)}{\frac{\partial |t_u(n; a)|}{\partial a}} + \underset{(+)}{\frac{\partial |t_u(n; a)|}{\partial n}} \cdot \underset{(-)}{\frac{dn}{da}}.$$
$$(-)$$

One can see from equation (34) that a reduction in a has two effects. The direct effect is

to increase the ad valorem trade subsidy for existing organized groups, while the indirect effect is to reduce it through entry of new groups into lobbying. Therefore, whether the tariff would increase or decrease will depend on which of the two effects dominates. The strength of the indirect effect relative to the direct effect is inversely related to the degree of heterogeneity in fixed costs since the slope of the fixed cost curve is directly related to the degree of heterogeneity and the extent of entry is related inversely to the slope of the fixed cost curve. With several sets of functional forms, it was found that the indirect effect dominates the direct effect when fixed costs are homogeneous. In Figure 3, setting $\theta = 1$, there is a positive trade subsidy when NB is at NB_1, while when a decreases, such that NB is NB_3, there is free trade and there is zero trade subsidy.[21] This is another example where the indirect effect is stronger than the direct effect. Even when the indirect effect is weaker than the direct effect, treating n as exogenous would lead to an overestimate of the positive effect of a reduction in a on the trade subsidy for the organized groups.

The magnitude of the tax on an unorganized group increases as a decreases. Here, both the direct and the indirect effects act in the same direction. Treating n as exogenous underestimates the effect of a decline in a on the tax on an unorganized group. A reduction in a increases the magnitude of the tax both directly for a given number of lobbies, and indirectly by facilitating more entry into lobbying.

(ii) In Figure 3, when $\theta = 1$, there is the possibility of free trade for very high values of a (when NB is NB_4 or below) and very low values of a (when NB is NB_3 or above). For high values of a, nobody is organized and so there is free trade, while for low values, everybody is organized and so, again, there is free trade. Therefore, free trade can be an equilibrium outcome when a government is highly responsive to special interests or when it is not too responsive. For values of a in between, there are trade subsidies protecting the organized groups and taxes on the unorganized groups.

---

[21] Plugging $\theta = 1$ and $n = N$ in equation (15) yields a zero trade subsidy.

II. Relaxing the Homogeneity Assumptions

Let us assume that the production functions for the nonnumeraire and numeraire goods are given by $X_i = K_i$, and $Z = L_Z$, respectively. The demand function for each nonnumeraire good is given by $C_{X_i} = A - \beta p_i$, which implies a quadratic subutility function in the overall quasi-linear utility function. The world price of each nonnumeraire good is p^*. Now, let us introduce heterogeneity along only one dimension, say, the capital stock. Let the fixed costs of lobby formation be homogeneous and equal F for each group. As before, I still deal with a continuum of groups. The total number of nonnumeraire groups N is normalized to unity, so that $n \in [0, 1]$. The net benefit of a marginal group from getting organized when n groups are organized is given by

$$(36) \qquad NB_M = \frac{K_M^2}{2(a + n\theta)\beta}$$

where K_M is the capital stock of this marginal group. (More precisely, NB_M is the net benefit per lobby of an infinitesimal mass of lobbies, each of which has a capital stock infinitesimally close to K_M.)[22]

In equilibrium, the net benefit to the marginal group equals the fixed cost of getting organized and each group with a higher net benefit (inframarginal groups), given the actions of other groups, is also organized. Any group with a lower net benefit remains unorganized. As can be easily seen, the inframarginal groups have higher levels of capital stock than the marginal group to make their net benefits higher, while the groups that are unorganized

have lower capital stock levels. Therefore, the easiest way to determine the marginal group when several groups are organized is to arrange groups in descending order of their capital stock levels, so that $K'(n) < 0$. When the first n groups get organized, the net benefit from getting organized for the marginal group is given by

$$(37) \qquad NB(n) = \frac{[K(n)]^2}{2(a + n\theta)\beta}.$$

In equilibrium, we have

$$(38) \qquad NB(n^0) = F.$$

In order to determine the equilibrium and perform comparative static exercises, one has to look at the following derivatives:

$$NB_n = \frac{-\theta[K(n)]^2}{2(a + n\theta)^2\beta} + \frac{2K(n)K'(n)}{2(a + n\theta)\beta} < 0,$$

$$NB_\theta = \frac{-n[K(n)]^2}{2(a + n\theta)^2\beta} < 0,$$

$$NB_a = \frac{-[K(n)]^2}{2(a + n\theta)^2\beta} < 0.$$

Differentiating the equilibrium condition (38) and from the above derivatives, it is easy to see that the earlier results still hold, since we have

$$\frac{dn^0}{d\theta} = -\frac{NB_\theta}{NB_n} < 0, \qquad \frac{dn^0}{da} = -\frac{NB_a}{NB_n} < 0.$$

Moreover, one can easily see that groups with high levels of capital stock get organized, while the ones with low levels of capital stock remain unorganized.

Now, let us assume that all groups have the same capital stock levels. They only differ in their demand functions. Let $C_{X_i} = A - \beta_i p_i$. In this case, groups differ only in their β_i's. It can easily be shown that the inframarginal lobbies would have lower β_i's than the marginal lobby. Thereforr, I arrange industries in increasing order of β_i's, so that $\beta'(n) > 0$. The net benefit

---

[22] Indexing the groups in the desired order, let $\Omega_O(i, n)$ be the equilibrium gross welfare of the ith organized group when groups indexed from $0 \cdots n$ are organized. The contribution by the nth group is given by $-[\int_0^n \Omega_{O2}(i, n)\,di + a\Omega'_A(n)]$. Reordering the groups as desired and using the envelope theorem to differentiate the government's maximand with respect to n as before, we have the equilibrium contribution by the ith lobby as $\check{C}(i, n) = \gamma(n)(GB(i, n) + \Delta D(i, n)) + a\Delta D(i, n)$ where (i, n) represents the relevant variable for the ith lobby when the first n groups are organized and $\gamma(n)$ is the proportion of the population that is organized. This gives us the net benefit formula as $NB(i, n) = (1 - \gamma(n))GB(i, n) - (a + \gamma(n))\Delta D(i, n)$.

of the marginal group when the first n groups are organized is given by

$$(39) \quad NB(n) = \frac{K^2}{2(a + n\theta)\beta(n)}$$

$$NB_n = \frac{-\theta K^2}{2(a + n\theta)^2 \beta(n)}$$

$$- \frac{K^2 \beta'(n)}{2(a + n\theta)(\beta(n))^2} < 0,$$

$$NB_\theta = \frac{-n K^2}{2(a + n\theta)^2 \beta(n)} < 0,$$

$$NB_a = \frac{-K^2}{2(a + n\theta)^2 \beta(n)} < 0.$$

Again we have

$$\frac{dn^0}{d\theta} = -\frac{NB_\theta}{NB_n} < 0, \qquad \frac{dn^0}{da} = -\frac{NB_a}{NB_n} < 0.$$

Moreover, one can clearly see that groups with lower β_i's get organized, while the ones with high β_i's remain unorganized.

Now, let groups vary in their size (number of members) and let everything else remain the same across groups. It can be seen that the larger groups benefit less than the smaller groups from organizing. The reason is that when groups get larger, they consume a significant proportion of their own product and so do not like a very high price for it. Hence, I arrange groups in increasing order of their size. Changing the definition of θ slightly, let $\theta'(n) > 0$ where $q\theta(n)$ is the number of members in the nth group as a proportion of the overall population. An increase in q means a reduction in asset inequality. The net benefit of the marginal group when the first n groups are organized is given by

$$(40) \quad NB(n) = \frac{K^2}{2\left(a + q \displaystyle\int_0^n \theta(i) \, di\right) \beta}$$

$$NB_n = \frac{-K^2 q \, \theta(n)}{2\left(a + q \displaystyle\int_0^n \theta(i) \, di\right)^2 \beta} < 0,$$

$$NB_q = \frac{-K^2 \displaystyle\int_0^n \theta(i) \, di}{2\left(a + q \displaystyle\int_0^n \theta(i) \, di\right)^2 \beta} < 0,$$

$$NB_a = \frac{-K^2}{2\left(a + q \displaystyle\int_0^n \theta(i) \, di\right)^2 \beta} < 0.$$

The comparative static results hold as before:

$$\frac{dn^0}{dq} = -\frac{NB_q}{NB_n} < 0, \qquad \frac{dn^0}{da} = -\frac{NB_a}{NB_n} < 0.$$

Moreover, one can clearly see that smaller groups get organized, while the bigger ones remain unorganized. In this case, one can even introduce heterogeneity in fixed costs where fixed costs are correlated with size. This would further strengthen the above result that smaller groups organize themselves, while the larger groups remain unorganized.

The introduction of heterogeneity in the world price does not add any new insights, since NB here is invariant to the world price.

From the above analysis, one can see that it is easy to determine the equilibrium when there is heterogeneity along one dimension. This kind of analysis is useful because it answers the following kind of question: If groups only differ in characteristic x, which are the groups that get organized? Groups with low x or groups with high x? The answer to this question is useful for empirical work where all kinds of different characteristics are thrown into the right-hand side of a regression, so that one can look at whether high x or low x groups get organized after controlling for all the other characteristics. In a multiple regression, such a question can be asked for every characteristic x.

It is also clear that when heterogeneities along different dimensions are correlated (e.g., size of groups and fixed costs), it is easy to solve for the equilibrium. However, there is, in general, no reason for other kinds of heterogeneities to be correlated. Yet, when all groups are heterogeneous in all respects, then groups would organize according to the dominant kind of heterogeneity if there is one and the model could be easily solved. For example, if the capital heterogeneity is by far the dominant heterogeneity, then high capital stock groups get organized and other groups remain unorganized. If no dominant heterogeneity exists, then all one can say is that groups with high capital stock levels, low demand elasticities, low level of geographical dispersion, and few members will get organized, while the groups with just the opposite characteristics will remain unorganized in equilibrium.

III. Conclusions

This paper endogenizes the formation of lobbies within the Grossman-Helpman (1994) "Protection for Sale" framework for trade policy determination. It uses the endogenous market structure approach from industrial organization theory and communication-based refinements of the Nash equilibrium.

The possibility of the entry of new groups into lobbying results in several new, surprising insights. The ad valorem trade subsidy may actually fall as a result of a reduction in the government's weight on aggregate social welfare relative to political contributions in its objective function. It is also shown that free trade can be an equilibrium outcome either when the government is highly responsive to special interests or when it is highly welfare oriented. This explains the presence of free trade in the United States, despite the high degree of responsiveness of the government to special interests through its high affinity for political contributions.

This paper also looks at the effects of changes in asset distribution on the equilibrium number of lobbies and trade taxes and subsidies and is able to explain the differences in the numbers of lobbies and the levels of protection between East Asia and Latin America.

Finally, I also look at the industry characteristics that determine whether an industry is organized or not. Industries that have large capital stocks, face inelastic demand functions, have very few capital owners, and are geographically less dispersed are the ones that get organized in equilibrium.

Appendix A

TO PROVE: (i) $(dt_O^0/dn) < 0$, $(dt_u^0/dn) < 0$ and (ii) $|dt_O^0/dn| > |dt_u^0/dn|$.

PROOF:

Equations (16) and (17) can be written as:

(A1) $t_O^0 = \dfrac{(N/\theta) - n}{(Na/\theta) + n} \cdot \dfrac{X(p_O^0)}{[-p^*I'(p_O^0)]}$ and

(A2) $t_u^0 = \dfrac{-n}{(Na/\theta) + n} \cdot \dfrac{X(p_u^0)}{[-p^*I'(p_u^0)]}$

respectively where $I(p_i)$ is import demand.

The above equations can in turn be written as

(A3) $t_O^0 = \delta_O(n) g(t_O^0)$ and

(A4) $t_u^0 = \delta_u(n) g(t_u^0)$

where $\delta_O(n) = [(N/\theta) - n]/[(Na/\theta) + n]$, $\delta_u(n) = -n/[(Na/\theta) + n]$ and $g(t) = X(p^*(1 + t))/[-p^*I'(p^*(1 + t))]$, $\delta_O'(n) = -(N/\theta)(a + 1)/[Na/\theta + n]^2 < 0$, $\delta_u'(n) = -(N/\theta)a/[Na/\theta + n]^2 < 0$. It can clearly be seen from above that $|\delta_O'(n)| > |\delta_u'(n)|$.

I impose the restriction that an increase in the price of a commodity should increase the output supplied proportionally at least as much as it increases the magnitude of the derivative of its import demand or export supply with respect to price, so that $g'(t) \geq 0$. This would always hold for linear demand and supply functions and also for most standard demand and supply functions.

Differentiating t_O^0 with respect to n,

(A5) $\dfrac{dt_O^0}{dn} = \delta_O'(n) g(t_O^0)$

$+ \delta_O(n) g'(t_O^0) \dfrac{dt_O^0}{dn} \Rightarrow \dfrac{dt_O^0}{dn}$

$= \dfrac{\delta_O'(n) g(t_O^0)}{1 - \delta_O(n) g'(t_O^0)} < 0$

since the numerator is negative and the denominator is positive. $1 - \delta_O(n) g'(t_O^0) > 0$ from the second-order condition of the government's maximization exercise (15).

Furthermore,

(A6) $\dfrac{dt_u^0}{dn} = \dfrac{\delta_u'(n) g(t_u^0)}{1 - \delta_u(n) g'(t_u^0)} < 0$

because the numerator is clearly negative and the denominator clearly positive.

Since $|\delta_O'(n)| > |\delta_u'(n)|$, $0 < g(t_u^0) \leq g(t_O^0)$ and $1 - \delta_u(n)g'(t_u^0) \geq 1 - \delta_O(n)g'(t_O^0) > 0$ [because $\delta_O > 0$, $\delta_u < 0$ and $g'(t) \geq 0$], we have $|dt_O^0/dn| > |dt_u^0/dn|$.

APPENDIX B

TO PROVE: NB is decreasing in n.

PROOF:

(B1) $NB_n = \theta NB_\gamma$ where $\gamma = n\theta$

(B2) $NB_\gamma = (1 - \gamma)GB_\gamma - (GB + \Delta D)$

$\qquad\qquad - (a + \gamma)\Delta D_\gamma.$

The first-order conditions of the government's maximization problem (15) with respect to p_O and p_u [multiplied respectively by $(\partial p_O/\partial \gamma)$ and $(\partial p_u/\partial \gamma)$] give us $(1 - \gamma)(\partial \tilde{\pi}_O/\partial \gamma) - (a + \gamma)(\partial D_O/\partial \gamma) = 0$ and $-\gamma(\partial \tilde{\pi}_u/\partial \gamma) - (a + \gamma)(\partial D_u/\partial \gamma) = 0$. These equations when plugged into (B2) yield

(B3) $NB_\gamma = -(GB + \Delta D) - \dfrac{\partial \tilde{\pi}_u}{\partial \gamma}.$

At $a = 0$, the second right-hand-side term $-(\partial \tilde{\pi}_u/\partial \gamma)$ is zero. Therefore, we have

(B4) $NB_\gamma (a = 0) < 0.$

It is easy to see that

(B5) $\lim_{a \to \infty} NB_\gamma = 0.$

We can also write $NB_\gamma = CT_O - CT_u - (\partial \tilde{\pi}_u/\partial \gamma)$ where CT stands for the consumer surplus plus tariff revenue generated by a sector for the entire economy. The subscripts O and u stand as before for organized and unorganized respectively. Differentiation of NB_γ with respect to a yields

(B6) $NB_{\gamma a} = \dfrac{\partial CT_O}{\partial a} - \dfrac{\partial CT_u}{\partial a} - \dfrac{\partial^2 \tilde{\pi}_u}{\partial \gamma \partial a} > 0.$

[It is easy to see that $(\partial CT_O/\partial a) > 0$ and $(\partial CT_u/\partial a) < 0$. The term $(\partial^2 \tilde{\pi}_u/\partial \gamma \partial a) <$

or > 0 depending on parameter values. However, it is a second-order term and (when positive) can be shown to be dominated (for all a and γ) by the two first-order terms using various sets of standard supply and demand functions including linear ones.[23]]

From (B4), (B5), and (B6), we have $NB_\gamma < 0$ for all γ and all finite a. Therefore, we have $NB_n < 0$.

APPENDIX C

TO PROVE: NB is decreasing in a.

PROOF:

(C1) $GB_a = \pi'(t_O^0) \dfrac{\partial t_O^0}{\partial a} - \pi'(t_u^0) \dfrac{\partial t_u^0}{\partial a} < 0$

since $\pi'(t_O^0)$, $\pi'(t_u^0) > 0$ and $(\partial t_O^0/\partial a) < 0$, $(\partial t_u^0/\partial a) > 0$.

(C2) $\tilde{C}_a = \underbrace{n\theta(GB_a + \Delta D_a)}_{-} + \dfrac{\Delta D}{+ (-)}$

$\qquad\qquad + \dfrac{a \Delta D_a}{- (+)}.$

The second and third terms are opposite in sign to each other. With a higher a, on the one hand, the magnitude of the change (positive for low $n\theta$ and negative for high $n\theta$) in the deadweight loss from the entry of another lobby is lower, while on the other hand, a larger proportion of this change is taken into account in the computation of contributions.

(C3) $NB_a = \underbrace{(1 - n\theta)GB_a}_{-}, \quad \dfrac{-\Delta D(n)}{-(+)}$

$\qquad\qquad \dfrac{-(a + n\theta)\Delta D_a}{+ (-)}.$

The first-order conditions of the government's maximization problem (15) with respect to p_O

---

[23] The following sets of supply and demand functions were used to assess the magnitude of the combination of the two first-order terms relative to that of the second-order term: (i) $X_i = \bar{X}$ and $C_{X_i} = A - \beta p_i$; (ii) $X_i = p_i$ and $C_{X_i} = A - p_i$; (iii) $X_i = p_i^2$ and $C_{X_i} = A - p_i^2$; and (iv) $X_i = p_i^3$ and $C_{X_i} = A - p_i^3$.

and p_u [multiplied respectively by $(\partial p_O/\partial a)$ and $(\partial p_u/\partial a)$] give us $(1 - n\theta)(\partial\tilde{\pi}_O/\partial a) - (a + n\theta)(\partial D_O/\partial a) = 0$ and $-n\theta(\partial\tilde{\pi}_u/\partial a) - (a + n\theta)(\partial D_u/\partial a) = 0$. These equations when plugged into (C3) yield

(C4) $NB_a = \underbrace{\dfrac{-\Delta D}{-(+)}}_{-} \; \underbrace{-\tilde{\pi}_{ua}}_{-}$.

From (C4), we can see that NB is decreasing in a at least for low values of $n\theta$. By further rearranging the right-hand terms, (C4) can be written as

(C5) $NB_a = \underbrace{-D_O}_{-} \; \underbrace{-(\tilde{\pi}_{ua} - D_u)}_{-} < 0$

which means that NB is decreasing in a for all values of $n\theta$. A sufficient condition for the second right-hand-side term to be negative is that $[I''(p)/I'(p)]$ is small in magnitude [i.e., the import demand function $I(p)$ is of negligible curvature] for all permissible values the unorganized sector price can take.[24] (The necessary and sufficient condition is much weaker.)

---

[24] Under this condition,

$-(\tilde{\pi}_{ua} - D_u) < 0 \Leftrightarrow \tilde{\pi}_{ua}$

$> D_u \Leftrightarrow \dfrac{\{n\theta[X(p_u)]^2\}/[(a + n\theta)^2(-I')]}{1 + \{n\theta X'/[(a + n\theta)(-I')]\}}$

$> \dfrac{(n\theta)^2[X(p_u)]^2}{2(a + n\theta)^2[-I']}$

$\Leftrightarrow \{[2/(n\theta)] - 1\}\{[a/(n\theta)] + 1\} > [X'/(-I')]$ which is always true since the left-hand side is greater than $1 + a$, while the right-hand side is less than one.

REFERENCES

Alesina, Alberto and Rodrik, Dani. "Distributive Politics and Economic Growth." *Quarterly Journal of Economics*, May 1994, *109*(2), pp. 465–90.

Becker, Gary. "A Theory of Competition among Pressure Groups for Political Influence." *Quarterly Journal of Economics*, August 1983, *98*(3), pp. 371–400.

Bernheim, B. Douglas; Peleg, Bezalel and Whinston, Michael D. "Coalition-Proof Nash Equilibria." *Journal of Economic Theory*, June 1987, *42*(1), pp. 1–12.

Cigler, Allan J. and Loomis, Burdett A. *Interest group politics.* Washington, D.C.: C.Q. Press, 1986.

Dixit, Avinash K. "Special-Interest Lobbying and Endogenous Commodity Taxation." *Eastern Economic Journal*, Fall 1996, *22*(4), pp. 375–88.

Findlay, Ronald. "The New Political Economy: Its Explanatory Power for LDCs," in G.M. Meier, ed., *Political economy and policy making in developing countries.* San Francisco, CA: ICS Press, 1991, pp. 13–40.

Findlay, Ronald and Wellisz, Stanislaw. "Endogenous Tariffs, the Political Economy of Trade Restrictions and Welfare," in J.N. Bhagwati, ed., *Import competition and response.* Chicago: University of Chicago Press, 1982, pp. 223–34.

Grossman, Gene M. and Helpman, Elhanan. "Protection for Sale." *American Economic Review*, September 1994, *84*(4), pp. 833–50.

_____. "Trade Wars and Trade Talks." *Journal of Political Economy*, August 1995a, *103*(4), pp. 675–708.

_____. "The Politics of Free Trade Agreements." *American Economic Review*, September 1995b, *85*(4), pp. 667–90.

Helpman, Elhanan. "Politics and Trade Policy." Eitan Berglas School of Economics, Tel Aviv University Working Paper No. 30-95, September 1995.

Hillman, Arye L. *The political economy of protection.* London: Harwood Academic, 1989.

_____. "Protectionist Policies as the Regulation of International Industry." *Public Choice*, November 1990, *67*(2), pp. 101–10.

_____. "Protection, Politics, and Market Structure," in Elhanan Helpman and Assaf Razin, eds., *International trade and trade policy.* Cambridge, MA: MIT Press, 1991, pp. 118–40.

Hillman, Arye L. and Moser, Peter. "Trade Liberalization as Politically Optimal Exchange of Market Access," in M.B. Canzoneri, W.J. Ethier, and V. Grilli, eds., *The new transatlantic economy.* Cambridge: Cambridge University Press, 1996, pp. 295–312.

Hillman, Arye L. and Ursprung, Heinrich W. "Domestic Politics, Foreign Interests, and International Trade Policy." *American Economic Review*, September 1988, *78*(4), pp. 719–45.

Krugman, Paul R. "Regionalism versus Multilateralism," in J. De Melo and A. Panagariya, eds., *New dimensions in regional integration.* Cambridge: Cambridge University Press, 1992, pp. 58–79.

Mayer, Wolfgang. "Endogenous Tariff Formation." *American Economic Review,* December 1984, *74*(5), pp. 970–85.

Moe, Terry M. *The organization of interests.* Chicago: University of Chicago Press, 1980.

O'Halloran, Sharyn. *Politics, process, and American trade policy.* Ann Arbor, MI: University of Michigan Press, 1994.

Olson, Mancur. *The logic of collective action.* Cambridge, MA: Harvard University Press, 1965.

———. *The rise and decline of nations.* New Haven, CT: Yale University Press, 1982.

Peltzman, Sam. "Toward a More General Theory of Regulation." *Journal of Law and Economics,* August 1976, *19*(2), pp. 211–40.

Ranis, Gustav. "Contrasts in the Political Economy of Developmental Policy Change," in G. Gereffi and D.L. Wyman, eds., *Manufacturing miracles: Paths of industrialization in Latin America and Latin America and East Asia.* Princeton, NJ: Princeton University Press, 1990, pp. 207–30.

Rodrik, Dani. "Tariffs, Subsidies, and Welfare with Endogenous Policy." *Journal of International Economics,* November 1986, *21*(3/4), pp. 285–99.

———. "King Kong Meets Godzilla: The World Bank and the East Asian Miracle," in Albert Fishlow, Dani Rodrik, and Catherine Gwin, eds., *Miracle or design? Lessons from the East Asian experience.* Washington, DC: Overseas Development Council, 1994, pp. 13–53.

———. "Political Economy of Trade Policy," in Gene M. Grossman and Kenneth Rogoff, eds., *Handbook of international economics,* Vol. 3. Amsterdam: North-Holland, 1995, pp. 1457–94.

Sachs, Jeffrey D. "External Debt and Macroeconomic Performance in Latin America and East Asia." *Brookings Papers on Economic Activity,* 1985, (2), pp. 523–64.

———. "Managing the LDC Debt Crisis." *Brookings Papers on Economic Activity,* 1986, (2), pp. 397–431.

Salisbury, Robert H. *Interest and institutions: Substance and structure in American politics.* Pittsburgh, PA: University of Pittsburgh Press, 1992.

Stigler, George. "The Theory of Economic Regulation." *Bell Journal of Economic Management and Science,* Spring 1971, *2*, pp. 3–21.

United Nations Development Programme (UNDP). *Human development report.* New York: UNDP, 1993, 1994.

Wilson, Graham K. *Interest groups in the United States.* Oxford: Oxford University Press, 1981.

World Bank. *World development report.* Washington, DC: World Bank, 1991.

Chapter 2

Endogenous political organization and the value of trade agreements

Devashish Mitra[*]

Department of Economics, Florida International University, Miami, FL 33199, USA

Received 27 April 2000; received in revised form 12 February 2001; accepted 20 June 2001

Abstract

In a bargaining model of endogenous protection, I introduce fixed costs of political-organization that need to be incurred by capitalists prior to actual lobbying. Unlike Maggi and Rodriguez-Clare [J. Pol. Econ. 106(3) (1998) 575] intersectoral capital mobility is disallowed. Nevertheless, I am still able to obtain their main result that a government with low bargaining power vis-à-vis the import-competing lobby precommits to a free-trade agreement. Further, with high fixed organizational costs, the government prefers to stay out of such agreements. Its maximum bargaining power consistent with signing a trade agreement has an inverse-V-shaped relationship with respect to the size of fixed costs. © 2002 Elsevier Science B.V. All rights reserved.

Keywords: Trade policy; Lobbying; Bargaining; Political organization; Trade agreements

JEL classification: F10; F11; F13

1. Introduction

The trade literature is rich in purely economic as well as political-economy explanations for the existence of free trade agreements. Johnson (1954) showed that a large country, which has an incentive to set a tariff to improve its terms of trade, imposes a negative externality on its trading partners. If all countries try to improve their respective terms of trade simultaneously, they may be worse off than

---

Tel.: +1-305-348-3893; fax: +1-305-348-1524.
E-mail address: mitrad@fiu.edu (D. Mitra).

0022-1996/02/$ – see front matter © 2002 Elsevier Science B.V. All rights reserved.
PII: S0022-1996(01)00156-8

474   D. Mitra / Journal of International Economics 57 (2002) 473–485

under free trade. Mayer (1981) rigorously analyzes conditions under which welfare-maximizing, large-country governments are better off signing trade agreements. Grossman and Helpman (1995) show that governments, subject to internal political pressures, also impose these terms-of-trade externalities on one another, creating a rationale for 'trade-talks' as opposed to 'trade wars'. Further, Bagwell and Staiger (1996, 1999) show that even when political economy considerations are taken into account, the only rationale for (reciprocal) trade agreements is the elimination of these terms-of-trade externalities.

Another interesting strand in the literature argues that free trade agreements provide governments with the ability to commit in situations where the setting of trade policy is ridden with time inconsistency problems (see Staiger and Tabellini, 1987; Tornell, 1991).

Maggi and Rodriguez-Clare (1998) have an elegant and interesting political economy explanation for the commitment to free trade agreements by small countries. They formally examine the often-heard informal explanation for trade agreements: ' . . . they (trade agreements) provide a way for the government to credibly distance itself from the domestic special-interest groups that lobby for protection; the idea is that, by committing to free trade, a government may be able to foreclose political pressures at home'. More specifically, they have a setting in which owners of capital first decide in which sector to invest and then those who invest in a particular sector (the import-competing sector) lobby the government for protection. The lobbying is modeled as a Nash bargaining game between the import-competing lobby and the government over tariffs and political contributions. The lobby ends up at least compensating the government for the deadweight losses purely generated in the second stage. However, it may not compensate the government for the welfare loss through the intersectoral misallocation of capital in the first stage in the expectation of protection in the second stage. In such a situation, it is possible that a government that has the option of committing to a free trade agreement in a prior (to stage one) stage zero may actually commit to such an agreement. Such a situation is one in which, in the absence of the agreement, the welfare loss from the resource misallocation in the first stage is valued more by the government than its gain from sharing the redistributed surplus in the second stage.

The Maggi–Rodriguez-Clare framework demands a government with a long enough horizon as intersectoral capital mobility is a fairly long-run phenomenon. Such an assumption is perfectly valid when the focus is on developed countries that have stable governments. However, in the recent past, quite a few developing countries have joined or have expressed a desire to join the GATT/WTO. In such countries, governments are generally weak and often do not last long. In such situations, governments could hardly be expected to care about long-term problems such as capital misallocation, whose effects on welfare or the quality of life take decades to show up. In such a setting, capital mobility may not be an aspect that one would like to focus on. With the frequent entry and exit of parties

D. Mitra / Journal of International Economics 57 (2002) 473–485 475

into and from power, lobbies need to constantly build new relationships and establish new contacts. In other words, certain fixed costs may have to be incurred to get politically organized (build relationships) with respect to the new government in power. However, as its reputation (at least some of it) might precede the government, the decision to incur this cost may be based on the expectation of success in lobbying for protection down the road once these organizational costs are incurred. Further, in quite a few developing countries, due to a politically unstable environment, political organizations (such as lobbies) form and disintegrate quite frequently. Thus, the fixed costs of political organization can alternatively be interpreted as lobby formation costs as in Mitra (1999) and as in Krishna and Mitra (2000).

In this context, I build on the Maggi–Rodriguez-Clare version of the Grossman–Helpman framework, augmenting it with the decision to incur fixed costs (build relationships with politicians in power and/or to form a lobby) prior to the actual lobbying, but, importantly, eliminating the capital-mobility portion considered by them (Maggi and Rodriguez-Clare) to be key in driving their results. As argued above, this story sounds more realistic at least in the case of developing countries. However, the main result of the Maggi–Rodriguez-Clare model goes through in this newly modified set up which does not have any intersectoral capital mobility. This is the result that generally governments with low bargaining power with respect to domestic lobbies are the ones that want to precommit to free trade agreements. In other words, this paper coupled with the Maggi–Rodriguez-Clare paper makes a more general point, a point that cannot be made by any one of these two papers in the absence of the other. This general point is that the precommitment to a free trade agreement does not have to be driven specifically by the possibility of capital misallocation alone (or solely by the possible incurring of organizational costs) arising in the expectation of protection. It is applicable to any kind of resource costs incurred prior to lobbying through actions taken in the expectation of successful lobbying in the next stage. In this respect, this paper and the one by Maggi and Rodriguez-Clare are complementary.

Additionally, this model provides several new and fairly surprising insights especially with respect to the comparative static effects of the organizational costs on the possibility of entering into a trade agreement. Firstly, holding constant the government's bargaining power, when fixed organizational costs are above a certain cut-off value (itself a function of the government's bargaining power), the government never has to commit to a trade agreement even when the lobby is expected to get formed down the road. Below, this cut-off value of fixed costs, the likelihood (in terms of the range of parameter values) of this commitment by the government keeps increasing (or at least remains constant) as fixed costs go down. This is because the likelihood of lobby formation increases. Secondly, the maximum bargaining power (of the government with respect to the lobby) needed for commitment to a trade agreement is increasing in the fixed organizational costs for low fixed costs, but is decreasing in fixed costs once a threshold fixed cost is

476   *D. Mitra / Journal of International Economics 57 (2002) 473–485*

reached. The comparative static effects of changes in organizational costs are important as these costs change with changes in communications technology which has made giant leaps in the last two decades. Moreover, these costs might vary across countries that differ in political stability, geographical concentration of firms, asset inequality, size, etc.

In Section 2, I present the model and the results. In Section 3, I analyze certain extensions and the consequences of relaxing some assumptions made in Section 2. Finally, in Section 4, I make a few concluding remarks.

2. The model

Consider a small open economy. Individuals are assumed to have identical preferences. There are two kinds of factor owners — workers and capitalists. There is a non-numeraire import-competing good, produced using capital and labor under constant-returns-to-scale. In addition, there is a numeraire exportable good which is produced under constant-returns-to-scale using only labor.

Each consumer chooses c_Z and c_X to maximize a utility function $U = c_Z + u(c_X)$ subject to her budget constraint $pc_X + c_Z = E$ where c_Z is consumption of the exportable, numeraire good Z, c_X is consumption of the import-competing, non-numeraire good X (whose exogenous world price is p^* and domestic price is p) and E is total income. $u' > 0$ and $u'' < 0$. The wedge between p and p^* arises from the presence of the import-tariff (to be derived endogenously). Thus we have the demand functions for the two goods given by $c_X = d(p)$ and $c_Z = E - pd(p)$ where $d(.)$ is the inverse of $u'(.)$.

Let L_Z be the amount of labor used in the production of the numeraire good whose production function is assumed to be $Z = L_Z$ (so that the wage rate $w = 1$ in a competitive equilibrium). The output of the non-numeraire, import-competing good is given by a constant-returns-to-scale production function $X = f(K, L_X)$ where K is capital used only in the production of the import-competing good and L_X is the amount of labor used in its production. Thus the supply function of the import competing good is $X(p) = \pi'(p)$ where $\pi(p)$ is the profit function and gives the total reward to capital.

I assume that the only policy instruments available to politicians are trade taxes and subsidies and the net revenue from them is distributed uniformly across the population. The total gross welfare levels of capitalists and workers are given by $\Omega_K(p) = \pi(p) + \gamma_K M[\tau(p) + \sigma(p)]$ and $\Omega_L(p) = L + (1 - \gamma_K)M[\tau(p) + \sigma(p)]$, respectively, where $\tau(p)$ and $\sigma(p)$ are, respectively, net tariff revenue and consumer surplus going to each individual in the economy, γ_K is the number of capitalists as a proportion of the total population, L is the total labor endowment of the economy, M is the total population.

The model has three stages.

Stage zero: The government decides whether or not to commit to a free trade agreement. If the government precommits to such an agreement the game ends. Otherwise, the game goes on to the next stage.

The gross cost of signing an agreement is assumed to be small and so is not modeled. This cost will only act as a tie-breaker when the government is indifferent between signing and not signing, i.e. in the case of such indifference, the government does not precommit to such an agreement.

First stage: If no commitment was made to the trade agreement in stage zero, then in this stage, capitalists decide whether to contribute to the financing of the fixed organizational costs (defined in labor terms). This fixed cost may consist of one or a combination of the following: the costs of forming an organization (as in Mitra, 1999), establishing links with politicians, hiring professional lobbyists, building a communications network among members, designing a scheme of punishments for defaulting members, etc. By incurring these costs, capitalists can get closer to the government, so that political influence can be exercised on government's decision making. By incurring these costs for the formation or alternatively, for the maintenance of a political organization in the first stage, capitalists might be able to reduce transactions costs in lobbying activity, coordinate campaign giving decisions and communicate political 'offers' to the politicians.

Second stage: As in Grossman and Helpman (1994), the government's objective function is a weighted sum of political contributions and overall social welfare. If capitalists are not able to form a lobby in the first stage, no offers are made to the government which then maximizes aggregate welfare by choosing free trade. If capitalists form a lobby in the previous stage, then in this stage, as in Maggi and Rodriguez-Clare, the government and the lobby engage in bargaining over trade policy and contributions. The bargaining process is modeled as a Nash bargaining game in which the government and the lobby have bargaining powers b and $(1-b)$, respectively. The threat point is the status-quo situation in which the lobby makes no contributions and the government maximizes aggregate welfare by choosing free trade.

The problem is solved by working backwards, i.e. by starting from the second stage. The government's objective function in the second stage is the following:

$$\Omega_G = C + a\Omega_A(p) \tag{1}$$

where $\Omega_A(p)$ is aggregate gross (of both fixed costs and contributions) social welfare and C is the contribution by the lobby. The parameter a is the weight the government attaches to aggregate social welfare relative to political contributions. The higher is a, the lower is the government's affinity for political contributions and the higher is its concern for social welfare.

Let C^*, Ω_K^*, Ω_G^* and Ω_A^* be the equilibrium values of contributions, capitalists' gross welfare, government's gross welfare and aggregate gross welfare in the presence of bargaining between the government and the capitalists' lobby over trade policy and contributions. If the lobby does not get formed in the first stage, the government implements free trade in the second stage and the corresponding welfare levels are denoted by Ω_K^{FT}, Ω_G^{FT} and Ω_A^{FT}. Note that $\Omega_G^{FT} = a\Omega_A^{FT}$.

The outcome of the second-stage bargaining game (if the lobby was formed in the first stage and the government did not commit to the trade agreement in stage zero) can be described as follows.

(a) The contribution paid by the lobby in the second stage is given by[1]

$$C^* = (1 - b)a[\Omega_A^{FT} - \Omega_A^*] + b[\Omega_K^* - \Omega_K^{FT}]. \tag{2}$$

(b) The tariff or rather the tariff-inclusive domestic price p is chosen such that the government maximizes the following

$$\Omega_K(p) + a\Omega_A(p). \tag{3}$$

In order to ensure that the second-order condition of the government's maximization problem holds and there is an interior solution, I impose the following fairly weak restriction:

Restriction R. $1 - g'(p) > 0$ where

$$g(p) = \frac{1 - \gamma_K}{a + \gamma_K} \cdot \frac{X(p)}{[-I'(p)]},$$

$I(p)$ being import demand (as a function of price). [For the special case of linear demand and supply functions of the form $D(p) = A - p$ and $X(p) = p$, this boils down to the condition $2a + 3\gamma_K - 1 > 0$. For all standard functional forms, unless a and γ_K are both extremely small at the same time, an interior solution will exist.]

The maximization of (3) yields an ad valorem tariff rate t on imports given by the following familiar Grossman–Helpman expression:

$$\frac{t}{1 + t} = \frac{1 - \gamma_K}{a + \gamma_K} \cdot \frac{1}{\mu e} \tag{4}$$

where μ is the ratio of imports to domestic output and e is (the absolute value of) the price elasticity of import demand.

The net (net of contributions but gross of fixed costs) benefit for capitalists of forming a lobby is given by

---

[1]It should be noted that contributions are independent of fixed costs already incurred, so that the welfare levels gross of fixed costs in the contribution formula can be easily replaced by those net of fixed costs and vice versa as fixed costs get cancelled out.

D. Mitra / Journal of International Economics 57 (2002) 473–485   479

$$NB = \Omega_K^* - \Omega_K^{FT} - C^* = (1-b)\{[\Omega_K^* - \Omega_K^{FT}] - a[\Omega_A^{FT} - \Omega_A^*]\}$$
$$= (1-b)S \qquad (5)$$

where $S = [\Omega_K^* + a\Omega_A^*] - [\Omega_K^{FT} + a\Omega_A^{FT}] > 0$ is simply the joint surplus of the lobby and the government under protection over the free trade situation. Capitalists in the import-competing sector will decide to form a lobby only if $NB > F$. Differentiating (5), we have

$$\frac{\partial NB}{\partial a} = -(1-b)D < 0 \qquad (6)$$

where $D = [\Omega_A^{FT} - \Omega_A^*] > 0$ and $\frac{\partial NB}{\partial b} = -S < 0$. $[\partial NB/\partial a = (1-b)\partial S/\partial a = (1-b)\ \partial\{[\Omega_K^* + a\Omega_A^*] - [\Omega_K^{FT} + a\Omega_A^{FT}]\}/\partial a$. As free trade welfare levels do not change with a, we have $\partial NB/\partial a = \{(1-b)\{[d\Omega_K^*/dp + a\ d\Omega_A^*/dp](\partial p/\partial a) - [\Omega_A^{FT} - \Omega_A^*]\}$. By the first order condition of the government's maximization problem, $d\Omega_K^*/dp + a\ d\Omega_A^*/dp = 0$ which implies that $\partial NB/\partial a = -(1-b)[\Omega_A^{FT} - \Omega_A^*]$. Further note that S is completely invariant to changes in b (as the domestic price and the tariff are not dependent on it) which explains the derivative of NB with respect to b.]

The government's net benefit from lobby formation is given by

$$NB_G = \Omega_G^* - \Omega_G^{FT} = C^* + a\Omega_A^* - a\Omega_A^{FT} = bS. \qquad (7)$$

The government benefits from lobby formation if $NB_G > aF \Rightarrow NB_G/a > F$, since the government weighs by a the loss in welfare through the dissipation of resources in the incurring of the fixed costs. Let us define the government's normalized net benefit (for comparison with the fixed costs of organization)[2] as

$$\tilde{NB}_G = NB_G/a = bS/a. \qquad (8)$$

Then we have

$$\partial\tilde{NB}_G/\partial a = -(bS/a^2) + (b/a)(\partial S/\partial a) = -(bS/a^2) - (bD/a)$$
$$< 0 \quad \text{and} \quad \partial\tilde{NB}_G/\partial b = S/a > 0. \qquad (9)$$

[After imposing the government's first order condition for tariff determination, it is easy to see that $\partial S/\partial a = -D$.]

In order to obtain the point of intersection between $\tilde{NB}_G$ and NB in Fig. 1, the two need to be equated. From (8) and (5), $\tilde{NB}_G = NB$ means $bS/a = (1-b)S \Leftrightarrow [b/(1-b)] = a$ or $b = a/(1+a)$. Furthermore, $\tilde{NB}_G >$ or $< NB$ as $[b/(1-b)] >$ or $< a$.

The above derivatives and the comparison of net benefit functions give rise to

---

[2]This normalized net benefit is measured in units of aggregate welfare, while one that is not normalized is measured in units of political contributions.

480   D. Mitra / Journal of International Economics 57 (2002) 473–485

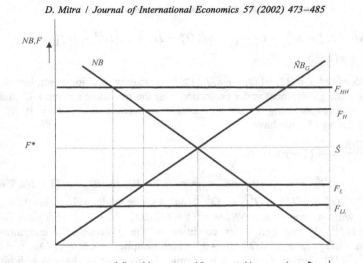

Fig. 1. The impact of a change in the governments bargaining power.

Fig. 1. As shown above, $\tilde{N}B_G$ and NB intersect at the point where $b^* = a/(1 + a)$. $\tilde{N}B_G$ is upward sloping with respect to the government's bargaining power b, while NB is downward sloping since b is also the government's (endogenously determined) share in the joint surplus S. When the bargaining power of the government is below b^*, the capitalists' net benefit from organization exceeds the normalized net benefit to the government. When the fixed cost is above F^* (but below the vertical intercept of the NB curve), say F_H, then in the absence of the trade agreement, these costs are incurred by the capitalists only if the government's bargaining power is below b'. Above b', these costs are not incurred and so the equilibrium outcome in the second stage is going to be free trade even without the government signing the trade agreement. So in stage zero, the government precommits to the trade agreement only if its bargaining power is below b'. This is the maximum bargaining power below which the government commits to the trade agreement. When the fixed cost goes up from F_H to F_{HH}, this maximum bargaining power falls to b'', making the trade agreement less likely in terms of the feasible parameter range. If the fixed cost is below F^*, at F_L, say, then absent the trade agreement, capitalists will incur organizational costs if the government's bargaining power is below $b^\wedge$. However, the government loses from this political organization only if its bargaining power is below b' in which case it signs the trade agreement. This maximum bargaining power falls to b'' if this fixed cost falls to F_{LL}. Therefore, we get an inverse-V-shaped relationship between the government's maximum bargaining power (for the signing of the trade agreement) and the fixed cost of political organization (see Fig. 2).

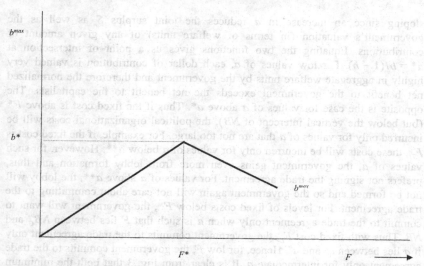

Fig. 2. The government's maximum bargaining power consistent with signing the trade agreement.

Fig. 3 shows the same net benefit levels as functions of a, the inverse measure of the government's affinity for political contributions (or rather the measure of the government's concern for aggregate welfare). Both functions are downward

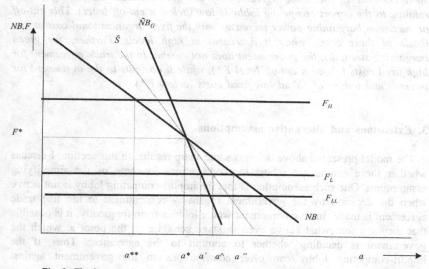

Fig. 3. The impact of a change in the governments concern for aggregate welfare.

sloping since an increase in a reduces the joint surplus S as well as the government's valuation (in terms of welfare units) of any given amount of contributions. Equating the two functions gives us a point of intersection at $a^* = b/(1 - b)$. For low values of a, each dollar of contribution is valued very highly in aggregate welfare units by the government and therefore the normalized net benefit to the government exceeds the net benefit to the capitalists. The opposite is the case for values of a above a^*. Thus if the fixed cost is above F^* (but below the vertical intercept of NB), the political organizational costs will be incurred only for values of a that are not too large. For example, if the fixed cost is F_H, these costs will be incurred only for values of a below a^{**}. However, for such values of a, the government gains even more from lobby formation and thus, prefers not signing the trade agreement. For values of a above a^{**}, the lobby will not be formed and so the government again will not care about committing to the trade agreement. For levels of fixed costs below F^*, the government will want to commit to the trade agreement only when a is such that F lies between $\tilde{NB}_G$ and NB. Thus with fixed cost F_L, the government commits to the trade agreement only if a lies between a' and a''. Hence, for low F, the government commits to the trade agreement only for intermediate a. It is clear from Fig. 3 that both the minimum and maximum values of a for commitment to the agreement will rise with a decline in the fixed costs. However, the range (of a) for this commitment increases in size. Thus, from the above analysis we have the following central proposition of the paper:

Proposition. *Imposing restriction R defined above, for a given 'a', the government commits to the trade agreement if the government's bargaining power relative to the import competing lobby is low (below a cut-off level). This cut-off or maximum bargaining power increases with the fixed organizational cost at low levels of these costs, while it decreases at high levels. Further, for given bargaining strengths, the government does not commit to the trade agreement for high fixed costs (above a cut-off level F^*), while it commits to the agreement for intermediate values of 'a' at low fixed costs (below F^*).*

3. Extensions and alternative assumptions

The model presented above delivers some sharp results. In this section, I discuss whether these results are robust to modifications in some of the simplifying assumptions. One such assumption is that the import-competing lobby is not active when the decision by the government regarding commitment to the free trade agreement is made. In an environment where lobbies form frequently, it is possible that they are somewhat active even in stage zero, i.e. at the point at which the government is deciding whether to commit to the agreement. Thus, if the import-competing lobby can offer contributions to the government against commitment to this trade agreement in period zero, it can easily be argued that the main results will still go through. Let F now be the total fixed costs of lobbying to be incurred by the import-competing sector in stages zero and one. The lobby will be able to prevent the government from committing to the agreement if the import-competing sector's net gain from incurring the fixed cost and being able to bargain in stage two exceeds the government's net loss (expressed in units of contributions), i.e. when $(1 - b)S - F > aF - bS > 0$. This implies that it is necessary to have $S > (a + 1)F$ for the government to be prevented from signing the agreement. This condition just means that the joint surplus of the lobby and the government under protection over the free trade situation (after the fixed cost has been incurred) should exceed the total loss perceived by the government and the lobby together from the incurrence of the fixed costs. If $\hat{S} = S/(a + 1) > F$, there is no commitment to the trade agreement by the government in period zero, while the reversal of this inequality leads to commitment. Thus in Fig. 1 (where all three curves can be shown to intersect simultaneously at the same point), if $F > \hat{S}$, the analysis is the same as before and the government's maximum bargaining power consistent with commitment to this agreement is decreasing in fixed costs. In Fig. 3, $\hat{S}$ (represented by the dotted line) is between the other two curves (again with a unique point of intersection) and is represented by the dotted line. For values of F below F^*, the range of a in which the government commits to the agreement clearly shrinks with the introduction of lobbying in stage zero. For example, with fixed cost F_L, this range is (a', a'') under no lobbying in stage zero and it shrinks to $(a', a^{\wedge})$ in the presence of stage zero lobbying.

The next question is regarding the ways in which the government can commit to free trade. Furthermore, there is also the issue of enforcement of trade agreements. The model in this paper relies on a WTO type system in the background. Of course, a repeated game setting with reputation, where expectations regarding the future behavior of the government are based on present behavior, may result in self-sustaining free trade. In this case, however, one will have to think of these fixed costs as the costs of reestablishing contact with the government or the expenses of getting to the bargaining table every period to negotiate with the government the level of import protection. So, even if the fixed costs have already been incurred in a prior stage (within the same period), the government may refuse to come to the bargaining table to prevent the formation of bad expectations regarding future behavior that would waste resources even further.[3] Also, even though there might be quite a few bad equilibria in addition to this good one, the fact that there exists such a free trade situation belonging to the overall set of

---

[3]It should be noted of course that in this repeated interactions setting whether the government would want to renegotiate protection with lobbies once fixed costs have been incurred will depend on the government's rate of time preference, the length of the electoral cycle, its probability of getting re-elected, etc. The renegotiability of trade agreements in a preferential trade context has been provided for and examined thoroughly in a recent paper by McLaren (2000).

equilibria ensures that signing the free trade agreement itself is at least self-enforcing.

Finally, in this context of enforcement, it is interesting to point out the case of Chile which unilaterally commits to a uniform tariff of 9% even though its bindings in the WTO are at 25% for manufactured products and 32% agricultural products, respectively (WTO, 1997). The framework presented in this paper can be used as follows to produce a result qualitatively quite close to this experience. Under no WTO tariff bindings, the bargaining between the government and the import-competing lobby is unconstrained. Let the net benefit function under such unconstrained bargaining be NB as before. Under the WTO binding, bargaining is constrained. The joint surplus of the government and the lobby over and above the free trade situation is lower under this constrained situation (where the maximum tariff that can be set is the WTO binding) and so the net benefit for the lobby is going to be lower. Let us call this constrained net benefit NB^C. Let b^U solve $NB(b) = F$, while b^C solve $NB^C(b) = F$. If the actual bargaining power lies in between b^U and b^C, then committing to a positive tariff binding in the WTO would actually lead to a zero equilibrium tariff. (Note that this amounts to the fixed cost lying between the constrained and unconstrained net benefit levels.) A similar analysis can be done by holding b constant and varying the parameter a. This result of this analysis is pretty consistent with what has happened in Chile. Just looking at the outcome, one would infer that the WTO binding is not a binding constraint. In the analysis presented above, it has the effect of lowering the net benefit, thereby preventing the import-competing sector from incurring the fixed costs. Thus, this binding, even though positive, ends up totally wiping out the tariff.

4. Conclusions

In this paper I augment a standard Nash bargaining model of endogenous protection with a prior decision for the import-competing capitalists to incur organizational costs (to build relationships with politicians in power and/or to form a lobby) before the actual lobbying. Unlike Maggi and Rodriguez-Clare (1998), I disallow intersectoral capital mobility. Nevertheless, their result (that is supposed to hinge on capital mobility), that governments with low bargaining power with respect to domestic lobbies want to precommit to free trade agreements, goes through. Further, surprisingly, when fixed organizational costs are above a certain cut-off value, the government never has to commit to a trade agreement even when down the road the lobby is expected to form. Below, this cut-off value, the likelihood of this commitment is decreasing in these fixed costs. The maximum bargaining power (of the government vis-à-vis the lobby) needed for commitment to the trade agreement is increasing in the fixed organizational costs for low fixed costs, but is decreasing for high values. This framework seems important in explaining the decisions of some of the developing countries to join the GATT/WTO. Most developing countries have unstable, short-lived governments that are unlikely to care about long-run problems arising from intersectoral misallocation of capital. On the other hand, the role of political organizational costs becomes more important in such settings as new political relationships have to be developed constantly.

Acknowledgements

I am indebted to Robert Staiger and two anonymous referees for very useful and constructive comments on an earlier version of this paper. The standard disclaimer applies.

References

Bagwell, K., Staiger, R., 1996. Reciprocal trade liberalization. NBER, Cambridge, MA, Working paper # 5488.

Bagwell, K., Staiger, R., 1999. An economic theory of GATT. American Economic Review 89 (1), 215–248.

Grossman, G., Helpman, E., 1994. Protection for sale. American Economic Review 84 (4), 833–850.

Grossman, G., Helpman, E., 1995. Trade wars and trade talks. Journal of Political Economy 103 (4), 675–708.

Johnson, H., 1954. Optimum tariffs and retaliation. Review of Economic Studies 21 (2), 142–153.

Krishna, P., Mitra, D., 2000. Reciprocated unilateralism: a political economy approach. Brown University and Florida International University, Mimeo.

Maggi, G., Rodriguez-Clare, A., 1998. The value of trade agreements in the presence of political pressures. Journal of Political Economy 106 (3), 575–601.

Mayer, W., 1981. Theoretical considerations on negotiated tariff adjustments. Oxford Economic Papers 33, 135–153.

McLaren, J., 2000. Free Trade Agreements, Customs Unions and the Dynamics of Political Influence. Paper presented at the Leitner Conference on Political and Economic Aspects of Regional Integration at Yale.

Mitra, D., 1999. Endogenous lobby formation and endogenous protection: a long-run model of trade policy determination. American Economic Review 89 (5), 1116–1135.

Staiger, R., Tabellini, G., 1987. Discretionary trade policy and excessive protection. American Economic Review 77 (5), 823–837.

Tornell, A., 1991. Time inconsistency of protectionist programs. Quarterly Journal of Economics 106, 963–974.

WTO, 1997. Trade Policy Review: Chile. WTO, Geneva.

Chapter 3

Reciprocated unilateralism in trade policy

Pravin Krishna[a,b,*], Devashish Mitra[b,c,1]

[a] *Brown University, USA*
[b] *NBER, USA*
[c] *Syracuse University, USA*

Received 5 November 2001; received in revised form 20 March 2003; accepted 24 October 2003

Abstract

Using the menu-auction approach to endogenous determination of tariffs and allowing additionally for lobby formation itself to be endogenous, this paper analyzes the impact of unilateral trade liberalization by one country on its partner's trade policies. We find that such unilateral liberalization may induce reciprocal tariff reductions by the partner country. Intuitively, unilateral liberalization by one country has the effect of increasing the incentives for the export lobby in the partner country to form and to lobby effectively against the import-competing lobby there for lower protection.
© 2004 Elsevier B.V. All rights reserved.

Keywords: Trade policy; Political economy; Lobby formation; Unilateralism; Reciprocity; GATT

JEL classification: F13; F10; F02

---

1. Introduction

In trade policy debates, the issue of unilateralism (i.e., the unilateral adoption of liberal trade policies) versus reciprocity (where reciprocity of access is insisted on instead) is a long standing one.[2] The theoretical arguments used by proponents of either policy stance

---

* Corresponding author. Current address: Economics Department, Brown University, 64 Waterman Street, Providence, RI 02912, USA. Tel.: +1-401-863-2170; fax: +1-401-863-1970.
E-mail addresses: Pravin_Krishna@Brown.edu (P. Krishna), dmitra@maxwell.syr.edu (D. Mitra).
[1] Contact address: Department of Economics, Maxwell School of Citizenship and Public Affairs, Syracuse University, 133 Eggers Hall, Syracuse, NY 13244, USA.

[2] Thus, one may consider the recent policy debates in the United States or go back a hundred and fifty years and examine the policy discussions preceding England's famous unilateral repeal of its Corn Laws to find free traders and reciprotarians actively pitted against each other. See Bhagwati and Irwin (1987).

0022-1996/$ - see front matter © 2004 Elsevier B.V. All rights reserved.
doi:10.1016/j.jinteco.2003.10.003

462   P. Krishna, D. Mitra / Journal of International Economics 65 (2005) 461–487

are well known: Unilateralists rely upon the demonstration that in the absence of "distortions," free trade is efficient, while a policy stance of reciprocity is theoretically supported by the presence of "terms-of-trade" and political economy motivations in the economy.[3]

In contrast to much of this literature, which has considered these two approaches to trade liberalization independently of each other, it is the goal of this paper to study the possible *causal interaction* between unilateral and reciprocal trade liberalization. Specifically, we are interested in examining the question of whether unilateral trade liberalization by one country could *induce* reciprocal liberalization by its partner in the absence of any communication or negotiation between these two countries. The theoretical platform that we use to investigate this point is the popular construct of Grossman and Helpman (1994), where tariffs are determined by the interaction between competing domestic lobbying groups and the government, and where the government's objective function itself includes political contributions from organized lobbies and also aggregate welfare. An important feature of our analysis is that formation of organized lobbies itself is treated as being endogenous, as in Mitra (1999). In this context, it is this paper's central finding that unilateral tariff liberalization by one country, by altering the political economy equilibrium in the partner country, may indeed result in reciprocal tariff reduction by the partner. We believe that this result carries interesting normative implications: It stands in contrast to the conventional policy wisdom on this matter regarding the use of (the threat of) one's trade barriers to remove those of others—as exemplified by the United States' recent use of the "Super-301" provision to "retaliate" by raising trade barriers against countries whose trade barriers are perceived as unreasonable.

The linkage between unilateralism and reciprocal liberalization that we have in mind is as follows: Consider a small open economy trading with a large partner. Further, to fix ideas, consider an initial situation in which the import-competing sector in the small country is represented by an organized lobby but the exportables sector is not (due to a fixed cost requirement faced by this sector which in this initial equilibrium exceeds the benefits it could get from the formation of the lobby). Consequently, its (Grossman–Helpman) trade policy vector (determined by lobbying by the import-competing lobby and the government preferences) is characterized by import tariffs (which raise the lobby's profits) and export taxes (which lower the lobby's cost of consuming the exportable good).[4] In this context, unilateral liberalization by the large partner country can be shown to generally increase the incentives for the formation of an export lobby in the small country. This happens for two reasons: First, a higher world price of the exportable good

---

[3] Thus, for instance, Mayer (1981) showed that in the presence of terms of trade motivations for tariffs, international negotiations could lead to a better outcome than the non-cooperative Nash outcome derived earlier by Johnson (1953). Equally, political economy influences have been considered in models explaining agreed-upon reciprocal trade liberalization in the work of Mayer (1984), Grossman and Helpman (1995), Hillman and Moser (1996) and Bagwell and Staiger (1999), among others.

[4] The export tax derived in the Grossman–Helpman model should not be taken literally. As is well known, in multi-sector general equilibrium models with perfect competition, the imposition of import taxes on all imports is itself equivalent to export taxes being imposed on all exports at the same ad valorem rate (Lerner symmetry). Further, if intermediates are used in production (specifically if the importable is used in the production of the exportable good), it should be clear to see that the import tax itself acts as a tax on the exportable sector.

(resulting from this liberalization) makes the existing trade policy vector more costly for the export lobby. Secondly, at higher export prices (in the absence of an export lobby), the import-competing lobby has incentives to lobby for a trade policy vector even more biased against the exporting lobby—further raising the incentives for formation of the export lobby. Once formed, this export lobby then competes effectively with the import-competing lobby to oppose the orientation of existing trade policies (i.e., to reduce domestic tariffs and export taxes). Unilateral liberalization by one country therefore has a "strategic" effect on the relevant groups in the partner country so that free trade is the outcome.[5]

Several additional points relating to the empirical validity of our results and their connection with the rest of the theoretical literature may be made here: First, we should note that the type of result demonstrated in the paper is indeed possible in the classic Johnson (1953) analysis of optimal tariffs if the tariff reaction functions there are upward sloping. There too, a unilateral tariff reduction by one country would result in tariff reductions by the partner (again, if the partner's tariff reaction function is upward sloping). However, it should be clear that our analysis differs in significant theoretical (and finally empirically relevant) ways from the Johnsonian analysis. In our framework, a unilateral liberalization by a country would affect even a "small" country's trade policies, whereas in the Johnsonian analysis, a small open economy keeps its tariffs fixed at zero— independently of the tariffs imposed by the large partner country. Furthermore, in Johnson's analysis, upward sloping reaction functions can only be derived if partner export supply elasticities are falling in partner country tariffs. Our results do not depend upon this monotonic elasticity relationship whose empirical validity itself may be questioned (indeed most textbook treatments consider the opposite case—that of down-ward sloping reaction functions).

Second, *without* making a strong empirical claim, we should note that the prediction of our model is consistent with a few major episodes of unilateral trade liberalization which are well known in the history of international economic relations.[6] As Coates and Ludema (1997) argue, these include the unilateral repeal of England's Corn Laws in the mid-19th century, "after decades of attempts to negotiate lower tariffs with its trading partners" and the more recent example of the United States, which, after the end of the Second World War sponsored the General Agreement on Trade and Tariffs (GATT) and engaged subsequently in major tariff reductions "without requiring substantive reciprocity from its major trading partners." "Waves of liberalization" by trading partners followed both these episodes. In the period immediately after England's repeal of its Corn Laws, numerous countries followed suit—with unilateral trade reforms of their own or with bilateral tariff agreements with England. Equally, the major trading partners of the United States reduced their trade barriers in the period leading up to the 1970s (see Kindleberger,

---

[5] This causal link is similar to the one suggested informally by Bhagwati (1990) that "concessions to the foreign exporters," through a reduction in home country tariffs, "may create new interests that counterbalance the interests that oppose trade liberalization" there.

[6] Separately, the role of sunk costs in political organization and the endogenous formation of lobbies in response to improved economic incentives to do so has been analyzed recently in the empirical investigation of the 1934 Reciprocal Trade Agreements Act (RTAA) by Irwin and Kroszner (1997).

1975, 1977; Coates and Ludema, 1997). In this context, the recent experiences of many developing countries also seem relevant. Following trade barrier reductions by full-obligation (i.e., developed country) GATT members in the several GATT rounds, there have been dramatic reductions of trade barriers by many developing countries that were exempt from the obligation to reciprocate by the articles (specifically, Article XVIII) of the GATT.[7] This is roughly consistent with the theoretical predictions of the model: Unilateralism may be reciprocated even in the absence of a formal obligation to do so.

We should note also the similarity in motivation of our work with that of Coates and Ludema (2001), who study the impact of unilateral tariff reduction on *negotiation* outcomes (specifically the likelihood of success of achieving bilateral agreements in the presence of the "political risk" of domestic opposition to trade agreements) and argue that unilateral trade liberalization may be the optimal policy for a large country. In their framework, "unilateral liberalization acts as insurance" by providing a "risk-sharing" role. Unilateral tariff reduction lowers the political stakes associated with trade liberalization in the foreign country, thereby lowering the overall political cost of reaching and implementing trade agreements and increasing the probability of successful agreements.

To sum up, we believe the contribution of the paper to be threefold: It is among the first formal analyses of the interaction between unilateralism and reciprocal liberalization that we are aware of. Second, in studying this interaction it articulates channels through which unilateralism could lead to the organization of export interests in partner countries and thus induce reciprocity—a result which we believe holds interesting normative implications. Finally, in serving as a potential explanation for some well-known historical episodes of trade reform that we have mentioned, we believe that our paper has some positive significance as well.

Before proceeding with the formal model, we should note a point regarding the modeling strategy here: While we treat explicitly the formation of lobbies and tariffs in the "small" economy, the tariff reduction in the large economy is modeled as being *exogenous* (i.e., the level of the tariff imposed by the large open economy is taken as given by agents in the small country). This is done for analytical convenience since it appears to us to be the simplest framework within which to communicate the central idea of the paper—i.e., that there exist channels through which tariff reductions in one country (however they come about) could lead to reciprocal tariff reductions by its partners. However, even taking this assumption of "exogenous tariff reduction" literally, several examples may be offered in justification: Thus, for example, the model may be interpreted as representing a situation in which developed country GATT members negotiate tariff reductions amongst themselves and bind their tariffs at the end of such negotiations. Developing country members are beneficiaries of these tariff reductions due to the most favored nation (MFN) principle of the GATT, but may not be under full obligation to reciprocate (due to Article XVIII of the GATT). The possible reciprocity (in the form of tariff reductions by the developing countries, for instance) that may nonetheless be induced by such tariff reductions by developed countries is what this model studies. An alternate interpretation is to think of the

---

[7] The relevance of interest groups in trade policy determination in developing countries has been established in a number of recent empirical papers, including De Melo et al. (2001) and Mitra et al. (2002).

model as studying the effects on partner countries of tariff reductions that may occur in certain countries due to regime shifts involving ideological changes (the ascension of committed free traders into political power, for instance). A third interpretation is to think of the model as studying the impact of trade policy changes undertaken by some countries due to conditionality imposed on them by international bodies such as the International Monetary Fund as part of a larger scheme to restructure the economy. In each of these cases, one may argue that agents in the partner countries (i.e., lobbies) take the tariff changes as being given rather than being endogenous to their own actions.

The rest of the paper proceeds as follows: Section 2 outlines the basic model describing endowments, technology and preferences in a small economy that is involved in trade with a "large" partner. Section 3 discusses the endogenous formation of lobbies and trade policy in the small country and derives the initial equilibrium. Section 4 demonstrates the scope for reciprocal liberalization by the small country when tariffs are liberalized by its large partner. Section 5 discusses the normative implications of this reciprocity mechanism for tariff policy in the large country. Section 6 describes the results of simulation analysis conducted with a view to exploring the implications of our framework under circumstances (i.e., initial conditions) other than those we focus on in the main section of the paper. Section 7 concludes.

2. The model

Consider a small open economy producing a numeraire good z with Ricardian technology and two non-numeraire goods (an import-competing and an exportable good), x_m and x_e,[8] each requiring a different kind of factor of production specific to that good and labor for their production. Individuals in this economy are assumed to have identical preferences with their utility functions taking the following form:

$$U = c_z + \sum_i u_i(c_{x_i}), \qquad i = m, e,$$

where c_z is consumption of the numeraire good, c_{x_i} is consumption of good x_i and $u_i(c_{x_i})$ denotes the sub-utility derived from the consumption of the ith non-numeraire good ($u'>0$ and $u''<0$). Consumers then solve the following optimization problem:

$$\max_{c_z, c_{x_i}} U = c_z + \sum_i u_i(c_{x_i}) \text{ subject to } \sum_i p_i c_{x_i} + c_z = E \qquad (1)$$

where E is total income and where p_m and p_e denote the domestic prices of the two non-numeraire goods (the world price of goods x_i is assumed to be exogenously given at p_i^*).

---

[8] As is standard in the literature, it is assumed that this numeraire good is freely traded between countries—indeed it is exchanges of this "numeraire" good that serve to settle the balance of trade. Thus, this good may be imported or exported by any country based on its balance of trade in the remaining goods. Regardless, we use the terms importable good and exportable good in this paper to refer exclusively to the goods x_m and x_e, respectively.

466   *P. Krishna, D. Mitra / Journal of International Economics 65 (2005) 461–487*

From the first-order conditions, we have demand for the non-numeraire goods given by:

$$c_{x_i} = d_i(p_i)$$

where $d(\cdot)$ is the inverse of $u_i'(\cdot)$.

The demand for the numeraire good, in turn, is given by

$$c_z = E - \sum_i p_i d_i(p_i). \tag{2}$$

Given our assumption regarding the form of the utility function, the indirect utility function is given by

$$v(\mathbf{p}, E) = E + \sigma(\mathbf{p}), \tag{3}$$

where $\mathbf{p} = (p_m, p_e)$ is the vector of domestic prices of the non-numeraire goods and

$$\sigma(\mathbf{p}) = \sum_i u_i(d_i(p_i)) - \sum_i p_i d_i(p_i), \tag{4}$$

is consumer surplus.

As stated earlier, good z is manufactured using labor alone under constant returns to scale (CRS). We set the input–output coefficient equal to one by choice of units (i.e., $z = L_z$), so that the wage rate $w = 1$ in a competitive equilibrium. The output of each non-numeraire good is given by the following production function

$$x_i = F_i(K_i, L_i) \tag{5}$$

where K_i is the sector specific factor used in the production of the ith good and L_i is the amount of labor used in the ith good. $F_i(\cdot)$ is assumed to be CRS and subject to diminishing returns to each factor.

The quantity of each non-numeraire good supplied domestically is then given by:

$$x_i = x_i(p_i) = \pi_i'(p_i) \tag{6}$$

where $\pi_i(p_i)$ is the profit function and gives the total reward to K_i.[9]

Individual income in this economy is augmented by lump-sum (and uniform) redistribution of income derived from trade taxes and subsidies.[10] The net revenue from taxes and subsidies, expressed on a per capita basis, is given by

$$\tau(\mathbf{p}) = \sum_i (p_i - p_i^*)[d_i(p_i) - (1/N)x_i(p_i)] \tag{7}$$

where N is the total population and p_i^* denotes the world price of good i.

---

[9] It can easily be shown that $\pi_i''(p_i) > 0$, i.e., the profit function is convex with respect to price—a property that we will use later in deriving our results.

[10] Following Grossman and Helpman (1994), we assume that the only policy instruments available to politicians are trade taxes and subsidies.

Thus, if l^h represents individual h's endowment of labor and if s_i^h denotes its share of the ith specific factor, the income of this individual is then given by

$$E^h = l^h + \sum_i s_i^h \pi_i(p_i) + \tau(\mathbf{p}) \qquad h = 1, 2 \ldots N. \tag{8}$$

Finally, the indirect utility function of individual h is given by

$$v^h(\mathbf{p}) = l^h + \sum_i s_i^h \pi_i(p_i) + \tau(\mathbf{p}) + \sigma(\mathbf{p}) \tag{9}$$

To get to endogenous determination of tariffs and lobbies, we make some simplifying assumptions regarding the structure of endowments and ownership of specific factors in this economy. First, we assume that each individual in the economy is endowed with exactly l units of labor. Further, we assume that each individual owns only *one* type of specific factor and that owners of any particular type of specific factor are symmetric (that is, they own identical amounts of that specific factor). Letting θ denote the fraction of the population that owns the kind of specific factor used in the production of the importable and $1 - \theta$ denote the proportion of population that owns the other specific factor,[11] we have the total gross welfare of the set of individuals owning the ith specific factor to be given by

$$\Omega^i(\mathbf{p}) = \alpha_i N l + \pi_i(p_i) + \alpha_i N[\tau(\mathbf{p}) + \sigma(\mathbf{p})] \tag{10}$$

where

$$\alpha_i = \begin{cases} \theta & \text{when } i = m \\ 1 - \theta & \text{when } i = e \end{cases}$$

3. Determination of the structure of lobbies and protection

As in Grossman and Helpman (1994), the government is assumed to care about the total level of political contributions that it may receive and about aggregate well-being. The government values contributions because they can be used to finance campaign spending or provide other direct benefits to office holders. Social welfare is of concern to the

---

[11] Thus, we assume that the entire population owns some specific factor. As will quickly become evident, this delivers strong results with changing lobby structure. However, we should note that the qualitative spirit of our results is preserved even with greater concentration of ownership of specific factors, i.e., if $\alpha_e + \alpha_m < 1$. Further, even at very high levels of concentration of ownership of factors, i.e., with $\alpha_e + \alpha_m$ approaching zero, the qualitative spirit of our results is maintained if we include and consider other features—such as intermediate inputs which are importables or the potential formation of consumer lobbies.

government since voters would more likely re-elect a government that has delivered a high standard of living. A linear objective function is assumed to represent these preferences:

$$\Omega^{G}(\mathbf{p}) = \left[\sum_{i \in \Lambda} C_i(\mathbf{p}) + a\Omega^{A}(\mathbf{p}) \right]$$

where Λ is the set of organized interest groups (lobbies), $\Omega^{G}(\mathbf{p})$ is the objective function of the government, $\Omega^{A}(\mathbf{p})$ is aggregate gross social welfare,[12] $C_i(\mathbf{p})$ is the contribution schedule of the ith lobby and a is the weight the government attaches to aggregate social welfare relative to political contributions. Clearly, the higher is a, the higher its concern for social welfare relative to its affinity for political contributions.

We are interested in the political equilibrium of the following three-stage non-cooperative game. In the first stage, specific factor owners in a sector decide whether to contribute to the financing of the fixed and sunk costs (defined in labor terms) of forming an organized lobby. This fixed cost consists of the costs of forming an organization, establishing links with politicians, hiring professional lobbyists, building a communications network among members, designing a scheme of punishments for defaulting members, etc. Forming a lobby can also be one way of getting closer to the government, so that political influence can be exercised on government's decision making. A lobby can be considered to be an organizational set up to reduce transactions costs in lobbying activity, coordinate campaign contributions and communicate political "offers" to the politicians. In sectors without lobbies, the individual owners consider themselves too small to communicate their offers or persuade the government to formulate economic policy one way or the other, since the transactions costs for these to be done at the level of the individual may be very high.

In the second stage, lobbies choose their political contribution schedules. As in Grossman and Helpman (1994), it is assumed that each organized industry provides the government with a contribution schedule that *truthfully* reveals its preferences taking into account the government's objective function. Finally, in the third stage, the government sets trade policy to maximize a weighted sum of political contributions and overall social welfare.

The problem is solved by working backwards, i.e., by starting from the third stage. Here, the government, facing the contribution schedules of organized lobbies, solves the following problem:

$$\max_{\mathbf{p} \in P} \ \Omega^{G}(\mathbf{p}) = \left[\sum_{i \in \Lambda} C_i(\mathbf{p}) + a\Omega^{A}(\mathbf{p}) \right] \tag{11}$$

where P is the set of domestic price vectors from which the government may choose. As already noted, attention in this paper is restricted to equilibria that lie in the interior of P.

---

[12] Since this paper is eventually concerned with causes and consequences of lobby formation, we shall shortly introduce additional notation in the form of subscripts attached to Ω that denote which lobbies are operational at any given time.

In the prior stage, lobbies are assumed to choose truthful contribution schedules. The schedule for each lobby $i \in \Lambda$ is given by

$$C_i(\mathbf{p}) = \max(0, \Omega_i(\mathbf{p}) - b_i)$$

where the scalars b_i's (the net welfare anchors for the different lobby groups) are determined in equilibrium. As in Grossman and Helpman, we focus on equilibria where lobbies make positive contributions. In other words, in the neighborhood of the equilibrium,

$$C_i(\mathbf{p}) = \Omega^i(\mathbf{p}) - b_i. \tag{12}$$

Substituting Eq. (12) into Eq. (11), we have,

$$\max_{\mathbf{p} \in P} \Omega^G(\mathbf{p}) = \left[\sum_{i \in \Lambda}(\Omega^i(\mathbf{p}) - b_i) + a\Omega^A(\mathbf{p})\right] \Rightarrow \max_{\mathbf{p} \in P} \left[\sum_{i \in \Lambda} \Omega^i(\mathbf{p}) + a\Omega^A(\mathbf{p})\right] \tag{13}$$

The solution to this maximization problem yields the following expressions for trade taxes and subsidies, t_i (Grossman and Helpman (1994)):

$$\frac{t_i}{1 + t_i} = \frac{I_i - \gamma}{a + \gamma} \cdot \frac{1}{\mu_i \epsilon_i} \tag{14}$$

where γ is the proportion of the population that belongs to any organized lobby in equilibrium, μ_i and ϵ_i denote the ratio of imports to domestic production and the absolute value of the price elasticity of import demand, respectively, if $i = m$, and denote the ratio of exports to domestic production of the exportable and the absolute value of the elasticity of export supply if $i = e$ instead. I_i is an indicator variable which takes a value of one if the ith sector is organized and zero otherwise.

The immediate implication of Eq. (14) is that if both the exporting and importing sector in our framework are organized, we have *free trade*—since $\gamma = 1$ and I_i takes on the value of one for both sectors. This can be seen intuitively from Eq. (13). We know that when both lobbies are formed, the government is simply maximizing the weighted sum of overall welfare on the one hand and the sum of the surplus that accrues to each group on the other. This is simply a multiple of overall welfare anyway—which is maximized with free trade.

We are interested in understanding what the implications are of a reduction in tariffs by a large partner country on the equilibrium structure of tariff protection in this country. To begin with, we assume that at least one sector is organized. Without loss of generality, let us assume that only the *import-competing sector* is organized to begin with.[13] Eq. (14) gives us then that the trade regime is one that favors the import competing sector and in

---

[13] As we discuss in the next section, the spirit of our theoretical results is unaffected if we start instead with only the exporting lobby being organized. However, as Rodrik (1995) notes, it is a stylized fact that the vast majority of trade regimes that were liberalized in the recent years started with regimes in which the import-competing sector enjoyed significant protection.

470   P. Krishna, D. Mitra / Journal of International Economics 65 (2005) 461–487

which the exporting sector is effectively taxed. The import tariff, t_m, and the export tax, t_e, are given respectively by:

$$\frac{t_m}{1 + t_m} = \frac{1 - \theta}{a + \theta} \cdot \frac{1}{\mu_m \epsilon_m} \tag{15}$$

$$\frac{t_e}{1 + t_e} = \frac{-\theta}{a + \theta} \cdot \frac{1}{\mu_e \epsilon_e} \tag{16}$$

Note that here, the tariff on imports, t_m, is positive and the protection to the export sector, t_e, is a negative number—indicating that it is a tax on exports. In both cases, $(1 + t_i)$ denotes the ratio p_i/p_i^*.[14]

We now go back to the first stage and analyze conditions under which we may have lobby formation (of the export lobby) itself, *taking the import sector as organized*.[15] To save on notation, for the present analysis, we set (without any loss of generality) the world price of the importable good to be one.[16] We also let $p_e^* = p^*$. Thus, p^* now denotes the world relative price of the exportable. In this context, members of the exportable group decide whether to form a lobby or remain unorganized. To form the lobby, they face a fixed labor cost denoted by F. Nash interaction among group members is assumed in their contribution decisions towards the provision of the fixed labor cost of lobby formation. However, once the lobby is formed, it is assumed here that the lobby machinery can enforce perfect coordination among the members of that group in the collection of political contributions, i.e., given the symmetry of capital ownership by members within a group, the lobby machinery can enforce collection of equal amounts of political contributions from each capitalist in the sector. To compare the costs and benefits of lobby formation, we set up some additional notation as promised: Using " ~ " to denote equilibrium values, we let $\tilde{\Omega}^k_{i,j}$ denote equilibrium gross welfare of the kth sector with both lobbies in place, $\tilde{\Omega}^k_i$ denote its equilibrium gross welfare with only the ith lobby in place and $\tilde{\Omega}^k$ denote its equilibrium gross welfare with no lobbies in place. Finally, we let $\tilde{C}$ denote the export lobby's equilibrium political contribution.

Now, depending upon the magnitude of the fixed costs relative to the benefits of lobby formation, there are three possibilities:

(1) The benefit to any one individual within the exportable lobby exceeds the cost of forming the lobby. Here, contributing to the full financing of the fixed cost F is the only Nash equilibrium outcome among the group members, i.e., a lobby is always formed when,

$$(\tilde{\Omega}^e_{m,e} - \tilde{\Omega}^e_m - \tilde{C})/(1 - \theta)N > F.$$

---

[14] Henceforth when we talk of a higher export tax, we mean a higher absolute value of the tax in Eq. (16).

[15] Again, it is straightforward to do a similar analysis of the incentives for the import-competing sector to organize taking the export sector as organized. This is discussed in greater detail at the end of Section 4.

[16] This is, of course, consistent with the small country assumption made here. In Section 5, where we consider a large country trading with a large number of small open economies instead, we allow the world price of the importable good to vary.

P. Krishna, D. Mitra / Journal of International Economics 65 (2005) 461–487 471

(2) Alternately, the cost of lobby formation exceeds the benefit to any one individual but is less than the total benefit to the lobby, i.e.,

$$\tilde{\Omega}^e_{m,e} - \tilde{\Omega}^e_m - \tilde{C} > F > (\tilde{\Omega}^e_{m,e} - \tilde{\Omega}^e_m - \tilde{C})/(1-\theta)N$$

In this situation, there are two possible Nash equilibrium outcomes—either there is no contribution to the provision of the lobby or the fixed cost is fully financed. We assume that pre-play communication can take place. For example, when capitalists in an industry feel that they are going to benefit from forming a lobby, they start communicating with each other—write letters, make phone calls, etc. Hence, one can use some popular communication-based refinements here. The better equilibrium for the group (i.e., the lobby is formed) satisfies the conditions for the three popular communication-based refinements—coalition proof Nash, strong Nash and the Pareto-dominance refinement, and hence, group coordination becomes the likely equilibrium outcome.[17]

(3) The cost of forming the lobby exceeds the benefit of lobby formation to the group, i.e.,

$$\tilde{\Omega}^e_{m,e} - \tilde{\Omega}^e_m - \tilde{C} < F.$$

The Nash equilibrium outcome is obviously "not providing the lobby" since the total benefit is less than the total fixed costs. From the analysis of the above three cases, the conclusion that emerges is that a lobby is formed under the following condition:

$$\tilde{\Omega}^e_{m,e} - \tilde{\Omega}^e_m - \tilde{C} > F. \tag{16}$$

Having described the initial equilibrium that we focus on and having derived conditions under which an (initially non-existent) export lobby may be formed, we proceed to analyze the impact of unilateral trade reform on this initial equilibrium.

4. Unilateral tariff liberalization, terms of trade changes and endogenous lobby formation

We are interested in how a unilateral tariff reduction by a large partner country (leading to an improvement in the export price p^* faced by the "small" home country) may affect the initial equilibrium. In particular, we are interested in how this may affect the equilibrium structure of lobbies and finally the equilibrium structure of tariffs.

---

[17] Bernheim et al. (1987) look at an important class of "non-cooperative" environments where players can freely discuss their strategies, but cannot make binding commitments. They introduce a refinement of the Nash set, the concept of coalition-proof Nash equilibrium. An agreement is coalition-proof if and only if it is Pareto efficient within the class of self-enforcing agreements. In turn, an agreement is self-enforcing if and only if no proper subset (coalition) of players, taking the actions of its complement as fixed, can agree to deviate in a way that makes all its members better off. A more demanding refinement is the strong Nash refinement which requires that no coalition (including the whole set), taking the actions of its complement as given, can cooperatively deviate in a way that benefits all of its members. The Pareto dominance refinement requires that the Nash equilibrium is Pareto efficient among all possible Nash equilibria.

To get to this, however, we need to develop a little additional notation. Thus, we let NB represent net benefit from lobby formation for the exportable sector. NB is net of political contributions, but gross of fixed costs. This net benefit is therefore given by

$$\text{NB} = \tilde{\Omega}_{m,e}^{e} - \tilde{\Omega}_{m}^{e} - \tilde{C} \tag{17}$$

With truthful contributions, as in Grossman and Helpman (1994), the equilibrium contribution level by the exportable sector when organized is given by

$$\tilde{C}(p^*) = \tilde{\Omega}_{m,e}^{e}(p^*) - \tilde{b}_{e}(p^*) \tag{18}$$

where $\tilde{b}_{e}$ is the net (of contributions) welfare or payoff anchor (determined in equilibrium) of the contribution schedule of the exportable group when organized. Note that this is different from the net benefit (gross of fixed costs) from lobby formation, NB, which is the difference between the net payoff $\tilde{b}_{e} = \tilde{\Omega}_{m,e}^{e} - \tilde{C}$ received as an organized group and the net payoff $\tilde{\Omega}_{m}^{e}$ as an unorganized group. Note also that the endogeneity of trade taxes and subsidies and thus domestic prices implies that equilibrium values of group welfare and contributions can now be written as functions of only the world price of the exportable, rather than as functions of domestic prices and trade taxes.

Importantly, with truthful contributions, any lobby when formed will have to pay the government an amount that makes it indifferent between treating that lobby as organized and treating it as unorganized, given the contribution schedule of the other lobbies.[18] Thus, from Eq. (14), we know that the export lobby should compensate the government for the reduction in the import lobby's welfare due to its entry and for changes in overall social welfare. Therefore, the contribution of the export lobby is given by:

$$\tilde{C} = \tilde{\Omega}_{m}^{m} - \tilde{\Omega}_{m,e}^{m} + a(\tilde{\Omega}_{m}^{A} - \tilde{\Omega}_{m,e}^{A}) \tag{19}$$

where the superscript "A" stands for aggregate as before. We can now state our first proposition:

Proposition 1. *With a pre-existing import-competing lobby, the net benefit to the exporting sector from the formation of an export lobby (gross of fixed costs) is proportional to the sum of the deadweight losses created (relative to the free trade level) in the importable and the exportable sectors by the equilibrium trade policies that result when only the import-competing sector is organized.*

This is seen by substituting Eq. (19) into Eq. (17). The net benefit to the export lobby from lobby formation can then be written as:

$$\text{NB} = \tilde{\Omega}_{m,e}^{e} - \tilde{\Omega}_{m}^{e} - [(\tilde{\Omega}_{m}^{m} - \tilde{\Omega}_{m,e}^{m}) + a(\tilde{\Omega}_{m}^{A} - \tilde{\Omega}_{m,e}^{A})] = (a+1)(\tilde{\Omega}_{m,e}^{A} - \tilde{\Omega}_{m}^{A}) \tag{20}$$

where the second equality derives from our assumption that all members of society own at least one specific factor. Eq. (20) tells us that the net benefit from lobby formation can

---

[18] This is analogous to the well-known Clark–Groves mechanism. See Bernheim and Whinston (1986) for a discussion.

simply be expressed in terms of the change in aggregate welfare due to the formation of the lobby. Since our utility functions are quasi-linear, aggregate change in welfare can simply be expressed in terms of surplus changes. The above expression for net benefit can then be usefully modified as follows:

$$\text{NB} = (a+1)(\Delta_m + \Delta_e) \tag{21}$$

where Δ_m and Δ_e are the dead weight losses created in the importable and exportable sector, respectively, when only the importable sector is organized relative to when both lobbies are organized (i.e., the free trade level). This proves our proposition.

Our assumption regarding the initial equilibrium is equivalent to assuming that at the initial level of world prices, NB $< F$, that is, that the net benefit from lobby formation is less than the fixed cost of lobby formation and so the lobby does not form. The particular exercise that we wish to undertake relates to the effects of unilateral liberalization by a large partner country. As such, this would raise the world price of the small country's exportable good. To see how this may affect the incentives for lobby formation, we take the derivative of the above expression with respect to p^*. Then, under the additional *sufficient* assumption (which we discuss shortly) that $E_s(\cdot)'' \geq 0$ where E_s is export supply from the small country, we have our second proposition:

Proposition 2. *The net benefit from lobby formation to the exporting sector, NB, is increasing in the world price of the exportable, p^*.*

Noting that the deadweight loss in the import competing sector, Δ_m, does not depend upon p^*, and noting that the deadweight loss in the other sector can simply be expressed as a function of the world price of the exportable and the absolute value of the per unit tax on the exportable, $T = |p^* t_e|$, we have;

$$\frac{d\text{NB}}{dp^*} = (a+1)\frac{d\Delta_e}{dp^*} = (a+1)\left(\underbrace{\frac{\partial \Delta_e}{\partial T}}_{>0} \cdot \underbrace{\frac{dT}{dp^*}}_{>0} + \underbrace{\frac{\partial \Delta_e}{\partial p^*}}_{>0} \right) > 0 \tag{22}$$

Eq. (22) has three components on the right-hand side which need to be signed:

The first component is the change in the dead weight loss in the exportable sector due to an increase in the absolute value of the tax. It is straightforward to see that this is positive.

The second component is the change in the absolute value of the export tax for a given change in international export prices. This is positive as well. While we save a formal proof for the Appendix A.1, we can state the intuition here: The reason that T is increasing in p^* is that at a high world price for the exportable, the gain to the organized group from a given reduction in the price of the exportable good is higher. This leads to more vigorous lobbying by the importable sector for a higher per unit export tax (since they are consumers of this good). In turn, this leads to a higher per unit export tax. This can be seen clearly in Fig. 1 which represents changes in surplus and tariff revenues at two different levels of the world price of the exportable, p^*, holding the per unit tax, T, fixed. Note first that changes in p^* affect the import-competing sector through changes in

474   P. Krishna, D. Mitra / Journal of International Economics 65 (2005) 461–487

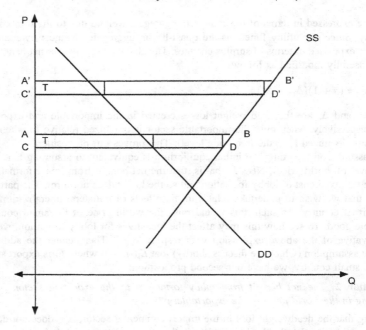

Fig. 1. Domestic demand and supply curves for the exportable good.

consumer surplus and tariff revenues (i.e, area ABCD minus the two Harberger triangles). Note further that change in surplus to this sector is a fixed proportion (i.e., the ratio θ) of the overall change (since all individuals in this economy consume goods in identical fashion and get the same share of tax revenues). Thus, at a higher p^*, for a given T, the change in surplus overall is higher (since A'B'C'D'>ABCD and the Harberger triangles are the same area). This implies a higher change in surplus to the import lobby. Thus there is a greater incentive to lobby for a higher export tax, which results in a higher per unit export tax, T, in equilibrium.[19]

As we show in Appendix A.2, the third term $\partial \Delta_e / \partial p^*$ is always ≥ 0 if $E_s'' \geq 0$, a condition that we assume here but that can be argued to be satisfied under fairly general conditions. To see this we note first that the condition holds for the linear supply and demand case where $E_s'' = 0$. Further, as we show in Appendix A.3, with constant export supply elasticities, for $E_s'' > 0$, we need that $\epsilon_s > 1$ where ϵ_s denotes export supply elasticity.

---

[19] We should point out that this holds even under alternate assumptions regarding tariff revenue redistribution. To see this, assume that the government holds onto tariff revenue instead of redistributing it uniformly to individuals. Now, with an increase in the world price of the exportable, the import-competing sector by itself would have less reason to lobby for an export tax (since its consumer surplus gain from such a tax on the margin is smaller). However, if it is assumed that the government places a premium on tariff revenues, then the government has a strong motivation to raise the export tax. On balance, with a strong enough emphasis on tax revenues placed by the government, the export tax would go up.

As we argue further in Appendix A.3, the condition that $\epsilon_s > 1$ itself should be satisfied for a very wide range of domestic supply and demand elasticities.[20] Conditions under which $E_s'' \geq 0$ holds even with non-constant export supply elasticities are discussed in Appendix A.3 as well.

Combining the three effects, we have that,

$$\frac{dNB}{dp^*} > 0$$

meaning that the net benefits to the export sector of forming an export lobby increase in p^*. This too can be seen from Fig. 1. Raising p^*, holding T fixed, the export lobby sees a larger reduction in producer surplus ($A'B'C'D'$ instead of ABCD) thereby increasing the incentive of the export lobby to form a lobby and lobby against the tax. Further, as we have already explained, the per unit export tax increases as p^* goes up, increasing the incentive to form the lobby even further.

Now, knowing that

$$\frac{dNB}{dp^*} > 0,$$

we let $p^* = \bar{p}$ solve the following equation:

$$NB(p^*) = F. \tag{23}$$

This allows us to state our third proposition:

Proposition 3. *When tariff reductions by the unilaterally liberalizing large country raise the world price of the small country's exportable (p^*) beyond $\bar{p}$, this unilateralism is reciprocated: the small partner country moves to free trade.*

This follows directly from Eqs. (22) and (23). From these, we know that when $p^* \geq \bar{p}$, the exportable sector gets organized. Now with both export and import sectors organized, there is *free trade*.[21,22]

---

[20] We should note here that even if we abandon our assumption regarding the curvature of the export supply function and it turns out to have the opposite sign (i.e., $E_s'' < 0$), NB would be increasing in p^* if the product of the first and second terms (both unambiguously positive) dominates.

[21] Note, interestingly, that this move towards free trade need not always be welfare improving for the small partner country. Thus, imagine that the initial world price of the exportable is just below $\bar{p}$ and that unilateral liberalization by the large country raises it to a level just above $\bar{p}$, so that NB just exceeds F. We know that the small country's export lobby would now form and in doing so will undertake a fixed resource cost of F. Gross aggregate welfare goes up by $(\Delta_m + \Delta_e)$. However, the fixed cost in this case would only be slightly below the net benefit to the export lobby which is given by NB=$(a+1)(\Delta_m + \Delta_e)$ and is therefore greater than $(\Delta_m + \Delta_e)$.

[22] With the specific assumptions on technology and preferences made here for the small country (and under identical assumptions for the large country), it is easy to show that we do not encounter the "Lerner case" and that a tariff reduction by the large country does increase the price of the small country's exportable in world markets.

This establishes our primary result that unilateral liberalization by a large partner country within this framework will induce reciprocal liberalization.[23] Profiles of the net benefit from lobby formation and the per unit trade taxes as functions of p^* are illustrated in Fig. 2. As shown there, once the export price, p^*, rises above the threshold level, i.e., once $p^* \geq \bar{p}$, we have free trade.[24] It may be noted that given the profile of export taxes, a gradual liberalization may generate an adverse initial welfare impact on the large country (if the partner were large enough) before bringing benefits.

It is also useful to interpret the political economy mechanism just stated in terms of how the welfare level of the exportable group varies with the world price of the exportable differently when this group is organized than when it is not. Fig. 3 illustrates that an increase in the world price of the exportable increases welfare of the exportable group whether it is organized or unorganized (see Krishna and Mitra, 2003 for a detailed mathematical derivation). Thus, the welfare levels are shown with positive slopes. Note that the welfare level of the exportable group when organized (net of political contributions but gross of the fixed cost of lobby formation) is higher than when it is not organized. Note also that NB increasing in p^* implies that the welfare locus when unorganized has flatter slope— implying, in turn, with large enough fixed costs, some point of intersection with the welfare locus when organized (net of both fixed costs and political contributions). The price at which this takes place is, again, $\bar{p}$. Beyond this price, the lobby is formed. Below it, it is not.

In the preceding discussion, in demonstrating the possibility that unilateral liberalization by a large country may induce reciprocity by its partner, we have made a number of explicit and implicit assumptions. The unilaterally liberalizing country was assumed to be large enough to affect world prices and, indeed reciprocal liberalization was shown to obtain only when tariff liberalization drove the world price p^* above the threshold level, $\bar{p}$ (which, it may be noted, need not happen even with full liberalization by the large country). Further, in order for there to be some connection between export and import lobbies (crucial for the mechanism we have proposed), it was assumed that lobbies are large enough (i.e., that α is big enough) for lobby owners to care about the prices of goods they consume—although, as we have discussed before, this will be the case even if each lobby was small but used output from the other sector as an intermediate in its own production. A sufficiency condition regarding export supply elasticities was stated and assumed to hold (and its empirical plausibility discussed). Finally, our analysis focused on the case where an active import lobby exists in the small country but there is no export lobby present. However, given Eq. (21), we can now discuss why our initial assumption regarding the pre-existence of the import-competing lobby rather than the exporting lobby is not crucial (see also Section 6 for a detailed discussion of alternate possibilities that

---

[23] Note that in the model, unilateral liberalization by one country results in reciprocity by the partner country through changes in the "demand" for protection in the partner country. However, one could interpret this as occurring through a change in the "supply" of protection instead. Specifically, with the formation of the export lobby, the final maximand of the "supplier" of protection, the government, changes—since it now takes into account contributions by this lobby as well. One could therefore think of this, loosely, as being an endogenous change in preferences of the supplier of the protection.

[24] As can also be seen in Fig. 2, when p^* is below the threshold level, the per unit export tax is rising with p^*—just as we have discussed earlier.

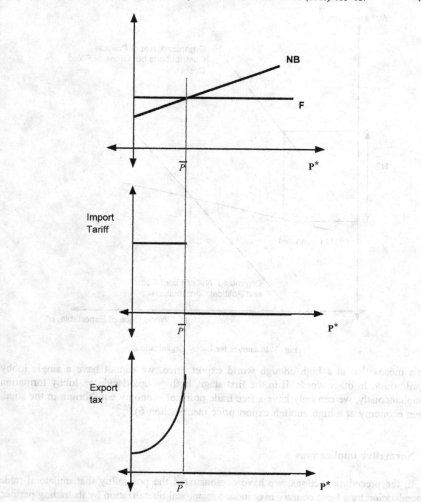

Fig. 2. Net benefits from lobby formation and trade taxes versus P*.

emerge with different initial conditions): Taking the other group as organized, the net benefit from organizing for any group of specific factor owners is proportional to the total deadweight loss caused prior to its entry as an organized group. When the export sector is the only organized group, the deadweight loss created by this sector is increasing in the world price of the exportable as the per unit export subsidy increases with the world price of the exportable. This makes the net benefit from organizing for the second group (the import-competing lobby) increasing in the world price of the non-numeraire exportable.

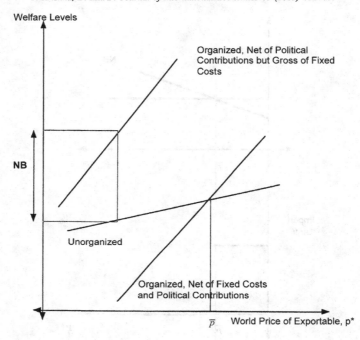

Fig. 3. Incentives for Lobby Organization.

This means that at a high enough world export price, we cannot have a single lobby equilibrium. In other words, if in the first stage, both groups decide on lobby formation simultaneously, we can only have a free trade political economy equilibrium in the small open economy at a high enough export price (see Section 6).[25,26]

5. Normative implications

In the preceding sections, we have demonstrated the possibility that unilateral trade liberalization by a large country may induce reciprocal liberalization by its trading partner.

---

[25] It should be noted that although the per unit export tax in the small open economy increases with an increase in the world exportable price, this is not true about the ad valorem export tax, as can be seen from the equilibrium export tax expressions. For example, with a constant price elasticity of export supply, we have an ad valorem export tax that is decreasing in p^*. When we have linear demand and supply with the additional requirement that the supply passes through the origin, the ad valorem export tax remains constant. When this supply has a positive price intercept, the ad valorem tax is again decreasing in p^*.

[26] If the initial situation was one where no lobbies were organized, it is possible that a unilateral reduction in tariffs by the large country induces a single lobby to form—thus taking the small country away from its initial free trade regime. However, further reductions in tariffs should lead to the formation of the second lobby taking the small economy back to free trade.

Would the large country benefit from such reciprocity? Our maintained assumption that the trading partner of the unilaterally liberalizing large country is small, clearly precludes this possibility—the movement of any single small country to free trade does not affect world prices and is therefore of little consequence to the large country. The (induced) reciprocity mechanism we have discussed is not without potentially important normative implications for the large economy, however. Indeed, in a simple extension of our framework where the large country trades with a number of small countries (which are individually small but collectively large), we are able to show that with unilateral liberalization, the large country may benefit if its trade partners reciprocally liberalize their trading regimes.[27]

Specifically, consider a situation in which the large open economy, A, trades with a continuum of small open economies (which are identical to each other with respect to technology, endowments and preferences) denoted by B. B's non-numeraire export good, e, and import good, m, are A's non-numeraire import and export goods, respectively.[28] Consider further, an initial situation in which import lobbies are organized in all the countries in B, but export lobbies are not. From Proposition 3, we have that the benefit of organization to export sectors (net of contributions but gross of fixed costs, F), NB, in B is decreasing in A's tariff, i.e., that $(\partial NB/\partial t^*) < 0$. With tariff reductions by A, if export lobbies in B get organized and move their countries to free trade, the collective size of these countries will bring terms-of-trade and thus welfare gains to A.

As we discuss in detail in Krishna and Mitra (2003), the responsiveness of countries in B to tariff reductions by A depends upon a number of parameters in the model. The movement of the various countries in B to free trade, may be, for instance, continuous or highly discrete. Nevertheless, setting aside concerns regarding stability and continuity for the moment (see Krishna and Mitra, 2003 for a comprehensive discussion), we can provide here a general discussion of how optimal tariff policy[29] for A may be modified in light of the reciprocity mechanism we have discussed so far. Two situations may be contrasted: one where the large country, A, chooses its tariffs taking the lobby structure in B as fixed and where the lobbies in the small open economies, B, are formed taking the large country's tariff as given (i.e., with simultaneous moves) and a second where A moves first, pre-committing to its tariff level, taking its effect on lobby formation in B into account (i.e., where A leads in Stackelberg-like fashion). In the present context (i.e.,

---

[27] The discussion that follows is intended as a brief and suggestive description of the results we have obtained regarding the normative implications of the reciprocated unilateralism mechanism. A detailed and formal treatment, dropped from this paper at the suggestion of our editor, can be found in Krishna and Mitra (2003).

[28] It is assumed that the general structure of the "large" economy is similar to that of the small open economies with which it trades (even though it may differ from them in endowments, the precise technologies used and in its exact preferences): Its consumers have quasi-linear and additively separable utility as in Eq. (1). It produces goods x_m and x_e using CRS technologies and employing sector specific capital and mobile labor and the numeraire good using Ricardian technology (just as in the small open economies). Also, we continue to assume that in each of the small open economies in B, trade policy is set in the political economy contexts discussed in the previous sections.

[29] It should perhaps be clarified that, given our normative concern, optimality here is in relation to the standard welfare-maximizing objective.

480   P. Krishna, D. Mitra / Journal of International Economics 65 (2005) 461–487

starting from an initial situation in which a large country trades with a number of identical small open-economies with politically organized import competing sectors) it can be shown that:

Proposition 4. *The large country's optimal (i.e., welfare maximizing) tariff is smaller when it takes into account its effect on the incentives for lobby formation in the exportables sector of its partner countries than when it takes the lobby structure in those partner countries as given.*

This follows intuitively from the discussion regarding the terms of trade gains to the large country that following reciprocal liberalization by its trading partners, which while individually small, are collectively large enough to impact world prices. Mathematical details (and a systematic analysis of the various possibilities that arise depending on the collective size of B in the markets for e and m) can be found in Krishna and Mitra (2003).

6. Simulations

Thus far, our argument regarding reciprocated unilateralism has been discussed in the context of particular (and, as we shall argue further below, empirically relevant) initial conditions. Specifically, the argument has been developed in the context of a small trading partner whose trade policy has been distorted due the *exclusive* initial presence of an import-competing lobby. A question arises here as to what happens under other different initial conditions. That is to say, what will be the effect of unilateral tariff liberalization by the large country if no lobbies are present in the small country initially? Or if it is an export lobby rather than an import lobby that is initially present? The complexity of the theoretical framework and multitude of parameters involved make analytical solutions to these questions hard to obtain and assess. However, simulation analysis using alternative functional forms and parameter values (treating the political organization decision of both the export and the import-competing lobby as endogenous) provides us with guidance on this issue. We discuss our findings below.

Our discussion of our findings using simulation analysis focuses on two illustrative cases. In both, demand functions and production functions are assumed to be linear and symmetric across sectors (see Appendix A.4 for details). We develop some additional notation as follows. $FNB_i( ) = NB_i - F_i$ denotes the *full* net benefit (benefit from organizing net of contributions *and* fixed costs) with the subscript $i=m,e$ indicating the sector whose full net benefit function it is. Included within the parentheses are *all* the sectors which are organized once the sector under consideration gets organized (for example, $FNB_e(e)$ denotes the full net benefit to the export sector from forming its lobby when the import-competing lobby is not organized, and $FNB_e(m,e)$ denotes the full net benefits to the export sector from lobby formation when the import-competing sector is organized as well). To see the effects of unilateral tariff reductions by the large country, we hold the import price of the small open economy constant at unity and vary the export price, p^*.

P. Krishna, D. Mitra / Journal of International Economics 65 (2005) 461–487 481

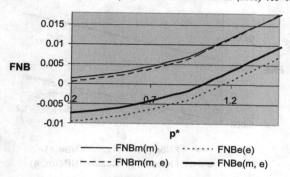

Fig. 4. $FNB = NB - F$ ($\theta = 1/3$, $a = 10$, F(export) = 0.02, F(import) = 0.01, export capital endowment = twice the import capital endowment).

In our first case (Fig. 4), our small open economy is assumed to have an endowment of capital (sector specific) in the exportable sector that is twice the amount of capital in the import-competing sector. We further assume that individuals in this economy own capital in identical amounts and in one or the other of the two sectors (but not both). Assuming further that the fixed cost of lobby organization, F, is proportional to the number of capital owners in a sector, we take the fixed cost of political organization in the export sector to be twice that in the import-competing sector. Fig. 4 presents the full net benefit curves as a function of the export price faced by the small open economy. The slopes of the full net benefit curves are positive for reasons that have already been discussed earlier in this paper. We can see from Fig. 4 that for low values of the export price, we have a unique equilibrium with just the import sector organized. As the export price rises, this initially continues to be the unique equilibrium—the FNB curves for the export sector (taking the import sector to be organized or not) are both below zero and the FNB curves for the import sector are both above zero. After FNB_e(m,e) rises above zero with yet higher p^*, the export lobby gets formed and the unique equilibrium here involves the formation of both lobbies (with free trade as the trade policy outcome) since FNB curves for both lobbies, each taking the other as organized, are above zero. This scenario is consistent with the one that we have focused on in the paper so far and illustrates our main argument. Note, however, that if fixed costs were a bit higher in the import-competing sector, both the FNB_m curves would shift down uniformly and, at low values of p^*, the import-competing sector would not be organized. If this were the initial condition, a reduction in tariffs by the large country would now induce the import-competing lobby to form first. Although the small economy now enjoys better terms of trade, it will have moved from an efficient trade regime (with free trade) to an inefficient one and will have incurred additionally the fixed costs of lobby formation. This may appear to be damaging to the argument regarding the use of unilateralism to induce reciprocity, but this is not the case since, of course, the argument is only relevant when there are some tariffs being imposed by the partner country in the first place. Also, with further tariff reductions (i.e., increases in the world price, p^*), the export lobby gets formed as well (after FNB_e goes above zero)

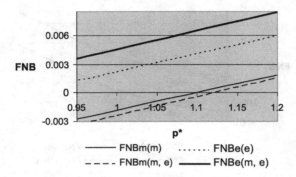

Fig. 5. FNB = NB − F (θ = 1/3, a = 10, F(export) = 0.015, F(import) = 0.02, export capital endowment = twice the import capital endowment).

and we have free trade. Thus, with high enough tariff reductions by the large country, free trade obtains in the partner country (even if the path to this is non-monotonic and fixed costs of lobby organization have been incurred along the way).[30]

In our second case, we continue to assume that the endowment of capital in the exportable sector is twice than in the importable sector. However, fixed costs of lobby organization for the export sector are assumed to be lower than that in the importable sector. As shown in Fig. 5, this gives us FNB curves for the exportable that are higher than those in the importable sector. Note that, as drawn, at low levels of p^*, it is now the export lobby that is organized while the import lobby is not. Trade policy is initially distorted with export subsidies and import subsidies. While it should be clear that this is an empirically nearly irrelevant case as virtually no countries can be characterized as having trade regimes of this nature, it is a clear theoretical possibility and so we analyze this nonetheless. Here too, a high enough increase in the world price of the exportable results in the formation of the import lobby with free trade emerging as the policy outcome. While such an outcome may benefit the small country, the large country would be faced with a policy regime less favorable to it. Finally, if fixed costs were a little higher, there would be no lobbies at low values of p^*. An increase in p^* would first lead to the formation of an export lobby which could be welfare worsening for the small country, causing it to move from free trade to a trade regime that was more favorable to the large country. Of course,

---

[30] We should note another interesting possibility that emerges in the setting just discussed. When only the import lobby is organized initially, an increase in tariffs by the large country also reduces the benefit to the import lobby of being active, as the FNB profiles show. To the extent that fixed costs of lobby organization are paid period by period, this suggests that tariff increases by the large country may also move the small country to free trade (if the import lobby drops out). However, if lobby organization costs are fully sunk, there will always be an incentive for the import sector to lobby (however small). The possibility of unilateral increases in tariffs by the large country leading to free trade in the partner then disappears.

further increases in p^*, as shown, will cause the formation of the import lobby as well and a movement back to free trade.

Finally, we should note that, for particular parameter values, other possibilities than those discussed in the two cases above arise as well. Specifically, with increases in p^*, it may be that we enter an intermediate zone where multiple equilibria are possible. Thus, the position of the FNB curves may be such that each lobby has an incentive to get organized only if the other lobby does as well. The outcome could then either be that both lobbies get organized or that neither does (with free trade as the policy outcome either way). In these cases too, however, it can be seen that with large enough values of p^* both lobbies get organized.

The simulations exercises, which examine a variety of "initial conditions," leave us with the following conclusions. First, the argument regarding reciprocated unilateralism has normative relevance primarily in contexts where the unilaterally liberalizing country faces countries that impose restrictions on its exports. Else, if the initial situation is one of free trade in the small country, liberalization by the large country might lead to protection in its small trading partner or might maintain free trade there but with resources wasted in organizational costs and political contributions.[31] Second, sufficiently large unilaterally tariff reductions can lead to free trade in the partner countries regardless of the initial conditions.

7. Summary and conclusions

Using the menu-auction approach to endogenous determination of tariffs pioneered by Grossman and Helpman (1994) and allowing for lobby formation itself to be endogenous, as in Mitra (1999), this paper analyzes the potential for unilateral trade liberalization by one country to impact trade policies in its partner in the absence of any formal agreement or communication between these countries.

We consider a large country trading with a small partner in which initially an organized import-competing lobby exists and where the trade regime is characterized by import tariffs (and export taxes). In this context, we find that unilateral liberalization by the large country may *induce* reciprocal tariff reductions by altering the political economy equilibrium there. Intuitively, unilateral liberalization by the large country has the effect of increasing the incentives for the export lobby in the partner country to form and to lobby effectively against the import-competing lobbies there for lower protection. Using simulation analysis, we confirm that the reciprocated unilateralism mechanism inducing the small country to move towards free trade may emerge even under quite different initial conditions than the ones considered centrally in the paper (although the path towards free trade may not always be monotonic, as we have discussed in Section 6). The induced reciprocity mechanism we have discussed has potentially important normative implications.

---

[31] One policy implication that might arise here concerns the merit of a rules-based system in which countries are not allowed to raise their tariffs (i.e., tariff bindings are agreed to). In this case, a tariff reduction by the large country will never be reciprocated by tariffs by the partner.

Acknowledgements

For helpful discussions and comments, we are very grateful to Jagdish Bhagwati, Elhanan Helpman, John McLaren, Dani Rodrik, Robert Staiger, two anonymous referees, and to seminar and conference participants at the Board of Governors of the Federal Reserve, Boston College, Brandeis University, University of British Columbia, Brown University, University of California at Irvine, Columbia University, University of Connecticut, Dartmouth, Florida International University, INSEAD, Korea Development Institute, New York University, University of Notre Dame, Syracuse University, Yale University, the NBER's 1999 Summer Institute in Cambridge, MA, the AEA's 2000 meetings in Boston, the Fall 1999 Mid-West International Economics Conference at the University of Illinois at Urbana-Champaign, the Fall 1999 Southeastern International Economics conference at Georgetown University and the Ford Foundation-American Enterprise Institute conference on "Unilateralism: The Case for Relaxed Reciprocity." Pravin Krishna gratefully acknowledges the hospitality and the intellectual and financial support of the Center for Research on Economic Development and Policy Reform at Stanford University and the Research Department of the International Monetary Fund, where some of this research was conducted.

Appendix A

A.1. To prove: (dT/dp*)>0

Proof. From Eqs. (15) and (16), when only the import-competing sector is organized, the ad valorem import tax and the ad valorem export tax are given by:

$$t_m = \frac{1-\theta}{a+\theta} \cdot \frac{x_m(p_m)}{[-p_m^* I_m'(p_m)]} \text{ and } t_e = \frac{-\theta}{a+\theta} \cdot \frac{x_e(p_e)}{[-p_e^* I_e'(p_e)]}, \text{ respectively,}$$

where $I_m(p_m)$ is import demand and $-I_e(p_e)$ is export supply. Normalizing $p_m^* = 1$ and letting $p_e^* = p^*$, we can write the magnitude of the per unit export tax as

$$T = |p^* t_e| = \frac{\theta}{a+\theta} \cdot \frac{x_e(p_e)}{[-I_e'(p_e)]} = g(p^* - T).$$

We impose the restriction that an increase in the price of a commodity should increase the output supplied proportionally more than it increases the magnitude of the derivative of export supply with respect to price, so that $g'>0$. This would always hold for linear demand and supply functions and also for most standard demand and supply functions.

Differentiating T with respect to p^*,

$$\frac{dT}{dp^*} = \frac{g'}{1+g'} > 0.$$

A.2. Sufficient condition for $(\partial \Delta_e/\partial p^*)>0$, $E_s''(p)\geq 0$

From Fig. 6, we have deadweight loss in the exportable sector due to the export tax given as:

$$\Delta(T,p^*) = \int_{p^*-T}^{p^*} E_s(p)\mathrm{d}p - TE_s(p^* - T)$$

$$= IE_s(p^*) - IE_s(p^* - T) - TE_s(p^* - T)$$

where I stands for integral evaluated at a particular value.

$$\Delta_2(T,p^*) = E_s(p^*) - E_s(p^* - T) - TE_s'(p^* - T)$$

$$\Delta_2 \geq 0 \Leftrightarrow E_s(p^*) - E_s(p^* - T) \geq TE_s'(p^* - T)$$

$$\Leftrightarrow \frac{E_s(p^*) - E_s(p^* - T)}{T} \geq E_s'(p^* - T).$$

By the mean value theorem,

there exists $p' \in [p^* - T, p^*]$, such that $\dfrac{E_s(p^*) - E_s(p^* - T)}{T} = E_s'(p')$

where $p' \geq p^* - T$.

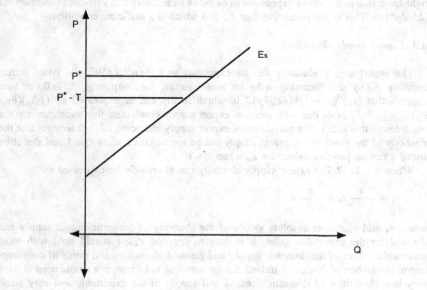

Fig. 6. Export supply curve.

486   P. Krishna, D. Mitra / Journal of International Economics 65 (2005) 461–487

Therefore,

$$E_s''(p) \geq 0 \Rightarrow E_s'(p^* - T) \leq E_s'(p') = \frac{E_s(p^*) - E_s(p^* - T)}{T}$$

which, in turn, implies that $\Delta_2 \geq 0$.

On necessary and sufficient conditions:

$$\frac{d\Delta}{dp^*} = \Delta_1 \frac{dT}{dp^*} + \Delta_2$$

$$= [E_s(p^* - T) - E_s(p^* - T) + TE_s'(p^* - T)]\frac{dT}{dp^*}$$

$$+ [E_s(p^*) - E_s(p^* - T) - TE_s'(p^* - T)]$$

$$= \underbrace{TE_s'(p^* - T)\frac{dT}{dp^*}}_{+} + \underbrace{[E_s(p^*) - E_s(p^* - T) - TE_s'(p^* - T)]}_{+/-}$$

We know that $E_s'' \geq 0$ is a sufficient condition for $(d\Delta/dp^*) > 0$, since it makes the second term ≥ 0. With $E_s'' < 0$, the second term is negative. However, we can still have $(d\Delta/dp^*) > 0$ as long as the first-term dominates the second. In other words, we only need the total on the right-hand side of the above expression to be > 0 as a necessary and sufficient condition for $(d\Delta/dp^*) > 0$. This is less restrictive then $E_s'' \geq 0$ which is a sufficient condition.

A.3. Export supply elasticities

The export supply elasticity can be expressed as $\epsilon_s = (p/E_s(p))E_s'(p)$. Twice differentiating $E_s(p)$ and requiring it to be non-negative, i.e., requiring, $E_s'' \geq 0$, in turn requires that $(\epsilon_s/p)[\epsilon_s - 1] + (\partial \epsilon_s/\partial p) \geq 0$, which finally can be expressed as: $(p/\epsilon_s)(\partial \epsilon_s/\partial p) \geq -[\epsilon_s - 1]$. Note that with constant export supply elasticities, this translates into the requirement that $\epsilon_s \geq 1$. For non-constant export supply elasticity, $E_s'' \geq 0$ requires that the elasticity of the elasticity of export supply not be too negative when $\epsilon_s \geq 1$ and that it be above a certain positive value, $1 - \epsilon_s$, when $\epsilon_s < 1$.

When is $\epsilon_s \geq 1$? The export supply elasticity can alternately be expressed as:

$$\epsilon_s = \frac{x}{x - c}\epsilon_x + \frac{c}{x - c}\epsilon_c,$$

where ϵ_x and ϵ_c denote absolute values of the elasticity of domestic output supply and demand for the exportable good. It is easy to see that $\epsilon_s \geq 1$ would hold with most reasonable values of the domestic supply and demand elasticities and ratios of consumption to production of this good. Indeed, for the converse to be true, one would need to have very low elasticities of domestic demand and supply of the exportable and very small ratios of domestic consumption relative to output.

P. Krishna, D. Mitra / Journal of International Economics 65 (2005) 461–487 487

A.4.

To conduct the simulation analysis, we make the following assumptions regarding supply and demand functions in the small economy: Total endowment of the export-specific capital in the economy is assumed to be twice that of the import-competing specific factor. The production functions of the two goods are assumed to be the same, so that, taking into account the endowment difference, we can write the supply functions of the exportable and import-competing goods, respectively, as $x_e = 2p_e$ and $x_m = p_m$. We also write the aggregate domestic demands as $A_e - p_e$ and $A_m - p_m$.

References

Bagwell, K., Staiger, R., 1999. An economic theory of GATT. American Economic Review, March 89 (1), 215–248.

Bernheim, D.B., Whinston, M.D., 1986. Menu auctions, resource allocation, and economic influence. Quarterly Journal of Economics, February 101 (1), 1–31.

Bernheim, D.B., Peleg, B., Whinston, M.D., 1987. Coalition-proof Nash equilibria. Journal of Economic Theory, June 42 (1), 1–12.

Bhagwati, J., 1990. Aggressive unilateralism. In: Bhagwati, J., Patrick, H. (Eds.), Aggressive Unilateralism. University of Michigan Press, Ann Arbor, MI.

Bhagwati, J., Irwin, D., 1987. The return of the reciprotarians: US trade policy today. World Economy 10 (2), 109–130.

Coates, D., Ludema, R., 1997. Unilateral Trade Liberalization as Leadership in International Trade, Working Paper Number 97-23, Georgetown, 1–29.

Coates, D., Ludema, R., 2001. A theory of trade policy leadership. Journal of Development Economics, June 65 (1), 1–29.

De Melo, J., Grether, J., Olarreaga, M., 2001. Who determines Mexican trade policy? Journal of Development Economics, April 64 (2).

Grossman, G., Helpman, E., 1994. Protection for sale. American Economic Review, September 84 (2), 833–850.

Grossman, G., Helpman, E., 1995. Trade wars and trade talks. Journal of Political Economy, August 103 (4), 675–708.

Hillman, A., Moser, P., 1996. Trade liberalization as politically optimal exchange of market access. In: Canzoneri, P. et al. (Eds.), The New Transatlantic Economy. Cambridge Univ. Press, Cambridge, pp. 295–316.

Irwin, D., Kroszner, R., 1997. Interests, Institutions and Ideology in the Republican Conversion to Trade Liberalization, 1934–1945, NBER Working Paper Number 6112.

Johnson, H., 1953. Optimum tariffs and retaliation. Review of Economic Studies 21, 142–153.

Kindleberger, C., 1975. The rise of free trade in Western Europe, 1820–1875. Journal of Economic History, 20–55.

Kindleberger, C., 1977. America in the World Economy. Foreign Policy Association, New York.

Krishna, P., Mitra, D., 2003. Reciprocated Unilateralism in Trade Policy: An Interest-Group Approach, NBER Working Paper 9631.

Mayer, W., 1981. Theoretical considerations on negotiated tariff adjustments. Oxford Economic Papers 33, 135–143.

Mayer, W., 1984. The political economy of tariff agreements. Schriften des Vereins fur Socialpolitik 148, 423–437.

Mitra, D., 1999. Endogenous lobby formation and endogenous protection: a long run model of trade policy determination. American Economic Review, December 89 (5), 1116–1134.

Mitra, D., Thomakos, D., Ulubasoglu, M., 2002. Protection for sale in a developing country: democracy vs. dictatorship. The Review of Economics and Statistics 84 (3), 497–508.

Rodrik, D., 1995. Political economy of trade policy. In: Grossman, G., Rogoff, K. (Eds.), Handbook of International Economics, vol. 3. North-Holland.

Part II

Majority Voting and Ideology: Implications
for Endogenous Trade Policy

Chapter 4

Endogenous trade policy through majority voting: an empirical investigation

Pushan Dutt[a], Devashish Mitra[b,*]

[a]*Department of Economics, University of Alberta, Edmonton, Canada T6G 2H4*
[b]*Department of Economics, Florida International University, Miami, FL 33199, USA*

Received 4 October 2000; received in revised form 14 May 2001; accepted 23 August 2001

Abstract

The median-voter approach to trade policy determination (within a Heckscher-Ohlin framework) as in Mayer [Am. Econ. Rev. 74(5) (1984) 970] predicts that an increase in inequality, holding constant the economy's overall relative endowments, raises trade barriers in capital-abundant economies and lowers them in capital-scarce economies. We find support for this prediction using cross-country data on inequality, capital-abundance and diverse measures of protection. We perform certain robustness checks that include controlling for the effects of political rights and schooling as well as using alternative datasets on factor endowments. © 2002 Elsevier Science B.V. All rights reserved.

Keywords: Protection; Openness; Median voter; Inequality

1. Introduction

The median-voter approach, with its focus on majoritarian electoral politics, has been applied quite extensively to diverse political economy issues. This approach and its predictions are best interpreted when the concept of the median voter is not taken literally, but viewed as a convenient analytical device that resolves the conflicting redistributive forces in an unequal society. As Alesina and Rodrik (1994) write:

---

*Corresponding author. Tel.: +1-305-348-3893; fax: +1-305-348-1524.
E-mail addresses:* pdutt@ualberta.ca (P. Dutt), mitrad@fiu.edu (D. Mitra).

0022-1996/02/$ – see front matter © 2002 Elsevier Science B.V. All rights reserved.
PII: S0022-1996(01)00162-3

"We appeal to this (median voter) theorem to capture the basic idea that any government is likely to be responsive to the wishes of the majority when key distributional issues are at stake. Even a dictator cannot completely ignore social demands for fear of being overthrown. Thus, even in a dictatorship, distributional issues affecting the majority of the population will influence policy outcomes."

In this paper, our aim is to empirically investigate the predictions of the median voter analysis in an important arena of economic policy, namely international trade.[1] Mayer (1984) applies the median voter approach to trade policy determination in standard Heckscher–Ohlin and specific factors (Jones–Ricardo–Viner) trade models. In a two-sector, two-factor (capital and labor) Heckscher–Ohlin version of the Mayer model, the political-economy equilibrium trade policies in an unequal society (one in which the relative capital endowment of the median individual is less than the mean) will be biased in favor of labor. More trade results in a higher factor reward for the abundant factor and a lower factor reward for the scarce factor. Hence, the model predicts an equilibrium trade policy biased against trade in capital-rich countries and in favor of trade in capital-scarce economies. However, in the real world, trade policies are almost everywhere and always biased against trade. This discrepancy between the median-voter prediction and the empirical evidence can be attributed to other kinds of redistributive pressures on the government, such as those from lobbies and special-interest groups. Real-world politics consists of both special interest and majoritarian politics among numerous other things. Thus, there might exist in reality elements of redistributive pressures similar to those captured by the median-voter argument but may be rendered invisible by other opposing elements.

Our paper, therefore, focuses on a second important prediction that can be derived from this median-voter approach to trade policy determination. This prediction is about cross-country variations in levels of trade barriers and *not* about the actual orientations (signs) of the levels. More precisely, we perform a simple comparative-static exercise in the Mayer–Heckscher–Ohlin (Mayer-H-O) framework to obtain the result that an increase in inequality (the difference between the mean and the median capital-labor ratio), holding constant the economy's overall relative endowments, raises trade barriers in capital-abundant economies and lowers them in capital-scarce economies.[2] It is exactly this

---

[1] The other approach focusses on pressure group politics. See, for instance, Feenstra and Bhagwati (1982), Findlay and Wellisz (1982), Grossman and Helpman (1994), Hillman (1989), Magee et al. (1989) and Mitra (1999).

[2] An increase in inequality increases the demand for redistribution from capital to labor. This can be achieved through trade policies that increase further the factor reward to labor but reduce the reward to capital, which in turn is achieved by increasing the domestic price of the labor-intensive good in a two-sector, two-factor Heckscher–Ohlin economy. Thus, an increase in inequality would result in a tightening of trade restrictions in capital-abundant economies and their reduction in capital-scarce countries.

prediction about cross-country variation in trade policy that we are able to investigate empirically using cross-sectional data on inequality, capital-abundance and diverse measures of trade restrictions and openness.

It is important to note here that in the Mayer-H-O framework, an increase in inequality makes the import tariff more positive (i.e. makes trade policies more antitrade) in a capital-abundant economy, while as a result of such an increase in inequality, the import tariff becomes more and more negative (i.e. trade policies become more protrade) in a labor abundant economy. However, as argued above, in the real world there are possibly other components of the tariff (arising from other factors or considerations) which are, in combination, always positive enough to make the overall tariff positive in countries of all degrees of capital abundance or scarcity. *Holding these other effects constant with respect to inequality, the overall import tariff can rise or fall with inequality to the extent that the positive or negative Mayer component becomes more positive or more negative.*

An alternative political economy model using a lobbying approach in a static setting (within the same two-sector, two-factor Heckscher–Ohlin framework) makes exactly the opposite prediction. As asset or capital inequality increases, the ownership of capital becomes more concentrated. Thus, in this one-period setting, we have a reduction in the free-riding related public-good provision problem for pro-capital lobbying relative to pro-labor lobbying. The result is an intensification of redistribution from labor to capital (as opposed to redistribution from capital to labor in the median-voter case). Thus, in a single-period lobbying model with capital and labor pitted against each other in a two-factor, two-sector Heckscher–Ohlin environment, an increase in inequality will lead to an increase in import protection in capital-scarce economies, but will lead to a reduction in import-protection in capital abundant economies.[3]

In a repeated-game setting, Pecorino (1998) shows that the effect of concentration on the free-rider problem is ambiguous. A reduction in concentration increases the current-period gain from defecting from the cooperative outcome and at the same time lowers the profits that each firm makes when punished (through a non-cooperative regime) as a result.[4] Thus, what we learn from the above lobbying

---

[3]The simplest way to obtain such a result is to consider a model of the type presented in Rodrik (1986) and perform a comparative static exercise there by varying the the number of capitalists, holding constant the aggregate stock of capital and the total population. In such a model, pro-capital redistribution is increasing in asset inequality, while in the median-voter model, pro-labor redistribution is increasing in asset inequality.

[4]Magee (2001) uses a political-contributions approach (and endogenizes the tariff-formation function used by Pecorino) in a repeated game setting to resolve some of this ambiguity. He is able to characterize the equilibria under different sets of parameter values and is able to derive conditions on the parameters (such as the discount rate and the government's bargaining power with respect to the import-competing lobby) that lead to monotonically increasing (decreasing) or even non-monotonic relationships between concentration, the ease of free riding and the maximum sustainable tariff. Which of these parameter values real-world lobbies face is not easy to identify.

110   P. Dutt, D. Mitra / Journal of International Economics 58 (2002) 107–133

models is that the relationship between inequality or concentration and trade protection can only be resolved empirically.

We employ two measures of inequality (or equality) in studying its impact on different measures of trade restrictiveness. One is the Gini-coefficient which is a summary measure of inequality and is consistent with a broad interpretation of the model we employ. The other is the share of the median quintile of the population in national income, which fairly accurately corresponds to the share of the median voter in the Mayer framework. In looking at the effects of inequality, we allow it to change direction and magnitude as the relative factor proportions change when we move across countries. We carry out our empirical investigation using three separate measures (Nehru–Dhareshwar, Summers–Heston and Easterly–Levine) of relative factor endowments (capital per worker), constructed using different methods and under different assumptions. Across all measures of trade restrictiveness and using different measures of the capital-labor ratio, we find strong evidence in favor of the above-mentioned median voter prediction. An increase in the Gini-coefficient or a reduction in the median quintile's share, holding constant the economy's overall relative endowments, does in fact, raise trade barriers in capital-abundant economies and lowers them in capital-scarce economies.[5] Further, this result is extremely robust to the use of controls.

In this context, our result is consistent with the results of econometric studies (using micro-level suvey data) on individual level trade policy preferences such as Balistreri (1997), Beaulieu (2001), and Scheve and Slaughter (1998). These authors find that for both Canada and the US in recent years, factor type has been the dominant determinant of support for or opposition to trade barriers. Individuals owning proportionally more of the scarce factors are in favor of trade barriers, while those owning proportionally more of the abundant factors do not like trade restrictions. If we can take the empirical findings on individual trade policy preferences as given, a simple application of the median-voter analysis over these preferences should theoretically deliver our non-monotonic results. For the sake of completeness, we present a framework in which even the empirically observed type of individual preferences over trade policy are derived from first principles using a two-sector, two-factor Heckscher–Ohlin set up.

The main theoretical proposition presented in our paper is driven by the Stolper–Samuelson effect and therefore, our empirical results can be interpreted only in the context of this effect. Besides the above individual-level, revealed preference evidence for the Stolper–Samuelson theorem, there are papers that have found support for it using data on Political Action Committee (PAC) contributions and congressional voting patterns. These studies specifically find support for the two-factor, capital-labor version of the Stolper–Samuelson effect and thus are specially relevant for our empirical investigation. Beaulieu (2000) finds some

---

[5]In addition to using inequality as a variable, an interaction term between inequality and the capital-labor ratio is used to endogenously determine from the data the threshold capital-labor ratio where the trade restrictiveness-inequality relationship changes sign or direction.

evidence of congressional voting patterns on trade policy in the US being affected by the factor-endowment composition of constituencies. One of the interesting empirical regularities unravelled by his study is a negative relationship between the likelihood that a candidate votes in favor of the CUSTA, GATT or NAFTA and the size of contributions from labor PACs. He also finds a positive effect of contributions from capital (corporate) PACs in the case of the CUSTA. In the case of the GATT and NAFTA, however, he finds no effect of capital contributions. Kahane (1996) finds that after controlling for state characteristics, the likelihood of voting against the NAFTA in both the House and the Senate was increasing in contributions by labor PACs. Steagall and Jennings (1996) find that the likelihood of a favorable House vote for the NAFTA was again decreasing in labor contributions, but also increasing in capital (corporate) contributions. However, contributions are endogenous to political and other leanings of the candidate. Baldwin and Magee (2000), after taking into account this endogeneity, find strong evidence that the likelihood of a favorable vote for NAFTA or GATT cast in the House was decreasing in labor contributions but increasing in business contributions. Beaulieu and Magee (2000) determine industry affiliation of these capital and labor PACs. They find that both the probability of a capital PAC contributing money to a candidate and the size of its contribution to a candidate were higher if he/she was a supporter of NAFTA, while the reverse was true for a labor PAC. Industry affiliation of these PACs did not seem to matter in their contributions decisions in this NAFTA context.[6]

The contribution of our paper is two-fold. Firstly, our results uncover a robust empirical regularity in the relationship between trade protection and inequality and provide some credibility to the median voter approach to political economy. Secondly, the paper adds to the empirical literature on cross-national variation in protection.[7]

---

[6]In contrast to the studies mentioned above, earlier studies (using older data) by Irwin (1994, 1996) and Magee (1978) find that industry of employment was the major determinant of individual level trade policy preferences in the British elections of the early twentieth century and in the testimonies of trade unions, management and industry associations before the House Ways and Means Committee on the Trade Reform Act of 1973 in the US, respectively. However, Rogowski (1987) shows how coalitions formed in the US, Britain and Germany in the nineteenth century are those predicted by the Heckscher–Ohlin model.

[7]See Rodrik (1995) for a discussion of the importance of (and the need for) empirical work on cross-country variations in protection.To our knowledge, there are only two cross-country empirical studies on protection. Magee et al. (1989) (Chapter 16) find that average tariff rates tend to decrease as capital-labor ratios increase. Mansfield and Busch (1995) examine cross-national variation in average protection levels among 14 advanced industrial countries pooled over 2 years, 1983 and 1986. They find that non-tariff barriers are increasing in country size, unemployment rate and number of parliamentary constituencies and are higher for countries that use proportional representation as their electoral system. Also, there are three well known cross industry studies on protection in the US—Goldberg and Maggi (1999), Gawande and Bandopadhyay (2000) and Trefler (1993)—all of which focus on the predictions of lobbying/political contributions models about cross-industry variation in protection.

The Political Economy of Trade Policy

112   P. Dutt, D. Mitra / Journal of International Economics 58 (2002) 107–133

In Section 2, we present a modified version of the Mayer (1984) model and perform a comparative-static exercise to derive the implications of increasing inequality for trade policy determination. Section 3 describes the specification of the econometric model and explains the various inferences that the model allows. Section 4 briefly discusses the data and the choice of regressors. In Section 5, we discuss our empirical results and finally, in Section 6, we make some concluding remarks.

2. Theoretical framework

Let us consider a two-factor, two-sector, small-open, Heckscher–Ohlin economy. Good 1 is the importable and good 2 the exportable. The domestic price of the importable is p while its world price is p^*, so that $p = p^*(1 + t)$. Let good 2 be the numeraire good. Both goods require both capital and labor in their production carried out under constant returns to scale. On the demand side, individual preferences are taken to be identical and homothetic. An individual h's indirect utility function can, therefore, be written as $V(p)I^h$.

For simplicity, we assume that each individual owns one unit of labor and k^h units of capital. Let the share of an individual h in the overall capital stock of the economy be denoted by σ^h, so that $k^h = \sigma^h K$ where K is the aggregate capital stock of the economy.[8] Let L be the total number of individuals and hence the aggregate labor endowment of the economy. The income of an individual is then given by

$$I^h(p) = w(p) + r(p)\sigma^h K + \phi^h(p - p^*)M(p) \tag{1}$$

where ϕ^h is the share of an individual h in the total tariff revenue (*equal to an individual's share in factor income by assumption*) and $M(p)$ the imports of good 1. $w(p)$ and $r(p)$ are the wage rate earned by labor and rental on capital, respectively, both being solely the functions of the domestic price of the importable.

An individual h's most preferred tariff is determined by maximizing $V(p)I^h(p)$ with respect to p, which yields

---

[8] Our assumption, in this theory section, that $L^h = 1$ for all h, is a simplifying assumption. The model can be easily modified to incorporate heterogeneity in labor holdings so that individuals differ in terms of $k^h = K^h/L^h$, the relative capital–labor endowment. In that case, the equilibrium tariff will be determined by the ratio of median K/L to the average K/L. However, whether this makes a difference depends on our interpretations of K and L, i.e. whether capital is interpreted to be just physical capital or also includes human capital and how labor is being measured-in terms of the number of workers or in terms of efficiency units. Our measure of labor (in the data we use) is in terms of the number of workers (i.e. one unit of labor per person) and we interpret the income gini (used in our empirical investigation) as reflecting heterogeneity in both physical and human capital.

$$t^h = \frac{-I}{p^*M'(p)} \frac{\partial \phi^h / \partial p}{\phi^h} \tag{2}$$

where I is aggregate income. Imports are negatively related to the domestic price of the importable and so we have $M'(p) < 0$. Furthermore, $\partial \phi^h / \partial p > (<)0$ if individual h is relatively well (poorly) endowed in the factor used intensively in the production of the importable and consequently such an individual's most preferred tariff will be positive (negative).

Assuming that the voters differ only along a single dimension, namely in their relative capital–labor endowment k^h and that there are no voting costs, the tariff under majority voting can be obtained using the median voter theorem and is the one that maximizes the utility of the individual with the median relative capital–labor endowment in the economy. In other words, it is obtained by maximizing $V(p)I^{mv}$ where mv stands for the median voter. This is equivalent to maximizing $v(p) + i^{mv}$ where $v(p) = \ln V(p)$ and $i^{mv} = \ln I^{mv}$. It is assumed that this objective function is concave with respect to price. Expanding the expression for i^{mv}, we have $i^{mv} = \ln[w(p) + r(p)\sigma^{mv}K] + \ln[1 + \delta(p, K/L)]$ where δ is the ratio of total tariff revenue to national factor income. The first order condition of our maximization problem gives us

$$v'(p) + \partial i^{mv} / \partial p = 0 \tag{3}$$

σ^{mv} is the median voter's share in the capital stock and is always below the average share in real world distributions (see Alesina and Rodrik, 1994). Thus, σ^{mv} can be considered to be an inverse index of inequality or an index of equality in the distribution of assets. Therefore, in order to study the effect of a change in the degree of inequality in asset distribution on the nature of trade policy, we look at the effect of a change in σ^{mv}, holding constant the economy's aggregate factor endowments. Let t^{mv} be the median voter's most preferred level of tariff (on the importable), also called the political–economic equilibrium tariff. Differentiating our first order condition to perform comparative statics we obtain

$$\frac{\partial t^{mv}}{\partial \sigma^{mv}} = \frac{-[r'(p)w(p) - r(p)w'(p)]K}{p^*[w(p) + r(p)\sigma^{mv}K]^2[v''(p) + \partial^2 i^{mv} / \partial p^2]} \tag{4}$$

Since an increase in the domestic price of the importable increases the reward to the scarce factor and reduces that for the abundant factor, we have $r'(p) < 0$ and $w'(p) > 0$ for a capital-abundant country, while $r'(p) > 0$ and $w'(p) < 0$ for a labor-abundant country. The denominator is always negative due to the restriction of concavity imposed on the objective function. Thus, the above derivative is negative when the economy is capital abundant, so that an increase in inequality leads to an increase in the equilibrium tariff. For a labor abundant country, the above derivative has a positive sign. In other words, an increase in inequality always results in an increase in the demand for redistribution through policies that would benefit labor at the expense of capital. In a capital abundant country, the

114   P. Dutt, D. Mitra / Journal of International Economics 58 (2002) 107–133

importable is the labor intensive good and an increase in the demand for redistribution from capital to labor would represent a demand for policies that increasingly favor the importable sector. In a labor abundant economy, the importable sector is the capital intensive sector and hence more redistribution towards labor requires policies that are more biased against the importable sector. This leads us to the following proposition whose empirical validity we test in this paper.

Proposition. *Holding other things constant, an increase in inequality leads to more restrictive or less open trade policies in capital abundant countries, while it leads to less restrictive or more open trade policies in capital scarce economies.*

While the predictions are not as precise once we allow for more than two factors,[9] we will attempt to argue that the median voter predictions stated in the above proposition are not as specific to the two-factor framework as they appear. First, let us assume that there are three factors-physical capital (K), human capital or skills (H) and raw, unskilled labor (L). Per capita income in any country is (National Income)$/L = r(K/L) + w_H(H/L) + w$ where w_H denotes the return on human capital. Thus, in order to be rich (poor), countries have to be relatively abundant (scarce) in K and H combined or relatively scarce (abundant) in L. In any country, concentration in the ownership of skills and physical assets leads to inequality.[10] Higher inequality (of this kind) implies greater dependence for the majority of the population on their raw, unskilled labor power, and a greater demand for redistribution (see Alesina and Rodrik, 1994), thereby leading to prolabor redistribution policies. In rich (poor) countries, this leads to higher (lower) trade barriers.[11]

---

[9]The median voter model is usually applied when individuals differ along a single dimension—in this case the capital labor ratio, which when combined with a monotonicity result, yields single peaked preferences. So even when allowing for multiple factors and heterogeneity in their ownership, it is crucial that voters and individuals differ along a single dimension.

[10]Endowments of physical and human capital should be correlated (both at the country and individual levels), as it is the marginal rate of time preference that determines the steady state levels of both in the absence of credit market imperfections, while in the presence of such imperfections, the ownership of physical assets directly affects the ability to acquire skills.

[11]If we go beyond three factors, our basic result qualitatively will still hold though it might be weakened a bit. The higher dimensional version of the Stolper-Samuelson theorem implies that if a factor is 'scarce enough' ('abundant enough'), it will be helped (harmed) by trade barriers (see Leamer and Levinsohn, 1995). Consider a continuum of types of skills (high level or high paying to low level or low paying) and types of physical assets (high tech and high return like computers to low tech and low return like hammers, screw-drivers, etc.). Further it would be realistic to assume that in all countries (rich and poor) the majority will possess the lower end of skills and assets. Rich countries will be abundant in the higher end factors, while poor countries in the lower end factors. Under these conditions, an increase in inequality through higher concentration of higher level assets and skills in the hands of fewer individuals, should increase the demand for redistribution from rich to the poor. Then, at least, in the very rich countries, this will generate high trade barriers and in the very poor ones lead to lower barriers.

P. Dutt, D. Mitra / Journal of International Economics 58 (2002) 107–133 115

3. Econometric methodology

The comparative static result of the previous section provides the foundation for our empirical work. In countries with high (K/L) ratios, inequality and trade restrictiveness should be positively related, but when (K/L) is low there is an inverse relationship between these two variables. A priori, we do not know at what level of (K/L), the relationship changes sign. The following specification takes care of this problem by allowing the data to tell us the exact location of this turning point:

$$TR_i = \alpha_0 + \alpha_1 INEQ_i + \alpha_2 INEQ_i \times (K/L)_i + \alpha_3 (K/L)_i + X_i \beta + \epsilon_i \qquad (5)$$

where TR_i is the extent of trade restrictions in country i, $INEQ_i$ is the level of inequality, $(K/L)_i$ the capital–labor ratio and X_i is a row vector of control variables.[12,13] Taking the partial derivative of TR_i with respect to $INEQ_i$, we have

$$\frac{\partial TR_i}{\partial (INEQ)_i} = \alpha_1 + \alpha_2 (K/L)_i \qquad (6)$$

The prediction of the comparative static exercise of the previous section is that $\alpha_1 < 0$ and $\alpha_2 > 0$ such that $\alpha_1 + \alpha_2 (K/L)_i \gtrless 0$ as $(K/L)_i \gtrless (K/L)^*$ where $(K/L)^* = -\alpha_1/\alpha_2$ is the turning point capital–labor ratio determined endogenously from the data, given our estimating equation. Another requirement for the prediction to hold is that $(K/L)^*$ should lie within the range of values of (K/L) in the dataset, i.e. $(K/L)^{MIN} < (K/L)^* < (K/L)^{MAX}$.

We start with the basic regression in which TR is regressed on (K/L), INEQ and INEQ $\times (K/L)$. The inclusion of (K/L) as a separate variable (in addition to INEQ and INEQ $\times (K/L)$) allows $\partial TR_i/\partial (K/L)_i$ and the variable component of $\partial TR_i/\partial (INEQ)_i$ to differ in sign. Otherwise, they are restricted to having the same sign. We then add controls such as schooling and democracy to see whether our results are robust to their inclusion. The reasons for their inclusion as controls is explained in Section 5.

---

[12] In our estimation, we use the capital–labor ratios in natural logs. The reasons are as follows: (1) For all measures (TARIFF, IMPORT DUTY, QUOTA and $(X + M)/GDP$), we have two to three outliers in regressions that use logs (of K/L), while there are 18–24 outliers in each regression when we use K/L in levels. Moreover, in the case of logs, the results are robust to the deletion of outliers. (2) For all protection measures, the J-test for the model with log (of K/L) vs. the model with the level clearly accepts the former as the null hypothesis against the latter as the alternative and rejects the latter as the null against the former as the alternative.

[13] We have also tested for non-linearities/non-monotononicities with respect to K/L by additionally including its square. This additional term is statistically insignificant at 15% and even much higher levels. Also, squares of INEQ and K/L thrown in simultaneously were statistically extremely insignificant. We also could not detect any non-linearities (at 15% and even higher levels of significance) in any of our variables $(K/L$, inequality, their cross product and other control variables) when we performed the Ramsey Reset test for all our regressions, both with and without controls. The detailed results are available at www.ualberta.ca/economics/dm/dm.htm.

116   P. Dutt, D. Mitra / Journal of International Economics 58 (2002) 107–133

As mentioned before, one index of inequality we use is the Gini-coefficient which is a broader measure than the interpretation of inequality used in the theoretical framework in Section 2. Alternatively, we use $Q3$, the share of the third quintile in national income, which corresponds much closer to the share of the median voter in the theoretical model. This is an inverse measure of inequality (or rather a measure of equality) and so the signs of the coefficients of this variable and its interaction with K/L are expected to be the reverse of those obtained when the Gini-coefficient is used.

We also do a few other robustness checks. Our measures of inequality are the income Gini-coefficient and the median quintile's share in national income or expenditure, both of which are indirect measures of asset inequality (or equality) since they are actually measures of income inequality.[14] There is the possibility of reverse causation running from trade policy to income inequality. Moreover, in a more dynamic context (for example in a multisectoral Solow model), K/L may be endogenous with respect to trade policy. Protection, by affecting the production structure, can affect accumulation and the steady state level of the capital stock. Even though our right-hand side variables generally are lagged with respect to the ones on the left-hand side, this would not take care of the endogeneity problem in cross-sectional analysis when variables exhibit stickiness. Therefore, we use tests suggested by Hausman (1978) and Smith and Blundell (1986). In a linear model, Hausman (1978) showed that an easy way of implementing the Hausman test for exogeneity is to first run reduced form regressions of each of the variables (in our case, INEQ, K/L and INEQ*K/L) that are suspected to be endogenous on all the exogenous variables from our main regression and other exogenous variables which theory suggests might affect any of these endogenous variables. The second step involves computing the residuals from each of these auxilliary regressions and inserting them as additional right-hand side variables in our main estimating regression. If these residuals are jointly significant (insignificant), our plain OLS estimation of the model produces inconsistent (consistent) estimates. However, in the case of the joint significance of auxilliary residuals and the consequent endogeneity, this Hausman regression will produce coefficient estimates that are consistent and identical to IV estimates. The standard errrors of the coefficient estimates, however, need to be corrected by multiplying those from the Hausman regression by an appropriate correction factor (which we do when required).

---

[14]The only measure of asset inequality on which cross-country data is available is the land-Gini. However, using data on land-ownership inequality directly in our regressions is not very meaningful, especially in a Heckscher–Ohlin framework. See the appendix for a more detailed analysis of the interpretation of regression coefficient estimates using income inequality as opposed to direct measures of asset inequality.

4. Data sources and some basic statistics

The detailed description of the data and their sources and the dataset itself are available at the following website: www.ualberta.ca/economics/dm/dm.htm. Here, we provide a very brief summary of the data used in this paper. Our dependent variable is trade protection and our independent variables of interest are inequality, the capital–labor ratio, indicators for democracy and political rights, and schooling. For the regional effects, we will be using region-specific dummies.

To test for the robustness of our results, we use a variety of trade policy measures: total import duties collected as a percentage of total imports (IMPORT DUTY), an average tariff rate calculated by weighing each import category by the fraction of world trade in that category (TARIFF)[15], a coverage ratio for non-tariff barriers to trade (QUOTA) and an indirect measure of trade restrictions-the magnitude of trade flows relative to GDP, defined as $(X + M)/\text{GDP}$.

The degree of income inequality is measured by the Gini-coefficient and alternatively, by an inverse index-the median quintile's share in national income or expenditure.

Using the Nehru–Dhareshwar data on capital in conjunction with the data on labor (defined as population between ages 15 and 64), we calculate the capital–labor ratio. The average for the 1980s is used. The data on capital stock at 1987 domestic prices are converted into 1987 constant dollars using the 1987 exchange rate. We perform robustness checks using the Summers–Heston and the Easterly–Levine capital per worker data whose country coverage is much smaller than the Nehru–Dhareshwar data.[16]

For a measure of democracy, we use the Freedom House (Gastil) measure of democracy that provides a subjective classification of countries on a scale of 1 to 7 on political rights, with higher ratings signifying less freedom. Again, the average for the 1980s is used. We use 'schooling' as a control variable, where schooling is defined as the average number of schooling years in total population over the age of 25. The summary statistics for these variables and the correlation across the various measures of trade restrictions are available at www.ualberta.ca/economics/dm/dm.htm.

For the Hausman regressions, the additional variables required are civil liberty (another Gastil index), schooling, $M2/\text{GDP}$, the Gini-coefficient for the distribution of land, savings rate and the population growth rate. The population growth rate and the savings rate are parameters in the Solow growth model in

---

[15]The variable is referred to as tariffs, although it includes all import charges, such as duties and customs fees.

[16]The Summers–Heston data are in constant 1985 international dollars, i.e. conversion into a common denominator is based on cost differentials and not the law of one price. The Easterly–Levine data are constructed using the Summers–Heston disaggregated sectoral investment data along with information on disaggregated sector-level depreciation, etc. to arrive at more accurate measures.

which the steady state per-capita capital stock is determined endogenously, while Li et al. (1998) explain intertemporal and international variation in income inequality in terms of variations in political and civil liberties (the Gastil indices), schooling, $M2/GDP$, and the Gini-coefficient for the distribution of land.

5. Results

Figs. 1 and 2 show some simple tariff vs. Gini scatter plots for capital-abundant and labor-abundant countries, respectively. The median capital–labor ratio from the Nehru–Dhareshwar dataset is used to classify countries as capital and labor abundant. There is clearly a positive correlation between tariffs and inequality in the case of capital-abundant countries and a negative correlation between the two for labor-abundant countries. Thus, even the very basic methods of data analysis can provide support for the theory presented in this paper.

5.1. OLS regressions (with and without controls)

Tables 1 and 2 present the regression results (with and without controls) for our main estimating equation (Eq. (5) in Section 3 of this paper). The sample size which ranges from 44 to 64, depends on the country coverage of the data on the different variables used. The regression models as a whole are always significant at the 5% level. The R^2 ranges from 0.15 (in the case of quota without controls and

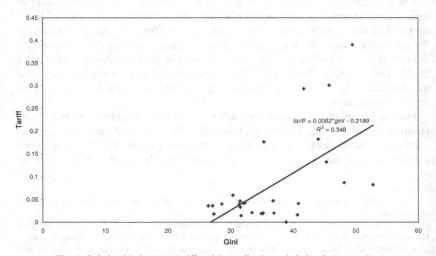

Fig. 1. Relationship between tariff and inequality in capital-abundant countries.

P. Dutt, D. Mitra / Journal of International Economics 58 (2002) 107–133 119

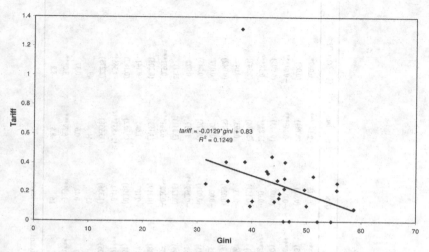

Fig. 2. Relationship between tariff and inequality in labor-abundant countries.

using the median quintile's share $Q3$) to 0.60 (in the case of import duty with controls, using the Gini coefficient).

Apart from the regressions based upon the quota coverage ratio, we find strong support for the predictions of the median voter model, both with and without controls. As predicted, $\alpha_1 < 0$ and $\alpha_2 > 0$ when the Gini coefficient is used and the reverse when $Q3$ is used.[17] For quotas, these coefficients are insignificant. In the quota regressions using the Gini coefficient, they even have the wrong signs.

The quota coverage ratio suffers from measurement error problems due to smuggling, coding problems and weaknesses in the underlying data. It also does not distinguish between highly restrictive barriers and non-binding ones, thus suggesting only their existence and being unable to measure their effect on imports. Harrigan (1993) has found that for OECD countries in 1983 both price and quantity NTB coverage ratios are, in most cases, not associated with lower imports. He points out that these coverage ratios are the noisiest indicators of trade policy as there are severe problems with their construction procedure and are not conceptually what is desired.[18] However, in subsequent sub-sections (where we use alternative capital per work measures), we show results even for the quota variable that are consistent with median-voter predictions.

---

[17]We also find support for the median-voter predictions using the Sachs–Warner binary measure of openness as the dependent variable in a logistic regression. However, we do not present those results as the Sachs–Warner measure has come under heavy criticism recently.

[18]For a detailed discussion of the problems with quantity and price NTB coverage ratios, see Leamer (1990).

120   P. Dutt, D. Mitra / Journal of International Economics 58 (2002) 107–133

Table 1
Gini coefficient-regression with and without controls

	Tariff	Quota	Import duty	(X + M)/GDP	Tariff	Quota	Import duty	(X + M)/GDP
Gini	-0.029**	0.012	-1.048*	0.049	-0.051***	0.016	-2.141***	0.082*
	(0.016)	(0.022)	(0.679)	(0.04)	(0.023)	(0.03)	(0.794)	(0.05)
Gini*capital–labor ratio	0.003***	-0.0002	0.144***	-0.006*	0.006***	-0.001	0.249***	-0.01***
	(0.001)	(0.002)	(0.067)	(0.004)	(0.002)	(0.003)	(0.083)	(0.005)
Capital–labor ratio	-0.189***	-0.037	-8.406***	0.341***	-0.328***	-0.03	-13.85***	0.58***
	(0.068)	(0.093)	(2.888)	(0.166)	(0.11)	(0.151)	(3.986)	(0.247)
Schooling					0.006	-0.03	0.593	-0.042
					(0.019)	(0.029)	(0.705)	(0.042)
Political rights (Gastil)					-0.025	-0.02	0.397	0.037
					(0.021)	(0.028)	(0.776)	(0.047)
Sub-saharan Africa					-0.068	-0.259***	1.537	0.022
					(0.095)	(0.126)	(3.341)	(21.7)
East Asia					-0.103	-0.202**	-6.981***	0.591***
					(0.088)	(0.119)	(3.189)	(0.203)
Oil					0.017	-0.107	1.085	-0.141
					(0.081)	(0.108)	(3.052)	(0.187)
Constant	1.942***	0.157	78.218***	-2.372	3.291***	0.414	129.835***	-4.365**
	(0.71)	(0.96)	(29.541)	(1.722)	(1.005)	(1.356)	(35.938)	(2.273)
No. of observations	51	50	50	56	45	45	44	49
R^2	0.36	0.25	0.44	0.22	0.47	0.42	0.6	0.37
F-statistic	8.82***	5.23***	11.97***	5.03***	4.01***	3.29***	6.79***	3.0***
Critical capital–labor ratio	9.7	55	7.3	8.2	8.5	16	8.6	8.2

Standard errors in parantheses; *** significant at 5% level, ** significant at 10% level, * significant at 15% level.

Table 2
Third quintile-regression with and without controls

	Tariff	Quota	Import duty	(X + M)/GDP	Tariff	Quota	Import duty	(X + M)/GDP
Q3	0.136***	0.081	6.752***	−0.196***	0.121***	0.021	5.15***	−0.09
	(0.042)	(0.06)	(1.821)	(0.062)	(0.055)	(0.075)	(1.879)	(0.068)
Q3*capital–labor ratio	−0.015***	−0.012**	−0.747***	0.025***	−0.013***	−0.005	−0.558***	0.012**
	(0.004)	(0.006)	(0.183)	(0.062)	(0.006)	(0.008)	(0.2)	(0.007)
Capital–labor ratio	0.18***	0.158**	8.803***	−0.324***	0.15***	0.07	6.508***	−0.154*
	(0.057)	(0.082)	(2.215)	(0.086)	(0.078)	(0.106)	(2.647)	(0.096)
Schooling					−0.025	−0.054**	−1.073**	0.041**
					(0.018)	(0.025)	(0.602)	(0.021)
Political rights (Gastil)					−0.015	−0.045**	−0.602	−0.001
					(0.018)	(0.025)	(0.653)	(0.023)
Sub-saharan Africa					−0.081	−0.162*	1.003	0.023
					(0.083)	(0.112)	(2.673)	(0.097)
East Asia					−0.051	−0.052	−2.717	−0.002
					(0.097)	(0.133)	(3.436)	(0.124)
Oil					−0.089	−0.223**	−2.142	0.017
					(0.097)	(0.133)	(3.813)	(0.125)
Constant	−1.431***	−0.863	−66.206***	2.687***	−0.995	0.435	−40.459*	1.207
	(0.58)	(0.827)	(24.942)	(0.855)	(0.798)	(1.081)	(26.87)	(0.979)
No. of observations	56	56	58	64	49	50	51	56
R^2	0.32	0.15	0.39	0.41	0.41	0.32	0.55	0.47
F-statistic	8.0***	2.95***	11.66***	13.86***	3.41***	2.36***	6.32***	5.2***
Critical capital–labor ratio	9.1	6.8	9.0	7.8	9.3	4.2	9.2	7.5

Standard errors in parantheses; *** significant at 5% level, ** significant at 10% level, * significant at 15% level.

122   P. Dutt, D. Mitra / Journal of International Economics 58 (2002) 107–133

Our regressions help us identify the critical level (which also are estimates with standard errors) of the capital-labor ratio, for each of the measures of trade restrictions, at which, the relationship between trade restrictions and inequality changes sign. In Tables 1 and 2, we also provide this turning point or the critical capital-labor ratio. Except for the quota regressions, these numbers are fairly close to the median (9.4) and the mean (9.8) capital–labor ratios. This is specially true for the tariff and import duty regressions. In Table 3, using the tariff regression with controls presented in Table 1, we categorize the countries in our sample into those that exhibit a negative relationship between protection and inequality (those with a low capital–labor ratio) and those that exhibit a positive relationship (those with a high capital–labor ratio). The critical (turning point) capital–labor ratio in this case is roughly 8.5 which is slightly lower than the capital–labor ratio for Korea.

Table 3
Countries (tariff-gini relationship)

Negative relationship	Positive relationship
Bangladesh	Korea, South
China	Jamaica
Rwanda	Iran, Islamic Republic of
Pakistan	Venezuela
India	Portugal
Indonesia	Greece
Sri Lanka	Trinidad and Tobago
Ghana	Algeria
Nigeria	Spain
Philippines	Singapore
Thailand	Ireland
Guatemala	United Kingdom
Cameroon	New Zealand
Uganda	Malaysia
Colombia	Canada
Turkey	Italy
Chile	Belgium
Peru	Netherlands
Costa Rica	France
Tunisia	United States
Mauritius	Sweden
Jordan	Denmark
	Japan
	Finland
	Luxembourg
	Norway
	Germany
	Morocco
	Mexico

Note: The above partitioning is based on the tariff regression with controls in Table 1.

A partial derivative of trade restrictions with respect to the capital–labor ratio in the regressions with the Gini-coefficient yields

$$\frac{\partial TR_i}{\partial (K/L)_i} = \alpha_3 + \alpha_2 (INEQ_i) \tag{7}$$

Our regression results show that $\alpha_3 < 0$ and $\alpha_2 > 0$ and their estimates are statistically significant except for the case of the quota-coverage ratio. Plugging in the values of $INEQ_i$ into the expression for the above partial derivative, we find a negative sign overall barring very few exceptions. For example, in Table 2, the partial derivative is always negative except for Guatemala. These results are in line with the findings of Magee et al. (1989). Tariffs are a dependable and important source of revenues in developing countries (countries with a low capital–labor ratio). Moreover, developing countries have used infant-industry reasoning to justify protecting domestic industries.

We now look at the coefficients of our control variables in Tables 1 and 2. Our controls are an inverse index of democracy (the Gastil index of political rights), schooling, and regional effects using regional dummies. The inclusion of democracy is motivated by several factors. First, if we believe the evidence that openness stimulates economic growth, dictatorships which are more concerned with the size of the pie rather than its distribution, are more likely to be open. Second, since unemployment is a major issue in most elections, democracies are also more likely to provide import protection to inefficient domestic firms and to public sector firms that may not survive foreign competition. Furthermore, Fernandez and Rodrik (1991) show that in the presence of individual-specific uncertainty regarding the costs of moving to the export sector, trade reforms that are beneficial to the majority ex-post may require a dictator to implement them in the first place. Third, Rodrik (1997) has argued that rising labor demand elasticities, brought about by more open trade, may hurt workers (the majority of the population) by shifting the wage or employment incidence of non-wage labor costs towards labor and away from employers, by triggering more volatile responses of wages and employment to labor demand shocks and by shifting bargaining power over rent distribution in firms away from labor and towards capital. This may generate some demand for protection, to which democracies may be more responsive. In Table 2, we find a weak, positive link between protection and democracy in the case of quotas.[19] This is shown by the negative sign of the

---

[19]Additionally, we also use another control variable which is the interaction of democracy and capital–labor ratio for the reason that redistributive labor-oriented trade policies can be anti-trade or pro-trade depending on the capital abundance of the economy and democracies might be more responsive to demands for such redistribution. This variable turns out to be statistically insignificant.

coefficient of Gastil's (inverse) index of political rights.[20] Somewhat stronger results of this kind are obtained when we use alternative measures of the capital–labor ratios (discussed in detail in the next section).

In Table 2, we also find that schooling has a negative and significant effect on trade restrictions. A possible reason for this is that schooling is higher and trade restrictions lower in developed countries and that schooling is simply an index of development. Another plausible reason, however, for our observed sign could be that a better educated public is better informed about government policies and can better figure out the dead-weight costs of distortionary government policies favoring special interest groups. Finally, the inclusion of regional dummies does not affect our conclusions. East Asian economies in general seem to have had lower protection (Table 1). Apart from that, we fail to find any significant evidence whether a particular region or group of countries have a tendency to be more open or more protectionist.

5.2. Robustness checks

5.2.1. The Hausman test for endogeneity

Finally, because of the possible endogeneity of the Gini coefficient, the capital–labor ratio and the interaction between the two (as explained in the previous section), we perform the Hausman test for contemporaneous correlation between the error and the three regressors, that are suspected to be endogenous. As mentioned in the previous section, this test can be used to test any potential failure of the orthogonality assumption so long as instrumental variables are available. We use a simple method of implementing this test as suggested by Hausman (1978) and extended in Smith and Blundell (1986), the details of which have already been discussed in Section 3.

Each of our suspected endogenous variables is regressed on all the exogenous variables from our main regression plus other exogenous variables that, we believe, affect any of the three endogenous variables. The residuals from these auxilliary regressions are calculated and inserted as additional regressors in our main regression. F-Hausman in Table 4 gives the F-statistic for the joint significance of these residuals. All these residuals turn out to be jointly insignificant except in the case of the tariff. The results of the Hausman test suggest that there is no loss in consistency from the use of the OLS estimates when our dependent variable is the quota, import duty or $(X + M)/$GDP. In addition, OLS estimates are efficient. However, in the case of the tariff, the consistent coefficient estimates are only the ones obtained from the Hausman regression (identical to instrumental variable estimates) presented in Table 4. Besides, the required standard error correction to produce the IV standard errors has also been done. After taking into account the endogeneity of the capital–labor ratio, inequality and

---

[20]It needs to be noted that this index increases with the extent of dictatorship and decreases with the degree of democracy.

Table 4
Hausman regressions

	Tariff	Quota	Import duty	$(X+M)/\text{GDP}$
Gini	−0.171***	0.0003	−3.198***	0.043
	(0.084)	(0.055)	(1.407)	(0.05)
Gini*capital–labor ratio	0.017***	0.001	0.368***	−0.006
	(0.008)	(0.005)	(0.136)	(0.005)
Capital–labor ratio	−0.722***	−0.109	−18.15***	0.365**
	(0.326)	(0.238)	(6.148)	(0.217)
Schooling	0.007	−0.014	0.816	−0.019
	(0.047)	(0.041)	(0.938)	(0.034)
Political rights (Gastil)	0.012	0.013	1.107	0.016
	(0.049)	(0.039)	(1.013)	(0.035)
Sub-saharan Africa	−0.192	−0.43*	−5.907	−0.244
	(0.345)	(0.278)	(7.065)	(0.261)
East Asia	−0.046	−0.283**	−8.041**	0.098
	(0.215)	(0.166)	(4.214)	(0.155)
Oil	0.018	−0.03	0.02	−0.021
	(0.17)	(0.134)	(3.45)	(0.128)
Residual (Gini)	0.039	0.012	0.408	0.024
	(0.032)	(0.024)	(0.596)	(0.021)
Residual (capital–labor)	−0.013	0.062	1.153	−0.004
	(0.077)	(0.059)	(1.565)	(0.056)
Residual (capital–labor*Gini)	−0.004***	−0.001	−0.073**	−0.001
	(0.002)	(0.002)	(0.043)	(0.001)
Constant	7.25***	1.031	165.195***	−2.425
	(3.22)	(2.273)	(60.05)	(2.121)
No. of observations	37	37	37	41
R^2	0.66	0.47	0.65	0.53
F-statistic	4.52***	2.03**	4.26***	3.01***
Joint signifcance of residuals (F-Hausman)	4.34***	0.62	1.76	0.6

For tariffs, the Hausman test suggests that there is an endogeneity problem. Therefore, for this case we have modified the standard error by a factor of 1.94 to obtain consistent IV standard error estimates. After correction our main coefficient estimates remain highly significant.

The residuals are obtained from auxiliary regressions where each of the suspected endogenous variables are regressed on all exogenous variables. The additional exogenous variables are savings rate, population growth, land gini, civil liverty and $M2/\text{GDP}$

Standard errors in parantheses; *** significant at 5% level, ** significant at 10% level, * significant at 15% level.

the product of the two in the case of the tariff, we have the results virtually unchanged and still statistically significant. The critical capital–labor ratio is around 10, again fairly close to the median and the mean.

5.2.2. Dictatorship vs. democracy

We have argued earlier in this paper that majoritarian concerns are important in both democracies and dictatorships. Nevertheless, these concerns may be relatively more important in democracies. There are two possible interpretations here: (a) the median-voter model fits the data better for democracies; and (b) the predicted relationship between trade policy and inequality is stronger (larger in magnitude) for democracies.

We investigate (a) by generating residuals from our main regressions and then regressing the absolute values and alternatively, squares of these residuals on the democracy/dictatorship (political rights) variable. In most cases, we do not get any statistically significant results, except in the case of the absolute values and squares of residuals obtained from the import-duty regression without controls (the quota residuals with the Nehru–Dhareshwar data also give us significant results, but those quota residuals are based on results which do not in the first place validate the median-voter predictions):

$$|\text{Import duty residual}| = \underset{(1.24)}{0.94} + \underset{(0.35)}{1.26}\text{***} \,(\text{political rights}) \quad R^2 = 0.22$$

$$[\text{Import duty residual}]^2 = \underset{(28.45)}{1.43} + \underset{(7.99)}{15.22}\text{**} \,(\text{political rights}) \quad R^2 = 0.07$$

(Note: The standard errors are shown in parentheses and asterisks represent significance). As the political rights variable is increasing in the extent of dictatorship, the above regression results at least provide some weak evidence that the median voter prediction works better in democracies than in dictatorships. We, however, find much stronger evidence when we generate predicted values of protection using our coefficient estimates and then find their correlation with the actual values separately for the dictatorship sample (countries with values of the political rights variable above 3) and the democracy sample (the rest). Using the regressions without controls, the correlation coefficients for the dictatorship sample are 0.42, 0.42, 0.3 and 0.3 for tariff, quota, import duty and $(X + M)/\text{GDP}$, respectively, while for democracies they are 0.71, 0.5, 0.8 and 0.71. The comparisons are very similar with controls.

Finally, we run regressions with additional interaction terms (Gini*pol rights and Gini*(K/L)*pol rights) to investigate the hypothesis (b) that the demand for prolabor (median-voter related) redistribution through trade policies is stronger in democracies than in dictatorships, for which we find support only with $(X + M)/\text{GDP}$ as the dependent variable. For the regression without controls, the cross-partial derivative is $\partial^2[(X + M)/\text{GDP}]/\partial\text{dictatorship} \,\partial\text{gini} = -0.013 + 0.001(K/L)$ so that democracies reinforce the positive (negative) relationship between inequality and openness in capital scarce (abundant) countries, predicted by the median voter model.[21]

5.2.3. Alternative data on capital–labor ratios

We do some robustness checks by using other data on capital per worker. Both with the Summers–Heston as well as the Easterly–Levine K/L data, it can be seen

---

[21]This result for $(X + M)/\text{GDP}$ is robust to the inclusion of controls. Detailed regression results can be found at www.ualberta.ca/economics/dm/dm.htm.

Table 5
Gini coefficient-regression with controls

	Summers–Heston capital–labor ratio				Easterly–Levine capital–labor ratio			
	Tariff	Quota	Import duty	(X + M)/GDP	Tariff	Quota	Import duty	(X + M)/GDP
Gini	-0.144***	0.021	-6.268***	0.126*	-0.152*	-0.035	-6.461***	0.352
	(0.059)	(0.075)	(1.877)	(0.082)	(0.095)	(0.105)	(2.464)	(1.788)
Gini*capital–labor ratio	0.014***	-0.003	0.666***	-0.015**	0.015*	0.003	0.675***	-0.047
	(0.006)	(0.008)	(0.199)	(0.009)	(0.01)	(0.011)	(0.258)	(0.186)
Capital–labor ratio	-0.936***	-0.067	-37.324***	0.714**	-0.963***	-0.289	-37.519***	4.639
	(0.256)	(0.33)	(8.444)	(0.364)	(0.389)	(0.446)	(10.515)	(7.685)
Schooling	0.034*	-0.017	1.29**	-0.004	0.036*	-0.014	1.249*	-0.93**
	(0.021)	(0.03)	(0.749)	(0.032)	(0.022)	(0.032)	(0.772)	(0.555)
Political rights (Gastil)	-0.005	0.098***	0.287	0.003	-0.001	0.101***	0.395*	0.33
	(0.032)	(0.043)	(1.182)	(0.048)	(0.034)	(0.044)	(1.224)	(0.83)
Sub-saharan Africa	-0.346**	-0.231	-5.594	0.341	-0.334**	-0.198	-4.9	2.727
	(0.187)	(0.246)	(6.2)	(0.289)	(0.199)	(0.256)	(6.377)	(4.932)
East Asia	-0.254**	-0.375***	-6.682	-0.01	-0.245*	-0.343**	-6.003	1.697
	(0.142)	(0.187)	(4.964)	(0.22)	(0.154)	(0.196)	(5.242)	(3.797)
Oil	0.208*	0.175	10.033***	-0.025	0.223*	0.147	10.527***	-2.836
	(0.134)	(0.177)	(4.453)	(0.205)	(0.148)	(0.193)	(4.742)	(3.594)
Constant	9.253***	1.236	354.941***	-5.909***	9.595***	3.33	361.65***	-33.71
	(2.414)	(3.082)	(78.978)	(3.462)	(3.723)	(4.202)	(100.479)	(73.884)
No. of observations	31	31	31	35	28	28	28	32
R^2	0.7	0.63	0.73	0.47	0.7	0.61	0.75	0.15
F-statistic	6.29***	4.73***	7.57***	2.89***	5.67***	3.68***	7.02***	0.5
Critical capital–labor ratio	10.3	7.0	9.4	8.4	10.1	11.7	9.6	7.5

Standard errors in parentheses; *** significant at 5% level, ** significant at 10% level, * significant at 15% level.

Table 6
Third quintile-regression with controls

	Summers–Heston capital–labor ratio				Easterly–Levine capital–labor ratio			
	Tariff	Quota	Import duty	(X + M)/GDP	Tariff	Quota	Import duty	(X + M)/GDP
Q3	0.321***	0.191*	10.698***	-0.167	0.293***	0.21*	9.841***	-1.649
	(0.087)	(0.125)	(3.024)	(0.135)	(0.125)	(0.13)	(3.416)	(2.224)
Q3*capital–labor ratio	-0.034***	-0.025**	-1.226***	0.021	-0.032***	-0.029***	-1.14***	0.231
	(0.01)	(0.014)	(0.33)	(0.015)	(0.013)	(0.014)	(0.364)	(0.239)
Capital–labor ratio	0.272***	0.365***	12.756***	-0.175	0.345***	0.445***	11.497***	-1.302
	(0.129)	(0.185)	(4.414)	(0.196)	(0.19)	(0.2)	(5.152)	(3.409)
Schooling	0.005	-0.039	-0.436	0.021	0.002	-0.025	-0.401	-0.962**
	(0.022)	(0.031)	(0.736)	(0.032)	(0.03)	(0.031)	(0.81)	(0.514)
Political rights (Gastil)	-0.051**	-0.053	-2.562***	0.006	-0.031	-0.055*	-2.266***	0.45
	(0.026)	(0.038)	(0.957)	(0.04)	(0.034)	(0.036)	(1.026)	(0.521)
Sub-saharan Africa	-0.208**	-0.029	3.978	0.143	-0.015	0.079	2.234	0.19
	(0.117)	(0.166)	(3.995)	(0.179)	(0.178)	(0.18)	(5.004)	(3.066)
East Asia	-0.124	-0.002	0.853	-0.025	-0.007	0.04	-0.103	1.205
	(0.132)	(0.188)	(4.594)	(0.204)	(0.178)	(0.186)	(5.04)	(3.143)
Oil	-0.036	-0.455**	-2.222	-0.104	-0.028	-0.465**	-2.017	-1.242
	(0.177)	(0.254)	(6.126)	(0.276)	(0.234)	(0.246)	(6.406)	(4.213)
Constant	-2.215**	-2.059	-88.009***	1.476	-2.874*	-2.731*	-75.765*	10.326
	(1.201)	(1.722)	(41.302)	(1.838)	(1.813)	(1.892)	(48.77)	(32.057)
No. of observations	33	34	35	38	30	31	31	36
R^2	0.65	0.43	0.66	0.48	0.44	0.44	0.67	0.15
F-statistic	5.59***	2.36***	6.22***	3.39***	2.08***	2.16***	5.67***	0.62
Critical capital–labor ratio	9.4	7.6	8.7	8.0	9.2	7.2	8.6	7.1

Standard errors in parantheses; ***significant at 5% level, **significant at 10% level, *significant at 15% level.

P. Dutt, D. Mitra / Journal of International Economics 58 (2002) 107–133   129

from Tables 5 and 6 that our main results remain qualitatively unchanged. Inequality, the capital–labor ratio and the product of the two are very significant and have the right signs. This is true even for quotas when the third quintile's share is used as an inverse measure of inequality (Table 6). *So, there is, at least, some weak evidence for the median voter prediction working in the case of quotas.* The critical capital–labor ratios presented in Tables 5 and 6 are in most cases quite close to the mean and median values. Again, there is some evidence that more democracy leads to more protection (Table 6). The results with schooling are somewhat mixed.

5.2.4. Regressions using changes in protection and changes in inequality

We also perform regressions of changes in import duty and alternatively, changes in $(X + M)/\text{GDP}$ (the other protection measures being purely cross-sectional, i.e. available only at one point in time) on changes in inequality and an interaction term of change in inequality interacted with the capital–labor ratio. Using Δ to denote changes, Eq. (6) from Section 3 can be written as $\Delta TR_i / \Delta INEQ_i = \alpha_1 + \alpha_2 (K/L)_i$ which in turn gives us our following new estimating equation:

$$\Delta TR_i = \alpha_1 \, \Delta INEQ_i + \alpha_2 (K/L)_i \, \Delta INEQ_i + e_i \qquad (8)$$

The changes in these variables are for the 1980 to 1990 period for each country, while the data on K/L as before are the averages for the 1980s. The result for import duty seems to support and strengthen our earlier results. For $(X + M)/\text{GDP}$ we failed to find any significant relationship, perhaps because the change in GDP dominates and is itself driven by extraneous factors. The following are the regression results with the change in import duty as the dependent variable, with and without the constant term, respectively (standard errors are shown in parentheses):

$$\Delta(\text{import duty}) = \underset{(0.74)}{0.55} - \underset{(0.89)}{2.21^{****}} \, \Delta(\text{gini}) + \underset{(0.096)}{0.224^{***}} (K/L) \, \Delta(\text{gini})$$

$$R^2 = 0.18, N = 33$$

$$\Delta(\text{import duty}) = -\underset{(0.88)}{2.31^{****}} \, \Delta(\text{gini}) + \underset{(0.094)}{0.233^{***}} (K/L) \, \Delta(\text{gini})$$

$$R^2 = 0.18, N = 33$$

The signs of the coefficients of $\Delta(\text{gini})$ and $(K/L) \, \Delta(\text{gini})$ are negative and positive respectively, exactly as predicted. The critical value of the K/L ratio is 9.8, again very close to the median.

6. Conclusion

The prediction of the median voter approach (within a Heckscher–Ohlin framework) is that trade policies will be biased towards trade in labor rich countries, and biased against trade in capital rich economies. However, trade policies, as we know, are always and everywhere biased against trade. This paper gives a second chance to the median-voter approach by focusing on cross-country variations in (rather than the orientations of) trade policies. The data show that an increase in inequality increases import protection in capital-abundant countries, but reduces trade barriers in capital-scarce economies. This is consistent with the predictions of the median-voter approach within a two-factor, two-sector Heckscher–Ohlin model. There is some evidence, that this relationship may hold better in democracies than in dictatorships.

Acknowledgements

We are grateful to Francisco Rodriguez for sharing his dataset with us and are indebted to Adolph Buse, Robert Feenstra, Raquel Fernandez, Kishore Gawande, Pravin Krishna, Priya Ranjan, Dani Rodrik, Dimitrios Thomakos and two anonymous referees for very detailed and useful comments on earlier drafts. We would like to thank Jim Anderson, Bob Baldwin, Cem Karayalcin, John Kennan, Robert Lemke, Giovanni Maggi, Debraj Ray, Bob Staiger, Scott Taylor, Giorgio Topa, Andres Velasco and seminar participants at the University of Alberta, Boston College, Canadian Economic Association Meetings (2001 at Montreal), Florida International University, Midwest International Economics Conference (Spring, 2001 at Madison), New York University and the University of Wisconsin-Madison for useful discussions. The standard disclaimer applies.

Appendix A

Here we tie our empirical results to the theoretical predictions in the context of the inequality measures used. Let the share of the median quintile in the capital stock be λ_K and its share in total income be λ_I. Since in the model, tariff revenue is distributed in proportion to a person's share in factor income, in the context of our two-factor (capital–labor) framework, we have $\lambda_I = [0.2wL + r\lambda_K K]/[wL + rK] = [0.2w + r\lambda_K k]/[w + rk]$ where $k = K/L$ is the economy's ratio of capital to labor endowment. $\partial\lambda_I/\partial\lambda_K = \frac{rk}{w + rk} > 0$, $\partial\lambda_I/\partial p = (0.2 - \lambda_K)k[rw'(p) - wr'(p)]/[w + rk]^2 > 0$ for a capital-abundant country and < 0 for a labor abundant country (as in any country with asset inequality, $\lambda_K < 0.2$). Thus, we can write $\lambda_I = \psi(\lambda_K, t, k)$ where t is the tariff and $\psi_1 > 0$, and $\psi_2 > 0$ for a capital-abundant country and < 0 for a capital-scarce economy. Holding λ_I constant and allowing λ_K and t to vary, we have $d\lambda_I = 0 \Rightarrow \psi_1 \partial \lambda_K / \partial t + \psi_2 = 0 \Rightarrow \partial \lambda_K / \partial t = -\psi_2/\psi_1 < 0$ for a capital-abundant country and > 0 for a capital-scarce country. Thus, we can write $\lambda_K = \phi(\lambda_I, t, k)$ where $\phi_1 > 0$, and $\phi_2 < 0$ for a capital-abundant country and > 0 for a capital-scarce one. The equilibrium tariff can be written as $t = f(k, \lambda_K)$ where $f_2 < 0$ for a capital-abundant country and > 0 for a capital-scarce economy. Therefore, we have $t = f(k, \phi(\lambda_I, t, k)) \Rightarrow dt/d\lambda_I = f_2 \phi_1 / [1 - f_2 \phi_2]$. We find from our regressions that $f_2 \phi_1 / [1 - f_2 \phi_2] < 0$ for a capital-abundant country and > 0 for a capital-scarce one. We know that with the two-factor (capital–labor) Stolper–Samuelson effect at work, we have support for the median-voter predictions only if $f_2 < 0$ for a capital-abundant country and > 0 for a capital-scarce one. The question here is whether, with the Stolper–Samuelson effect at work, the signs of the estimated derivative $dt/d\lambda_I$ from our regressions support the median-voter predictions. In a capital–abundant country $f_2 \phi_1 / [1 - f_2 \phi_2] < 0 \Rightarrow$ either $\{f_2 \phi_1 \underset{(-)(+)}{<} 0, 1 - f_2 \phi_2 \underset{(-)(-)}{>} 0\}$ or $\{f_2 \phi_1 \underset{(+)(+)}{>} 0, 1 - f_2 \phi_2 \underset{(+)(-)}{<} 0\}$ (Note that we have already established ϕ_2's negative sign for a capital-abundant country and ϕ_1's positive sign in general). Only $\{f_2 \phi_1 \underset{(-)(+)}{<} 0, 1 - f_2 \phi_2 \underset{(-)(-)}{>} 0\}$ consists of mutually consistent inequalities. Similarly when we find that $f_2 \phi_1 / [1 - f_2 \phi_2] > 0$, for a capital-scarce economy we have $\{f_2 \phi_1 \underset{(+)(+)}{>} 0, 1 - f_2 \phi_2 \underset{(+)(+)}{>} 0\}$ or $\{f_2 \phi_1 \underset{(-)(+)}{<} 0, 1 - f_2 \phi_2 \underset{(-)(+)}{<} 0\}$, of which only the first set consists of mutually consistent inequalities. Thus, our derivatives from our regressions imply that $f_2 < 0$ (> 0) for a capital-abundant (capital-scarce) country. Thus, finding a positive (negative) relationship between inequality and protection in a capital-abundant (scarce) economy provides support for the median-voter predictions.

References

Alesina, A., Rodrik, D., 1994. Distributive politics and economic growth. Quarterly Journal of Economics 109 (2), 465–490.

Baldwin, R., Magee, C., 2000. Is Trade Policy for Sale? Congressional Voting on Recent Trade Bills, Public Choice 105, 79–101.

Balistreri, E., 1997. The performance of the Heckscher–Ohlin–Vanek model in predicting endogenous policy forces at the individual level. Canadian Journal of Economics 30 (1), 1–17.

Beaulieu, E., 2000. The Stolper–Samuelson Theorem Faces Congress, Review of International Economics, in press.

Beaulieu, E., 2001. Factor or Industry Cleavages in Trade Policy? An Empirical Analysis of the Stolper–Samuelson Theorem, mimeo. Department of Economics, University of Calgary.

Beaulieu, E., Magee, C., 2000. Campaign Contributions and Trade Policy: Simple Tests of Stolper–Samuelson, mimeo, Department of Economics, University of Calgary and Department of Economics, Bard College.

Fernandez, R., Rodrik, D., 1991. Resistance to reform: status-quo bias in the presence of individual-specific uncertainty. American Economic Review 81 (5), 1146–1155.

Feenstra, R., Bhagwati, J., 1982. Tariff seeking and the efficient tariff. In: Bhagwati, J. (Ed.), Import Competition and Response. The University of Chicago Press, Chicago, IL.

Findlay, R., Wellisz, S., 1982. Endogenous tariffs, the political economy of trade restrictions and welfare. In: Bhagwati, J.N. (Ed.), Import Competition and Response. The University of Chicago Press, Chicago, IL, pp. 223–234.

Gawande, K., Bandopadhyay, U., 2000. Is protection for sale? A test of the Grossman–Helpman theory of endogenous protection. Review of Economics and Statistics 82 (1), 139–152.

Goldberg, P., Maggi, G., 1999. Protection for sale: an empirical investigation. American Economic Review 89 (5), 1135–1155.

Grossman, G., Helpman, E., 1994. Protection for Sale, American Economic Review, 84, September 1994, 833–850.

Harrigan, J., 1993. OECD imports and trade barriers in 1983. Journal of International Economics 35 (1), 91–111.

Hausman, J., 1978. Specificfication tests in econometrics. Econometrica 46, 1251–1271.

Hillman, A., 1989. The Political Economy of Protection. Harwood Academic, London and New York.

Irwin, D., 1994. The political economy of free trade: voting in British general election of 1906. Journal of Law and Economics 37, 75–108.

Irwin, D., 1996. Industry or class cleavages over trade policy? evidence from the British general election of 1923. In: Feenstra, R., Grossman, G., Irwin, D. (Eds.), The Political Economy of Trade Policy: Papers in Honor of Jagdish Bhagwati. MIT Press, Cambridge, MA, pp. 53–75.

Kahane, L., 1996. Congressional voting patterns on NAFTA; an empirical analysis. American Journal of Economics and Sociology 55, 395–409.

Leamer, E., 1990. The Structure and Effects of Tariff and Non-tariff Barriers in 1983. In: Jones, R., Krueger, A. (Eds.), The Political Economy Economy of International Trade: Essays In Honor of Robert E. Baldwin. Basil Blackwell, Cambridge, MA, pp. 224–260.

Leamer, E., Levinsohn, J., 1995. International Trade Theory: The Evidence. In: Grossman, G., Rogoff, K. (Eds.). Handbook of International Economics, Vol. 3. North-Holland, Amsterdam, pp. 1339–1394.

Li, H., Squire, L., Zou, H., 1998. Explaining international and intertemporal variations in income inequality. The Economic Journal 108 (446), 26–43.

Magee, C., 2001. Endogenous Trade Policy and Lobby Formation: An Application to the Free-Rider Problem, mimeo. Bard College, Annandale-on-Hudson.

Magee, S., 1978. Three simple tests of the Stolper–Samuelson theorem. In: Oppenheimer, P. (Ed.), Issues in International Economics. Oriel Press, Stockfield.

Magee, S., Brock, W., Young, L., 1989. Black Hole Tariffs and Endogenous Policy Theory. Cambridge University Press, Cambridge and New York.

Mansfield, E., Busch, M., 1995. The political economy of nontariff barriers: a cross-national analysis. International Organization 49 (4), 723–749.

Mayer, W., 1984. Endogenous tariff formation. American Economic Review 74 (5), 970–985.

Mitra, D., 1999. Endogenous lobby formation and endogenous protection: a long run model of trade policy determination. American Economic Review 89 (5), 1116–1134.

Pecorino, P., 1998. Is there a free-rider problem in lobbying? Endogenous tariffs, trigger strategies, and the number of firms. American Economic Review 88, 652–660.

Rodrik, D., 1986. Tariffs, subsidies, and welfare with endogenous policy. Journal of International Economics 21 (3/4), 285–299.

Rodrik, D., 1995. Political economy of trade policy. In: Grossman, G., Rogoff, K. (Eds.). Handbook of International Economics, Vol. 3. North-Holland, Amsterdam, pp. 1457–1494.

Rodrik, D., 1997. Has Globalization Gone Too Far?. Institute for International Economics, Washington, DC.

Rogowski, R., 1987. Political cleavages and changing exposure to trade. American Political Sceince Review 81 (4), 1121–1137.

Scheve, K., Slaughter, M., 1998. What Determines Individual Trade Policy Preferences?, NBER Working Paper 6531.

Smith, R., Blundell, R., 1986. An exogeneity test for a simultaneous equation tobit model with and application to labor supply. Econometrica 54, 679–685.

Steagall, J., Jennings, K., 1996. Unions, PAC contributions and the NAFTA vote. Journal of Labor Reasearch 17, 515–521.

Trefler, D., 1993. Trade liberalization and the theory of endogenous protection. Journal of Political Economy 101, 138–160.

Chapter 5

POLITICAL IDEOLOGY AND ENDOGENOUS TRADE POLICY: AN EMPIRICAL INVESTIGATION

Pushan Dutt and Devashish Mitra*

Abstract—In this paper, we investigate empirically how government ideology affects trade policy. The prediction of a partisan, ideology-based model (within a two-sector, two-factor Heckscher-Ohlin framework) is that left-wing governments will adopt more protectionist trade policies in capital-rich countries, but adopt more pro-trade policies in labor-rich countries, than right-wing ones. The data strongly support this prediction in a very robust fashion. There is some evidence that this relationship may hold better in democracies than in dictatorships, though the magnitude of the partisan effect seems stronger in dictatorships.

I. Introduction

POLITICAL ideology has been conceptualized in a number of ways, giving rise to a multiplicity of meanings and interpretations. One view is that it stands for the self-defined notions of public interest and altruistic goals of politicians and political parties, which form the basis for most of economic policymaking (Kau & Rubin, 1979). Another view is that the interests of constituents and ideological preferences of politicians are interrelated, with the former probably determining the latter (Peltzman, 1984; Alt, 1986).[1,2] However, in between these two extremes is the position that both pure altruistic, public-interest motivations and constituents' interests are important determinants of the ideological positions of political parties and politicians (Kalt & Zupan, 1984).[3,4]

In this paper, we investigate how trade policy depends on the political ideology of the government (the party or the ruler in power). We examine how trade policy varies with the extent of the government's leftist (prolabor, as opposed to procapital) orientation. Our analysis is independent of which of the above definitions of ideology one adopts. A left-wing party adopts a prolabor stance either because its constituents are workers whose welfare they need to care about to be guaranteed their support in votes and political contributions, and/or because they really place a high weight on egalitarianism. Similarly, a right-wing party may be taking care of its constituents, the capitalists, and/or may truly believe in providing incentives for capital accumulation to foster growth and generate jobs. In our analysis, we just assume that a government that is more left-oriented places a higher weight on the welfare of workers relative to that of capitalists, which can be consistent with any or all of the above reasons. This is consistent with the findings of Hibbs (1977), who shows in his cross-sectional investigation of 14 major, industrialized countries (as well as in his time series analysis of U.S. and U.K. data) that countries (and periods) with left-wing governments had lower unemployment and higher inflation than others.[5] This cross-country evidence provides support for his *partisan* theory according to which politicians are "partisan"—left-wing and right-wing governments have different objective functions, the former attributing a higher cost to unemployment relative to inflation than the latter. Alesina (1987) develops his *rational partisan* theory using a two-party model in which the left-wing party attaches a higher weight to un-employment relative to inflation (and a higher target inflation rate) in its loss function than the right-wing party.[6] Hibbs and Vasilatos (1982) and Hibbs, Rivers, and Vasilatos (1982), in different studies of survey data for the United States and the United Kingdom, show that the electorate's preferences and concerns about macroeconomic issues are class-related, with blue-collar groups being relatively more concerned about unemployment and white-collar groups being more concerned about inflation.[7] Magee, Brock, and Young (1989) have also argued that in the United States, the low-unemployment–high-inflation combinations under Democratic presidents benefit workers (debtors), and the opposite combinations under Republican presidents benefit capitalists (creditors).[8] Thus, it is fairly standard in the

Received for publication December 12, 2002. Revision accepted for publication October 7, 2003.

* University of Alberta, and Syracuse University and NBER, respectively.

We are indebted to Andrew Bernard, Lawrence Broz, Marc Busch, Gary Engelhardt, Robert Feenstra, Jeffry Frieden, Gordon Hanson, Cem Karayalcin, Pravin Krishna, Philip Levy, Chris Magee, Will Martin, Doug Nelson, Dani Rodrik, Matt Slaughter, Connie Smith, Alan Taylor, Dimitrios Thomakos, Daniel Traca, and two anonymous referees for valuable comments and suggestions, and to Michael Hiscox for sharing his data set with us. We also thank seminar audiences at Baruch College, the Canadian Economic Association Meetings (2002, Calgary), the East-West Center (Honolulu), the GEP conference (Summer 2003, University of Nottingham), the International Monetary Fund, McGill University, INSEAD, NBER Summer Institute 2002, National University of Singapore, Syracuse University, Tulane University, the University of Alberta, the University of Calgary, the World Bank, and Yale University for useful discussions. We gratefully acknowledge the financial support of the SSHRC (410-2003-1309). The standard disclaimer applies.

[1] Peltzman (1984) finds empirical support for this position using Senate voting records across a wide range of issues.

[2] Alt (1986) writes: ". . .class-party modelers from Kalecki to Hibbs say, . . .parties are policy-oriented, ideological agents of their supporters. . .".

[3] Empirically, Kalt and Zupan (1984) find the effects of both pure "ideology" and the constituents' interests to be fairly important in Senate voting (on strip-mining controls).

[4] For an informational aspect to ideology, see Glazer and Grofman (1989).

[5] Also, see Alt (1985), who analyzes data from 14 western industrial nations between 1960 and 1983 and finds that unemployment falls (rises) following a change from a right-wing (left-wing) to a left-wing (right-wing) government.

[6] Alesina and Roubini (1992) find empirical support for the rational partisan model using OECD data.

[7] In fact, for the United Kingdom, they also find that manual working class voters are far more supportive of Labor governments than of Conservative governments.

[8] This is the standard textbook argument in macroeconomics that a sudden increase in the inflation rate benefits debtors at the expense of creditors.

The Review of Economics and Statistics, February 2005, 87(1): 59–72
© 2005 by the President and Fellows of Harvard College and the Massachusetts Institute of Technology

political economy literature to use left-wing (right-wing) and prolabor (procapital) interchangeably.[9,10]

In this paper, we use the political support function approach of Hillman (1989) and Van Long and Vousden (1991) in a two-sector, two-factor (capital and labor) Heckscher-Ohlin framework.[11] The government's objective function, also called the political-support function, is a weighted sum of the welfare of workers and capitalists.[12] Maximization of this objective function yields the political-economy equilibrium tariff. In this model, the effect of an increase in the leftist orientation of the government is studied by increasing the weight on labor welfare relative to capital welfare in the government's maximand. This increase in the labor-welfare weight results in policies that are more prolabor and that make the domestic terms of trade move in favor of the labor-intensive sector. In a capital-abundant country, the labor-intensive good is the importable good, and therefore an increase in the leftist orientation of the government will result in a rise in import protection. In a labor-abundant country, however, the capital-intensive good is the importable and the labor-intensive good is the exportable. Therefore, an increase in leftist orientation in such a country that calls for a change in the domestic price ratio in favor of the labor-intensive exportable good will result in a decline in import protection. It is exactly this prediction about cross-country variation in trade policy that we are able to investigate empirically, using cross-country data on government ideology (left, center, or right), capital abundance, and diverse measures of trade restrictions and openness.

It is important to note here that in this kind of Heckscher-Ohlin framework, a left-wing (right-wing) government may

want to make the import tariff negative in a labor-abundant (capital-abundant) country if free trade is considered the neutral situation (arising from equal weights on labor and capital). However, in the real world there are possibly other components of the tariff (arising from other factors or considerations) which are, in combination, always positive enough to make the overall, observed tariff levels positive in countries of all degrees of capital abundance or scarcity, and with governments of all ideologies. Holding these other effects constant with respect to ideology, the overall import tariff can rise or fall with left-wing ideology to the extent that the positive or negative component that we focus on becomes more positive or more negative.

We perform our empirical investigation using three separate measures of relative factor endowments (capital per worker), constructed using different methods and under different assumptions. In looking at the effects of ideology, we allow it to change direction and magnitude as the relative factor proportions change when we move across countries.[13] Across all measures of trade restrictiveness and using different measures of the capital-labor ratio, we find strong evidence in favor of the above-mentioned prediction of the impact of ideology: an increase in the left-wing ideology, holding constant the economy's overall relative endowments, does in fact raise trade barriers in capital-abundant economies and lower them in capital-scarce economies.[14] Further, this result is extremely robust to the use of controls, to the treatment of the relative capital and labor endowments as endogenous to trade policy, to the correction of measurement errors in the ideology measure, and to controlling for differences in the endowments of other factors of production.

It is important to note here that our results are consistent with the results of econometric studies (using micro-level survey data) on individual-level trade policy preferences such as Balistreri (1997), Beaulieu (2001), and Scheve and Slaughter (2001). These authors find that for both Canada and the United States in recent years, factor type has been

---

[9] See, for instance, Magee, Brock, and Young (1989) or Persson and Tabellini (2000). The tradition of linking political parties to classes or factors can be traced back to traditional theories of party systems, where classification is generally in terms of capitalists versus workers, urban versus rural, or the like (see Lipset & Rokkan, 1967)).

[10] See also the work by Garrett (1998), Swank (2002), and Adsera and Boix (2002) on the effects of partisanship on different kinds of economic policies. Using OECD data, Garret looks at how globalization has changed the way in which fiscal policy responds to partisanship, and Swank looks at how the response of welfare expenditure to globalization depends on the nature of the state and the relative strengths of interest groups. Adsera and Boix model the endogenous trade regime (free trade versus autarky) as well as government size and show the possibility of multiple equilibria—autarky (free trade) with small (large) government, and an authoritarian free-trade, small-government model.

[11] There are other approaches to modeling endogenous trade policy. See Rodrik (1995) for an excellent and comprehensive survey of the political economy literature on trade policy.

[12] Grossman and Helpman (1994) use their political-contributions approach to provide micro foundations to the political-support function approach. Furthermore, the political-contributions approach and the associated objective function of the government in terms of contributions and aggregate welfare can be derived from a model of electoral competition (Grossman & Helpman, 1996), which also shows the possibility of nonconvergence of party platforms. In this sense we are using a reduced-form approach. In terms of the approach taken by Grossman and Helpman (1994), an increase in the weight on labor welfare in our framework can be, interpreted for instance, as a switch in power from a right-wing government receiving contributions from the capital lobby to a left-wing government receiving contributions from the labor lobby.

---

[13] In addition to using ideology as a variable, an interaction term between ideology and the capital-labor ratio is used to endogenously determine from the data the threshold capital-labor ratio where the trade-restrictiveness–ideology relationship changes sign or direction.

[14] Besides the above explanation that relies on the Stolper-Samuelson theorem and right-(left-)wing parties being aligned to capital (labor), there is an alternative explanation based on the ideological preferences of right-(left-)wing parties for lower inflation (unemployment). Right-wing governments that dislike inflation tighten monetary policy, exacerbating unemployment. To mitigate the costs of recession in import-sensitive sectors, they may favor protectionism. Though this would explain the protectionist instincts of right-wing governments in capital-scarce economies, it would imply that right-wing governments are protectionist in capital-abundant countries as well—a proposition clearly rejected by our empirical findings. A third explanation relies on the relationship between trade openness and government spending (see Rodrik, 1998; Garrett, 1998; and Adsera & Boix, 2002). If lowering trade barriers requires a substantial increase in government spending (to insure against income risk/volatility), it is quite possible that right-wing governments are not willing to move in that direction, especially in developing nations, where tax systems are not advanced enough to raise revenues at reasonable cost. We thank an anonymous referee for this explanation.

the dominant determinant of support for or opposition to trade barriers. Individuals owning proportionally more of the scarce factors favor trade barriers, whereas those owning proportionally more of the abundant factors do not like protection. Mayda and Rodrik (2001) also find, using cross-country survey data, that protrade preferences are related to individual human-capital levels in the manner predicted by the Heckscher-Ohlin model. Besides the above individual-level, revealed-preference evidence for the Stolper-Samuelson theorem (on which this paper's main proposition rests), there are papers that have found support for it using data on political action committee (PAC) contributions and congressional voting patterns.[15]

Thus, our results uncover a robust empirical regularity in the relationship between trade protection and political ideology, thereby making a contribution to the literature on the political economy of trade policy,[16] as well as to the one on cross-national variation in protection.[17] Our findings suggest that a left-wing government that is generally more interventionist and believes in state control of the economy may surprisingly have a preference for free trade.

II.   Theoretical Framework

We now present an outline of a model that is presented in detail in Dutt and Mitra (2002). Consider a two-factor, two-sector, small-open, Heckscher-Ohlin economy. Both goods require both capital and labor in their production, carried out under constant returns to scale. On the demand side, individual preferences are taken to be identical and homothetic. For simplicity, we assume that there are two kinds of factor owners, workers (who only own labor) and capitalists (who only own capital). We also assume that tariff revenues are distributed in proportion to the factor incomes earned by individuals. The government chooses the level of the import tariff to maximize its objective function,

which is a weighted sum of the aggregate welfare of workers and capitalists. Our main comparative-static exercise here is to see how this tariff varies with the government's weight on the welfare of workers (relative to that of capitalists). This leads us to the following proposition, whose empirical validity we test in this paper:

Proposition. Holding other things constant, an increase in the left orientation (prolabor bias) of the government leads to more restrictive or less open trade policies in capital-abundant countries, and leads to less restrictive or more open trade policies in capital-scare ones.

This result is very intuitive. An increase in leftist orientation always results in redistributive policies that would benefit labor. In a capital-abundant country, the importable is the labor-intensive good, and an increase in redistribution from capital to labor is brought about by an increase in the bias of policies in favor of the importable sector. In a labor-abundant economy, the importable sector is the capital-intensive one, and hence more redistribution toward labor requires policies that are more biased against the importable sector.[18]

III.   Econometric Methodology

As the comparative-static result of the previous section shows, in countries with high K/L ratios, left-wing ideology of the government and trade restrictiveness should be positively related, but when K/L is low there is an inverse relationship between these two variables. A priori, we do not know at what level of K/L this relationship changes sign. The following specification takes care of this problem by allowing the data to tell us the exact location of this turning point:

$$TR_i = \alpha_0 + \alpha_1 Ideology_i + \alpha_2 Ideology_i \times (K/L)_i$$
$$+ \alpha_3 (K/L)_i + X_i\beta + \epsilon_i, \tag{1}$$

where TR_i is the extent of trade restrictions in country i, $Ideology_i$ is a measure of the extent of the government's left-wing ideology, $(K/L)_i$ the capital-labor ratio, and X_i is a row vector of control variables.[19,20] The inclusion of K/L as a separate variable [in addition to $Ideology$ and $Ideology \times (K/L)$] allows $\partial TR_i/\partial(K/L)_i$ and the variable component of

---

[15] See, for instance, Beaulieu (2002), Baldwin and Magee (1998), and Beaulieu and Magee (2000). In contrast, earlier studies (using older data for the United Kingdom and the United States, respectively) by Irwin (1996) and Magee (1978) find that industry of employment was the major determinant of individual-level trade policy preferences.

[16] There are two studies, namely O'Halloran (1994) and Magee, et al. (1989), that link partisanship to protection levels. However, they only look at time series, aggregate-level evidence for the United States for the periods 1877–1934 and 1900–1983, respectively, and find that Republicans (Democrats) have tended to raise (reduce) tariffs. This is not totally inconsistent with the Heckscher-Ohlin model; for the United States, at least until the end of World War I, was relatively poor in capital and rich in labor and land. By the 1970s, owing to the change in the country's comparative advantage, the two parties had switched sides as regards trade but not as regards factors of production (see Rodrik, 1995, and Ray, 1987). This switch is not obvious upon casual observation, because changes in macroeconomic conditions complicate matters (see Magee et al., 1989; O'Halloran, 1994; and Rodrik, 1995). There is also an interesting paper by Schonhardt-Bailey (1991) on the lack of partisanship with respect to trade policy in nineteenth-century Britain. Finally, Hiscox (2001), in his study of six western nations, looks at how historically the nature and structure of partisanship on the trade issue changes over time and depends on the extent of intersectoral factor mobility, which itself keeps changing.

[17] See Rodrik (1995) for a discussion of the importance of (and the need for) empirical work on cross-country variations in protection.

[18] Though the predictions are not as precise once we allow for more than two factors, one can argue that the above proposition is not as specific to the two-factor framework as it appears. See Dutt and Mitra (2002) for a more detailed argument.

[19] We could not find any nonmonotonicities with respect to K/L by including an additional term in $(K/L)^2$. We did not detect any nonlinearities (at 15% and even higher levels of significance) in any of our variables (K/L, ideology, their cross product, and other control variables) when we performed the Ramsey reset test for all our regressions, both with and without controls.

[20] In our estimation, we use the capital-labor ratios in natural logs (whose use results in very few outliers) and not in levels (whose use results in a very large number of outliers).

$\partial TR_i/\partial Ideology_i$ to differ in sign. Otherwise, they are restricted to having the same sign.

Taking the partial derivative of TR_i with respect to $Ideology_i$, we have

$$\frac{\partial TR_i}{\partial Ideology_i} = \alpha_1 + \alpha_2(K/L)_i . \tag{2}$$

The prediction of the comparative-static exercise of the previous section is that $\alpha_1 < 0$ and $\alpha_2 > 0$ such that $\alpha_1 + \alpha_2 (K/L)_i \gtreqless 0$ as $(K/L)_i \gtreqless (K/L)^*$, where $(K/L)^* = -\alpha_1/\alpha_2$ is the turning point capital-labor ratio determined endogenously from the data, given our estimating equation.[21] Another requirement for the prediction to hold is that $(K/L)^*$ should lie within the range of values of (K/L) in the data set, that is, $(K/L)^{MIN} < (K/L)^* < (K/L)^{MAX}$.

We first run the basic (without controls) ordinal and cardinal versions (explained in detail in section V A) of the above estimating equation. We then add controls such as democracy and special dummies for east Asia, for oil countries, and for sub-Saharan African countries to see whether our results are robust to their inclusion.[22] Hausman tests suggested the endogeneity of the capital-labor ratio with respect to trade protection. We therefore performed two-stage least squares regressions to control for such endogeneity. We also take advantage of the fact that some of our measures of protection have a time series dimension to create a panel data set and validate our results using a fixed-effects model with time-specific and comprehensive region-specific effects. Furthermore, we investigate whether this model works better in democracies than in dictatorships, and where the magnitude of this predicted relationship is stronger. A number of other robustness checks are also performed (explained in detail in section VI).

IV. Data Sources and Some Basic Statistics

Our dependent variable is trade protection, and our independent variables of interest are a measure of ideological orientation (left-, center-, and right-wing), the capital-labor ratio, and indicators for democracy and political rights. The cross-sectional analysis averages all variables for the decade of the 1980s; the panel analysis covers the time period 1980–1989. For running our regression in changes, the change in each variable is calculated as its average value in the eighties minus its average value in the seventies.

To test for the robustness of our results, we use a variety of trade policy measures: total import duties collected as a percentage of total imports (*IMPORT DUTY*), an average

tariff rate calculated by weighing each import category by the fraction of trade in that category (*TARIFF*),[23] a coverage ratio for nontariff barriers to trade (*QUOTA*), an indirect measure of trade restrictions [the magnitude of trade flows relative to GDP, denoted $(X + M)/GDP$], and the newly available Hiscox-Kastner measure. For the panel analysis, only *IMPORT DUTY*, $(X + M)/GDP$, and the Hiscox-Kastner measure are used, because these are the only measures for which data are available over time. *IMPORT DUTY* and $(X + M)/GDP$ are taken from the World Development Indicators, *TARIFF* and *QUOTA* (both available for only one point in time for each country in the 1980s) are taken from Barro and Lee (1994), and the Hiscox-Kastner measure of protection is taken from Hiscox and Kastner (2002).

The data on political orientation are obtained from the Database of Political Institutions (DPI) (Beck et al., 2001), which is a large cross-country database of political institutions that covers 177 countries over 25 years, 1971–1995. We use the ideological orientation (left, center, or right) of the chief executive (that of the chief executive's party or, when considered appropriate, that of the chief executive himself/herself) for political systems classified as presidential in the database, that of the largest government party for systems classified as parliamentary, and the average of these two orientations for systems classified as assembly-elected president.[24] We also verified the robustness of our results by using the ideological orientation of the chief executive for political systems that are classified as assembly-elected president instead of using an average measure.

The data on capital-labor ratios are obtained from Easterly and Levine, who use aggregate investment and depreciation data to construct capital-per-worker series for 138 countries. To check for and ensure the robustness of our results we also use the Easterly-Levine capital-per-worker data that are based on disaggregate sectoral investment and depreciation data to arrive at more accurate measures. However, the country coverage for the second measure is much smaller.[25]

---

[21] We will first give ideology a categorical interpretation and subsequently check if it may be given a cardinal interpretation as well. If ideology has an exclusively categorical (dummy variable) interpretation, then the derivatives shown here are not meaningful. However, the coefficients will still have similar interpretations, enabling the calculation of critical capital-labor ratios where the relationships switch sign.

[22] We have also tried using, in addition to these controls, a dummy for Latin America. The results remain completely unaffected.

[23] The variable is referred to as tariffs, although it includes all import charges, such as duties and customs fees.

[24] For details regarding the coding of parties as left, right, and center, see Beck et al. (2001). However, an important thing to note in the context of this paper is that their definition of these three categories is not based on trade policy orientation, but rather on how much the party advocates "the strengthening of private enterprise" (which could be interpreted as implicitly procapital) versus the extent to which "it supports a redistributive role for the government" (prolabor). See also some of the original sources Beck et al. (2001) cite.

[25] We also tried the Nehru-Dhareshwar data on capital in conjunction with the data on labor (defined as population between ages 15 and 64), to calculate an alternative measure of capital-labor ratio. The data on capital stock at 1987 domestic prices are converted into 1987 constant dollars using the 1987 exchange rate. However, this results in a number of outliers (both unrealistically high capital-labor ratios for countries such as Argentina, and in the results of multivariate outlier tests) owing to appreciated exchange rates. The results (with and without the inclusion of these outliers) here bear out our predictions as well.

TABLE 1.—EASTERLY-LEVINE (AGGREGATE) REGRESSION WITH DUMMIES

	Left versus Nonleft				Left versus Center versus Right			
	TARIFF	QUOTA	IMPORT DUTY	(X + M)/GDP	TARIFF	QUOTA	IMPORT DUTY	(X + M)/GDP
Left	-0.574***	-1.225***	-12.075	114.692***	-0.734***	-1.51***	-13.189	75.762*
	(0.181)	(0.477)	(10.204)	(48.577)	(0.194)	(0.553)	(11.507)	(49.907)
Left × capital-labor ratio	0.055***	0.115***	1.247	-11.914***	0.072***	0.142***	1.365	-7.972*
	(0.017)	(0.045)	(1.011)	(5.183)	(0.018)	(0.053)	(1.17)	(5.441)
Center					-0.365	-1.526***	-4.092	-164.819*
					(0.373)	(0.644)	(24.58)	(111.235)
Center × capital-labor ratio					0.039	0.141***	0.406	15.904
					(0.034)	(0.06)	(2.287)	(11.451)
Capital-labor ratio	-0.08***	-0.116***	-3.645***	18.432***	-0.097***	-0.143***	-3.762***	14.49***
	(0.014)	(0.042)	(0.736)	(4.974)	(0.016)	(0.05)	(0.934)	(5.237)
Constant	0.952***	1.391***	45.217***	-144.551***	1.112***	1.676***	46.331***	-105.621***
	(0.155)	(0.45)	(7.604)	(47.31)	(0.169)	(0.529)	(9.194)	(48.644)
No. of observations	67	66	65	88	67	66	65	88
R^2	0.32	0.15	0.35	0.32	0.34	0.19	0.35	0.35
F-statistic	14.07***	2.7***	12.9***	13.88***	12.6***	1.8*	7.58***	8.45***
Critical capital-labor ratio	10.4	10.6	9.7	9.6				
Joint test for cardinality (F-statistic)					0.38	0.62	0.55	1.32*

Standard errors in parentheses; ***significant at 5% level, **significant at 10% level, *significant at 15% level.

For a measure of democracy, we use the Freedom House (Gastil) measure of democracy, which provides a subjective classification of countries on a scale of 1 to 7 on political rights, with higher ratings signifying less freedom. Finally, as instruments, the additional variables used are the natural logarithm of the savings rate and the population growth rate obtained from the World Development Indicators. Note that the population growth rate and the savings rate are parameters in the Solow growth model, in which the steady-state per capita capital stock is determined endogenously.

The summary statistics for our data and the correlation matrix for our basic protection measures can be found in Dutt and Mitra (2002).

V. Results

A. Regressions Using Conventional Trade Policy Measures

OLS Regressions: We first show that our basic theoretical prediction is supported when we give ideology an exclusively ordinal or categorical (dummy variable) interpretation. Under this interpretation, our estimating equation is

$$TR_i = \alpha + \beta_0 left_i + \beta_1 left_i (K/L)_i$$
$$+ \gamma_0 center_i + \gamma_1 center_i (K/L)_i \quad (3)$$
$$+ \theta (K/L)_i + \epsilon_i,$$

where $left_i = 1$ (0 otherwise) if the ith country has a left-wing government, and $center_i = 1$ (0 otherwise) if the ith country has a centrist government. Both β_0 and γ_0 are predicted to be negative, whereas β_1 and γ_1 are predicted to be positive. Also, theory predicts that the β's are greater in magnitude than the respective γ's. Next, we perform tests to check if, in fact, the ideology measure can be treated as

cardinal, where it takes the value 1 if the government is right-wing, 2 if it is centrist, and 3 if it is left-wing. Under this interpretation, equation (1) is our estimating equation. In order for the cardinal specification (a special case of the ordinal specification) to be the correct one,

$$\beta_0 = 2\gamma_0 \quad \text{and} \quad \beta_1 = 2\gamma_1$$

should hold simultaneously.[26] If we cannot reject this joint hypothesis, then there are efficiency gains from treating ideology as a cardinal measure, with equal distances between right and center and between center and left.

In table 1, we present our first set of cross-section results.[27] In the first four regressions, we use a single dummy variable that takes the value 1 for left-wing governments (and 0 otherwise) to represent ideology. For the last four columns we have another dummy for *center* that additionally distinguishes countries with centrist governments from those with right-wing ones. Classification of political ideology was done as follows: The time period of our study is the decade of the 1980s. Any country that had a left-wing (centrist right-wing) government in office for at least 6 years was coded as left (centrist, right). There were three countries in our sample (Bolivia, New Zealand, and Norway) that had a left-wing and a right-wing government for exactly 5 years each during the 1980s, and one country

[26] Note that the test of cardinality versus ordinality is performed strictly in distance terms. We cannot and do not perform a test of levels of right, left, and center in terms of each other, because regression results are independent of scale and origin of the variable. For example, if instead of a 1, 2, 3 scale we had a 0, 1, 2 or a 5, 6, 7 scale, only the constant term would change, and all the slope coefficients would remain unchanged. On the other hand, if we had a 2, 4, 6 scale, the slope coefficients would be halved (and thus the interpretations of results would remain unchanged).

[27] In these results and the ones that follow in the rest of this paper, all standard errors are White-corrected.

TABLE 2.—EASTERLY-LEVINE (AGGREGATE) REGRESSION WITH AND WITHOUT CONTROLS

	Regressions without controls				Regressions with Controls			
	TARIFF	QUOTA	IMPORT DUTY	(X + M)/GDP	TARIFF	QUOTA	IMPORT DUTY	(X + M)/GDP
Ideology	−0.394***	−0.783***	−10.011*	58.493***	−0.36***	−0.93***	−9.938*	47.005**
	(0.095)	(0.263)	(6.22)	(25.975)	(0.113)	(0.307)	(6.49)	(25.921)
Ideology × capital-labor ratio	0.04***	0.073***	1.043*	−6.209***	0.035***	0.087***	1.027*	−4.857**
	(0.009)	(0.025)	(0.652)	(2.819)	(0.011)	(0.029)	(0.679)	(2.806)
Capital-labor ratio	−0.138***	−0.221***	−5.327***	25.228***	−0.138***	−0.253***	−5.014***	23.041***
	(0.023)	(0.07)	(1.543)	(8.022)	(0.025)	(0.076)	(1.53)	(7.988)
Political rights (Gastil)					0.003	−0.001	−0.216	−3.8***
					(0.009)	(0.02)	(0.604)	(1.224)
Sub-Saharan Africa					−0.054	0.031	2.353	21.47***
					(0.063)	(0.127)	(3.016)	(7.972)
East Asia					−0.067	−0.238**	1.694	5.671
					(0.043)	(0.136)	(2.506)	(5.006)
Oil					0.076**	−0.094	2.498***	5.955
					(0.044)	(0.066)	(1.437)	(16.591)
Constant	1.518***	2.5***	61.389***	−206.722***	1.531***	2.87***	58.587***	−180.358***
	(0.242)	(0.745)	(15.12)	(75.454)	(0.266)	(0.818)	(15.598)	(75.306)
No. of observations	67	66	65	88	66	65	64	87
R²	0.34	0.2	0.36	0.31	0.38	0.25	0.36	0.4
F-statistic	22.47***	3.52***	12.31***	11.22***	11.34***	2.06***	6.48***	7.47***
Critical capital-labor ratio	9.9	10.7	9.6	9.4	10.3	10.7	9.7	9.7

Standard errors in parentheses; ***significant at 5% level, **significant at 10% level, *significant at 15% level.

(Ecuador) that had a left-wing and a right-wing government for exactly 4 years each, and a centrist government for a year.[28] These countries we classified as centrist.[29] There was no other country that had the decade of the 1980s split up into all three types (left, right, and center). As the first four columns of table 2 show, left-wing governments are more protectionist in capital-abundant countries, but less protectionist in labor-abundant countries.[30] The critical capital-labor ratio varies from 9.6 for (X + M)/GDP to 10.6 for QUOTA, not far from the mean and median capital-labor ratios. Though the result for IMPORT DUTY is somewhat weak in terms of the significance of the individual coefficients, the model as a whole is significant. The R²'s for these regressions range from 0.15 to 0.35.

In the next four columns, we use two dummies (two intercept dummies as well as their interactions with the capital-labor ratio)—one for left and one for center. Here we can see that our results do not change qualitatively from the first four columns. Generally, left-wing governments are more protectionist than right-wing ones in capital-abundant countries, but less protectionist in labor-abundant countries. This result also holds for centrist versus right-wing governments with QUOTA as the dependent variable. The two critical capital-labor ratios (not shown in the table—one for

[28] For Ecuador, we have data for only 9 out of the 10 years in the decade of the 1980s.
[29] To check for the robustness of this classification, we tried the following permutations: (a) classifying these three countries as left-wing, (b) classifying them as right-wing, and (c) dropping them from the sample. Our results are robust to all such variations.
[30] We have similarly performed regressions where we look at right versus nonright nations; we find that right-wing governments are more protectionist than nonright ones in labor-abundant countries. The relationship is reversed for capital-abundant countries.

right versus center and another for right versus left) per regression are all around 10, again very close to the mean and median K/L. As before, the model as a whole is significant, and the R² ranges from 0.19 to 0.35.

Importantly, we see here that we cannot reject the hypothesis that ideology can be treated as cardinal (i.e., the joint hypothesis that $\beta_0 = 2\gamma_0$ and $\beta_1 = 2\gamma_1$) for any of the measures except (X + M)/GDP. Thus, we replace these ideology dummy variables with a cardinal measure of ideology to obtain more efficient parameter estimates. Therefore, for most of the rest of the paper we will treat ideology as cardinal. In order to provide further accuracy to our cross-sectional ideology measure, we recoded the ideological orientation of the government of each country for each single year to reflect the extent to which the relevant government authority can be classified as leftist—left was coded as 3, center as 2, and right as 1. For our cross-sectional regressions here, we take the average of this variable for the 1980s. Therefore, our ideology variable in the regressions is best interpreted as the extent to which the policy and decision-making authority can be considered left-wing, with higher numbers signifying a more leftist orientation. In addition to being a cardinal variable (that will yield more efficient estimates, because the cardinality hypothesis cannot be rejected) as opposed to being an ordinal variable, this variable, in our cross-sectional regressions, captures the variation in the proportion of years a country had regimes of various ideologies (which our ordinal variables do not).

Tables 2 and 3 present the regression results (with and without controls) for our main estimating equation [equation (1) in section III of this paper] with the cardinal

POLITICAL IDEOLOGY AND ENDOGENOUS TRADE POLICY   65

TABLE 3.—EASTERLY-LEVINE (DISAGGREGATE) REGRESSION WITH AND WITHOUT CONTROLS

	Regressions without Controls				Regressions with Controls			
	TARIFF	QUOTA	IMPORT DUTY	(X + M)/GDP	TARIFF	QUOTA	IMPORT DUTY	(X + M)/GDP
Ideology	−0.392***	−0.996***	−9.448	91.587**	−0.392***	−1.634***	−12.703	66.465
	(0.165)	(0.514)	(11.526)	(47.726)	(0.166)	(0.438)	(9.178)	(48.571)
Ideology × capital-labor ratio	0.042***	0.095**	0.98	−10.144**	0.041***	0.157***	1.245	−7.401
	(0.017)	(0.051)	(1.179)	(5.293)	(0.017)	(0.044)	(0.954)	(5.373)
Capital-labor ratio	−0.154***	−0.277**	−6.498***	38.141***	−0.129***	−0.389***	−4.795**	33.349***
	(0.037)	(0.147)	(2.832)	(14.502)	(0.047)	(0.156)	(2.692)	(14.879)
Political rights (Gastil)					0.008	−0.009	0.368	−5.608***
					(0.013)	(0.03)	(0.708)	(1.784)
Sub-Saharan Africa					0.073	0.303***	9.142***	28.573**
					(0.075)	(0.128)	(4.368)	(16.101)
East Asia					0.034	−0.352**	−0.337	13.598**
					(0.051)	(0.191)	(2.074)	(7.968)
Oil					0.086***	−0.093**	6.068***	−24.318***
					(0.032)	(0.05)	(1.674)	(7.587)
Constant	1.588***	3.005***	70.507***	−313.06***	1.315***	4.166***	53.413**	−258.669**
	(0.369)	(1.499)	(28.044)	(133.005)	(0.488)	(1.604)	(27.268)	(137.695)
No. of observations	37	36	38	44	36	35	37	43
R²	0.43	0.3	0.45	0.28	0.46	0.5	0.55	0.39
F-statistic	11.8***	2.83**	7.63***	4.93***	18.79***	11.08***	14.18***	4.39***
Critical capital-labor ratio	9.3	10.5	9.6	9	9.6	10.4	10.2	9

Standard errors in parentheses; ***significant at 5% level, **significant at 10% level, *significant at 15% level.

measure of ideology. Table 2 corresponds to the Easterly-Levine aggregate capital-labor ratio, and table 3 to the Easterly-Levine disaggregate capital-labor ratio. The sample size, which ranges from 35 to 89, depends on the country coverage of the data on the different variables used.

In table 2, all our regression models as a whole are significant at the 5% level. In addition, as predicted, we obtain a negative sign for ideology and a positive sign for the interaction term for TARIFF, QUOTA, and IMPORT DUTY, where these coefficients are individually as well as jointly significant. For (X + M)/GDP (a measure of openness), as predicted, the signs are reversed and significant. The table also reports the critical capital-labor ratio at which the relationship between trade protection and left-wing ideology switches from negative to positive. This critical ratio ranges from 9 [for (X + M)/GDP without controls] to 10.5 [for QUOTA without controls]. These values are very close to the median and mean capital-labor ratios in the sample.[31] The R² ranges from 0.2 (in the case of quota without controls) to 0.38 (in the case of tariffs with controls). The results are the strongest and most robust for TARIFF and QUOTA, which are the most direct measures of trade restrictions.

Even though our model can explain less than 40% of the cross-country variation in protection, we still are able to analyze the magnitudes of some of the partial derivatives of protection with respect to ideology. For example, let us consider two capital-scarce countries, Bangladesh (K/L = 7.34) and Senegal (K/L = 7.17). Whereas Bangladesh had a

right-wing government (Ideology = 1), Senegal had a left-wing government (Ideology = 3) in the 1980s. At the average of the two K/L ratios (K/L = 7.255), from our tariff regression without controls, we have ∂TARIFF/∂Ideology = −0.1. Bangladesh had a TARIFF of 0.41, and Senegal had a TARIFF of 0.19, a difference of 0.22, resulting in a slope of TARIFF with respect to ideology of approximately −0.11, which is very close to the estimated slope from our regression. Let us now compare two capital-abundant countries, Canada (K/L = 11.12) and the United States (K/L = 11.2). While the United States had Ideology = 1.2 (average for the 1980s), Canada had Ideology = 1.8. At the average of the two K/L ratios (K/L = 11.16), from our tariff regression without controls, we have ∂TARIFF/∂Ideology = 0.05. Canada had a TARIFF of 0.046, and the United States had a TARIFF of 0.02, a difference of 0.026, resulting in a slope of TARIFF with respect to Ideology of 0.043, which is very close to the estimated slope from our regression. Brazil, Korea, Algeria, Costa Rica, Jamaica, and Guyana, which have capital-labor ratios close to the critical values, also have roughly similar tariff rates even though the political ideologies of their governments are quite different.

In table 3, which uses the disaggregate capital-labor ratio, our estimates (Ideology, K/L, and the interaction term) have the right signs and are significant, except for the IMPORT DUTY regressions, where Ideology and the interaction term are insignificant[32] (even here they do have the correct signs, and the model as a whole is significant at the 5% level and accounts for up to 45% of the cross-country variation). The R² ranges from 0.28 for the (X + M)/GDP regression

[31] Of course, the critical capital-labor ratio is itself an estimate and has a standard error. For most of our regressions, the 2-standard-error confidence interval around this estimate includes the median and mean capital-labor ratios.

[32] Notice that the country coverage for the disaggregate capital-labor ratio is nearly half that for the aggregate capital-labor ratio.

TABLE 4.—COUNTRIES (TARIFF-IDEOLOGY RELATIONSHIP)

Negative Relationship	Positive Relationship
Madagascar	Uruguay
Ethiopia	Taiwan
Uganda	Portugal
Mozambique	Algeria
Sierra Leone	Mexico
Burkina Faso	Argentina
Angola	Cyprus
Guinea	Trinidad & Tobago
Tanzania	Greece
Senegal	Venezuela
Bangladesh	United Kingdom
Benin	Ireland
Pakistan	Japan
China	Spain
Congo	Denmark
Sri Lanka	Austria
Zimbabwe	Sweden
El Salvador	New Zealand
Papua New Guinea	Canada
Thailand	Belgium
Zambia	Netherlands
Guatemala	Italy
Mauritius	United States
Nicaragua	France
Paraguay	Finland
Bolivia	Germany
Tunisia	Norway
Jamaica	Luxembourg
Colombia	Switzerland
Guyana	
Turkey	
Costa Rica	
Barbados	
Peru	
South Korea	
Brazil	
Chile	
Ecuador	

Partition based on tariff regression without controls in table 2.

without controls to 0.55 for the *IMPORT DUTY* regression with controls.

In table 4, using the tariff regression without controls presented in table 2, we categorize the countries in our sample into those that exhibit a negative relationship between protection and left-wing ideology (those with a low capital-labor ratio) and those that exhibit a positive relationship (those with a high capital-labor ratio). The critical (turning point) capital-labor ratio in this case is roughly 9.9, which is slightly lower than the capital-labor ratio for Ecuador. Adding controls increases the number of countries that exhibit a negative relation between left-wing ideology and trade protection and diminishes the number of countries that exhibit a positive relation.

A partial derivative of trade restrictions with respect to the capital-labor ratio in the regressions [using the notation from equation (1)] yields

$$\frac{\partial TR_i}{\partial (K/L)_i} = \alpha_3 + \alpha_2 Ideology_i. \tag{4}$$

Our regression results show that $\alpha_3 < 0$ and $\alpha_2 > 0$ and that their estimates are statistically significant. Plugging in the

values of $Ideology_i$ into the expression for the above partial derivative, we find a negative sign for all countries in our sample. These results are in line with the findings of Magee et al. (1989). Tariffs are a dependable and important source of revenues in developing countries (countries with a low capital-labor ratio). Moreover, developing countries have used infant-industry reasoning to justify protecting domestic industries.

We now look at the coefficients of our control variables in tables 2 and 3. Our controls are an inverse index of democracy (the Gastil index of political rights),[33] and regional effects using regional dummies. The inclusion of democracy is motivated by several factors. First, if we believe the evidence that openness stimulates economic growth, then dictatorships, which are more concerned with the size of the pie than with its distribution, are more likely to be open. Second, because unemployment is a major issue in most elections, democracies are also more likely to provide import protection to inefficient domestic firms and to public-sector firms that might not survive foreign competition. Furthermore, Fernandez and Rodrik (1991) show that in the presence of individual-specific uncertainty regarding the costs of moving to the export sector, trade reforms that are beneficial to the majority ex post may require a dictator to implement them in the first place.[34] However, as tables 2 and 3 show, we fail to find any evidence that democracies are more protectionist. The relationship between democracy and the partisan model is addressed in more detail in later sections. Finally, in terms of regional effects, all we find is that quota coverage is lower for East Asian countries and that quotas and import duties are higher for sub-Saharan African countries.

Two-Stage Least Squares: In a dynamic context (for example, in a multisector Solow model), the capital-labor ratio may be endogenous with respect to trade policy. Protection, by affecting the production structure, can affect accumulation and the steady-state level of the capital stock. Because of the possible endogeneity of the capital-labor ratio and the interaction term, we performed a two-stage least squares estimation where we instrument the suspected endogenous terms by the log of the population growth rate and the log of the savings rate. In the case of the cardinal regressions we have two endogenous terms, K/L and $Ideology \times (K/L)$, and so the above two instruments are enough to ensure that the estimating equation is identified. For the ordinal regressions, there are three endogenous terms, and so we use both the first-order and second-order terms in the

[33] Note that this index increases with the extent of dictatorship and decreases with increasing degree of democracy. The results with the polity measure of democracy are qualitatively extremely similar (which is not surprising, in view of the high correlation between the two measures).
[34] Also, Rodrik (1997) has argued that rising labor demand elasticities, brought about by more open trade, may hurt workers (the majority of the population). This may generate some demand for protection, to which democracies may be more responsive.

POLITICAL IDEOLOGY AND ENDOGENOUS TRADE POLICY   67

TABLE 5.—EASTERLY-LEVINE (AGGREGATE) 2SLS REGRESSION CARDINAL AND ORDINAL

	Cardinal Interpretation				Ordinal Interpretation			
	TARIFF	QUOTA	IMPORT DUTY	(X + M)/GDP	TARIFF	QUOTA	IMPORT DUTY	(X + M)/GDP
Ideology	−1.057***	−1.493***	−45.591***	165.015***				
	(0.417)	(0.581)	(19.793)	(73.004)				
Ideology × capital-labor ratio	0.109***	0.147***	4.773***	−17.23***				
	(0.044)	(0.061)	(2.133)	(7.739)				
Capital-labor ratio	−0.315***	−0.41***	−15.795***	55.277***	−0.214***	−0.312***	−11.177***	35.183***
	(0.107)	(0.153)	(4.963)	(19.917)	(0.058)	(0.107)	(3.520)	(12.180)
left					−2.141***	−3.267***	−90.469***	285.685***
					(0.658)	(1.292)	(41.017)	(142.102)
left × capital-labor ratio					0.218***	0.321***	9.396***	−29.445***
					(0.067)	(0.135)	(4.291)	(14.895)
Center					−1.456*	−4.062***	−61.115	208.762
					(0.956)	(1.332)	(62.491)	(228.266)
Center × capital-labor ratio					0.150**	0.393***	6.390	−20.899
					(0.092)	(0.131)	(6.072)	(22.003)
Constant	3.239***	4.347***	162.79***	−501.897***	2.266***	3.333***	118.340***	−309.886***
	(1.034)	(1.504)	(47.407)	(192.246)	(0.583)	(1.074)	(34.296)	(119.224)
No. of observations	64	63	62	79	64	63	62	79
R^2	0.27	0.18	0.3	0.26	0.25	0.17	0.25	0.24
F-statistic	9.75***	3.93***	16.74***	13.07***	4.48***	2.65***	6.88***	6.25***
Critical capital-labor ratio	9.7	10.2	9.6	9.6				

The R^2's reported in this table are the coefficients of determination between the actual and the predicted value of the dependent variable. The instruments used for the cardinal regressions are the natural logs of the saving rate and the population growth rate; for the ordinal regression the squares and the cross product of the log of saving rate and the population growth rate are additionally used as instruments. Standard errors in parentheses; ***significant at 5% level, **significant at 10% level, *significant at 15% level.

saving rate and the population growth rate (levels, squares, and cross products) as instruments to ensure the identification of the equation.[35]

As table 5 shows, across all measures of protection the prediction of the partisan model is supported. The relevant terms are all significant, and the critical capital-labor ratios are again very close to the mean and the median. These results are also robust to the inclusion of controls.

Panel Regressions: We also test our model using cross-sectional time series data available for two measures of protection—*IMPORT DUTY* and (X + M)/GDP. We use a fixed-effects model with time and comprehensive region-specific effects.[36] In general, time-specific shocks seem more reasonable because historically the world as a whole has exhibited a pattern, where either all countries have tended to become more protectionist (e.g., the interwar years), or they all have tended to become less protectionist (the mid-1990s, following the Uruguay Round). Further,

[35] In fact, with the levels, their squares, and the cross product of the saving rate and the population growth rate, the estimating equation is overidentified, so that we were able to perform the appropriate tests for overidentifying restrictions and confirm that our instruments are valid and of good quality. We also performed these tests, using extra instruments, in the case of our 2SLS regressions with the cardinal ideology measure, where we could again confirm the high quality and validity of the instruments. The regression results are very similar to those with only levels as instruments.

[36] A fixed-effects model with country-specific effects, on the other hand, will not be able to identify the estimates for some of our variables that do not vary within a country over time. Moreover, with 50–60 countries in each regression, such an approach uses up many degrees of freedom and results in high multicollinearity between the country-specific effects and some of the right-side variables (especially the more time-invariant ones), making the interpretation of the coefficients difficult.

there has been a tendency for countries within a region to organize themselves into free-trade areas or customs unions—an effect that should be captured by our comprehensive region-specific effects. Finally, due to the endogeneity of the capital-labor ratio with respect to tariffs, we use instrumental variables—the log of the savings rate and the log of the population growth rate. Even though one would expect that the preferences of the government and those of the interest groups influencing it would take time to affect the level of protection, our predictions are borne out here as well in the case of *IMPORT DUTY*, the only direct measure of protection in our data set that has a time dimension. The following panel regression result with time-specific and very comprehensive region-specific effects (with K/L and *Ideology × K/L* instrumented by the log of the saving rate and the log of the population growth rate) has the expected signs for the relevant variables whose coefficients are significant at the 1% level:

$$IMPORT\ DUTY = -63.35^{***}Ideology$$
$$(12.82)$$

$$+ 6.31^{***}Ideology \times K/L$$
$$(1.26)$$

$$- 19.84^{***}K/L + \text{fixed effects},$$
$$(3.79)$$

$$R^2 = 0.22, \qquad N = 610.$$

The critical K/L is 10, again very close to the mean and the median value. A left versus nonleft regression based on the ordinal measure gives us similar results:

$$IMPORT\ DUTY = -105.26{***}left + 10.42{***}left$$
$$\qquad\qquad\qquad\quad (19.63)\qquad\qquad (1.93)$$

$$\times K/L - 11.08{***}K/L + \text{fixed effects},$$
$$\qquad\quad (1.94)$$

$$R^2 = 0.26, \quad N = 610.$$

Note that the *center* intercept and interaction slope dummies, when added to the above regression, are individually and jointly insignificant. Our indirect measure that has a time dimension; $(X + M)/GDP$ produces the correct signs but insignificant coefficient estimates.

Regression in Differences: In section III, we saw that the partial derivative of protection with respect to ideology can be written as $\partial TR_i/\partial ideology_i = \alpha_1 + \alpha_2(K/L)_i$, which as an approximation can be written as $\Delta TR_i/\Delta Ideology_i = \alpha_1 + \alpha_2 (K/L)_i$, where we use Δ to represents changes in the relevant variables (the difference between the decade average for the 1980s and that for the 1970s). Moving $\Delta Ideology$ to the right-hand side and accordingly running regressions, we obtain the following results:

$$\Delta IMPORT\ DUTY = -6.00{***}\Delta Ideology$$
$$\qquad\qquad\qquad\qquad (2.61)$$

$$+ 0.55{***}(K/L)\Delta Ideology, \quad R^2 = 0.03, \quad N = 63,$$
$$(0.25)$$

$$\Delta[(X + M)/GDP] = 28.68{***}\Delta Ideology$$
$$\qquad\qquad\qquad\qquad (13.39)$$

$$- 3.09{***}(K/L)\Delta Ideology, \quad R^2 = 0.02, \quad N = 80.$$
$$(1.28)$$

Again, we have the signs predicted by our theory, and our coefficient estimates are significant at the 5% level.[37]

Dictatorship versus Democracy: Next we investigate whether partisan concerns are more important in democracies or in dictatorships. Democratic governments, to ensure their reelection, may adopt policies that benefit their electoral base (groups that provide large blocks of votes and/or provide campaign contributions)—capitalists (business groups) for right-wing parties, and labor (trade unions) for left-wing parties. Dictatorships on the other hand face few such incentives. On the other hand, dictatorships are less constrained in their redistributive attempts.

In order to investigate the relationship between partisan concerns and the extent of democracy, we generate residuals from our main regressions and then regress the absolute values of these residuals on the democracy dictatorship (political rights) variable. These regressions show that for

[37] These regressions are equivalent to running a panel regression with country-specific fixed effects with two observations (the 1970s average and the 1980s average) for each country.

all our direct measures of trade policy (*TARIFF, QUOTA,* and *IMPORT DUTY*), the absolute residuals are higher for dictatorships. Next, we generate predicted values of protection from our coefficient estimates, using our regressions without controls, and find that their correlation with the actual values is considerably lower for the dictatorship sample (Gastil measure above 4) than for the democracy sample (the rest). Both findings suggest that our model fits democracies better. Finally, we run regressions with additional interaction terms (*Ideology* × *Democracy* and *Ideology* × *(K/L)* × *Democracy*) to investigate whether prolabor redistribution through trade policies is stronger in democracies or in dictatorships. These interaction terms are significant at the 5% level for tariffs, import duty and $(X + M)/GDP$ (but not for the quota regressions). For the regression with controls, the cross-partial derivative is

$$\frac{\partial^2 TARIFF}{\partial Democracy\ \partial Ideology} = 0.04 - 0.004(K/L),$$

$$\frac{\partial^2 IMPORT\ DUTY}{\partial Democracy\ \partial Ideology} = 3.01 - 0.322(K/L),$$

$$\frac{\partial^2[(X + M)/GDP]}{\partial Democracy\ \partial Ideology} = -6.4 + 0.814(K/L),$$

so that dictatorships reinforce the negative (positive) relationship between ideology and trade protection in capital-scarce (−abundant) countries, predicted by the partisan model.[38]

Thus the partisan model fits the data better for democracies, but the magnitudes of the effects are smaller in democracies. This may mean that dictators who have consolidated their position may not face any electoral threats and may have fewer incentives to formulate trade policies according to their ideological affinities. However, if they do decide to favor their core constituent groups, they are likely to face lesser constraints in implementing redistributive trade policies.

B. Regressions Using a More Comprehensive Trade Barrier Measure

Hiscox and Kastner (2002) have created two alternative measures of protection, using the importing-country-specific and time-specific effects in two versions of the gravity model, one being the standard gravity model and the other being an amended one with relative factor endowment differentials used as additional variables to capture factor-proportions effects. The advantage of such a measure is that it captures the implicit protection through substitutes (including domestic policies adopted)

[38] For more detailed results, see our working paper version, Dutt and Mitra (2002). Our results regarding the model fit and the size of the partisan effect go through with the polity measure of democracy as well, and are extremely similar.

TABLE 6.—EASTERLY-LEVINE (AGGREGATE) REGRESSION WITH HISCOX-KASTNER MEASURE AS DEPENDENT VARIABLE

	Cross-Sectional Results					Panel: Instrumented; Region and Time Fixed Effects	
	Ordinal (One Dummy)	Ordinal (Two Dummies)	Cardinal (1–3)	Cardinal (Controls)	Cardinal (2SLS, Controls)	Ordinal (One Dummy)	Cardinal (1–3)
left (or Ideology)	−54.318***	−74.268***	−40.863***	−29.157**	−124.074***	−195.075***	−119.562***
	(19.023)	(26.084)	(11.858)	(17.003)	(58.131)	(34.19)	(22.455)
left (or Ideology) × capital-labor ratio	5.475***	7.484***	4.264***	3.112**	12.754***	19.131***	11.748***
	(1.885)	(2.585)	(1.201)	(1.655)	(5.911)	(3.309)	(2.174)
center		−48.999*					
		(33.007)					
center × capital-labor ratio		4.842*					
		(3.176)					
Capital-labor ratio	−6.766***	−8.775***	−13.309***	−9.484***	−33.255***	−12.441***	−28.646***
	(1.698)	(2.447)	(3.237)	(4.354)	(14.059)	(2.823)	(5.776)
Political rights (Gastil)				1.286**	0.288		
				(0.787)	(1.548)		
Sub-Saharan Africa				−5.173	6.696		
				(6.949)	(12.215)		
East Asia				0.194	−10.156		
				(3.462)	(9.907)		
Oil				3.517	−1.676		
				(4.232)	(6.467)		
Constant	99.859***	119.808***	162.35***	120.19***	360.43***	156.338***	323.04***
	(17.543)	(24.983)	(32.815)	(45.916)	(143.478)	(30.462)	(61.018)
No. of observations	57	57	57	56	55	490	490
R^2	0.26	0.29	0.31	0.34	0.21	0.3	
F-statistic	7.12***	4.5	8.66***	6.97***	3.5***		
Wald statistic (Chi-squared)						37.50***	35.74***
Critical capital-labor ratio	9.9		9.6	9.4	9.7	10.2	10.1
Joint test for cardinality (f-statistic)		0.89					

Standard errors in parentheses; ***significant at 5% level; **significant at 10% level; *significant at 15% level.

of standard trade policy measures that governments use once they have committed to tariff levels in international agreements. We certainly believe that even if trade policy is determined through multilateral negotiations, domestic ideological orientations can be an important determinant of what kind of trade policy a country commits to in these negotiations. For those who do not buy this argument, the use of these new measures (as alternatives to actual trade policy) in our regressions will be useful. Table 6 provides those estimates using the Hiscox-Kastner measure generated from their basic gravity equation (our results using their measure from the amended gravity model are no different). Note that all the different kinds of regressions we ran for the conventional trade policy measures are also run for the Hiscox-Kastner measure. Again, in both the cross-sectional and the panel regressions (in our cardinal as well as ordinal versions), we get very strong results in the direction predicted by the theoretical model in section II. All our relevant variables have the correct signs and are highly significant (at the 1%–5% levels), both individually and jointly. The critical capital-labor ratios are in the range of 9.4 to 10.2, again very close to the mean and the median. As in the case of conventional measures, we cannot reject the null hypothesis of cardinality.

VI.   Robustness Checks

A.   International Comparability and Quality of the DPI Ideology Measure

Some readers may question the comparability of our ideology measure across nations, supposing that leftist and rightist orientations may be relative to the country-specific and not international notions of the center. Because the inclusion of country-specific dummies is clearly impossible in the case of cross-sectional regressions, we created nine very comprehensive *region-specific* dummies.[39] We consider it very plausible that countries from the same region have a common notion of a center around which party and government ideologies are classified. As before, we instrument the capital-labor ratio and its interaction with the ideology variable. (The measurement error of the interaction term is corrected by the instrumentation.) Our results remain qualitatively unchanged in coefficient signs, significance, and the estimate of the critical capital-labor ratio.

Furthermore, based on discussions with some regional experts, we decided to experiment with some adjustments to

[39] For our region-specific effects we use the following regional categories: east Asia, the rest of Asia, Oceania, eastern Europe, western Europe, north America, Latin America (excluding Mexico), oil-producing countries, sub-Saharan Africa, and the rest of Africa.

our ideology measure We increase the magnitude of the scale, 1 being the most right-oriented and 5 the most left-oriented. For the United States, the Republicans and Democrats remain at 1 and 3, respectively, as before. For Latin America, right is coded as 1, center as 3, and left as 5. The left-wing governments of China and eastern Europe are coded as 5. For western Europe (excluding Ireland and the United Kingdom), right, center, and left are coded as 2, 3, and 4, respectively. All other countries are coded the same as before. Again, our results survive this adjustment.

We also verify the quality of the DPI ideology measure by checking whether it is a good predictor of inequality after controlling for the Kuznets effect (captured by per capita GDP and its square). We find that the coefficient of the ideology variable is negative and highly significant. Because this is a long-run relationship, we believe that finding this relationship with data that are decade-wide averages clearly shows that our measures are fairly comparable across countries. We also find that the ideology measure is a good predictor of public health and education expenditure as a proportion of GDP, controlling for per capita GDP. We also constructed a revealed ideology measure (using the principal-components method) from the residuals of the regressions of the ratios of health and education expenditure to GDP on per capita GDP. When our DPI measure is replaced by this revealed measure in our original regressions, our results remain unchanged [detailed results in Dutt and Mitra (2002)].

Finally, the Swank data, available only for the OECD countries but considered to be of higher quality, provide us with two substitutes of the DPI measure: the percentage of cabinet portfolios by left parties, and left governing party seats as a percentage of all legislative seats. The correlations of these with our ideology measure (on limiting the data to OECD countries) are over 0.7, and rise to approximately 0.9 if the Swank data, like our DPI data, are classified on a 1, 2, 3 scale (the Swank ideology measure). Running panel regressions using the Swank measure give us exactly the result for capital-abundant OECD countries predicted by our model—protection is increasing in left-wing ideology. Regressions using a new ideology measure (which equals the Swank measure for OECD countries and DPI for the rest) produce exactly the same nonmonotonic results as with the DPI.

B. Controlling for the Endowments of Other Factors and the Level of Development

Next we control for the size of the endowment of land. We introduce the land-labor ratio and the interaction of ideology with it as additional variables. Our original results with respect to the capital-labor ratio and its interaction with ideology remain qualitatively unaffected. However, the derivative of protection with respect to ideology is increasing (decreasing) in capital (land) abundance, suggesting that the government's weight on land relative to other factors combined generally increases as the government becomes more left-oriented. We also ran several regressions where we included only the capital-land ratio and its interaction with the ideology variable (in addition to the ideology variable itself), and some others where we had the land-labor ratio in place of the capital-labor ratio. All these regressions seem to indicate that there is a possibility that land and labor generally tend to form coalitions against capital [details in Dutt and Mitra (2002)].[40]

Instead of using the capital-labor ratio and/or the land-labor ratio in the regressions, we use the per capita GDP (by itself and in its interaction with ideology) to allow for the relative abundance (scarcity) of capital, human capital, and productive assets in rich (poor) countries. The results are very similar to the ones obtained with the K/L ratio, thereby indicating that in countries abundant (scarce) in such factors and/or assets, a more left-wing (right-wing) government raises protection.

We also tried using both the per capita GDP and the capital-labor ratio in the same regression. Given that there is a serious multicollinearity problem associated with the simultaneous use of both these variables (the correlation between per capita GDP and the capital-labor ratio being very high, around 0.9), such regressions result in each of these variables (their levels and their interactions with the ideology variable) being individually insignificant but jointly very significant. For each of these two variables, a very small proportion of the variation is independent of the variation in the other, and therefore inserting both of them simultaneously to yield separate and precise identification of the effect of each on protection. Therefore, we then regressed per capita GDP on the capital-labor ratio, thereby generating both the predicted value and the residual to be inserted simultaneously in our main estimating equation. Whereas, the residual and its interaction with ideology turned out to be insignificant, the predicted value of per capita GDP and its ideology interaction were generally very significant and had the correct signs. Thus, it is mainly the part of per capita GDP, fully explained by the capital-labor ratio, that drives our results. The unexplained part does not seem to have any significant role to play. Finally, we also used principal-component analysis to take care of the multicollinearity between per capita GDP and the capital-labor ratio. Using the first component (which captures 71% of the variation) qualitatively preserves our main results.

C. The Role of GATT Bindings

In this subsection, we address the concern that some countries may have committed to GATT bindings several years earlier. We argue here that this is not a problem with our analysis. Firstly, in addition to doing our analysis with

---

[40] Note that in the context of this analysis for the third factor, land, the classification of parties into left, right, and center is independent of their classification into rural and urban. The correlation between the two classifications is only 0.05.

the nontariff barrier (NTB) measure, we have done it with the Hiscox-Kastner measure which captures other policies (industrial, labor, etc.) that can implicitly act as trade barriers; and our results are strong here as well. Secondly, we also find that the correlation of the ideology measure across decades turns out to be 0.8, which is very high. Thirdly, it turns out that only for eight countries in our data set would the GATT bindings have been binding constraints, that is, most other countries either had not bound their tariffs by early 1980s or had actual tariffs that were below their GATT commitments. The countries for which past bindings would have mattered in the 1980s are the United States, Japan, Canada, and (by the 1970s) the members of the European Union. When we throw away these countries or use a dummy for them, our results are qualitatively the same.[41] Finally, bindings do not rule out contingent tariffs, and the GATT did not have an effective dispute settlement mechanism of the type the WTO has.

D. Other Robustness Checks

Here we simply list all the other robustness checks. Firstly, we performed weighted least squares regressions using different weights, namely, GDP, GDP per capita, capital-labor ratios, population, and capital (both in levels and squares). Our results remain unchanged and sometimes become even stronger. Secondly, our results also survive the use of inflation (a macro variable that affects capitalists and workers differently) as a control.[42] Guided by the theory of tariff-jumping foreign direct investment (FDI), we also tried using FDI (alternatively in logs and levels) as a control. FDI does not seem to be significant except for $(X + M)/GDP$, whereas all our earlier results remain unchanged for all protection or openness measures. Our results are also robust to the use of dummy variables representing crisis and international organization interventions. A final robustness check (based on results from our recent research) shows that both partisan effects and the distribution of factor ownership (possibly through its effect on voting and/or lobbying outcomes) are important at the same time in the determination of protection levels. In other words, our results here are robust to controlling for the distribution or inequality variable.

---

[41] As expected, the correlation between the actual and model-predicted protection values is much higher for the countries which either had not committed to GATT bindings or had actual tariffs below the GATT bindings. We thank Will Martin of the World Bank (an expert on tariff bindings) for very useful discussions on this issue.

[42] We also try using unemployment as an additional control (simultaneously with inflation). The signs of our relevant variables still remain the same, but their significance falls. This is not surprising, in that, due to the limited availability of data on unemployment for developing countries, our sample size for this regression gets reduced to 32, with only three labor-abundant countries. Moreover, (a) developed and developing countries have different types of unemployment and therefore are not comparable, and (b) the relevant unemployment rate (for this analysis) itself will depend on the prevailing inflation rate for given expected inflation.

VII. Conclusion

In this paper, we empirically investigate how the ideology of the government in power affects trade policy. The prediction of a partisan, ideology-based model (within a two-sector, two-factor Heckscher-Ohlin framework) is that left-wing governments will adopt more protectionist trade policies in capital-rich countries, but adopt more protrade policies in labor-rich ones. The data strongly support this prediction in a very robust fashion. There is some evidence that this relationship may hold better in democracies than in dictatorships, though the magnitude of the partisan effect seems stronger in dictatorships.

Of late, economic policy reforms that foster growth, reduce inequality, and alleviate poverty have been attracting increasing attention from both academicians and policymakers. Simultaneously, there is a growing recognition that political institutions matter for these economic goals as well. In order to design effective economic policies to achieve these goals, it is critical that we have a thorough understanding of the interrelationship between policy variables and political institutions. Although the theoretical and empirical results in this paper are positive rather than normative, this paper takes a step in that direction by delineating the role of political ideology in trade policy determination.

REFERENCES

Adsera, Alicia, and Carles Boix, "Trade, Democracy and the Size of the Public Sector," *International Organization* 56:2 (2002), 229–262.

Alesina, Alberto, "Macroeconomic Policy in a Two Party System as a Repeated Game," *Quarterly Journal of Economics* 102 (1987), 651–678.

Alesina, Alberto, and Nouriel Roubini, "Political Cycles in OECD Economies," *Review of Economic Studies* 59 (1992), 663–688.

Alt, James, "Political Parties, World Demand and Unemployment: Domestic and International Sources of Economic Activity," *American Political Science Review* 79 (1985), 1016–1040.

—— "Party Strategies, World Demand, and Unemployment: The Political Economy of Economic Activity in Western Industrial Nations," *American Economic Review (AEA Papers & Proceedings)* 76:2 (1986), 57–61.

Baldwin, Robert, and Christopher Magee, "Is Trade Policy for Sale? Congressional Voting on Recent Trade Bills," NBER working paper no. 6376 (1998).

Balistreri, Edward J., "The Performance of the Heckscher-Ohlin-Vanek Model in Predicting Endogenous Policy Forces at the Individual Level," *Canadian Journal of Economics* 30:1 (1997), 1–17.

Barro, Robert J., and Jong-Wha Lee, "Sources of Economic Growth," *Carnegie-Rochester Conference Series on Public Policy* 40 (1994), 1–46.

—— "Factor or Industry Cleavages in Trade Policy? An Empirical Analysis of the Stolper-Samuelson Theorem," Department of Economics, University of Calgary, mimeograph (2001).

Beaulieu, Eugene, "The Stolper-Samuelson Theorem Faces Congress," *Review of International Economics* 10:2 (2002), 343–360.

Beaulieu, Eugene, and Chistopher Magee, "Campaign Contributions and Trade Policy: Simple Tests of Stolper-Samuelson," Department of Economics, University of Calgary, and Department of Economics, Bard College, Mimeograph (2000).

Beck, Thorsten, George Clarke, Alberto Groff, and Philip Keefer, "New Tools and New Tests in Comparative Political Economy: The Database of Political Institutions," *World Bank Economic Review* 15:1 (2001), 165–176.

Downs, Anthony, 1957, *An Economic Theory of Democracy* (New York: Harper Collins, 1957).

Dutt, Pushan, and Devashish Mitra, "Political Ideology and Endogenous Trade Policy: An Empirical Investigation," NBER working paper no. 9239 (2002).

Easterly, William, and Ross Levine, "It's Not Factor Accumulation: Stylized Facts and Growth Models," *World Bank Economic Review* 15:2 (2001), 177–219.

Fernandez, Raquel, and Dani Rodrik, "Resistance to Reform: Status-Quo Bias in the Presence of Individual-Specific Uncertainty," *American Economic Review* 81:5 (1991), 1146–1155.

Garrett, Geoffrey, *Partisan Politics in the Global Economy* (New York: Cambridge University Press, 1998).

Glazer, Amihai, and Bernard Grofman, "Why Representatives Are Ideologists though Voters Are Not," *Public Choice* 61:1 (1989), 29–39.

Grossman, Gene M., and Elhanan Helpman, "Protection for Sale," *American Economic Review* (September 1994), 833–850.

—— "Electoral Competition and Special Interest Politics," *Review of Economic Studies* 63 (1996), 265–286.

Hibbs, Douglas A., "Political Parties and Macroeconomic Policy," *American Political Science Review* 7 (1977), 1467–1487.

Hibbs, Douglas A., and Nicholas Vasilatos, "Economic Outcomes and Political Support for British Governments among Occupational Classes: A Dynamic Analysis," *American Political Science Review* 76:2 (1982), 259–279.

Hibbs, Douglas A., R. Douglas Rivers, and Nicholas Vasilatos, "The Dynamics of Political Support for American Presidents among Occupational and Partisan Groups," *American Journal of Political Science* 26:2 (1982), 312–332.

Hillman, Arye L., *The Political Economy of Protection* (London and New York: Harwood Academic, 1989).

Hiscox, Michael J., *International Trade and Political Conflict: Commerce, Coalitions and Mobility* (Princeton, NJ: Princeton University Press, 2001).

—— "Interindustry Factor Mobility and Technological Change: Evidence from Wage and Profit Dispersion across U.S. Industries, 1820 and 1990," *Journal of Economic History* 62:2 (2002a), 383–416.

—— "Commerce, Coalitions, and Factor Mobility: Evidence from Congressional Votes on Trade Legislation," *American Political Science Review* 96:3 (2002b).

Hiscox, Michael J., and S. Kastner, "A General Measure of Trade Policy Orientations: Gravity-Model-Based Estimates for 82 Nations, 1960–1992," Harvard University mimeograph (2002).

Irwin, Douglas, "Industry or Class Cleavages over Trade Policy? Evidence from the British General Election of 1923" (pp. 53–75), in R. Feenstra, G. Grossman, and D. Irwin (Eds.), *The Political Economy of Trade Policy: Papers in Honor of Jagdish Bhagwati* (Cambridge, MA: MIT Press, 1996).

Kalt, Joseph P., and Mark A. Zupan, "Capture and Ideology in the Economic Theory of Politics," *American Economic Review* 74:3 (1984), 279–300.

Kau, James B., and Paul H. Rubin, "Self Interest, Ideology and Logrolling in Congressional Voting," *Journal of Law and Economics* 22:2 (1979), 365–384.

Leamer, Edward "The Structure and Effects of Tariff and Non-tariff Barriers" (pp. 224–260), in R. Jones and A. Krueger (Eds.), *The Political Economy of International Trade: Essays In Honor of Robert E. Baldwin* (Cambridge MA: Basil Blackwell, 1990).

Lipset, Seymour M., and Stein Rokkan, *Party Systems and Voter Alignments: Cross-National Perspectives* (New York: Free Press, 1967).

Magee, Stephen P., "Three Simple Tests of the Stolper-Samuelson Theorem," in P. Oppenheimer (Ed.), *Issues in International Economics* (Stockfield, U.K.: Oriel Press, 1978).

Magee, Stephen P., William Brock, and Leslie Young, *Black Hole Tariffs and Endogenous Policy Theory* (Cambridge and New York: Cambridge University Press, 1989).

Mayda, Anna M., and Dani Rodrik, "Why Are Some People (and Countries) More Protectionist Than Others?" NBER working paper no. w8461 (2001).

Nehru, Vikram, and Ashok Dhareshwar, "A New Database on Physical Capital Stock: Sources, Methodology, and Results," *Rivista de Analisis Economico* 8 (1993), 37–59.

O'Halloran, Sharyn, *Politics, Process and American Trade Policy* (Ann Arbor: University of Michigan Press, (1994).

Peltzman, Sam, "Constituent Interest and Congressional Voting," *Journal of Law and Economics* 27:2 (1984), 181–210.

Persson, Torsten, and Guido Tabellini, *Political Economics: Explaining Economic Policy* (Cambridge, MA: MIT Press, 2000).

Ray, Edward J., "The Impact of Special Interests on Preferential Tariff Concessions by the United States, *Review of Economics and Statistics* 69:2 (1987), 187–193.

Rodrik, Dani, "Political Economy of Trade Policy," (pp. 1457–1494), in G. Grossman and K. Rogoff, (Eds.), *Handbook of International Economics*, vol. 3 (Amsterdam: North-Holland, 1995).

—— *Has Globalization Gone Too Far?* (Washington, DC: Institute for International Economics, (1997).

—— "Why Do More Open Economies Have Bigger Governments?" *Journal of Political Economy* 106:5 (1998), 997–1032.

Rogowski, Ronald, "Political Cleavages and Changing Exposure to Trade," *American Political Science Review* 81:4 (1987), 1121–1137.

Scheve, Kenneth, and Matthew Slaughter, "What Determines Individual Trade Policy Preferences?" *Journal of International Economics* 54:2 (2001), 267–292.

Schonhardt-Bailey, Cheryl, "Specific Factors, Capital Markets, Portfolio Diversification and Free Trade," *World Politics* 43:4 (1991), 545–569.

Swank, Duane, *Global Capital, Political Institutions and Policy Change in Developed Welfare States* (New York: Cambridge University Press, 2002).

Van Long, Ngo, and Neil Vousden, "Protectionist Responses and Declining Industries," *Journal of International Economics* 30:1–2 (1991), 87–103.

Chapter 6

Labor versus capital in trade-policy: The role of ideology and inequality

Pushan Dutt [a,1], Devashish Mitra [b,c,*]

[a] INSEAD, 1 Ayer Rajah Avenue, Singapore 138676, Singapore
[b] Department of Economics, The Maxwell School of Citizenship & Public Affairs,
Syracuse University, Eggers Hall, Syracuse, NY 13244, USA
[c] NBER, 1050 Massachusetts Avenue, Cambridge, MA 02138, USA

Received 24 October 2003; received in revised form 10 October 2004; accepted 31 May 2005

Abstract

Trade policy depends on the extent to which the government wants to redistribute income as well as on a country's overall factor endowments and their distribution. While the government's desire to redistribute income itself is dependent on asset distribution, it is to a large extent also driven by the partisan nature of the government, i.e., whether it is pro-labor or pro-capital. Using cross-country data on factor endowments, inequality and government orientation, we find that, conditional on inequality, left-wing (pro-labor) governments will adopt more protectionist trade policies in capital-rich countries, but adopt more pro-trade policies in labor-rich economies than right-wing (pro-capital) ones. Also, holding government orientation constant, higher inequality is associated with higher protection in capital-abundant countries while it is associated with lower protection in labor-abundant countries. These results are consistent with the simultaneous presence of both inequality as well as ideology as determinants of protection within a two-factor, two-sector Heckscher–Ohlin framework. Overall, various statistical tests support an umbrella model (that combines both the ideology and inequality models) over each of the individual models.
© 2005 Elsevier B.V. All rights reserved.

Keywords: Protection; Openness; Ideology; Inequality; Median voter

JEL classification: F10; F11; F13

---

* Corresponding author. Tel.: +1 315 443 6143; fax: +1 315 443 3717.
  E-mail addresses: Pushan.Dutt@insead.edu (P. Dutt), dmitra@maxwell.syr.edu (D. Mitra).
[1] Tel.: +65 6799 5388.

0022-1996/$ - see front matter © 2005 Elsevier B.V. All rights reserved.
doi:10.1016/j.jinteco.2005.05.011

P. Dutt, D. Mitra / Journal of International Economics 69 (2006) 310–320   311

1. Introduction

An important effect and sometimes an objective of trade policy is the redistribution of income from capital to labor or vice versa. A possible determinant of such redistribution is the political valence or the partisanship of the government, which we call "ideology." It refers to whether the government is pro-labor (left-oriented), pro-capital (right-oriented) or relatively neutral (centrist). Another possible determinant is asset inequality. In a model with policy determined by majority voting (Mayer, 1984), any government, due to the inherently unequal nature of asset and income distribution, will have a tendency to redistribute income from those who are well endowed in assets ("capital") to those who are relatively poorly endowed in it.

The precise manner in which the political ideology affects trade policy (the "ideology" hypothesis) can be derived using the political-support function approach, popularized by Hillman (1989) and Van Long and Vousden (1991). The effect of an increase in the government's leftist orientation can be viewed as an increase in the weight placed by it on the welfare of individuals predominantly dependent on labor income relative to the welfare of those who mainly derive their income from capital ownership. This increase in the labor-welfare weight results in policies that are more pro-labor and that move the domestic terms of trade in favor of the labor-intensive sector. In a capital-abundant country, the labor-intensive good is the importable good and therefore, an increase in the leftist orientation of the government will result in a rise in import protection. In a labor-abundant country, however, the labor-intensive good is the exportable. Therefore, an increase in leftist orientation in such a country will result in a decline in import protection.

The median-voter prediction (or the "inequality" hypothesis) we test is based on a simple comparative-static exercise in the Mayer–Heckscher–Ohlin framework (as in Mayer, 1984) — an increase in inequality (the difference between the mean and the median capital–labor ratio), holding constant the economy's overall relative endowments, raises trade barriers in capital-abundant economies and lowers them in capital-scarce economies. An increase in inequality increases the general demand for redistribution from capital to labor. This can be achieved through trade policies that increase further the factor reward to labor but reduce the reward to capital.

In Dutt and Mitra (2002) we empirically investigate the median-voter model of trade policy, followed by an investigation of a political ideology model in Dutt and Mitra (2005). We now address the issue of complementarity versus substitutability of these two models. One possibility is that ideology and inequality are correlated, and therefore, these models are observationally equivalent (substitutes). The other possibility is that there is extra information from each of the models and so a combination of the two, which we call the "umbrella" model, is a better predictor of trade policy than each of the individual models. Therefore, we empirically examine the two hypotheses (ideology and inequality) within a unified, nesting model. Using standard F-tests as well as other Bayesian and non-Bayesian criteria, we find overall that each component model provides additional information and so the umbrella model generally dominates each of them.

2. Estimation framework and econometric methodology

As explained in the previous section (Introduction), we focus on the following two hypotheses:

"Ideology" Hypothesis: Holding other things constant, an increase in the left orientation (pro-labor bias) of the government leads to more restrictive or less open trade policies in capital-abundant countries, while it leads to less restrictive or more open trade policies in capital-scarce economies.

"Inequality" Hypothesis: Holding other things constant, an increase in inequality leads to more restrictive or less open trade policies in capital-abundant countries, while it leads to less restrictive or more open trade policies in capital-scarce economies.

We next write down the following "umbrella" specification that nests both these hypotheses:

$$TR_i = \alpha_0 + \alpha_1 Ideology_i + \alpha_2 Ideology_i \times (K/L)_i + \alpha_3 Ineq_i + \alpha_4 Ineq_i$$
$$\times (K/L)_i + \alpha_5 (K/L)_i + \epsilon_i \tag{1}$$

where TR_i measures trade restrictions in country i, $Ideology_i$ measures the extent of the government's left-wing ideology, $Ineq_i$ is the level of inequality and $(K/L)_i$ the capital–labor ratio.[2] Taking the partial derivative of TR_i with respect to $Ideology_i$ and $Ineq_i$ respectively, we have $\frac{\partial TR_i}{\partial (Ideology)_i} = \alpha_1 + \alpha_2 (K/L)_i$, $\frac{\partial TR_i}{\partial (Ineq)_i} = \alpha_3 + \alpha_4 (K/L)_i$. The prediction of the "ideology" hypothesis is that $\alpha_1 < 0$ and $\alpha_2 > 0$ such that $\alpha_1 + \alpha_2 (K/L)_i \gtrless 0$ as $(K/L)_i \gtrless (K/L)^*$ where $(K/L)^* = -\alpha_1/\alpha_2$ is the turning point capital–labor ratio determined endogenously from the data, given our estimating equation. Another requirement for the prediction to hold is that $(K/L)^*$ should lie within the range of values of (K/L) in the dataset, i.e., $(K/L)^{MIN} < (K/L)^* < (K/L)^{MAX}$. Similarly the "inequality" hypothesis predicts $\alpha_3 < 0$ and $\alpha_4 > 0$ such that $\alpha_3 + \alpha_4 (K/L)_i \gtrless 0$ as $(K/L)_i \gtrless (K/L)^{**}$ where $(K/L)^{**} = -\alpha_3/\alpha_4$ is the turning point capital–labor ratio for inequality and again has to be within the range of values of K/L in our dataset.

We perform Hausman tests to investigate the possible endogeneity of the capital–labor ratio (suggested by the two-sector Solow model) and inequality (due to the use of income inequality measure implying reverse causation) with respect to trade protection and then correct for any detected endogeneity through instrumental variable estimation.

Finally, imposing the restriction $\alpha_1 = \alpha_2 = 0$ gives us our stand-alone inequality model, while $\alpha_3 = \alpha_4 = 0$ gives us our stand-alone ideology model. We compare these restricted models to the umbrella model using a variety of Bayesian and non-Bayesian criteria.

---

[2] We present regression results with capital-ratios in natural logs (and not in levels) as they generate very few outliers, to which our estimation is extremely robust for the majority of our protection measures.

The Political Economy of Trade Policy

3. Data sources and some basic statistics

Our trade policy measures are an average tariff rate calculated by weighing each import category by the fraction of trade in that category (TARIFF), a coverage ratio for non-tariff barriers to trade (QUOTA), total import duties collected as a percentage of total imports (IMPORT DUTY), an indirect measure of trade restrictions — the magnitude of trade flows relative to GDP, defined as $(X+D)/GDP$, and the newly available Hiscox–Kastner measure. While the first two (both available for only one point in time for each country in the 1980s) are taken from Barro and Lee, the next two (which are averages for the 1980s) are taken from the World Development Indicators (WDI). The Hiscox–Kastner measure of protection, based on the standard gravity model from Hiscox and Kastner (2002), captures also the implicit protection through substitutes (including domestic policies adopted) of standard trade policy measures that governments use after commitment to tariff levels in international agreements.

The data on political orientation are obtained from the Database of Political Institutions (DPI) (Beck et al., 2001). For each year, we use the ideological orientation ("Left", "Center" or "Right" coded as 3, 2 and 1 respectively to capture the extent of left orientation) of the chief executive (that of the chief executive's party or when considered appropriate that of the chief executive himself/herself) for political systems classified as presidential in the database, that of the largest government party for systems classified as parliamentary, and the average of these two orientations for systems classified as assembly-elected president. We take the average of this variable for the 1980s. For inequality we use the Dollar–Kraay data on the Gini-coefficient and the share of the third quintile in national income, $Q3$ which is an inverse measure of inequality. The Easterly–Levine data on capital–labor ratios are based on aggregate investment and depreciation. Finally, we use the Freedom House (Gastil) measure of democracy that provides a subjective classification of countries on a scale of 1 to 7 on political rights, with higher ratings signifying less freedom. Our instruments, savings rate and the population growth rate are obtained from the WDI.[3,4]

---

[3] 40% of our sample are dictatorships (Gastil index 4–7), which becomes 36% with Gastil scores of 5–7 as dictatorships. In terms of ideology in dictatorships, about a third of the countries are right wing (average 1980s ideology measure 1–1.5), almost half are left wing (ideology 2.5–3) and the rest centrists (ideology 1.5–2.5). For democracies, the split is a third right wing, a fourth left wing and the rest centrists (a large proportion due to governments oscillating between left and right as a result of elections). Note that in the case of dictatorships, as expected, it is the chief executive's orientation, in most cases, that gets coded as the government's ideology.

[4] The summary statistics for all the variables are available at: http://faculty.maxwell.syr.edu/dmitra/umbrella.htm. Note that even though each of our variables has 90 or more observations, the sample size for each of our regressions ranges from 54 to 79, depending on the measure of protection or openness used. The sample size turns out not to be a function of the type of inequality measure (Gini or $Q3$) used. The main limiting factor are the protection data, followed by ideology.

4. Results

4.1. The umbrella model and model comparisons

4.1.1. OLS estimates

All our regression models as a whole are significant at the 5% level (Table 1). As predicted, across all measures of protection save import duty, we find that the variables relevant to the ideology model (left-wing ideology and its interaction with the capital–labor ratio) and the variables relevant to the inequality model (inequality and its interaction with the capital–labor ratio) are strongly significant. Further as predicted, we obtain negative signs on ideology and inequality and positive signs on each of the interaction terms. For $(X+M)/\text{GDP}$ a measure of openness, the signs are reversed (as predicted by theory) and significant. The critical capital–labor ratios range from 8 to 11.2, and include the median capital–labor ratio within the 2 standard error confidence-interval. The R^2 ranges from 0.17 in the case of quotas, to 0.47 for the Hiscox–Kastner measure. The results are the strongest and most robust for tariffs and quotas, and for the Hiscox–Kastner measure which also captures implicit protection.

4.1.2. IV estimates

Consistent with the theoretical prediction of a multi-sector Solow model, the Hausman test suggests the endogeneity of the capital–labor with respect to the measures of trade

Table 1
The umbrella model

	Tariff	Quota	Import duty	Hiscox–Kastner	$(X+M)/\text{GDP}$
Ideology	−0.367***	−0.433**	−9.793*	−34.096***	49.506**
	(0.114)	(0.232)	(6.846)	(13.205)	(26.57)
Ideology * capital–labor ratio	0.036***	0.039**	1.119*	3.673***	−5.538**
	(0.011)	(0.022)	(0.707)	(1.377)	(2.946)
Inequality	−0.017**	−0.019**	−0.284	−1.845***	3.746***
	(0.009)	(0.011)	(0.626)	(0.786)	(1.854)
Inequality * capital–labor ratio	0.002**	0.002**	0.034	0.19***	−0.408**
	(0.001)	(0.001)	(0.062)	(0.088)	(0.217)
Capital–labor ratio	−0.198***	−0.205***	−7.027	−20.158***	39.624***
	(0.032)	(0.06)	(2.93)	(3.568)	(11.355)
Constant	2.09***	2.131***	74.293	224.049***	−336.88***
	(0.339)	(0.626)	(30.567)	(36.162)	(99.638)
No. of observations	59	58	62	54	79
R^2	0.4	0.17	0.36	0.47	0.39
F-statistic	12.98***	2.51***	10.12***	9.83***	8.07***
Joint test for inequality	1.83	1.81	0.33	3.03**	2.02*
Joint test for ideology	4.33***	2.75***	1.62	3.73***	2.43**
Critical capital–labor ratio (ideology)	10.1	11.2	8.8	9.3	8.9
Critical capital–labor ratio (inequality)	9.3	8	8.3	9.7	9.2

Standard errors in parentheses; *** — significant at 5% level; ** — significant at 10% level; * — significant at 15% level.

The Political Economy of Trade Policy

P. Dutt, D. Mitra / Journal of International Economics 69 (2006) 310–320

Table 2
The umbrella model (IV estimates)

	Tariff	Quota	Import duty	Hiscox–Kastner	$(X+M)$/GDP
Ideology	−0.605***	−0.648***	−32.427***	−58.147***	123.559***
	(0.227)	(0.318)	(16.169)	(19.036)	(46.015)
Ideology * capital–labor ratio	0.061***	0.061**	3.465***	6.052***	−13.056***
	(0.023)	(0.032)	(1.653)	(1.895)	(4.702)
Inequality	−0.048***	−0.052***	−2.258**	−3.627***	9.118***
	(0.018)	(0.026)	(1.398)	(1.298)	(3.472)
Inequality * capital–labor ratio	0.005***	0.006***	0.237**	0.362***	−0.951***
	(0.002)	(0.003)	(0.144)	(0.133)	(0.365)
Capital–labor ratio	−0.4***	−0.4***	−21.293***	−33.442***	82.443***
	(0.092)	(0.165)	(7.959)	(8.001)	(20.703)
Constant	4.09***	4.066***	214.027***	360.765***	−764.075***
	(0.924)	(1.623)	(80.316)	(83.453)	(208.598)
No. of observations	58	57	60	53	73
R^2	0.36	0.15	0.27	0.43	0.34
F-statistic	6.58***	1.56	6.81***	9.14***	7.11***
Critical capital–labor ratio (ideology)	9.9	10.6	9.4	9.6	9.5
Critical capital–labor ratio (inequality)	9.6	8.7	9.5	10	9.6
OID test (p-value)	0.55	0.95	0.16	0.2	0.3

Standard errors in parentheses; *** — significant at 5% level; ** — significant at 10% level; * — significant at 15% level.

protection. Therefore, we perform a two-stage, least-squares estimation where we instrument capital–labor ratio by the log of the population growth rate and the log of the savings rate.[5] Based on the Hausman test results, we do not instrument for inequality. As Table 2 shows, across all measures of protection the predictions of both models are supported. The relevant terms are all significant and the critical capital–labor ratios are again very close to the mean and the median capital–labor ratios. More importantly, we see that now for the import duty measure as well, we obtain support for the umbrella model.

4.1.3. Umbrella vs. Stand-Alone Models

Next we examine whether the umbrella model is an improvement on the individual ideology and the inequality models. First, for tariffs, the Hiscox–Kastner measure and $(X+M)$/GDP the adjusted R^2 is highest in the umbrella model. For import duty and quota, the adjusted R^2 is highest in the ideology model and in fact in the latter it is higher than the umbrella model by only 0.0019. Second, we run regressions of the actual measure of trade policy on the predicted values of protection from both component models thrown in together (run in levels and logs) and find both coefficients to be individually and jointly significant for all trade policy measures, except import duty. This suggests that the two

---

[5] Hausman tests did not indicate any endogeneity problems for either of the interaction terms. For these Hausman tests, we used ideology and inequality interacted with the saving and population growth rates as additional instruments, resulting in the estimating equation being overidentified. Moreover, overidentifying (OID) tests confirm that our instruments are valid and of good quality (last row of Table 2).

316   *P. Dutt, D. Mitra / Journal of International Economics 69 (2006) 310–320*

individual models complement one another. Third, we see in Table 1 that for all measures of protection, both the ideology and inequality related variables are individually significant. The *F*-test for the inequality-related variables (inequality and its interaction with the capital–labor ratio) shows joint significance for the Hiscox–Kastner measure (our most comprehensive measure) and $(X+M)$/GDP, while the test for the ideology-related variables shows their joint significance for all protection measures except for import duty. The Akaike Information Criterion (AIC) selects the umbrella model for tariffs, Hiscox–Kastner and $(X+M)$/GDP over each of the stand-alone models whereas it selects the ideology model over the umbrella model for quotas and import duty. The same is the case for the Bayesian Information Criterion (BIC) except that it selects the ideology model over the umbrella model in the case of tariffs as well. None of these criteria ever suggest that the inequality model is better than the umbrella model.

With IV estimation, across all measures of protection, our tests and model selection criteria unambiguously favor the umbrella model, thereby removing all ambiguity (when comparing models) and providing strong evidence to reject the assertion that ideology or inequality on its own can explain variations in protectionism. Rather, the two seem to be complementary.[6]

4.2. Other robustness checks

First, the extent of political rights, as an additional independent variable to control for the degree of democracy, turns out to be insignificant and does not alter our earlier results qualitatively. Per capita income, which is highly correlated with capital–labor ratio ($r=0.94$) as an additional control also does not affect any of our results. It is not itself significant, but K/L is always significant. Using land gini in place of the income gini drastically reduces our sample size and produces statistically insignificant results, which is understandable in the light of the small correlation between the two ginis. Next, using membership in free trade areas and customs unions (obtained from Andrew Rose's website) on the right hand side does not alter any of our results while this variable itself is significant and has a negative effect on protection. If this same variable is treated as a dependent variable (an indicator of openness) in a probit model, all our ideology and inequality variables (along with their K/L interactions) have the correct signs and are jointly significant, but only inequality and its interaction with K/L are individually significant. Similar results are obtained with GATT membership. Next, we use an alternative (inverse) measure of inequality — the share of the third quintile ($Q3$) in national income. The regressions show that both inequality and ideology considerations significantly influence trade policies in the predicted direction for tariffs, quotas and the Hiscox–Kastner measure, marginally for $(X+M)$/GDP, but not for import duty. Critical capital–labor ratios are indistinguishable from those in Table 1.[7]

---

[6] We failed to find support for an argument that the political ideology of the government is endogenous with respect to the level of inequality. First, the correlation between left-wing ideology and income inequality is only 0.01. Second, when we used the generated residuals from the ideology-on-inequality regression as a proxy for left-wing ideology in the umbrella model, our results remain completely unaffected.

[7] All the robustness results are available at http://faculty.maxwell.syr.edu/dmitra/umbrella.htm.

Table 3
The ideology hypothesis

| | Low inequality | | | | | High inequality | | | | |
	Tariff	Quota	Import duty	Hiscox–Kastner	(X+M)/GDP	Tariff	Quota	Import duty	Hiscox–Kastner	(X+M)/GDP
Ideology	-0.534***	-0.306**	-6.945	-45.727***	67.114*	0.03	-1.163	-13.294	-19.105	-48.397**
	(0.145)	(0.183)	(11.862)	(15.341)	(43.419)	(0.314)	(0.803)	(13.389)	(21.296)	(24.283)
Ideology* capital–labor ratio	0.054***	0.028*	0.963	5.191***	-7.804**	-0.005	0.112	1.37	1.772	5.845***
	(0.015)	(0.019)	(1.234)	(1.497)	(4.389)	(0.033)	(0.085)	(1.491)	(2.253)	(2.683)
Capital–labor ratio	-0.18***	-0.091**	-5.432**	-17.163***	31.473***	-0.001	-0.313	-6.422*	-7.109	-10.419
	(0.037)	(0.047)	(3.041)	(4.05)	(11.115)	(0.095)	(0.243)	(3.981)	(6.214)	(7.338)
Constant	1.96***	1.097***	58.343***	190.988***	-255.692***	0.202	3.4	71.976**	101.741*	111.447*
	(0.37)	(0.468)	(30.292)	(42.652)	(113.349)	(0.904)	(2.313)	(36.386)	(59.521)	(67.58)
No. of observations	29	28	31	27	39	30	30	31	27	40
R^2	0.58	0.19	0.4	0.74	0.43	0.06	0.17	0.28	0.15	0.31
F-statistic	11.69***	2.0*	6.1***	22.63***	8.68***	0.54	1.8	3.5***	1.4	5.45***
Critical capital–labor ratio	9.9	11	7.2	8.8	8.6	5.9	10.4	9.7	10.8	8.3

Standard errors in parentheses; *** — significant at 5% level; ** — significant at 10% level; * — significant at 15% level.

Table 4
The inequality hypothesis

	Pro-labor government					Pro-capital government				
	Tariff	Quota	Import duty	Hiscox-Kastner	(X+M)/GDP	Tariff	Quota	Import duty	Hiscox-Kastner	(X+M)/GDP
Inequality	−0.017**	−0.02**	−0.51	−1.576**	3.393**	−0.061***	−0.037	−0.217	−2.562	−9.356**
	(0.009)	(0.011)	(0.72)	(0.786)	(2.031)	(0.022)	(0.058)	(0.792)	(2.374)	(4.832)
Inequality* capital–labor ratio	0.002**	0.002**	0.047	0.138*	−0.36**	−0.006***	0.004	−0.006	0.288	−1.008***
	(0.001)	(0.001)	(0.069)	(0.091)	(0.219)	(0.002)	(0.006)	(0.082)	(0.242)	(0.496)
Capital–labor ratio	−0.091***	−0.082*	−4.398	−8.356***	23.875***	−0.309***	−0.211	−2.736	−16.112**	−55.419***
	(0.04)	(0.051)	(3.065)	(3.595)	(8.957)	(0.078)	(0.201)	(2.955)	(9.003)	(20.155)
Constant	1.034***	0.898***	54.309	119.608***	−195.349***	3.174***	2.091	29.24	177.234**	491.462***
	(0.432)	(0.468)	(33.066)	(33.455)	(86.083)	(0.789)	(2.056)	(29.458)	(90.098)	(204.252)
No. of observations	38	37	39	33	52	33	32	35	31	41
R^2	0.2	0.05	0.3	0.4	0.37	0.52	0.15	0.4	0.43	0.38
F-statistic	3.32***	1.46***	4.7***	5.23***	9.39***	20.99***	2.84***	17.26***	7.83***	7.55***
Critical capital–labor ratio	9.9	9.3	10.8	11.4	9.4	9.6	8.7	35.8	8.9	9.3

Standard errors in parentheses; *** — significant at 5% level; ** — significant at 10% level; * — significant at 15% level.

4.3. Ideology–inequality interactions and the role of democracy

We analyze whether the importance of ideology as a determinant of trade policy varies with inequality. With very high levels of inequality, we expect governments to eschew partisan considerations and adopt the preferred policies of the median voter to ensure re-election or to prevent revolution. From Table 3, we see that for the majority of the regressions, the ideology model has greater explanatory power and that the estimated coefficients are individually as well as jointly significant in countries with low levels of inequality. In contrast, it fares poorly in countries with high levels of inequality. The absolute value of residuals from the ideology model is increasing in inequality for tariff, quota, and the Hiscox–Kastner measure. Moreover, the predicted values of protection from the same ideology model have a much greater correlation with the actual values for the low-inequality sample (Gini coefficient less than 40) than for the high-inequality sample. Thus the fit of the ideology model is superior in countries with low levels of inequality.

Next we test the efficacy of the median voter models and evaluate its explanatory power separately in countries with pro-labor governments and those with pro-capital ones. In countries with pro-labor governments in power, inequality and ideology considerations overlap. On the other hand, it can also be argued that left-wing governments who have already adopted pro-labor policies have less room to manoeuvre. Table 4 shows that the relevant coefficients for the inequality model are significant for tariffs and $(X+M)/GDP$ regardless of whether pro-labor or pro-capital governments are in power. But for quotas and the Hiscox–Kastner measure, inequality and its interaction with the capital–labor ratio are significant only when pro-labor governments are in power. We again fail to find any significant effect of inequality on import duties regardless of the government's ideological orientation. Finally, using residuals and predicted values from the inequality model, as we did above for the ideology model, we are unable to find a relationship between the model fit for the inequality model and ideology of the government.

Next, we investigate the relationship between redistributive concerns and the extent of democracy. We generate residuals from our umbrella model and regress the absolute values of the residuals on the Gastil political rights variable. We find that for all our direct measures of trade protection (tariff, quota, import duty, and Hiscox–Kastner measure), the absolute residuals are higher for dictatorships. Also, the predicted values of protection from Table 1, have a lower correlation with the actual values in the dictatorship sample (Gastil measure above 4) than for the democracy sample. Overall, this suggests that the extent of democracy matters less in determining the level of trade policy, but that the umbrella model fits democracies better. Democratic governments, to ensure their re-election, seem to be more sensitive to demands for redistributive policies from the majority and as well as their electoral base.

5. Conclusion

Using cross-country data on factor endowments, inequality and government orientation, we find that, conditional on inequality, left-wing (pro-labor) governments will adopt more protectionist trade policies in capital-rich countries, but adopt more pro-trade policies in

320   P. Dutt, D. Mitra / Journal of International Economics 69 (2006) 310–320

labor-rich economies than right-wing (pro-capital) ones. Also, holding government orientation constant, higher inequality is associated with higher protection in capital-abundant countries while it is associated with lower protection in labor-abundant countries. These results hold simultaneously within a unified econometric model. Overall, using various Bayesian and non-Bayesian statistical tests, we find strong support for using such an umbrella model over the component, ideology and inequality models, especially when we control for the endogeneity of the capital–labor ratio. Finally we show that the umbrella model works better for democracies than for dictatorships.

Acknowledgements

We are indebted to Jonathan Eaton and an anonymous referee for very detailed and useful comments. We also thank Chris Magee, Doug Nelson, Nina Pavcnik, Alan Taylor, Henry Van Egteren, Daniel Traca and participants at the GEP Conference on Trade and Labor Perspectives on Worker Turnover (University of Nottingham, June 2003) for useful discussions and gratefully acknowledge the SSHRC (410-2003-1309) for financial support. The standard disclaimer applies.

References

Beck, T., Clarke, G., Groff, A., Keefer, P., 2001. New tools and new tests in comparative political economy: the database of political institutions. World Bank Economic Review 15 (1), 165–176.
Dutt, P., Mitra, D., 2002. Endogenous trade policy through majority voting: an empirical investigation. Journal of International Economics 58 (1), 107–134.
Dutt, P., Mitra, D., 2005. Political ideology and endogenous trade policy: an empirical investigation. Review of Economics and Statistics 87 (1), 59–72.
Hillman, A.L., 1989. The Political Economy of Protection. Harwood Academic, London.
Hiscox, M.J., Kastner, S., 2002. A General Measure of Trade Policy Orientations: Gravity-model-based Estimates for 82 Nations, 1960–1992. mimeo, Harvard University.
Mayer, W., 1984. Endogenous tariff formation. American Economic Review 74 (5), 970–985.
Van Long, N., Vousden, N., 1991. Protectionist responses and declining industries. Journal of International Economics 30 (1–2), 87–103.

Chapter 7

Impacts of Ideology, Inequality, Lobbying, and Public Finance

Pushan Dutt and Devashish Mitra[1]

Barring very few exceptions, international trade has never and nowhere been free, even though only under extraordinary circumstances are deviations from free trade optimal. To explain this puzzle, an entire literature on the political economy of trade policy has emerged over the last three decades. In this literature, one common feature is that trade policies are chosen not with the aim of maximizing national economic efficiency and aggregate welfare, but set by politicians and policy makers whose objective functions diverge from aggregate welfare. Trade policies, in this view, are often used as indirect tools to redistribute income to certain targeted groups. The identity of these groups depends on (a) the type of political economy framework (lobbying or majority voting) assumed, (b) the actual economic, political, and geographic characteristics of the various sectors in the economy that determine which of them are politically organized, and (c) the political and economic ideology of the government.

The objective of this chapter is to explain both the cross-country variations in agricultural protection and the within-country evolution of this protection over time. The general trend has been an increase in agricultural protection in developed countries over time as their per capita incomes have increased.[2] This protection has taken the form of tariff and nontariff barriers on imports plus substantial subsidies provided by governments to their farmers. While membership in the GATT/WTO has attempted to control the growth of such protection in developed countries, it has so far not succeeded in eliminating or reducing it. In fact, agricultural support

[1] The authors are grateful for very useful comments and discussions from seminar participants, particularly Johan Swinnen and Will Martin.
[2] For detailed theoretical and empirical analyses of the evolution of agricultural protection during the process of economic development, see Anderson, Hayami and Others (1986) and Hai (1991).

278

or protection is one of the primary reasons behind the current impasse in the Doha Round of trade talks. In developing countries, by contrast, the bias has been against agriculture and in favor of the manufacturing sector that has historically been highly protected. This has resulted in negative effective rates of protection for agriculture. This bias against agriculture has been reduced in recent times. It is these trends in agricultural protection in developed and developing countries and the differences in their levels across countries that we are proposing to explain. In doing so, we draw upon the vast theoretical literature on the political economy of trade policy.

To examine the political economy drivers of the variation in agricultural protection across countries and within countries over time, we set up a basic framework that allows us to put forth various testable hypotheses on the variation and evolution of agricultural protection. We find that both the political ideology of the government and the degree of income inequality are important determinants of agricultural protection. Thus, both the political support function approach as well as the median-voter approach can be used in explaining the variation in agricultural protection across countries and within countries over time. In other words, while the government's decision making has some partisan elements, the concerns of the majority are also important.

We find that our results are consistent with the predictions of a model that assumes that labor is specialized and sector-specific in nature. The predictions of a model in which labor is assumed to be a general, intersectorally mobile factor do not hold. Finally, some aspects of protection also seem to be consistent with predictions of a lobbying model in that agricultural protection is negatively related to agricultural employment and positively related to agricultural productivity. Public finance aspects of protection also seem to be empirically important. Moreover, lobbying considerations are relatively more important in high-income countries, while public finance aspects are empirically relevant for developing countries.

This chapter is organized as follows. The next section provides a review of pertinent literature review before we set up a theoretical framework where we lay out all the hypotheses that we are going to test. We then briefly discuss our data sources and econometric methodology and present the results before drawing some conclusions.

LITERATURE REVIEW

Political economy models of trade are of two main types. In the first type, called "median voter" models, the approach taken is one of majority voting.

The second type, "lobbying models," may be further classified (following the typology in Rodrik 1995) into four approaches: (1) the tariff-formation function approach, (2) the political support function approach, (3) the political contributions approach, and (4) the campaign contributions approach. Within these lobbying models, (1) and (2) adopt a black-box approach to the modeling of lobbying in trade policy, whereas (3) and (4) have much stronger microfoundations.

Under the tariff-formation function approach, the tariff is a direct increasing function of resources going into lobbying in favor of the tariff and a decreasing function of lobbying resources devoted against the tariff. No microfoundations are provided for the function itself. Examples of this approach include Findlay and Wellisz (1982), Feenstra and Bhagwati (1982), and Rodrik (1986).

In models using the political support function approach, the government maximizes an objective function where different groups in the general population are given different weights depending on their political importance to the incumbent government (Hillman 1989, van Long and Vousden 1991).

In political contribution models, policies are determined through contributions by lobbies to incumbent politicians (Grossman and Helpman 1994), whereas in campaign contribution models, political competition between parties is fully modeled and contributions are made to competing parties (Magee, Brock and Young 1989).

In the theoretical modeling of endogenous protection, Grossman and Helpman (1994) made the biggest advance in providing strong microfoundations to the behavior of lobbies and the government, where the government maximizes a weighted sum of contributions and aggregate welfare, taking as a given contribution schedules provided by lobbies in a prior stage. Mitra (1999) endogenizes the formation of lobbies within this framework and analyzes its implications for sectoral tariffs.

Empirical Implications of the Median-Voter Approach

In the median-voter approach to tariff formulation, preferences on tariffs are assumed to be "single peaked," and conditions are imposed such that the most-preferred policy of each individual is monotonic in a certain characteristic. Then, holding other individual characteristics constant across the population, the tariff chosen under two-candidate electoral competition is the median voter's most-preferred tariff. The median voter here is the median individual in the economy when all individuals in the economy are ranked according to the characteristic under consideration. Mayer (1984) applied this median-voter principle to the Heckscher-Ohlin and specific-factors trade models. In the Heckscher-Ohlin case, the political economy equilibrium tariff is the most-preferred tariff of the median individual in the economy-wide ranking of the ratio of capital to labor ownership. If this median individual's capital-to-labor ratio is less than the economy's overall capital-to-labor ratio, that is, if the asset distribution in the economy is unequal, the equilibrium trade policy is different from free trade and is one that redistributes income from capital to labor. Hence it is protrade in a labor-abundant economy and antitrade in a capital-abundant economy.

In the Heckscher-Ohlin version of the Mayer median-voter model, a simple comparative static exercise produces the following result which is the main hypothesis that is empirically tested in Dutt and Mitra (2002): *A rise in asset inequality will make trade policy more protrade in a labor-abundant economy and more protectionist in a capital-abundant economy.*

Dutt and Mitra (2002) estimate the following protection equation using cross-country data on inequality, capital-abundance, and diverse measures of protection:

$$t_c = \alpha_0 + \alpha_1 (K/L)_c + \alpha_2 (Inequality)_c + \alpha_3 (Inequality)_c (K/L)_c + \nu_c$$

where the "c" is an index for country c. The theory predicts that $\alpha_2 < 0$ and $\alpha_3 > 0$ such that the partial derivative of protection with respect to inequality is positive if K/L is above a threshold, and negative if K/L is below that threshold. Dutt and Mitra (2002) find empirical support for this hypothesis.[3] Besides running the above regression cross-sectionally, Dutt and Mitra also run the regression in time differences (difference between the 1990s and 1980s) and find strong empirical support. Thus, not only does the above median-voter prediction help explain variations in overall trade protection levels across countries, but it also can explain long-run policy changes within a country.

[3] In this context, it is also important to mention Milner and Kubota (2005) who use a median-voter approach to empirically investigate the relationship between democratization and trade reforms in developing countries. Dutt and Mitra (2005) also perform a cross-country empirical investigation of the role of political ideology in trade policy determination. They use a political support function approach within a two-sector, two-factor Heckscher-Ohlin model. See Milner and Judkins (2004) on this issue. Also, see Hiscox (2001), who performs a study of six western nations to look at how historically the nature and structure of partisanship on trade issues change over time and depend on the extent of intersectoral factor mobility. Hiscox (2002) looks at the same question exclusively for the U.S., analyzing major pieces of congressional trade legislation between 1824 and 1994.

Empirical Implications of the Special-Interest Approach

The special-interest approach has evolved from the simple Findlay-Wellisz (1982) "tariff-formation function" approach to the state-of-the-art Grossman and Helpman (1994) "political-contributions" model. The latter is a very significant advance in several directions. Firstly, it is multisectoral. Secondly, it provides strong microfoundations to the behavior of the different actors in the model. A "menu-auctions" approach is used in modeling policy bidding by interest groups. Multiple principals, namely the various organized lobbies, try to influence the common agent, namely the government. The government's objective function is linear in political contributions and aggregate welfare, while each lobby maximizes its welfare net of political contributions. The level of protection for each industry is derived as an econometrically estimable function of industry characteristics and other political and economic factors. Most importantly, especially from an empirical perspective, the model provides the following hypothesis: *Holding everything else constant, organized sectors are granted higher protection than unorganized sectors. Further, protection to organized sectors is negatively related to import penetration and the (absolute value of the) import demand elasticity, while protection to unorganized sectors is positively related to these two variables.*

The following protection equation comes directly from the theory:

$$\frac{t_i}{1+t_i} = \frac{I_i - \alpha_L}{a + \alpha_L} \cdot \frac{z_i}{e_i}$$

where t_i denotes the ad valorem tariff (export subsidy in the case of an exportable) to sector i, z_i represents the output-to-import ratio (output-to-export ratio in the case of an exportable) in that sector, e_i its import demand elasticity (export supply elasticity in the case of an exportable), α_L the proportion of the total population of the economy that is politically organized, and a is the weight placed by the government on aggregate welfare relative to political contributions in its objective function. I_i is an indicator variable that takes the value 1 if the sector is politically organized and 0 otherwise.

The predictions of the Grossman and Helpman (1994) model are very intuitive: If an industry is import-competing and is organized ($I_i = 1$) then it buys protection and receives a positive tariff. If an industry is an exporter and organized, it is able to "buy" an export subsidy. Next, a high import-penetration ratio (high volume of imports relative to domestic output of importables) implies that specific-factor owners have less to gain from the increase in domestic price induced by the tariff, and the economy has more to lose from protection. So we are likely to see lower levels of protection. Similarly, when the import elasticity is higher, the deadweight loss from protection is also higher, so the government will grant it lower levels of protection. Next, an unorganized sector gets negative protection according to this theory if $\alpha_L > 0$ and gets zero protection if $\alpha_L = 0$, which is the case where factor ownership and political organization are concentrated in the hands of a few people that form a negligible proportion of the population. Thus, this theory leads to the estimation of the following estimating equation:

$$\frac{t_i}{1+t_i} = \frac{1}{a+\alpha_L} \cdot \frac{I_i z_i}{e_i} + \frac{-\alpha_L}{a+\alpha_L} \cdot \frac{z_i}{e_i} + u_i$$

where this equation can be linearly estimated with $\dfrac{1}{a+\alpha_L}$ and $\dfrac{-\alpha_L}{a+\alpha_L}$ as the two coefficients that are directly estimated, and then a and α_L can be inferred from the two coefficient estimates. Alternatively, these parameters can be directly estimated by nonlinear estimation.

Goldberg and Maggi (1999) and Gawande and Bandyopadhyay (2000) estimate the Grossman-Helpman "Protection for Sale" tariff expressions using industry-level data from the United States. Using slightly different econometric specifications from each other, both papers confirm empirically the Grossman-Helpman prediction regarding the relationship of protection to import protection and import demand elasticity. Holding everything else constant, organized sectors are granted higher protection than unorganized sectors. Both these papers find that the weight on aggregate welfare in the government's objective function (a) is several times higher than that on contributions. This finding is somewhat puzzling and perhaps worrisome. Although the Grossman-Helpman model does not provide any indication on the expected magnitude of the parameter a, the higher the weight governments put on aggregate welfare, the less compelling seems the raison d'être for the entire political economy literature. Moreover, the estimates of the proportion of population who are organized are very high in both the Goldberg-Maggi and Gawande-Bandyopadhyay papers.

Mitra, Thomakos and Ulubasoglu (2002) and McCalman (2004) obtain similarly high parameter estimates of the Grossman-Helpman model for Turkey and Australia, respectively. An interesting result that comes out of the empirical exercise by Mitra, Thomakos, and Ulubasoglu is that the relative weight on aggregate welfare was higher in the democratic regime than under the dictatorial regime in Turkey for the period spanned by the dataset. Due to the panel nature of the dataset, this study is able to explain both the cross-industry as well as the time series variation in protection.

Gawande, Krishna and Robbins (2006) use a new dataset on foreign political activity in the United States and extend the "Protection for Sale" model to include foreign lobbies. In line with the Grossman-Helpman's prediction, they find that foreign lobbying activity has significantly reduced US trade barriers. As a result, foreign lobbying has increased consumer surplus and overall welfare in the United States. In another empirical application, through an extension of the Grossman-Helpman model, Gawande and Krishna (2006) investigate the effects of US trade policy lobbying competition between upstream and downstream producers. Their parameter estimates are a significant improvement over those in the earlier literature even though they do not completely resolve the puzzle.

Finally, the most relevant paper from the point of view of the present study is the recent paper by Gawande, Krishna and Olarreaga (2009). This paper looks at the cross-country and cross-industry variations in protection at the same time. The Grossman-Helpman tariff expression for an organized sector can be written as:

$$\frac{t_{ict}}{1+t_{ict}} = \frac{1-\alpha_{Lc}}{a_c+\alpha_{Lc}} \cdot \frac{z_{ict}}{e_{ict}}$$

where the subscript "ict" denotes industry i in country c at time t. Assuming ownership of specific factors and political organization to be fully concentrated among a negligible proportion of the population, we have:

$$\frac{t_{ict}}{1+t_{ict}} = \frac{1}{a_c} \cdot \frac{z_{ict}}{e_{ict}}$$

which in turn can be written as

$$\frac{t_{ic}}{1+t_{ic}} \cdot \frac{e_{ict}}{z_{ict}} = \frac{1}{a_c}$$

and can be estimated as

$$\frac{t_{ic}}{1+t_{ic}} \cdot \frac{e_{ict}}{z_{ict}} = \beta_c + \xi_{ict}$$

The variance of the disturbance term is allowed to vary by country, and the coefficient $\beta_c = \dfrac{1}{a_c}$ is a measure of a government's affinity for political contributions, and its inverse gives us the weight the government puts on aggregate welfare relative to contributions in its objective function. The ranking of countries on the basis of the estimates of a and $1/a$ obtained by Gawande, Krishna and Olarreaga is quite realistic. The Spearman rank correlation of this estimate with Transparency International's corruption index turns out to be 0.67. Several political variables from the Database on Political Institutions (Beck et al. 2001), such as constraints on the executive, competition for executive, party concentration, and number of government seats, do very well in explaining the variation in a and $1/a$. In addition, institutional variables such as the nature of the legal system also perform well. This study, therefore, provides useful insights into the institutional and political variables that may potentially explain the variation in protection to agriculture both across space and over time.

Empirical Implications of the Political Ideology or Partisan Government Approach

Dutt and Mitra (2005) use a reduced form special-interest approach (earlier referred to as the "political support function" approach) to study how variations in political ideology of governments can explain international and intertemporal variations in protection. Ideology of the government is labeled as right, center, and left. Using the same Stolper-Samuelson intuition as in their median-voter paper, they arrive at the following testable hypothesis: *A more left-wing government (i.e., that attaches a higher weight to the welfare of workers/labor) is more protectionist in the case of capital-abundant countries but is less protectionist in the case of capital-scarce countries.* That hypothesis results in the following estimating equation:

$$t_c = \alpha_0 + \alpha_1 (K/L)_c + \alpha_2 (\text{Ideology})_c + \alpha_3 (\text{Ideology})_c (K/L)_c + \nu_c$$

Dutt and Mitra (2002) find support for their ideology hypothesis. In another paper, Dutt and Mitra (2006) combine both their ideology and their inequality (median-voter) hypotheses into the following umbrella model to show that protection is determined both by general-interest and special-interest concerns:

$$t_c = \alpha_0 + \alpha_1 (K/L)_c + \alpha_2 (\text{Ideology})_c + \alpha_3 (\text{Inequality})_c$$
$$+ \alpha_4 (\text{Ideology})_c (K/L)_c + \alpha_4 (\text{Inequality})_c (K/L)_c + \nu_c$$

Again, these models provide some guidance for the present study of agricultural protection.

Lessons from the "First Generation" Empirical Work

Unlike recent work described above, the early empirical literature, or what Gawande and Krishna (2003) call "first generation" empirical work on endogenous trade policy, is not driven by formal models. Nevertheless, we believe it does provide very useful insights and guidance for future research. It is important here to note that there were some important correlations revealed between tariffs and a number of political and economic variables by this early literature. For example Baldwin (1985) found that tariffs are higher for industries that are labor-intensive, have low wages, have a small number of firms and employ a large number of workers, and experience a high degree of import penetration. Also, he finds that tariff cuts from the GATT's Tokyo round were the lowest for the most unskilled labor-intensive industries.

Another well-known empirical piece from the early literature on the political economy of trade policy is by Trefler (1993), who finds that import penetration and other comparative advantage measures are more important in the determination of the nontariff barrier coverage ratios than industry concentration, scale, and capital measures.

Other important papers in the old literature include Caves (1976), Saunders (1980), Ray (1981), Marvel and Ray (1983), Ray (1991) and Trefler (1993).[4] The main finding of this early empirical literature is that protection is higher for sectors that are labor-intensive, low-skill and low-wage, for consumer-goods industries, for industries facing high import penetration when geographical concentration of production is high but that of consumers is low, and in sectors with low levels of intra-industry trade.[5]

Lessons from the Literature on Agricultural Protection

A large proportion of the theoretical research on the political economy of trade policy prior to the Grossman and Helpman (1994) model was on agricultural protection. Noteworthy in this literature is Swinnen (1994), who uses a Hillman-type of political support function approach within a fairly rich structure of the economy (three factors, of which one is mobile

---

[4] See Rodrik (1995) for a detailed survey of this literature.
[5] For an examination of the cross-national variation in average protection levels across industrialized countries, see Mansfield and Busch (1995). They find that nontariff barriers are increasing in country size, unemployment rate, and number of parliamentary constituencies and are higher for countries that use proportional representation as their electoral system.

and two are fixed), to study the relationship between agricultural protection and economic development.[6]

Honma (1993), who uses the Anderson and Hayami (1986) framework, finds support for the Anderson (1992) hypothesis that the shrinking of the agricultural sector makes opposition to agricultural protection more diffused and the lobbying for it more concentrated.[7] Honma uses panel data from fourteen industrial countries for the period 1955–87. He further finds that agricultural protection is inversely related to agricultural industry productivity and positively related to deterioration in its terms of trade.

Olper (1998) tries to explain cross-country variations in agricultural protection among the European Union (EU) countries in the 1970s and 1980s. Specifically, he looks at the Common Agricultural Policy (CAP) of the EU. He shows that agricultural protection is countercyclical to market conditions and is positively related to the extent of comparative disadvantage in agriculture. Also, agricultural protection is greater in countries with a smaller number of farms, finding evidence for the free-rider problem in lobbying.[8]

Finally, a recent paper by Gawande and Hoekman (2006) tests a modified version of the Grossman and Helpman (1994) "Protection for Sale" model for US agriculture. The modification is the uncertain outcome of lobbying, and the dataset they use contains both agricultural protection (tariffs and subsidies) and PAC contributions in the United States during the late 1990s. This is the first empirical piece in the agricultural protection literature that is completely structural in that the estimating equation is derived exclusively from theory.

THEORETICAL FRAMEWORK FOR THE PRESENT STUDY

In the theory we develop here, we recognize the existence of land as a factor that is of primary importance to agriculture. To do this, we make the extreme assumption that land is a factor of production specific to

[6] For an application, see Swinnen, Banerjee and de Gorter (2001). The literature on the political economy of agricultural protection until the early 1990s is comprehensively surveyed in de Gorter and Swinnen (2002).

[7] For a CGE study, based on a similar argument, trying to explain the bias against agriculture in poor countries and high agricultural protection in rich countries, see Anderson (1995).

[8] Also, see Olper (2007), where he looks at the interaction between ideology and inequality in the determination of agricultural protection. This work builds on Dutt and Mitra (2002, 2005, 2006).

agriculture. We develop our hypotheses under two scenarios: one where labor is intersectorally mobile and one where it is sector-specific.

Consider a two-sector specific-factors model. In the economy under consideration, assume there are two sectors, manufacturing and agriculture. The manufacturing sector uses capital (specific to manufacturing) and labor under constant returns to scale (CRS), while agriculture uses land (specific to agriculture) and labor, also under CRS. An unconditional prediction of this set of assumptions is that an increase in agricultural protection increases the real incomes (welfare) of landowners, while it reduces the real incomes of capitalists. In this framework, if labor is also sector-specific and immobile across sectors, then the prediction gets modified to the following: An increase in agricultural protection increases the real incomes (welfare) of landowners and agricultural workers, while it reduces the real incomes of capitalists and manufacturing workers. On the other hand, if labor is mobile across sectors, then the effect of agricultural protection on labor's welfare is ambiguous – it depends on labor's share of expenditure on agricultural products (food).

Political Ideology and Inequality

Clearly, in the mobile labor framework described above, a right-wing government (one that puts a higher weight on the well-being of capitalists) will try to keep protection as low as possible for agriculture. In such a framework, what will a left-wing government do? Remember that a left-wing government has an affinity for workers, which means they attach a higher weight to labor's welfare than to the welfare of others in the country. Protecting agriculture raises the overall demand for workers in the economy and increases their real wages in terms of the manufactured good, but lowers real wages when measured in terms of the agricultural good (food). Thus, if the share of expenditure on food is small enough, workers will be made better off through agricultural protection. A left-wing government will in such situations want to protect agriculture. There will be labor-land coalitions formed in such situations. The opposite will be the case when the expenditure share of food is high. Since the expenditure share of food varies inversely with per capita income, a left-wing government will want to protect agriculture in rich countries and not in poor countries.

In the immobile labor case, with a move from right-wing to centrist to left-wing governments, we will get an increase in agricultural protection if a large proportion of employment is in the agricultural sector. Since a left-wing government is pro-labor, it will support the sector that has relatively more workers. In general, the share of agriculture in employment is higher in poor countries. Therefore, the poorer a country the more likely it is that a left-wing government (relative to a right-wing or centrist government) will provide assistance to agriculture.

This brings us to **Competing Hypotheses 1:**

   (a) *Mobile Labor Case: Countries with left-wing governments will exhibit higher levels of agricultural protection when per capita income is high. At high levels of income, agricultural protection goes up when the political ideology of the government changes from rightist to centrist to leftist.*

   (b) *Immobile Labor Case: Countries with left-wing governments will exhibit higher levels of agricultural protection when per capita income is low. At low levels of income, agricultural protection goes up when the political ideology of the government changes from rightist to centrist to leftist.*

Majority Voting and Inequality

In a model where governments set policies that have the support of the majority of the population, agricultural protection will respond to income inequality. The predicted direction of response (to such changes in inequality) will once again depend on whether labor is intersectorally mobile or immobile.

In the mobile labor case, in a setting where the government tries to put in place policies that get majority support, agricultural protection will again be conditional on the food expenditure share. When this expenditure share is low, the majority, who are mainly workers, are likely to demand higher agricultural protection since this will increase the real incomes of workers in terms of their consumption baskets. When the expenditure share of food is low, which is the case when income is high, an increase in asset inequality will increase agricultural protection. This happens since, with an increase in inequality, the share of labor income in the incomes of the majority of the people goes up.[9] The opposite is the case when income is low and the share of food in overall expenditure is high.

In the immobile labor case, with an increase in inequality, there will be a demand for inequality reduction and we will get an increase in agricultural protection if a large proportion of employment is in the agricultural sector.

---

[9]   In the median voter model, it is common to assume that the median voter is labor-rich and asset-poor. From an empirical perspective as well, such an assumption seems plausible.

In general, the share of agriculture in employment is higher in poor countries. Therefore, the poorer a country the more likely it is that an increase in inequality will lead to an increase in assistance to agriculture.

Therefore, we have **Competing Hypotheses 2**:

(a) *Mobile Labor Case: Countries with higher levels of inequality will exhibit higher levels of agricultural protection provided income levels are high enough. Countries that experience an increase in inequality will increase their levels of agricultural protection over time, provided income levels are high enough.*

(b) *Immobile Labor Case: Countries with higher levels of inequality will exhibit higher levels of agricultural protection provided income levels are low enough. Countries that experience an increase in inequality will increase their levels of agricultural protection over time, provided income levels are low enough.*

Lobbying

With economic development and rising per capita incomes, agriculture's share in overall employment goes down. There are two main reasons for this. Firstly, in line with the traditional Engel effect, the share of expenditure on food goes down. Secondly, technological progress in agriculture means that fewer workers are required to produce a given level of output. As the employment share of agriculture goes down, agricultural workers and landowners will probably find it easier to organize and mitigate the inherent free-rider problem of lobby formation. As a result, a decline in the share of employment in agriculture is likely to be accompanied by an increase in agricultural protection. Second, if agricultural productivity goes up, lobbying becomes more beneficial and we are likely to see more agricultural protection.

This brings us to the following **Noncompeting (Complementary) Hypotheses 3**:

(a) *Countries with a lower share of employment in agriculture and higher agricultural productivity will exhibit higher levels of agricultural protection.*

(b) *Countries that experience a falling share of employment in agriculture and rising agricultural productivity will increase the levels of agricultural protection over time.*

Public Finance

During the initial stages of development, a country's tax infrastructure to raise revenues through direct taxes is weak. So revenues are raised through indirect taxes including tariffs on imports, which at that stage of development are mainly manufactured goods (but could include some agricultural goods). Over time, incomes increase and the returns to having a strong direct tax infrastructure rise, which results in government investment in an effective internal revenue service. Most of the revenue now comes from income taxes. Some of these revenues can now be used to give agricultural subsidies (especially since most rich countries have a comparative disadvantage in agriculture).

Thus, we have the following **Noncompeting (Complementary) Hypotheses 4**:

(a) *Countries with a small direct tax base (income taxes as a proportion of total tax revenues or government expenditure) will exhibit higher levels of agricultural tariffs.*

(b) *Countries whose direct tax revenues (as a proportion of total tax revenues or government expenditure) rise over time will exhibit a fall in their agricultural tariff rates and a rise in agricultural subsidies.*

EMPIRICAL RESULTS

To test these hypotheses we gather data on political variables from a variety of sources. Table 11.1 lists the data sources and the coverage for each of our explanatory variables.

We examine both the cross-country variations in agricultural protection as well as the within- country variation in agricultural protection over time. Table 11.2 shows the regressions that we run and the predicted coefficients on the independent variables to test our cross-country hypotheses as well as those which are within country and over time. To investigate cross-country variations, we use pooled ordinary least squares (OLS). For the within-country variation over time, we use panel data estimation techniques. This allows us to control for unobserved and time-invariant country-specific effects by using country-fixed effects.

Table 11.1. *Description of variables*

Variable	Years	Description
Relative Rate of Assistance to agriculture (RRA)	1955–2007	Anderson and Valenzuela (2008). (Methodology in Anderson et al. 2008.)
Nominal Rate of Assistance to agriculture (NRA)	1955–2007	Anderson and Valenzuela (2008). (Methodology in Anderson et al. 2008.)
Political Ideology	1975–2000	Political Ideology of chief executive (the President for Presidential systems and largest ruling party for Parliamentary system). *Source*: Database of Political Institutions 2004 (update of Beck et al. 2001).
Income Inequality	1960–1999	Gini coefficients from Dollar and Kraay (2002) and Deininger and Squire (1996, 1998). Data for the latter at http://www.worldbank.org/research/inequality/data.htm
Land Inequality	One year	Land Gini from Li, Squire and Zou (1998).
Per capita GDP	1960–2000	GDP per capita on a PPP basis. *Source*: World Bank (2007).
Share of agriculture in employment	1960–2000	Total workers employed in agriculture as a proportion of labor force. *Source*: World Bank (2007).
Comparative Disadvantage in Agriculture	1960–2000	Measured as $(X - M)/(X + M)$, where X is exports of agricultural products and M is the imports of agricultural products.
Direct taxes (% of total taxes)	1970–2000	Direct taxes include income taxes, profits, and capital gains tax. *Source*: World Bank (2007).
Constraints on Executive	1960–2000	Extent of institutionalized constraints on the decision-making powers of chief executives, whether individuals or collectivities. *Source*: Polity IV Project, (Marshall, Jaggers and Gurr 2000).
Rural party	1975–2000	Dummy equals 1 if chief executive's party can be classified as rural. *Source*: Database of Political Institutions 2004 (update of Beck et al. 2001).

Source: Authors' compilation.

Table 11.2. *Hypotheses and predicted signs*

Hypotheses	Description	Predicted signs
1: *Political Ideology*	Regress agricultural protection on left-wing ideology and leftist ideology×per capita income	Mobile labor case: Negative on leftist ideology and positive on the interaction term.
		Immobile labor case: Positive on leftist ideology and negative on the interaction term.
2: *Inequality*	Regress agricultural protection on income inequality and inequality×per capita income	Mobile labor case: Negative on inequality and positive on the interaction term.
		Immobile labor case: Positive on inequality and negative on the interaction term.
3: *Lobbying*	Regress agricultural protection on share of agriculture in employment and agricultural productivity	Negative on employment share and positive on agricultural productivity
4: *Public Finance*	Regress agricultural protection on share of direct taxes in total taxes/ expenditure	Negative on direct tax share

Source: Authors' compilation.

Ideology, Inequality, and Agricultural Protection

To examine the role played by ideology and inequality in influencing agricultural protection, we first estimate the following equations:

$$agprot_{ct} = \alpha_1 (per\ capita\ income)_{ct} + \alpha_2 (\text{Ideology})_{ct}$$
$$+ \alpha_3 (\text{Ideology})_{ct} (per\ capita\ income)_{ct} + \epsilon_{ct}$$

$$agprot_{ct} = \alpha_1 (per\ capita\ income)_{ct} + \alpha_2 (\text{Inequality})_{ct}$$
$$+ \alpha_3 (\text{Inequality})_{ct} (per\ capita\ income)_{ct} + \epsilon_{ct}$$

where the subscript "c" is for country and "t" denotes time. "Agprot" stands for agricultural protection. For the within-estimates, we add country (as well as time) fixed effects to the above specification.

In Table 11.3, we see how political ideology and inequality affect the Relative Rate of Assistance (RRA) to agriculture. In column 1, the

Table 11.3. *Ideology and per capita GDP as determinants of RRAs*

	(1)	(2)	(3)	(4)
	RRA	RRA	RRA	RRA
Left–wing ideology	0.555*** (0.148)	0.726*** (0.177)	0.270** (0.124)	0.240* (0.133)
Ideology*per capita GDP	-0.064*** (0.017)	-0.082*** (0.021)	-0.030** (0.013)	-0.027* (0.014)
per capita GDP	0.528*** (0.046)	0.562*** (0.057)	0.385*** (0.054)	0.376*** (0.063)
Constraints on executive		-0.002 (0.002)		0.001** (0.000)
Presidential system		-0.091*** (0.018)		0.097*** (0.026)
Rural party in power		0.634*** (0.221)		0.446*** (0.144)
Constant	-4.444*** (0.408)	-4.687*** (0.508)	-3.328*** (0.513)	-3.265*** (0.576)
Observations	1261	1077	1261	1077
R^2	0.39	0.43	0.17	0.22
Number of countries	60	58	60	58
Country-fixed effects	No	No	Yes	Yes
Year-fixed effects	No	No	Yes	Yes

Robust standard errors in parentheses; * significant at 10%; ** significant at 5%; *** significant at 1%. The dependent variable is the relative rate of assistance (RRA) calculated as $((1+NRA_{ag})/(1+NRA_{nonag})-1)$, where NRA_{ag} is the nominal rate of assistance to tradable agricultural products and NRA_{nonag} is the nominal rate of assistance to tradable nonagricultural products. Ideology is coded as 1 for Right-wing governments, 2 for Centrist, and 3 for Left-Wing governments. We use the political ideology of the executive for Presidential systems; of the largest governing party in the parliament for parliamentary system and average of the Executive and largest party for mixed systems. Columns 1 and 2 present pooled OLS estimates; columns 3 and 4 present within-estimates with country and time-fixed effects.
Source: Authors' computations.

coefficient on the ideology variable is positive and significant, whereas the coefficient on the interaction of ideology with per capita income is negative and significant. The signs of the ideology term and its interaction with per capita income suggest that the intersectoral mobility of labor is quite low and so the immobile labor model is a better approximation to reality than the mobile labor model. Column 2 shows that this finding is robust to the addition of three political institution controls: Constraints on the executive, which captures checks and balances on the chief executive (higher in democracies); a dummy equal to 1 for Presidential systems; and a dummy equal to 1 if the ruling party can be classified as rural. Columns 3 and 4 present within-estimates, where again we see that political ideology influences agricultural protection. The signs of the estimated coefficients are compatible with the immobile labor scenario.

The coefficient of the ideology term divided by the absolute value of the coefficient of the interaction term gives us the critical per capita income at which the relationship changes sign. Per capita income is measured in natural logarithms, and the threshold is about 8.7 in column 1, which in levels is about $6,000. When we add country-fixed effects, we observe a decline in the magnitude of the coefficient estimates. However, the critical per capita income remains substantively unchanged in column 3 (equal to 9).

Table 11.4 presents regressions analyzing the effects of inequality. Columns 1–3 show pooled OLS estimates, whereas columns 4 and 5 present within-estimates. All columns use the income Gini coefficient as the measure of inequality, except column 2, which uses the land inequality measure from Li, Squire and Zou (1998). The estimated coefficient on the Gini coefficient is positive and significant, and its interaction with per capita income is negative and significant. As with political ideology, these signs are consistent with the immobile labor scenario. The threshold per capita income is only $3,000 in this case, except for column 2 (where the land Gini is used), where the threshold is even lower. The results hold for the within-estimates as well, with the critical per capita income rising to $3,500.

We next explore whether it is actually the relative size of agricultural employment that is driving these results. In Table 11.5, instead of per capita income, we use the share of agriculture in total employment. As expected from the first set of regressions, we now have the political ideology coefficient negative and significant. The coefficient of the interaction between political ideology and the share of agriculture in employment is positive and significant in column 1 (where no fixed effects are used) but insignificant in column 2 where country and year-fixed effects are used. When inequality is used in place of ideology in these regressions (columns 3, 4, and 5), the inequality variable is positive and significant, and the interaction of inequality with the share of agricultural employment is negative and significant, both in the absence and presence of country

Table 11.4. *Inequality and per capita GDP as determinants of RRAs*

	(1)	(2)	(3)	(4)	(5)
	RRA	RRA	RRA	RRA	RRA
Inequality	0.109***	0.054*	0.107***	0.049**	0.050**
	(0.020)	(0.029)	(0.021)	(0.023)	(0.023)
Inequality*per capita GDP	−0.014***	−0.008**	−0.014***	−0.006**	−0.006**
	(0.002)	(0.003)	(0.002)	(0.003)	(0.003)
per capita GDP	0.800***	0.792***	0.768***	0.484***	0.488***
	(0.084)	(0.237)	(0.088)	(0.110)	(0.111)
Constraints on executive			−0.004***		0.001
			(0.001)		(0.001)
Presidential system			−0.063**		0.037
			(0.025)		(0.028)
Rural party in power			0.068		0.205
			(0.187)		(0.227)
Constant	−6.308***	−6.091***	−6.031***	−3.680***	−3.944***
	(0.724)	(1.993)	(0.755)	(0.854)	(0.948)
Observations	450	43	441	450	441
R^2	0.46	0.67	0.46	0.31	0.30
Number of countries	62	43	62	62	62
Country-fixed effects	No	No	No	Yes	Yes
Year-fixed effects	No	No	No	Yes	Yes

Robust standard errors in parentheses; * significant at 10%; ** significant at 5%; *** significant at 1%. The dependent variable is the relative rate of assistance (RRA) calculated as $((1+NRA_{ag})/(1+NRA_{nonag})-1)$, where NRA_{ag} is the nominal rate of assistance to tradable agricultural products and NRA_{nonag} is the nominal rate of assistance to tradable nonagricultural products. Columns 1 and 2 present pooled OLS estimates; columns 3 and 4 present within-estimates with country and time-fixed effects. Column 2 uses Land Gini as the measure of inequality. All others use income Gini. *Source*: Authors' computations.

and year-fixed effects. In other words, these results hold in both cross-sectional and within-country, across-time variations in the data.

Lobbying and Agricultural Protection

As the employment share of agriculture goes down, agricultural workers and landowners will probably find it easier to organize, as a result of which protection to agriculture is likely to go up. In Table 11.6, the negative and

Table 11.5. *Ideology, inequality, and share of employment as determinants of RRAs*

	(1)	(2)	(3)	(4)	(5)
	RRA	RRA	RRA	RRA	RRA
Left-wing ideology	−0.119*** (0.040)	−0.036* (0.021)			
Ideology*share of agric. in emplt.	0.002** (0.001)	0.001 (0.001)			
Gini			−0.026*** (0.005)	−0.038*** (0.010)	−0.015** (0.007)
Gini* share of agriculture in emplt.			0.000*** (0.000)	0.002* (0.001)	0.000* (0.000)
share of agriculture in employment	−0.018*** (0.002)	−0.026*** (0.004)	−0.031*** (0.005)	−0.018*** (0.005)	−0.032*** (0.010)
Constraints on executive	−0.011*** (0.001)		−0.014 (0.016)	−0.055 (0.048)	0.009 (0.015)
Presidential system	−0.243*** (0.027)		−0.119*** (0.038)	−0.064 (0.074)	0.031 (0.040)
Rural party in power	0.784*** (0.282)		0.084 (0.240)	0.000 (0.000)	0.276 (0.271)
Constant	1.137*** (0.095)	0.749*** (0.108)	1.691*** (0.222)	2.065*** (0.480)	1.159*** (0.342)
Observations	645	645	284	27	284
R^2	0.25	0.31	0.37	0.63	0.33
Number of countries	49	49	50	27	50
Country-fixed effects	No	Yes	No	No	Yes
Year-fixed effects	No	Yes	No	No	Yes

Robust standard errors in parentheses; * significant at 10%; ** significant at 5%; *** significant at 1%. The dependent variable is the relative rate of assistance (RRA) calculated as $((1+NRA_{ag})/(1+NRA_{nonag})-1)$, where NRA_{ag} is the nominal rate of assistance to tradable agricultural products and NRA_{nonag} is the nominal rate of assistance to tradable nonagricultural products. Ideology is coded as 1 for Right-wing governments, 2 for Centrist, and 3 for Left-Wing governments. We use the political ideology of the executive for Presidential systems; of the largest governing party in the parliament for parliamentary system and average of the Executive and largest party for mixed systems. Columns 1, 3, and 4 present pooled OLS results; the rest present results with country and time-fixed effects. Column 4 uses Land Gini as the measure of inequality. Columns 3 and 5 use income Gini.
Source: Authors' computations.

Table 11.6. *Lobbying and RRAs*

	(1)	(2)	(3)	(4)
	RRA (all countries)	RRA (all countries)	RRA (OECD only)	RRA (OECD excl. Cairns group)
Employment in agriculture (% of total employment)	−0.913*** (0.134)	−2.712*** (0.406)	−2.991*** (0.821)	−3.423*** (0.894)
Agricultural productivity	0.069*** (0.021)	0.194*** (0.035)	0.261*** (0.082)	0.269*** (0.101)
Constraints on executive	−0.005* (0.003)	0.003* (0.001)	0.004 (0.003)	0.004 (0.003)
Presidential system	−0.134*** (0.022)	−0.005 (0.028)	0.020 (0.066)	0.023 (0.071)
Rural party in power	0.389*** (0.150)	0.385*** (0.095)	0.398*** (0.114)	0.405*** (0.121)
Constant	0.052 (0.198)	−0.908*** (0.330)	−1.577** (0.794)	−1.469 (0.967)
Observations	746	746	376	313
R^2	0.30	0.28	0.43	0.48
Number of countries	58	58	20	17
Country-fixed effects	No	Yes	Yes	Yes
Year-fixed effects	No	Yes	Yes	Yes

Robust standard errors in parentheses; * significant at 10%; ** significant at 5%; *** significant at 1%. Column 1 presents pooled OLS results; columns 2–4 present results with country and time-fixed effects. Columns 1 and 2 include all countries; column 3 includes only OECD countries; from which column 4 excludes the Cairns group of countries (Australia, Canada and New Zealand). *Source:* Authors' computations.

significant coefficient of the employment share of agriculture provides support for this hypothesis. This is true for all countries pooled together (column 1), when we restrict the sample to only OECD countries (column 2), and when we restrict the sample to OECD but exclude the Cairns group of countries.[10] We see that this variation is both cross-sectional as well within-country across time. The positive and significant coefficients of agricultural productivity in Table 11.6 provide support for the hypothesis that as agricultural productivity rises, lobbying becomes more beneficial,

[10] The Cairns countries are those who favor free trade and open market access in agriculture.

and we are likely to see more agricultural protection. The rise in the magnitude of the coefficient between columns 2 and 3 suggests that lobbying plays a more important role in rich OECD countries.

Revenue Motive for Agricultural Protection

In Table 11.7, the variable of interest is direct taxes as a percentage of total tax revenue. If the government has a well-developed tax infrastructure, it can raise revenue through direct taxes, and it can use some of this revenue to provide agricultural subsidies. In this case, there should be a complementarity between the government's ability to raise direct taxes and agricultural assistance. On the other hand, if the government is not able to raise direct tax revenues, it might have to resort to indirect taxation, which can take the form of import tariffs. If these tariffs are agricultural tariffs, then we might see some substitutability between direct taxes and agricultural assistance. Whether the ability to raise direct taxes negatively or positively affects agricultural assistance is therefore an empirical question. All but one of our regressions in Table 11.7 show a negative sign for the coefficient of direct taxes as a share of total tax revenues. This result holds both for nominal and relative rates of assistance to agriculture. For the latter, it is driven primarily by non-OECD countries.

CONCLUSION

Our main objective in this chapter is to identify the political economy drivers in the evolution of international trade policies with respect to agriculture. Understanding these determinants should not only help provide deeper insights into trade policy formulation in general, but also allow us to understand what makes agriculture a particularly contentious issue in recent trade talks.

We have set up a basic framework that allows us to put forth various testable hypotheses on the variation and evolution of agricultural protection. We find that both the political ideology of the government and the degree of inequality are important determinants of agricultural protection. Thus, both the political support function approach as well as the median-voter approach can be used in explaining the variation in agricultural protection across countries and within countries over time. The results are consistent with the predictions of a model that assumes that labor is specialized and sector-specific in nature. Some aspects of protection also seem to be consistent with predictions of a lobbying model in that agricultural protection

Table 11.7. Revenue motive for agricultural assistance

	(1) NRA	(2) NRA	(3) RRA	(4) RRA	(5) RRA (OECD only)	(6) RRA (non–OECD only)
Direct taxes (% of total taxes)	-0.002** (0.001)	-0.003** (0.001)	-0.002* (0.001)	-0.003** (0.001)	0.005 (0.009)	-0.004*** (0.001)
Revealed comp adv in agriculture		-0.047 (0.057)		-0.091 (0.057)	-0.182 (0.270)	-0.023 (0.051)
Constraints on executive		0.001*** (0.000)		0.001*** (0.000)	0.000 (0.000)	0.001** (0.000)
Presidential system		0.114*** (0.023)		0.172*** (0.027)	0.000 (0.000)	0.124*** (0.019)
Constant	0.223*** (0.055)	0.356*** (0.084)	0.132** (0.064)	0.285*** (0.069)	0.943* (0.477)	-0.049 (0.047)
Observations	554	301	531	285	100	185
Number of countries	64	50	64	49	19	30
R^2	0.13	0.14	0.13	0.14	0.51	0.34
Country-fixed effects	Yes	Yes	Yes	Yes	Yes	Yes
Year-fixed effects	Yes	Yes	Yes	Yes	Yes	Yes

Robust standard errors in parentheses; * significant at 10%; ** significant at 5%; *** significant at 1%.

The dependent variable in columns 1 and 2 is the nominal rate of assistance to agriculture. The dependent variable in columns 3–6 is the relative rate of assistance to agriculture (RRA) calculated as $((1+NRA_{ag})/(1+NRA_{nonag})-1)$, where NRA_{ag} is the nominal rate of assistance to tradable agricultural products and NRA_{nonag} is the nominal rate of assistance to tradable nonagricultural products. Direct taxes include income taxes, profits, and capital gains tax. Revealed comparative advantage in agriculture is defined as $(X-M)/(X+M)$, where X is exports and M is imports of agricultural products. All columns include country and time-fixed effects. Column 5 shows results with only OECD countries; column 6 shows results with only non-OECD countries.

Source: Authors' computations.

is negatively related to agricultural employment and positively related to agricultural productivity. Public finance aspects of assistance to agriculture also seem to be empirically important.

References

Anderson, K. (1992), "International Dimensions of the Political Economy of Distortionary Price and Trade Policies," pp. 290–310 in I. Goldin and L.A. Winters (eds.), *Open Economies: Structural Adjustment and Agriculture*, Cambridge and New York: Cambridge University Press.

(1995), "Lobbying Incentives and the Pattern of Protection in Rich and Poor Countries," *Economic Development and Cultural Change* 43(2): 401–23, January.

Anderson, K., Y. Hayami and Others (1986), *The Political Economy of Agricultural Protection: East Asia in International Perspective*, London: Allen and Unwin.

Anderson, K. and E. Valenzuela (2008), *Global Estimates of Distortions to Agricultural Incentives, 1955 to 2007*, database available at http://www.worldbank.org/agdistortions.

Anderson, K., M. Kurzweil, W. Martin, D. Sandri and E. Valenzuela (2008), "Measuring Distortions to Agricultural Incentives, Revisited," *World Trade Review* 7(4): 1–30.

Baldwin, R.E. (1985) *The Political Economy of U.S. Import Policy*, Cambridge MA: MIT Press.

Beck, T., G. Clarke, A. Groff and P. Keefer (2001), "New Tools in Comparative Political Economy: The Database of Political Institutions," *World Bank Economic Review* 15(1): 165–76.

Caves, R. (1976), "Economic Models of Political Choice: Canada's Tariff Structure," *Canadian Journal of Economics* 9(2): 278–300.

de Gorter, H. and J. Swinnen (2002), "Political Economy of Agricultural Policies,", pp. 2073–2123 in B. Gardner and G. Rausser (eds.), *Handbook of Agricultural Economics*, Volume 2, Amsterdam: Elsevier.

Dollar, D. and A. Kraay (2002), "Growth is Good for the Poor," *Journal of Economic Growth*, 7(3): 195–225.

Deininger, K. and L. Squire (1996), "A New Data Set Measuring Income Inequality," *World Bank Economic Review* 10(3): 565–91.

(1998), "New Ways of Looking at Old Issues: Inequality and Growth," *Journal of Development Economics* 57: 249–87.

Dutt, P. and D. Mitra (2002), "Endogenous Trade Policy Through Majority Voting: An Empirical Investigation," *Journal of International Economics* 58: 107–33.

(2005), "Political Ideology and Endogenous Trade Policy: An Empirical Investigation," *Review of Economics and Statistics* 87: 59–72.

(2006), "Labor versus Capital in Trade-Policy: The Role of Ideology and Inequality," *Journal of International Economics* 69(2): 310–20.

Feenstra, R. and J. Bhagwati (1982), "Tariff Seeking and the Efficient Tariff," in J. Bhagwati (ed.), *Import Competition and Response*, Chicago IL: University of Chicago Press.

Findlay, R. and S. Wellisz (1982), "Endogenous Tariffs, the Political Economy of Trade Restrictions, and Welfare," in J. Bhagwati (ed.), *Import Competition and Response*, Chicago IL: University of Chicago Press.

Gawande, K. and S. Bandyopadhyay (2000), "Is Protection for Sale? A Test of the Grossman–Helpman Theory of Endogenous Protection," *Review of Economics and Statistics* 82: 139–52.

Gawande, K. and B. Hoekman (2006), "Lobbying and Agricultural Policy in the United States," *International Organization* 60(3): 527–61.

Gawande, K. and P. Krishna (2003), "The Political Economy of Trade Policy: Empirical Approaches," in J. Harrigan and E.K. Choi (eds.), *Handbook of International Trade*, Malden MA: Basil Blackwell.

(2005), "Lobbying Competition over U.S. Trade Policy," Working Paper No. 11371, Cambridge, MA: NBER.

Gawande, K., P. Krishna and M. Olarreaga (2009), "What Governments Maximize and Why: The View from Trade," *International Organization* 63(3): 491–532, July.

Gawande, K., P. Krishna and M. Robbins (2006), "Foreign Lobbies and U.S. Trade Policy," *Review of Economics and Statistics* 88(3): 563–71.

Goldberg, P. and G. Maggi (1999), "Protection for Sale: An Empirical Investigation," *American Economic Review* 89: 1135–55.

Grossman, G.M. and E. Helpman (1994), "Protection for Sale," *American Economic Review* 84: 833–50.

Hai, W. (1991), *Agricultural Trade Protection and Economic Development*, unpublished Ph.D. Dissertation, University of California, Davis.

Hillman, A. (1989), *The Political Economy of Protection*, Chur: Harwood Academic Publishers.

Hiscox, M. (2001), *International Trade and Political Conflict: Commerce, Coalitions and Mobility*, Princeton NJ: Princeton University Press.

(2002), "Commerce, Coalitions, and Factor Mobility: Evidence From Congressional Votes on Trade Legislation," *American Political Science Review* 96: 593–608.

Honma, M. (1993), "Japan's Agricultural Policy and Protection Growth," pp. 95–114 in T. Ito and A. Krueger (eds.), *Trade and Protectionism*, Chicago: University of Chicago Press.

Li, H., L. Squire and H. Zou (1998), "Explaining International and Intertemporal Variations in Income Inequality," *Economic Journal* 108(446): 26–43.

Magee, S., W. Brock and L. Young (1989), *Black Hole Tariffs and Endogenous Policy Theory*, Cambridge and New York: Cambridge University Press.

Mansfield, E. and M. Busch (1995), "The Political Economy of Trade Barriers: A Cross-National Analysis," *International Organization* 49: 723–49.

Marshall, M.G., K. Jaggers and T.R. Gurr (2000), "Political Regime Characteristics and Transitions, 1800–2002," Polity IV Project, Center for International Development and Conflict Management, University of Maryland, College Park MD.

Marvel, H. and E. Ray (1983), "The Kennedy Round: Evidence on the Regulation of Trade in the US," *American Economic Review* 73(1): 190–7.

Mayer, W. (1984), "Endogenous Tariff Formation," *American Economic Review* 74: 970–85.

McCalman, P. (2004), "Protection for Sale and Trade Liberalization: An Empirical Investigation," *Review of International Economics* 12: 81–94.

Milner, H., and B. Judkins (2004), "Partisanship, Trade policy, and Globalization: Is There a Left–right Divide on Trade Policy?" *International Studies Quarterly* 48: 95–119.

Milner, H. and K. Kubota (2005), "Why the Move to Free Trade? Democracy and Trade Policy in the Developing Countries," *International Organization* 59: 107–43.

Mitra, D. (1999), "Endogenous Lobby Formation and Endogenous Protection: A Long Run Model of Trade Policy Determination," *American Economic Review* 89: 1116–34.

Mitra, D., D. Thomakos and M. Ulubasoglu (2002), "Protection for Sale in a Developing Country: Democracy vs. Dictatorship," *Review of Economics and Statistics* 84: 497–508.

Olper, A. (1998), "Political Economy Determinants of Agricultural Protection Levels in EU Member States: An Empirical Investigation," *European Review of Agricultural Economics* 25: 463–87.

(2007), "Land Inequality, Government Ideology and Agricultural Protection," *Food Policy* 32: 67–83.

Ray, E. (1981), "The Determinants of Tariff and Non-tariff Restriction in the United States," *Journal of Political Economy* 89: 105–21.

(1991), "Protection of Manufactures in the United States", in D. Greenaway (ed.), *Global Protectionism: Is The US Playing on a Level Field?* London: Macmillan.

Rodrik, D. (1986), "Tariffs, Subsidies and Welfare with Endogenous Policy," *Journal of International Economics* 21: 285–96.

(1995), "Political Economy of Trade Policy," in G. Grossman and K. Rogoff (eds.), *Handbook of International Economics*, vol. 3, Amsterdam: North-Holland.

Saunders, R. (1980), "The Political Economy of Effective Protection in Canada's Manufacturing Sector," *Canadian Journal of Economics* 13: 340–8.

Swinnen, J. (1994), "A Positive Theory of Agricultural Protection," *American Journal of Agricultural Economics* 76(1): 1–14.

Swinnen, J., A. Banerjee and H. de Gorter (2001), "Economic Development, Institutional Change and the Political Economy of Agricultural Protection: An Empirical Study of Belgium since the 19th Century," *Agricultural Economics* 26(1): 25–43.

Trefler, D. (1993), "Trade Liberalization and the Theory of Endogenous Protection," *Journal of Political Economy* 101: 138–60.

van Long, N. and N. Vousden (1991), "Protectionist Responses and Declining Industries," *Journal of International Economics* 30: 87–103.

World Bank (2007), *World Development Indicators 2007*, Washington DC: World Bank.

Chapter 8

Reciprocated unilateralism in trade reforms with majority voting

Pravin Krishna [a,b,*], Devashish Mitra [b,c,d]

[a] John Hopkins University, United States
[b] NBER, United States
[c] Syracuse University, United States
[d] IZA, Germany

Received 26 September 2004; received in revised form 11 May 2006; accepted 30 May 2006

Abstract

This paper shows how unilateral liberalization in one country can increase the voting support for reciprocal reduction in trade barriers in a partner country. When trade policies are determined simultaneously in the two countries, we show the possibility of multiple political equilibria — one in which the countries are both protectionist and another in which they trade freely with each other. Starting with trade protection in both countries, a unilateral reform in one country is shown to bring about a free trade equilibrium that obtains majority support in both countries.

JEL classification: F13; F10; F02; O24
Keywords: Unilateralism; Reciprocity; Voting; Tariff; Liberalization

1. Introduction

Reciprocal tariff reductions in the context of trade negotiations have been extensively studied in the theoretical literature on international trade.[1] Recently, however, the literature has also begun studying the potential interdependence of trade policies across countries, specifically the role of unilateral (i.e., unconditional) liberalization in securing a reciprocal reduction in trade barriers by partners.[2]

---

* Corresponding author.
  E-mail address: Pravin_Krishna@Jhu.edu (P. Krishna).
[1] See, for instance, Johnson (1953), Mayer (1981) and, more recently, Bagwell and Staiger (1999), among others.
[2] See Coates and Ludema (2001) and Krishna and Mitra (2005). See also Bhagwati (2002) for a general discussion.

In this paper, we explore the link between unilateralism and reciprocity in a context in which the decision to carry out a trade reform is determined by its popular political support. That is, trade policy changes are voted upon by the public and outcomes are determined by the majority (as, for instance, in Mayer, 1981 and Fernandez and Rodrik, 1991). We model a two-good, two-country trading world in which output in each country is produced by individuals with differing relative productivities in the two sectors (as in Mayer, 1998). In the home country, any proposed trade reforms pit (loosely speaking) individuals in the losing (import-competing) sector against those in the winning (exportable) sector but to varying extents (as workers vary in their relative productivities). In this setting, we demonstrate how unilateral trade liberalization by a trade partner may increase the voting support for trade liberalization in the home country. Specifically, a reduction in tariffs by a partner country that increases the world price of the exportable of the home country (and thus lowers the relative price of the importable) lowers the relative wage advantage from working in the home country's import-competing sector. Some workers in the import-competing sector prior to the reforms who would have previously opposed a move to free trade in the home economy now support this policy. With a large enough downward movement in the relative price of the importable good, the protected home economy may then gain majority support for free trade.

When trade policies are determined simultaneously in the two countries, we show the possibility of multiple political equilibria — one in which both countries are protectionist and another in which both freely trade with each other. Starting with trade protection in both countries, a unilateral reform in one country is thus shown to bring about a free trade equilibrium (a self-enforcing state) that is consistent with majority voting in both countries.

Interdependencies of the type discussed in this paper carry important normative implications. The policy of using unconditional liberalization to induce reciprocity by partners stands in contrast to conventional policy wisdom regarding the use (or the threat) of raising one's trade barriers to remove those of others. Understanding the channels that link trade policies across countries is important from a positive standpoint as well, as it may help us understand better particular episodes of reforms undertaken by countries. Specifically, we should note that the prediction of our model is consistent with a few major episodes of unilateral trade liberalization that are well known in the history of international economic relations. As Coates and Ludema (1997) argues, these include the unilateral repeal of England's Corn Laws in the mid-nineteenth century, "after decades of attempts to negotiate lower tariffs with its trading partners," and the more recent example of the United States, which, after the end of the Second World War sponsored the General Agreement on Trade and Tariffs (GATT) and engaged subsequently in major tariff reductions "without requiring substantive reciprocity from its major trading partners." "Waves of liberalization" by trading partners followed both these episodes. In the period immediately after England's repeal of its Corn Laws, numerous countries followed suit — with unilateral trade reforms of their own or with bilateral tariff agreements with England. Equally, the major trading partners of the United States reduced their trade barriers in the subsequent period leading up to the 1970s.

Perhaps closer in spirit to the theoretical framework and assumptions articulated in the paper is the more recent experience of developing countries in the world trading system: Following (chronologically) trade barrier reductions by full-obligation (i.e., developed country) GATT members in the several GATT rounds, and despite the exemption from the obligation to reciprocate afforded by the articles (specifically, Article 18) of the GATT, there was by the late 1980s a "rush to free trade" among countries in the developing world (see Rodrik, 1994). Unilateralism was thus reciprocated even in the absence of a formal obligation to do so. We may also cite the specific example of Uruguay, whose trade reforms in early 1990s seem roughly consistent with the predictions of our model. Thus, for instance, Forteza et al. (2004) has described the liberalization in the early 1990s as having been driven by trade policy changes in Brazil which "altered the domestic equilibrium in Uruguay in favor of pro-export groups." Thus, in understanding the reform experiences of developing countries, it seems important to consider interdependencies in trade policy of the sort that we model here.

Finally, a few points regarding the links between this present paper and our earlier work may be worth noting. Krishna and Mitra (2005), like the present paper, considers the question of whether unilateral trade liberalization in one country may induce reciprocity in partner countries *absent* any trade negotiations.[3] In a setting where organized interest groups influence trade policy, it argues that unilateral trade liberalization in one country may impact policies in partner countries by encouraging the formation (or increasing the relative strength) of the relevant interest groups there. The key difference between our earlier work and the present analysis is the institutional setting in which policy is determined. While interest groups influence policy in our earlier analysis, policy is determined by majority voting in this paper.[4] This is not a minor difference, since the trade policy predictions that are obtained in the two settings generally differ widely from each other. The finding that unilateral reforms by one country may, regardless of the institutional setting, have similar (positive) effects on the incentives for reforms in partner countries is therefore significant.

The rest of the paper proceeds as follows. In Section 2, we develop a simple majority voting framework in which we demonstrate the mechanism of reciprocated unilateralism. Section 3 considers policy interdependence between large countries and demonstrates the interesting possibility of multiple policy equilibria. Sections 4 and 5 develop the analysis with tariff revenue redistribution and with endogenous tariffs — demonstrating the robustness of the results in both cases. Section 6 concludes.

2. Trade policy with majority voting

Consider a small economy with two sectors, M (import-competing) and E (exportable). We assume that both goods in this economy are produced under constant returns to scale using labor alone. However, different individuals have different levels of productivities in the production of the two goods. Thus, we denote by $h^M(i)$ the labor productivity of individual i in sector M and by $h^E(i)$ her productivity in sector E. Let p^* be the world relative price of good M. Thus, its domestic price is $p=p^*(1+t)$ where t is the ad valorem import tariff, which takes the value $\bar{t}$ prior to the trade reform and zero once the reform takes place.

A person works in the sector that pays her a higher wage determined by her productivity. She decides to work in sector E if $h^E(i)>ph^M(i)$, i.e., if $h^E(i)/h^M(i)>p$. Thus, her comparative advantage in the production of the export good is $h^E(i)/h^M(i)$, which needs to be greater than the relative price p of the import-competing good for her to decide to work in the export sector. Let us

---

[3] See also Coates and Ludema (2001) which argues that in the presence of "political risk" of domestic opposition to trade agreements, unilateral tariff reduction – by lowering the political stakes associated with trade liberalization in the foreign country – may increase the likelihood of a successful outcome in a trade negotiation.

[4] Moreover, while in Krishna and Mitra (2005) the political economy structure and policy endogenously respond to exogenous changes in the partner country, the model here is fully closed in the sense that policies in both countries are completely endogenous and determined in equilibrium.

150   The Political Economy of Trade Policy

rank individuals in decreasing order of their comparative advantage in E production. This comparative advantage denoted by

$$R(n) = h^E(n)/h^M(n) \tag{1}$$

is therefore decreasing in n. Henceforth, we use i to represent individuals in general and use n when we have in mind their ordering according to comparative advantage given by Eq. (1).

Let there be a continuum of individuals in the economy and let their total mass or measure be normalized to unity. In equilibrium, the marginal worker will be indifferent between working in the export and import sectors. Thus, the equilibrium mass of individuals n^* working in the export sector is the solution to the equation

$$R(n) = p \tag{2}$$

and so the equilibrium mass working in the other sector is $1 - n^*$. Fig. 1 illustrates.

Let us assume that individuals have identical Cobb–Douglas preferences, so that each individual has an indirect utility function given by

$$V(p, I) = v(p)I = I/p^\gamma, \tag{3}$$

where γ is the exponent on the consumption of the importable in the Cobb–Douglas utility function.

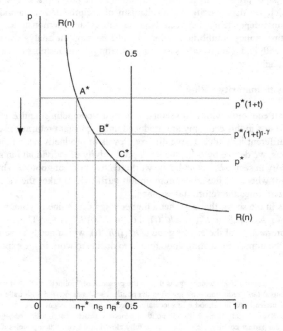

Fig. 1. The political support for a trade reform.

P. Krishna, D. Mitra / Journal of Development Economics 85 (2008) 81–93

85

Ignoring, for now, the issue of tariff revenues and how they are distributed across the population (we return to this in Section 4), it can be shown that individuals in the E sector prior to the reforms unambiguously benefit from these reforms. This is seen from the following inequality:

$$[p^*(1+\bar{t})]^{-\gamma}h^E(i) < p^{*-\gamma}h^E(i), \tag{4}$$

where the left-hand side is the pre-reform utility and the right-hand side is the post-reform utility. Thus, all individuals who remain in the E sector prior to the reforms support reforms.

We compare next the pre- and post-reform utility levels of those individuals who were originally in the M sector and remain there in the post-reform equilibrium. As can be seen from inequality Eq. (5) below, all of them are worse off since the pre-reform utility of such an individual (appearing on the left-hand side of Eq. (5)) is clearly less than the post-reform level (expressed on the right-hand side),

$$[p^*(1+\bar{t})]^{1-\gamma}h^M(i) > p^{*1-\gamma}h^M(i). \tag{5}$$

Finally, we look at the individuals who were in sector M prior to the reforms but are in sector E in the post-reform equilibrium. In other words, they end up moving from M to E, which is the relatively lucrative sector for them after the reforms. Note that given the post-reform relative prices, E might be relatively lucrative but some of those who moved may be worse off relative to their pre-reform situation (in which the domestic relative price was different). Prior to the reform, the utility of such an individual was $[p^*(1+\bar{t})]^{1-\gamma}h^M(i)$ and after the reform, her utility is $p^{*-\gamma} h^E(i)$. It is easy to show that the ranking of the two states is not the same for all individuals who moved at the implementation of reforms. All we know is that for all the people who are in sector E following the reforms, we have

$$p^{*-\gamma}h^E(i) \geq p^{*1-\gamma}h^M(i), \tag{6}$$

that is, post-reform, they are better off in sector E than they would have been in sector M. However, it is possible to have

$$[p^*(1+\bar{t})]^{1-\gamma}h^M(i) > p^{*-\gamma}h^E(i) \geq p^{*1-\gamma}h^M(i) \tag{7}$$

for some of these individuals. Thus, in order to calculate how many people support the reforms we need to solve the equation

$$[p^*(1+\bar{t})]^{1-\gamma}h^M(n) = p^{*-\gamma}h^E(n), \tag{8}$$

which in turn is

$$p^*(1+\bar{t})^{1-\gamma} = R(n). \tag{9}$$

We denote the solution to this equation by n_s, the number of people supporting the reforms.[5]

---

[5] Let n_R^* and n_T^* be the proportion of the population working in the export sector in the reformed and in the tariff-ridden states of the economy respectively. Then, all the n_T^* people that originally were and remain in sector E support the reforms. In addition, $(n_s - n_T^*)$ of the $(n_R^* - n_T^*)$ people moving to E after the reforms also support the reforms.

Next, we see how this support for reforms responds to the world relative price of imports and to the size of the original tariffs. It is easy to see by differentiating the above equation that

$$\frac{\partial n_s}{\partial p^*} = \frac{(1+\bar{t})^{1-\gamma}}{R(n)} < 0 \ \ and \ \ \frac{\partial n_s}{\partial \bar{t}} = \frac{p^*(1-\gamma)(1+\bar{t})^{-\gamma}}{R(n)} < 0. \tag{10}$$

In other words, the support for the reform is decreasing in the world relative price of imports as well as the initial tariff. And so a trade reform takes place when the world price is below a certain threshold. Since, with majority voting, more than half (i.e., $n=0.5$) the voters need to support the reform, this threshold world price is the one that solves the following equation:

$$p^*(1+\bar{t})^{1-\gamma} = R(0.5) \tag{11}$$

With the aid of Fig. 1, we try to illustrate the political support for reforms. Domestic voters, indexed by n, are represented on the x-axis while prices are represented on the y-axis. $R(n)=h^E(n)/h^M(n)$ is the downward sloping curve indicating the relative productivity of workers in the exportable sector. The pre-reform domestic relative price of the importable initially is given by p^* $(1+t)$ and the initial equilibrium is represented by A^*, with workers to the left of A^* allocated to the exportable sector and the rest to the import-competing sector. The post-reform domestic relative price is given by p^* and the post-reform equilibrium is represented by C^*. In other words, after the reform workers to the left of C^* are allocated to the exportable sector and the rest to the import competing sector. As argued above, workers to the left of A^* (i.e., the workers who are always in the export sector, both pre- and post-reform) will always support the reform because for them the reforms just mean a pure terms of trade gain. Workers to the right of C^* (i.e., the workers who are always in the import-competing sector, both pre- and post-reform) will always oppose the reform because for them the reforms are a pure terms of trade loss. The workers in between A^* and C^* (i.e., the workers who were in the import-competing sector prior to the reform but work in export sector after the reform) will be split in their support for the reforms. Everyone to the left of B^* supports the reform and everyone to the right of it is against it. The downward arrow in the figure shows the point of political support for the reform corresponding to the initial (pre-reform) equilibrium. Clearly, the supporters of the reform include people who always work in the export sector and some of the people who, after the reforms, move from the import-competing sector to the export sector. These are the movers who have a greater comparative advantage in producing the export good than the other movers, and therefore find their post-reform position in the export sector relatively more attractive than their pre-reform position in the import-competing sector.

It follows that, with trade policy determined by majority voting, a small country may liberalize its own trade regime in response to the unilateral liberalization of trade undertaken by a large partner country. Fig. 2 illustrates the effects of tariff reductions by a large partner country and an improvement of the world terms of trade in favor of the small home country. The world relative price of the importable goes down as a result from p^* to p'. A^*, B^* and C^* change to A', B' and C' respectively. In other words, the labor allocation to the export sector and therefore output in that sector increase both pre- and post-reform. The support for the reform also increases. Both the world terms of trade and the domestic terms of trade have shifted in favor of the home country's export sector, which makes

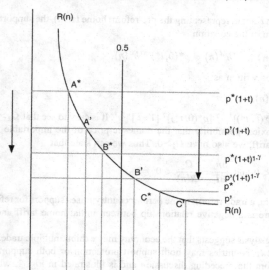

Fig. 2. Comparative statistics: the effect of a change in the world price on the political support for a trade reform.

working in this sector relatively more attractive, which also increases the support for the reform. Liberalization in the partner country, then, can increase support for the lowering of trade barriers from below 50% (at B^*) to above 50% (at B'). Thus reforms in the partner country lead to reforms at home.[6]

3. Large countries: multiple trade policy equilibria

We consider next the case of two large open economies trading with each other. The home country's exportable and importable are E and M, respectively, while it is the reverse for the foreign country. In this case, the world relative price of the importable will be a function of the tariffs of the two countries. If the domestic and foreign tariffs are t and t^* respectively, we have that

$$p^* = p^*(t, t^*) \text{ where } p_1^* < 0, p_2^* > 0,$$ (12)

with p_1^* and p_2^* denoting partial derivatives of p^* with respect to its first and second arguments respectively.

---

[6] Our theoretical result regarding reciprocal reforms at home clearly depends on changes in the terms of trade that come about due to the initial reforms in the partner country. In an interesting study investigating (somewhat analogously) the impact of terms of trade changes on domestic policy, Hanson and Spilimbergo (2001) finds that positive price shocks to sectors in the United States that use "undocumented labor" intensively result in reductions of border enforcement preventing illegal immigration.

88   *P. Krishna, D. Mitra / Journal of Development Economics 85 (2008) 81–93*

In this case (with $\bar{t}$ again representing the pre-reform home tariff), the support for the reform at home is the solution to the equation

$$[p^*(\bar{t}, t^*)(1 + \bar{t})]^{1-\gamma} h^M(n) = p^*(0, t^*)^{-\gamma} h^E(n), \qquad (13)$$

which in turn can be written as

$$\Omega(\bar{t}, t^*) = R(n), \qquad (14)$$

where $\Omega(\bar{t}, t^*) = [p^*(\bar{t}, t^*)]^{1-\gamma} [p^*(0, t^*)]^{\gamma} [1+\bar{t}]^{1-\gamma}$. It is easy to see that $\Omega_2 > 0$ as $p_2^* > 0$. If we rule out the paradoxical possibility that the domestic price of the importable may fall with an increase in home tariff, we also have $\Omega_1 > 0$. Thus we can state that

$$\frac{\partial n_s}{\partial t^*} = \frac{\Omega_2}{R(n)} < 0 \text{ and } \frac{\partial n_s}{\partial \bar{t}} = \frac{\Omega_1}{R(n)} < 0 \qquad (15)$$

In this case, again, a trade reform in the partner country raises support for reforms in the home country. Again there is a negative relationship between initial home tariff and the support for reform.

The preceding analysis suggests that the economy may exhibit multiple trade policy equilibria. Majorities in the two countries may both support protection or both support free trade. This follows directly from the preceding discussion and is illustrated in Fig. 3, where we draw the home tariff as a function of the foreign tariff. If the foreign tariff is very high, there is insufficient support at home for reform and the initial tariff persists. For a foreign tariff below a critical level (given by the solution to the equation $\Omega(\bar{t}, t^*) = R(0.5)$), there is majority support for the reform and the tariff drops to zero. Thus, R (Home) is the home country's reaction function. The foreign

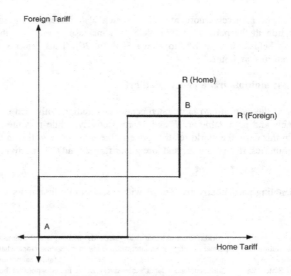

Fig. 3. Multiple Nash equilibria with two large countries.

country's reaction function R (Foreign) conveys the same idea. Fig. 3 shows the possibility of multiple equilibria — either both countries liberalize or both countries remain at their respective initial tariffs. Interestingly, a reform forced on either of these countries (either by a dictatorial leader or a multilateral agency such as the IMF or the World Bank) *against* the will of the majority can result in a popularly supported reciprocal reform in the partner country, which can create popular political support for trade liberalization in the country in which trade reform was imposed.

The intuition underlying the preceding results may be summarized as follows: the popular support for a tariff is decreasing in the world relative price of a country's importable good, which in turn is an increasing function of its partner country's import tariff. Thus, protectionism in the home country undermines support for reform in the partner country, which, in turn, discourages support for reform in the home country. Similarly, when there is no tariff in the home country, the relative price of the importable of the partner country is low and, therefore, the support for reforms increases. This, in turn, results in strong support for reforms in the home country as well.

Two final points about the magnitude of external tariffs are worth emphasizing here. For the case analyzed in Fig. 3, in order to induce a reciprocal tariff reduction by the partner country, the home country's initial tariff reduction has to be large enough. Second, small changes in policy around either equilibrium bring the system back to the equilibrium point (as also implied by Fig. 3). Thus, once the free trade equilibrium has been achieved in both countries, it is a relatively stable outcome. Removal of external pressures for free trade (from say, multilateral organizations, as we have suggested above) will not easily cause these countries to revert to the equilibrium with tariffs.

4. Tariff revenue redistribution

Considering the issue of tariff revenue redistribution does not substantively alter the results. Consider again the case of a small open economy (as modeled in Section 2). As before, we assume that individuals have identical Cobb–Douglas preferences, so that each individual has an indirect utility function given by

$$V(p,I) = v(p)I = I/p^{\gamma}, \ 0 \le \gamma \le 1, \tag{16}$$

where I is the individual's income. Let $\Upsilon(\bar{t}, p^*)$ denote tariff revenue as a proportion of national income (=national factor income plus total tariff revenue). Since tariff revenue is now redistributed in proportion to factor income, individual i's income prior to the reform now is given by $h^E(i)[1 - \Upsilon(\bar{t}, p^*)]^{-1}$ when she works in the export sector and $ph^M(i)[1 - \Upsilon(\bar{t}, p^*)]^{-1}$ if she works in the import-competing sector. Since there is no tariff revenue after reforms, the post-reform incomes are the same as those in the original model. With tariff revenues distributed in proportion to factor incomes, an individual who was originally in the export sector (prior to reforms) will benefit from these reforms if the utility of such an individual prior to these reforms is less than post-reform utility:

$$[p^*(1+\bar{t})]^{-\gamma} h^E(i)[1 - \Upsilon(\bar{t}, p^*)]^{-1} < p^{*-\gamma} h^E(i), \tag{17}$$

which holds when $(1+\bar{t})^{-\gamma}[1 - \Upsilon(\bar{t}, p^*)]^{-1} < 1$, which in turn always holds, for all $\bar{t}$, if $\gamma = 1$, i.e., when everyone consumes only good M. At the other extreme, when $\gamma = 0$, i.e., when everyone consumes only good E, the inequality is reversed. For an intermediate γ, the inequality will hold for a high enough tariff. For instance, it holds when $\bar{t}$ equals the prohibitive tariff since at that tariff $\Upsilon = 0$. However, the minimum tariff at which this inequality will start holding is much lower than the prohibitive tariff. Thus, we assume that the values of γ and $\bar{t}$ are such that the inequality holds and so all individuals who remain in the E sector prior to the reforms support reforms.

Next we look at all those individuals who were originally in the M sector and remain there in the post-reform equilibrium. All of them are worse off since the pre-reform utility of such an individual is greater than the post-reform level, as can be seen from the following inequality:

$$[p^*(1+\bar{t})]^{1-\gamma}h^M(i)[1-\Upsilon(\bar{t},p^*)]^{-1} > p^{*1-\gamma}h^M(i) \tag{18}$$

which always holds as it is always true that $(1+\bar{t})^{1-\gamma}[1-\Upsilon(\bar{t},p^*)]^{-1} > 1$.

Finally, we look at the individuals who were in sector M prior to the reforms but are in sector E in the post-reform equilibrium. Note that, given the post-reform relative prices, E might be relatively lucrative but some of these people may be worse off relative to their pre-reform situation (when the domestic relative price was higher). Prior to the reform, the utility of such an individual was $[p^*(1+\bar{t})]^{1-\gamma}h^M(i)[1-\Upsilon(\bar{t},p^*)]^{-1}$, and after the reform, her utility is $p^{*-\gamma}h^E(i)$. The ranking of the two states is not the same for all individuals who moved with the implementation of reforms. All we know is that for all the people who are in sector E following the reforms, we have

$$p^{*-\gamma}h^E(i) \geq p^{*1-\gamma}h^M(i). \tag{19}$$

However, it is possible to have

$$[p^*(1+\bar{t})]^{1-\gamma}h^M(i)[1-\Upsilon(\bar{t},p^*)]^{-1} > p^{*-\gamma}h^E(i) \geq p^{*1-\gamma}h^M(i) \tag{20}$$

for some of these individuals. Thus, in order to calculate how many people support the reforms we need to solve the equation

$$[p^*(1+\bar{t})]^{1-\gamma}h^M(n)[1-\Upsilon(\bar{t},p^*)]^{-1} = p^{*-\gamma}h^E(n) \tag{21}$$

which in turn may be written as

$$p^*(1+\bar{t})^{1-\gamma}[1-\Upsilon(\bar{t},p^*)]^{-1} = R(n). \tag{22}$$

As before, we denote the solution to this equation by n_s, the number of people supporting the reforms.

Next, we see how this support for reforms responds to the world relative price of imports and to the size of the original tariffs. By differentiating the above equation with respect to p^*, we get

$$\frac{\partial n_s}{\partial p^*} = \frac{(1+\bar{t})^{1-\gamma}[1-\Upsilon(\bar{t},p^*)]^{-1} + p^*(1+\bar{t})^{1-\gamma}[1-\Upsilon(\bar{t},p^*)]^{-2}\Upsilon_2}{R(n)} \tag{23}$$

It is easily shown that $\frac{\partial n_s}{\partial p^*} < 0$ if the elasticity of the tariff revenue share with respect to p^*, i.e., $\varepsilon_{\Upsilon,p^*} = \frac{p^*\Upsilon_2}{\Upsilon} > \frac{-(1-\Upsilon)}{\Upsilon}$.[7] (Here, γ_2 represents the partial derivative of γ with respect to p^*.) The

---

[7] We should note that it is a restriction that is quite easily met in practice. To see this, suppose imports (evaluated exclusive of tariffs) are 5% of national income. Also, suppose the ad valorem tariff rate is 20%. In that case, $\Upsilon = 0.01$ and $\frac{-(1-\Upsilon)}{\Upsilon} = -99$. In this example, for the above derivative to be negative, all we are saying is that if the elasticity $\varepsilon_{\Upsilon,p^*}$ is negative, it should not be more negative than -99. In other words, the reduction in tariff revenue as a proportion of national income as a result of a 1% rise in the world price of the importable should not exceed 99%.

P. Krishna, D. Mitra / Journal of Development Economics 85 (2008) 81–93 91

support for the reform is then decreasing in the world relative price of imports. And so a trade reform takes place when the world price is below a certain threshold price. The threshold world price at which the majority starts supporting reforms is the one that solves the following equation:

$$p^*(1+\overline{t})^{1-\gamma}[1-\Upsilon(\overline{t},p^*)]^{-1} = R(0.5) \tag{24}$$

since n_s decreases with p^* for a given $\overline{t}$, a small enough p^* can make n_s a majority (i.e., $n_s > 0.5$).

We have also considered the case of two large open economies trading with each other allowing for uniform tariff revenue redistribution in both. Under the same condition that $\varepsilon_{\Upsilon,p^*} = \frac{p^* \Upsilon_2}{\Upsilon} > \frac{-(1-\Upsilon)}{\Upsilon}$, it is straightforward to show that $\frac{\partial n_s}{\partial t^*} < 0$. Trade reform in the partner country raises support for reforms in the home country. We therefore obtain the same type of reaction functions and multiple equilibria as in the main model.

5. Endogenous tariffs

So far, the pre-reform tariff $\overline{t}$ has been exogenously (and arbitrarily) specified. In this section, we allow for endogenous determination of the tariff. As before, we develop the analysis without tariff revenue considerations and subsequently analyze the case with tariff revenue redistribution formally modeled.

Consider again the small country case. In the absence of tariff revenue redistribution, since individual utilities are monotonic in tariffs (given sector of employment), we assume (in order to be able to always derive a finite most preferred tariff for the median voter) that there are upper limits on the tariff that can be chosen in equilibrium. In other words, $t \in [0, t^{max}]$, where t^{max} is the maximum permissible tariff, which, say, is the prohibitive tariff (that leads to autarky). If p^* is low, the median individual (in terms of comparative advantage) always lies in sector E and her most preferred tariff is zero, while with high p^*, the median individual always produces M and so her most preferred tariff is t^{max}. Note that the median individual, in such cases, never prefers an interior value of the tariff to both extremes because her utility is monotonic in the tariff.

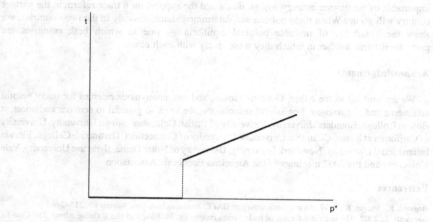

Fig. 4. The tariff as a function of the world relative price of the importable.

Next, we see what happens for intermediate values of p^*. In such cases, for low values of the tariff, the median individual works in the E sector and her utility is decreasing in the tariff. However, at a high enough tariff, she switches sectors and from then on her utility is increasing in the tariff. Since we have a continuum of individuals and we assume that $R(n)$ is continuous in n, the median voter's utility in this intermediate p^* case is a V-shaped function of the tariff and thus she (the median voter) again chooses one of the extreme values. A reduction in p^* will increase her utility under zero tariff and will reduce her utility when the tariff is t^{max}. Thus, a lower world price always makes it more likely that the median voter will choose the zero tariff.

When we extend the analysis with endogenous tariffs to the case of two large countries, multiple trade policy equilibria emerge as a possibility again. Median voters in both countries choose a zero tariff (autarky) or they choose their maximum permissible tariff.

We are also able to endogenize the tariff when tariff revenues are redistributed in proportion to factor incomes. In the case of a small country, placing standard restrictions that result in the concavity of the median voter's objective function and imposing the earlier restriction that $\varepsilon_{T,p^*} = \frac{p^* T_2}{T} > \frac{-(1-T)}{T}$, we have free trade below a cut-off value of p^*, with the equilibrium tariff jumping to a positive value at the cut-off value (and thereafter increasing or decreasing in p^*). One possible case is shown in Fig. 4. If a small country is trading with a large partner, a large enough reduction in this partner's tariff will lead to a large enough decrease in p^* leading, in turn, to a drop to a zero tariff (free trade). This analysis easily extends to the case with two large countries.

6. Conclusions

Can unilateral trade liberalization by one country lead to reciprocal liberalization by its partner in the absence of negotiations? In this paper, we explore this causal linkage between unilateralism and reciprocity in the context of a model in which the decision to carry out a trade reform is determined by its popular political support. In this framework, trade policy changes are voted upon by the public and outcomes are determined by the majority. We demonstrate that unilateral trade liberalization by a trading partner increases the voting support for trade liberalization in the home country. More specifically, if the home country reduces its tariff, the world price of the importable of the partner country will go down and the support for a trade reform in the partner country will go up. When trade policies are determined simultaneously in the two countries, we show the possibility of multiple political equilibria — one in which both countries are protectionist and another in which they trade freely with each other.

Acknowledgements

We are grateful to the editor, Gordon Hanson, and two anonymous referees for many helpful comments and suggestions. For helpful discussions, we are also grateful to seminar audiences at Boston College, Brandeis University, University of British Columbia, Brown University, University of California at Irvine, Columbia University, University of Connecticut, Dartmouth College, Florida International University, New York University, University of Notre Dame, Syracuse University, Yale University and the 2002 meetings of the American Economic Association.

References

Bagwell, K., Staiger, R., 1999. An economic theory of GATT. American Economic Review 89, 215–248.
Bhagwati, J., 2002. The unilateral freeing of trade versus reciprocity. In: Bhagwati (Ed.), Going Alone: The Case for Relaxed Reciprocity in Freeing Trade. MIT Press.

Coates, D., Ludema, R., 1997. Unilateral Trade Liberalization as Leadership in International Trade, Working Paper, Number 97–23, Georgetown University.

Coates, D., Ludema, R., 2001. A theory of trade policy leadership. Journal of Development Economics 65 (1), 1–29.

Fernandez, R., Rodrik, D., 1991. Resistance to reform: status-quo bias in the presence of individual specific uncertainty. American Economic Review 81 (5), 1146–1155.

Forteza, A., Buquet D., Ibarburu, M., Lanzaro, J., Pereyral, A., Siandra, E., Vaillant, M., 2004. Understanding Reform: The Uruguayan Case, Mimeo, Universidad de la Republica, Uruguay.

Hanson, G., Spilimbergo, A., 2001. Political economy, sectoral shocks, and border enforcement. Canadian Journal of Economics 34, 612–638.

Johnson, H., 1953. Optimum tariffs and retaliation. Review of Economic Studies 21, 142–153.

Krishna, P., Mitra, D., 2005. Reciprocated unilateralism in trade policy. Journal of International Economics 65 (2), 461–487.

Mayer, W., 1981. Theoretical considerations on negotiated tariff adjustments. Oxford Economic Papers 33, 135–143.

Mayer, W., 1998. Endogenous corrections of economic policies under majority voting. Finanzarchiv 55 (1), 41–58.

Rodrik, D., 1994. The rush to free trade. Why so late? Why now? Will it last? In: Haggard, S., Webb, S.B. (Eds.), Voting For Reform: Democracy, Political Liberalization, and Economic Adjustment. Oxford University Press, New York.

Part III

Political Contributions Approach
to Endogenous Trade Policy: Empirics

Chapter 9

"PROTECTION FOR SALE" IN A DEVELOPING COUNTRY: DEMOCRACY VS. DICTATORSHIP

Devashish Mitra, Dimitrios D. Thomakos, and Mehmet A. Ulubaşoğlu*

Abstract—For a "genuine" small open economy that has experienced both dictatorship and democracy, we find support for the predictions of the Grossman-Helpman (1994) "Protection for Sale" model. In contrast to previous studies, we use various protection measures (including tariffs, the direct measure of the theoretical model) and perform both single-year and panel regressions. Using Turkish industry-level data, the government's weight on welfare is estimated to be much larger than that on contributions. More importantly, we find that this weight is generally higher for the democratic regime than for dictatorship.

I. Introduction

THE literature on the political economy of trade policy has evolved over the last two decades into two strands, one focusing on majority voting and the other emphasizing special-interest politics. The majority voting approach to trade policy was introduced by Mayer (1984),[1] and the pioneering model in the special-interest strand is Findlay and Wellisz (1982), where the tariff itself is assumed to be an exogenously given function of resources into lobbying by different types of factor owners.[2] Electoral competition was introduced into lobbying models by Magee, Brock, and Young (1989), and Hillman (1989) provided an altogether different approach to modeling special-interest politics by introducing the idea of the "political support" function (which the government maximizes) that incorporates the government's preferential treatment of an organized industry as well as the cost of protecting this industry given by the excess burden on society.

Following this path, the special interest literature on trade policy has evolved into the state-of-the-art Grossman and Helpman (1994) "Protection for Sale" model.[3] This model is path-breaking for several reasons. Firstly, its framework is multisectoral. Secondly, it provides microfoundations to the behavior of lobbies and politicians. The government's objective function is a weighted sum of political contributions and aggregate welfare, and each lobby maximizes its welfare net of political contributions. Most importantly, the level of protection is derived as an estimable function of industry characteristics and other political and economic factors.

Two recent empirical papers, Goldberg and Maggi (1999) and Gawande and Bandyopadhyay (2000) estimate the Grossman-Helpman protection expressions using industry-level data from the United States.[4,5] The two papers are similar in the questions they address, but they are somewhat different in the details of their approaches. Whereas Goldberg and Maggi restrict focus on the protection expressions, Gawande and Bandyopadhyay concentrate more on the lobbying aspects and the determinants of the magnitude of contributions. Goldberg and Maggi use the basic Grossman-Helpman framework, whereas Gawande and Bandopadhyay introduce intermediate goods. The econometric specifications are somewhat different in the two papers. However, the results from both these papers are very similar in that they find that the weight on aggregate welfare in the government's objective function is several times higher than that on contributions. As predicted by the Grossman-Helpman model, both papers find that protection to organized sectors is negatively related to import penetration and the (absolute value of) import demand elasticity, while protection to unorganized sectors is positively related to these two variables.

We investigate these Grossman-Helpman predictions using industry-level data from Turkey. Our paper differs from the existing papers in the literature in the following respects. (i) We look at the cross-industry protection levels in a developing country for four different years in the period 1983 to 1990 (as opposed to a developed country for a single year). (ii) Our data set spans both dictatorial and democratic regimes. (iii) We use a variety of protection measures: nominal protection rates (the direct measure suggested by the theoretical model), effective protection rates

Received for publication July 11, 2000. Revision accepted for publication May 30, 2001.

* Syracuse University and NBER, Florida International University, and Deakin University, Australia, respectively.

We are indebted to Gene Grossman for detailed comments and suggestions on an earlier draft. We also thank two anonymous referees and the co-editor, Jim Campbell, whose comments improved the quality of the paper. Halis Akder, Adolf Buse, Don Davis, Cem Karayalçin, Euysung Kim, Pravin Krishna, Chris Magee, John McLaren, Paul Pecorino, and seminar participants at the International Atlantic Society Conference (Charleston S.C.), the Southern Economic Association Meetings (Washington D.C.), Florida International University, and the University of Alberta provided useful comments. Thanks are also due to Abdullah Akyüz and Giyas Gökkent who provided some of the data used in the paper. The standard disclaimer applies.

[1] The Mayer (1984) framework has been extended to the issue of the choice of instruments in a series of papers by Mayer and Riezman (1987, 1989, 1990).

[2] Papers using a similar approach are Feenstra and Bhagwati (1982) and Rodrik (1986).

[3] The basic framework of Grossman and Helpman (1994) has been used to analyze issues of trade negotiations and free trade areas in Grossman and Helpman (1995a, 1995b), commitment to trade agreements by Maggi and Rodriguez-Clare (1998), issues of lobby formation by Mitra (1999), and the relationship between lobby formation and reciprocity in trade policy in Krishna and Mitra (2000).

[4] There is a recent unpublished paper by McCalman (2000) that empirically investigates the "Protection for Sale" model for Australia for two separate years (1968–1969 and 1991–1992) and, unlike the two papers on the United States, focuses on tariffs (and not on NTB coverage ratios). Again, McCalman finds the model to be consistent with the data. He is also able to analyze the endogeneity of the Australian trade liberalization and attributes it to the increase in the fraction of the population that is politically organized and the government's weight on welfare relative to contributions.

[5] Other empirical papers investigating endogenous trade policy issues (but outside the Grossman-Helpman framework) are Baldwin (1985), Trefler (1993), Ray (1981), and Gawande (1997a, 1997b, 1998).

The Review of Economics and Statistics, August 2002, 84(3): 497–508
© 2002 by the President and Fellows of Harvard College and the Massachusetts Institute of Technology

and NTB coverage ratios (the measure used in the previous studies on the United States). (iv) We perform cross-sectional analysis for each year separately as well as panel regressions for the entire time span.

We find strong support for the validity of the fundamental predictions of the Grossman-Helpman "Protection for Sale" model. As in the previous studies, the government's weight on welfare is estimated to be much larger than that on contributions. Additionally, this weight on welfare is higher for the democratic regime than for dictatorship.

In this context, it is useful to discuss the rationale for our particular choice of country. Firstly, the Grossman-Helpman (1994) "Protection for Sale" model makes a "small, open economy" assumption that is certainly more apt for Turkey than for the United States.

Secondly, the use of Turkish data can tell us something about the applicability of this model to a developing country. In almost any country, interest-group contributions (although well documented only in the United States) are an integral part of the political environment. They are made mainly to finance election campaigns or take the form of bribes to politicians and other key government officials. In Turkey, there have been newspaper reports of well-known industrialists contributing in various forms to election campaigns.[6] Such support has included even the provision of personal airplanes and helicopters.[7] Further, in local newspaper reports, we find allegations of politicians accepting bribes in exchange for help in obtaining government contracts.

Going back to the choice of country, the third issue is the applicability of the "Protection for Sale" framework across different political systems. Turkey has had both dictatorial and democratic regimes and our data set spans both these regimes. In a democracy, on the one hand, there is need for political contributions as governments need to spend on advertising (campaigns) to get reelected. On the other hand, there is a cost of receiving political contributions because in exchange the government has to provide preferential treatment to the donors even if that leads to a reduction in average welfare or the quality of life. In dictatorships, the need for such contributions is lower, but the affinity for contributions (on the part of the ruler) may still exist.[8]

[6] For example, the daily newspaper *Milliyet* had a report on September 3, 1991, about some top businessmen (Kamhi, Boyner, Ekinci, Alaton, and Bodur) providing substantial support in different forms for the election campaign of the Motherland-True Path Party coalition.

[7] For instance, there are reports that Cavit Caglar, a well-known textile producer, provided an airplane and two helicopters for the election campaign of Suleyman Demirel, the president of the True Path Party.

[8] Grossman and Helpman (1994) write "Organized interest groups are able to offer political contributions, which politicians value for their potential use in the coming election (and perhaps otherwise)" (p. 834). It is this "perhaps otherwise" component that might be fairly important in dictatorships, and dictators might, for their own benefit, want to auction off policies. Often dictators also might rely on the support of politically and economically powerful individuals and groups for their existence. In return, they have to provide these powerful individuals or groups with different kinds of concessions. Thus, Grossman and Helpman (1994) write "Such an objective function seems plausible for a government that is

Additionally, the dictator may not need to care as much about the contributions-welfare tradeoff. Therefore, what kind of political system would assign a greater weight to welfare relative to contributions is an important empirical question.

Extensive data on different measures of protection, import penetration, import-demand elasticities, and so on are available for Turkey. Because no data were available on trade-related (or other) political contributions, we determine whether sectors are politically organized from the membership data for the Turkish Industrialists and Businessmen Association (TUSIAD) and then statistically validate this determination using classification methods based on discriminant analysis.

Besides the use of classification methods in constructing the political organization variable, our paper features a few other methodological advances. We depart from the estimated linear specifications of the previous studies and directly estimate, using nonlinear methods, the parameters (and their standard errors) in the structural equation of interest. The availability of data on a large number of exogenous (instrumental) variables enables us to perform nonlinear 2SLS. Allowing for year-specific effects, we also estimate (by both nonlinear 2SLS as well as generalized method of moments (GMM)) our structural parameters for the data pooled across years. Some hypotheses of economic interest, involving the structural parameters, are also tested.

In section II, we discuss the theoretical framework. The econometric methodology is presented in section III. Section IV describes the data and their sources. In section V, we present the results of our estimation. Finally, section VI concludes.

II. Theoretical Framework

In this section, we provide an abridged description of the "Protection for Sale" model of Grossman and Helpman (1994).

Consider a small, open economy. Individuals are assumed to have identical preferences. Each individual possesses labor and at most one kind of specific factor of production. There are N nonnumeraire goods, each requiring a different kind of factor of production specific to that good and labor. In addition, there is a numeraire good that is produced under constant returns to scale using only labor. A quasi-linear utility function (linear in numeraire good consumption, concave in the consumption of each nonnumeraire good, and additively separable across all goods) is assumed.

It is also assumed that the only policy instruments available to politicians are trade taxes and subsidies. Further, the government redistributes revenue uniformly to all its citizens.

In sectors that are politically organized, the specific-factor owners are able to lobby the government for prefer-

concerned about the next election, but *broader interpretations* [emphasis added] also are possible" (p. 836).

ential treatment in the form of higher trade protection for their own sectors and lower protection for other sectors. The interaction between the government and the lobbies takes the form of a "menu auction" as in Bernheim and Whinston (1986). Thus, we have the following two-stage game.

In the first stage, lobbies provide the government with their contribution schedules taking into account the government's objective function (described later). Each lobby takes the contribution schedules of other lobbies as given.

In the second stage, taking into account the contribution or offer schedules from the previous stage, the government sets trade policy to maximize a weighted sum of political contributions and overall social welfare.

The government's objective function is

$$\Omega_G(p) = \sum_{j \in \Lambda} C_j(p) + a\Omega_A(p), \qquad (1)$$

where Λ is the set of organized interest groups (lobbies),
$p \in P$ is the domestic price vector,
$\Omega_A(p)$ is aggregate social welfare,
$C_j(p)$ is the contribution schedule of the jth lobby and,
P is the set of domestic price vectors from which the government may choose.

The set P is bounded such that each domestic price lies between some minimum and some maximum value. Grossman and Helpman (1994) restrict attention to equilibria that lie in the interior of P. The parameter a in equation (1) is the weight that the government attaches to aggregate social welfare relative to political contributions. The higher a, the lower is the government's affinity for political contributions and the higher is its concern for social welfare.

Grossman and Helpman show that, with contribution schedules that are continuous in the price vector in the neighborhood of the equilibrium, the government's problem of choosing its most preferred tariff vector (on receiving all the contribution schedules) is equivalent to maximizing the following function with respect to the domestic price vector p:

$$\sum_{j \in \Lambda} \Omega_j(p) + a\Omega_A(p), \qquad (2)$$

where $\Omega_j(p)$ is welfare of sector j.[9] This maximization yields trade taxes and subsidies that satisfy the following, familiar Grossman-Helpman modified "Ramsey Rule":

$$\frac{t_i}{1 + t_i} = \frac{I_i - \alpha_L}{a + \alpha_L} \cdot \frac{z_i}{e_i} \qquad (3)$$

[9] This new reduced-form maximand is an additively separable form of the more general Hillman (1989) political support function; that is, Grossman and Helpman (1994) provide microfoundations for models that use the political support function approach. Alternatively, in Goldberg and Maggi (1999) and Maggi and Rodriguez-Clare (1998), the interaction between the government and lobbies is modeled as a Nash bargaining game over trade policy and contributions.

where z_i is the ratio of domestic output to imports or exports (depending on whether the sector is import competing or an exporting one),
e_i is the absolute value of price elasticity of import demand or export supply,
I_i is an indicator variable that takes a value 1 if the sector is politically organized and 0 for an unorganized sector, and
α_L is the proportion of the country's population that is organized.

This tariff expression can be written as the following empirically estimable form:

$$\frac{t_i}{1 + t_i} = \frac{1}{a + \alpha_L} \left[I_i \cdot \left(\frac{z_i}{e_i} \right) \right] - \frac{\alpha_L}{a + \alpha_L} \left[\frac{z_i}{e_i} \right] \qquad (4)$$

Because $a \in [0, \infty)$ and $\alpha_L \in [0, 1]$, the coefficient of $[I_i \cdot (z_i/e_i)]$ should be positive and that of (z_i/e_i) should be negative. Also, the coefficient of the former is larger in magnitude than the latter. This means that the protection is increasing in (z_i/e_i) for an organized industry, but decreasing in (z_i/e_i) in the case of an unorganized sector. In fact, in the theoretical model, organized sectors are given positive protection, whereas unorganized sectors are exploited through negative protection (which will be modified in the empirical model through the use of a constant term). Thus, there is deviation from free trade in opposite directions for organized and unorganized sectors, and the size of this deviation is increasing in (z_i/e_i) because (i) the deadweight costs of this deviation are increasing in the magnitude of the trade elasticities, (ii) the benefits to lobbies from protection are higher if their output levels are higher, and (iii) the costs of deviation from free trade are lower, the lower is the volume of actual and potential trade.

Because, in Turkish agriculture, median voter as well as political support concerns other than contributions could be important in determining tariffs, we also experiment with the following specification:

$$\frac{t_i}{1 + t_i} = \frac{1}{a + \alpha_L} \left[I_i \cdot \left(\frac{z_i}{e_i} \right) \right] - \frac{\alpha_L}{a + \alpha_L} \left[\frac{z_i}{e_i} \right] + \beta \left[I_{Ai} \cdot \left(\frac{z_i}{e_i} \right) \right], \qquad (5)$$

where I_{Ai} takes the value 1 if sector i is agricultural and 0 otherwise. β, thus, captures the populist protection to agriculture, which was viewed as a large source of votes.[10] Further, this specification takes care of mistakes made in our judgment of whether agricultural sectors are organized.

[10] Helpman (1995) shows how median-voter and political-support forces can affect tariffs within the kind of multisectoral, specific-factors framework presented in this paper. He shows that $\left(\frac{z_i}{e_i} \right)$ is still the main determinant of a sector's tariff under those forces.

III. Econometric Methodology

We deviate from Goldberg and Maggi (1999) and Gawande and Bandyopadhyay (2000) in that we directly estimate the structural coefficients and their standard errors by putting the estimation problem in its appropriate nonlinear regression form.[11] Although the linear regressions considered in the previous papers are appealing and straightforward to implement, the additional computational cost of directly estimating the structural coefficients is minimal. Moreover, we can immediately obtain the appropriate standard errors for the structural coefficients.

In proceeding, we are faced with two alternatives: we could either keep the elasticity in the tariff expression on the right-hand side, as in Gawande and Bandyopadhyay, or transfer it to the left-hand side, as in Goldberg and Maggi. For the Turkish data, we feel we are better off with the import-demand elasticity on the right-hand side for the following two reasons:

• Our elasticity estimates are estimated with much greater precision (lower measurement error), almost all of them being significant at the 1% through 5% significance levels. In addition, the presence of any remaining measurement error is handled through the use of instrumental variables in estimation, as explained later.
• Only when we keep the elasticity on the right-hand side do we have a consistent set of instrumental variables as we move from one year to another.

We next give a brief description of the model we estimate in this paper.

A. Single Year Estimation

Let $\theta_j = (c_j, \alpha_{Lj}, a_j)'$ be the (3×1) vector of structural parameters of the model for year j, where c_j is the constant term. Let $y_{ij} = t_{ij}/(1 + t_{ij})$ denote the left-side variable, for sector i and year j, and $x_{ij} = \{1, [I_i \cdot (z_{ij}/e_{ij})], (z_{ij}/e_{ij})\}$ be the (1×3) vector of explanatory variables. We denote by $g(x_{ij}; \theta)$ the right-side nonlinear function

$$g(x_{ij}, \theta_j) = c_j + \frac{1}{a_j + \alpha_{Lj}} \left[I_i \cdot \left(\frac{z_{ij}}{e_{ij}} \right) \right]$$
$$- \frac{\alpha_{Lj}}{a_j + \alpha_{Lj}} \left[\frac{z_{ij}}{e_{ij}} \right] \tag{6}$$

so that the estimable equation has a standard nonlinear regression format with additive errors:

$$y_{ij} = g(x_{ij}, \theta_j) + u_{ij}. \tag{7}$$

$\{u_{ij}\}_{i=1}^{x=37}$ is the regression error term that captures possible measurement errors in the right-side variables, as well as

[11] As can be seen from equation (4), the right-side expression is nonlinear in both variables and parameters.

other factors (outside the theoretical model) that affect the determination of the tariff.

Equation (7) cannot be estimated by nonlinear least squares because the right-side variables may be correlated with the regression error term because of the endogeneity of our right-side variables (z, e, and I) with respect to the tariff (see Goldberg and Maggi (1999), Mitra (1999), and Gawande and Bandyopadhyay (2000)), and also because of the measurement error associated with the political organization variable, I (from the possibility of misclassification) and the import demand elasticity, e (because it is estimated). Both the problem of endogeneity and measurement error of the right-side variables can be handled by using instrumental variables. These should be variables that are correlated with the right-side variables themselves but not correlated with the regression error. Shifts and rotations of the import demand function will affect both the import demand elasticity and the import penetration ratio, at any given tariff. Thus, we try to identify such shift variables affecting import demand. These variables include different forms of domestic (nontrade) governmental concessions, sector-specific minimum wages, incentives to freight, and so on. As regards the organization indicator, I, the degree of unionization may be an important determinant of the political organization of skilled workers (owners of sector-specific human capital) in any sector. Besides, as lobby formation costs are sunk in nature, import growth (by helping the formation of expectations regarding the future intensity of import competition) may also determine I.[12] It is important to note in this context that no existing theory suggests that any of the preceding instrumental variables are either endogenous to the tariff or are the determinants of the tariff missing from the right-side of the regression equation (7). Also, these instruments are correlated with the true values of the right-side variables (and are not expected to be correlated with any of the measurement errors). Finally, and very importantly, after estimation we perform the appropriate test for the validity of our instruments (see following).

Thus, the preceding regression is estimated by nonlinear two-stage least squares (NL2SLS)[13] so as to retrieve an estimator of θ_j directly, say $\hat{\theta}_{jn}$. Let y_j denote the $(n \times 1)$ vector of observations of the left-side variable, X_j denote the $(n \times 3)$ matrix of observations of the right-side variables, and W_j denote the $(n \times k)$ matrix of instrumental variables.[14]

[12] Decisions to get politically organized are based on the expected magnitude of protection on being organized relative to that on remaining unorganized. Thus, because z and e determine protection, the determinants of z and e will also determine I.

[13] See chapter 7 and 17 of Davidson and McKinnon (1993) or chapter 6 of Dhrymes (1994) for textbook discussions on estimation and testing of nonlinear regression models using NL2SLS and GMM.

[14] Standard practice in NL2SLS does not restrict the list of instrumental variables used in estimation to the levels of the instruments, but permits the use of their squares and cross-products as well. We follow this practice: using a small set of exogenous variables as instruments, almost exclusively levels and squares, is sufficient for producing economically meaningful results across all years.

Finally, let $\Theta \subseteq R^3$ denote the admissible parameter space. The estimator $\hat{\theta}_{jn}$ is then obtained as

$$Q_n(y_j, X_j; \hat{\theta}_{jn}) = \inf_{\theta \in \Theta} \{[y_j - g(X_j; \theta_j)]' W_j (W_j' W_j)^{-1} \\ \times W_j'[y_j - g(X_j; \theta_j)]\}. \tag{8}$$

The corresponding standard errors of $\hat{\theta}_{jn}$ are obtained from the diagonal elements of the estimated covariance matrix of $\hat{\theta}_{jn}$,

$$\text{Est. Cov } (\hat{\theta}_{jn}) = \hat{\sigma}_j^2 G_j(\hat{\theta}_{jn})' W_j (W_j' W_j)^{-1} W_j' G_j(\hat{\theta}_{jn}), \tag{9}$$

where $\hat{\sigma}_j^2$ is the estimated residual variance and $G_j(\hat{\theta}_{jn})$ is the $(n \times 3)$ Jacobian matrix of $g(X_j; \theta_j)$ evaluated at $\hat{\theta}_{jn}$.

With enough instruments at our disposal ($k > \#$ parameters to be estimated $= 3$), all equations are overidentified. Thus, after estimation, we test whether the $k - 3$ additional instrumental variables are correlated with the regression error term. The (overidentification) test statistic is given by nR_u^2, where R_u^2 is the coefficient of determination of an auxilliary LS regression of the estimated NL2SLS residuals $\hat{u}_{ij} = y_{ij} - g(x_{ij}, \hat{\theta}_{jn})$ on the matrix of instrumental variables W_j. The statistic is distributed as χ_{k-3}^2.[15]

Some hypotheses of interest were tested after estimation. We summarize these hypotheses here.

1. $H_0(1) : 1/a_j = 0$, an approximate test of the hypothesis that the government maximizes aggregate welfare and that the composite coefficient of $I_i(z_{ij}/e_{ij})$ is significant. Note that this hypothesis is equivalent to the hypothesis $H_0'(1) : 1/(a_j + \alpha_{Lj}) = 0$, contingent on α_{Lj} lying in the relevant economic range of $[0, 1]$.[16]
2. $H_0(2) : \alpha_L/(a_j + \alpha_{Lj}) = 0$, a test for the hypothesis that the composite coefficient of (z_{ij}/e_{ij}) is significant. Note that this test is affected by both the value of α_{Lj} and a_j; a large a_j will tend to reduce the value of the composite coefficient independently of the value of α_{Lj}.
3. $H_0(3) : \alpha_{Lj} = 0$ and $1/a_j = 0$, a (joint) test for the significance of the model. This is the most appropriate test in examining the joint significance of the composite coefficients of (z_{ij}/e_{ij}) and $I_i(z_{ij}/e_{ij})$.

All hypotheses involve nonlinear restrictions and were tested using a Wald-type test statistic.[17]

B. Panel Estimation

As a final step in our empirical analysis, we estimated the specification of equation (7) by pooling our data across years and including year dummy variables using a common list of instruments for all years, presented as NL2SLS(DV) in our tables, and by using panel fixed-effects NL2SLS and GMM estimation with year-specific instruments, to account both for year-specific intercepts and year-specific error variances (presented as NL2SLS (FE-SI) and GMM (FE-SI), respectively).[18]

We define the vector of year dummies, D_{ij}, with corresponding coefficient vector, δ. We excluded 1983 (the dictatorship year) from the dummy variable list so that the dummy coefficients represent contrasts with respect to that year. Let $\beta = (\theta', \delta')'$ denote the new coefficient vector. Equation (7) can now be rewritten as

$$y_{ij} = g^*(x_{ij}, D_{ij}; \beta) + u_{ij}, \tag{10}$$

where $g^*(x_{ij}, D_{ij}; \beta) = g(x_{ij}; \theta) + D_{ij}\delta$.

Estimation of equation (10) by pooled NL2SLS (DV) is based on the same objective function as in equation (8) by defining W to denote the common instrumental variables matrix. For the panel NL2SLS (FE-SI), estimation is based on the same objective function as in equation (8), but we now define W as the block diagonal matrix $W = \text{diag} (W_{1983}, W_{1984}, W_{1988}, W_{1990})$ and we substitute (y, X) for (y_j, X_j), where $y = (y'_{1983}, y'_{1984}, y'_{1988}, y'_{1990})'$ and $X = (X'_{1983}, X'_{1984}, X'_{1988}, X'_{1990})'$. Letting $B \subseteq R^6$ denote the new admissible parameter space, the panel-GMM estimator, $\hat{\beta}_n$ is obtained as

$$Q_n^*(y, X, D; \hat{\beta}_n) = \inf_{\beta \in B} \{[y - g^*(X, D; \beta)]' WV^{-1} \\ \times W'[y - g^*(X, D; \beta)]\}, \tag{11}$$

where now W is as in the case of panel NL2SLS (FE-SI).[19]

---

[15] The acceptance of the null hypothesis effectively supports lack of correlation of any of the instrumental variables with the regression error.

[16] Note that the distribution of the relevant test statistic is well defined. What is being tested is whether a_j is large enough so that its reciprocal $1/a_j$ is statistically indistinguishable from 0 (even though this reciprocal cannot take the value 0 for any finite a_j).

[17] Let $R(\theta_j) = 0$ denote the nonlinear function imposing J restrictions, and let $r(\theta_j) = \partial R(\theta_j)/\partial \theta_j$. The actual test statistic takes the following form:

$$\mathcal{W}_{jn} = (n/J) R(\hat{\theta}_{jn})' [r(\hat{\theta}_{jn}) \text{Est. Cov } (\hat{\theta}_{jn}) r(\hat{\theta}_{jn})']^{-1} R(\hat{\theta}_{jn}),$$

whose values we can compare to the critical values from the $F_{(J, n-3)}$ distribution. For a single restriction $J = 1$, we have that $\sqrt{\mathcal{W}_{jn}}$ has an asymptotic standard normal distribution.

[18] The list of instruments used in estimating the pooled equation with dummy variables includes the (union of the) exogenous variables and their squares used in single-year equations as well as some cross products of these variables, pooled across years. On the other hand, the list of instruments used in estimating the other panel equations include the year-specific instrumental variables used in single-year equations.

[19] In the case of FE-SI regressions, we report the coefficients of four year-specific constants instead of a constant and the coefficients on three year dummy variables, as in the case of the DV regressions.

The weighting matrix V is the covariance of the moment restriction; that is,

$$V = E(W'[y - g^*(X, D; \beta)][y - g^*(X, D; \beta)]'W),$$

where we use White's heteroskedastic covariance matrix estimator in obtaining an estimate of V, to account for different error variances, σ_j^2, across years.

IV. Data

We need data on imports and output to calculate the import penetration ratio. Data on imports are obtained from the *UN International Trade Statistics Yearbook* (various issues), and those on domestic output are obtained from the *U.N. Statistical Yearbook* (various issues), *Monthly Bulletin of Statistics* (various issues), the web site of the *U.N. Food and Agriculture Organization* (http://www.fao.org), *OECD Industrial Structure Statistics* (various issues), and *U.N. Industrial Statistics Yearbook* (various issues).[20]

Import-demand elasticities for thirteen of the 37 product categories in our study are directly obtained from Thomakos and Ulubaşoğlu (2000), who followed the methodology of Shiells, Stern, and Deardorff (1986). The remaining 24 elasticities were estimated for this study with the same techniques as in Thomakos and Ulubaşoğlu.

Data on nominal rates of protection (NRP), effective rates of protection (ERP), and non-tariff barrier coverage ratios (NTB) are obtained from Togan (1994).[21]

As explained in subsection IIIA, our estimating equation requires instrumental variables due to the endogeneity/measurement error of the right-side variables. We generally have a common set of instruments for all years. This set consists of unionization, hourly wage,[22] index of intra-industry trade, incentives to freight, nominal and effective subsidies (unrelated to trade protection), and specific components of nominal subsidies for each year subject to availability.[23] More precisely, effective subsidy data is not

available for 1988. Labor unions were banned until 1983, and, as one would expect, were effectively nonexistent in 1984. Thus, unionization is not there in the list of instruments for those two years. Incentives to freight are available for only 1988. Finally, the index of intra-industry trade is not available for 1990.

Unionization data (UNION) are for 1994 and used for each year except 1983 and 1984 (when unionization was nonexistent). They are obtained from the Household Labor Force Survey of Turkish State Institute of Statistics (SIS) (http://www.die.gov.tr).

The data on nominal hourly wage rate in each industry are obtained for 1994 from the Employment and Wage Structure Survey of SIS. The nominal wages for other years are constructed from the 1994 data by adjusting it using the inflation rate (based on the GDP deflator), as each year workers' wages are increased based on inflation.

The data on nominal subsidies (and some components), effective subsidies (modified),[24] index of intra-industry trade, and import growth are from Togan (1994).

A. Construction of the Political Organization Variable

Because no data were available on trade-related (or other) political contributions, the political organization dummy variable is constructed by other means. Our approach involves two steps: in the first step, membership data for the Turkish Industrialists and Businessmen Association (TUSIAD) are obtained,[25] and an initial determination of organized sectors is made. In the second step, we use discriminant analysis methods to statistically validate the choice made in the first step.[26] We next describe each step in some detail.

After mapping individual members of TUSIAD to their respective sectors, we count the members per sector. Using a cutoff of at least five members, we classify twelve of the 37 sectors as organized.[27] We then augment this list by an additional four sectors with fewer than five members each

---

[20] It is important to note here that we are covering 86.2% of all imports of 1990.

[21] NRP is the total customs duties plus other charges and expenses related to imports divided by the c.i.f. value of the imports of a particular commodity. ERP is the percentage increase in value added solely due to the presence of import protection measures (both on output and inputs). Finally, NTB is the share of imports "subject to permission" in sectoral imports.

[22] In the Grossman-Helpman (1994) model, the wage rate is exogenous to protection, as it is solely determined by the technology of the Ricardian numeraire sector. As explained later in this section, we use nominal wages that (especially in developing countries) are determined through minimum-wage legislation, which in turn depends on the cost of subsistence.

[23] Except for the case in which a complete system of structural equations is specified, finding appropriate variables to serve as instruments is a difficult problem. Although economists can write new models in which they endogenize variables that were previously treated as exogenous, we strictly follow the Grossman-Helpman model to set our minimum standards in classifying variables as endogenous or exogenous. Thus, as in the Grossman-Helpman model, all policies or incentives other than trade protection are treated as exogenous to the model. In fact, all the variables that we use as instruments are truly exogenous in the context of the Grossman-Helpman model. This is in contrast to the choice of instrumen-

tal variables in the existing empirical literature on endogenous trade protection. For example, in Goldberg and Maggi (1999) and Gawande and Bandyopadhyay (2000), the list of exogenous variables includes factor shares, sectoral unemployment, sectoral employment size, output growth, firm scale, and so on that can be considered "somewhat endogenous," even purely in the context of the Grossman-Helpman model.

[24] We construct purely nonimport protection effective subsidy rates that capture the relative increase in value added solely through domestic subsidies or incentives (over the value added in the absence, solely, of these measures) from those presented by Togan (1994), which effectively combine the effective rate of protection with the nonimport protection effective subsidy rate.

[25] We are grateful to Mr. Abdullah Akyuz, the Washington DC representative of TUSIAD, for his generosity in providing us with the list of TUSIAD members.

[26] TUSIAD is a private organization consisting of 470 individual members that hold business positions in a variety of sectors. Large import-competing firms are heavily represented. The organization is very active in Turkish public life, and some of its members are household names. It has representative offices in Washington DC and Brussels and publishes its own newsletter and quarterly economic survey.

[27] The cutoff point has been selected by looking at the frequency tabulation of members per sector.

but whose members are well known for their political and economic clout (based on national newspaper reports).

Because this choice of organized sectors contains elements of subjective judgment, we next examine whether our choice could somehow be statistically validated. We try two alternative methods: discriminant analysis and probit regressions. We see which sectors were ex ante misclassified and calculate the classification error.

A brief summary of the discriminant analysis procedure that we use is as follows. The overall set of all sectors is partitioned into two subsets: subset 1 (organized) and subset 2 (unorganized) based on TUSIAD membership data as explained previously. There is theoretical literature that deals with the (measurable) characteristics that are correlated with whether a sector is organized or unorganized. These measurable characteristics are in most cases the determinants of protection (z and e) and protection itself.[28] In addition, we use other measurable characteristics (that determine the extent of ease or difficulty in organizing): namely four-firm concentration ratios, the data for which have been obtained from the SIS Web site. Therefore, based on the sample means and correlations of all these characteristics of organized and unorganized subsets respectively, we estimate their multivariate normal joint density functions separately for the organized population (of sectors) and for the unorganized population. For our initial classification/partitioning (based on TUSIAD membership data) to be validated, the two joint density functions and their respective estimated parameter vectors should be significantly different (which is what we check in this analysis). To compute the extent of error in our classification, we use a two-stage procedure. Based on the two estimated density functions, we first perform a new ex post classification and compare this new one with our ex ante classification whose percentage error we then calculate.

In general, the discriminant analysis results support our ex ante choice of politically organized sectors, with an average ex post apparent error rate of less than 23%, which is fairly small for a sample size of 37 sectors.[29]

We also used some probit regressions to further scrutinize our classification. The dependent variable was the political organization dummy, and the right-side variables were the import penetration ratio and the import demand elasticity, both purely import-related variables. The variables are jointly significant and have the expected signs (negative for both the import demand elasticity, e, and the import penetration ratio, $1/z$, e being individually significant at the 1%

through 5% levels for the last two years and the 5% through 10% levels for the first two years. We then construct an ex post classification by categorizing a sector as organized if the predicted probability of being organized (using the estimated probit regression) is 0.6 or higher. The average percentage error (from misclassification) in this case is around 26.75% and was as low as 24% for 1983 and 1990.

We also do some sensitivity analysis in which we replace in our main tariff regressions the ex ante data on political organization with the ex post classification from our discriminant analysis and our probit regressions. The results are discussed in the section on sensitivity analysis.

V. Results

As explained in section III, we estimate a and α_L, our parameters of interest directly using nonlinear 2SLS and GMM. We present year-specific as well as pooled/panel regressions. We have one set of pooled regressions that includes all years and another one that has all years except 1983. We present results obtained with NRP in considerable detail and then outline the main results with ERP and NTB.

A. Results with NRP

Table 1 presents our results with NRP/(1 + NRP) as the dependent variable. In other words, NRP is the empirical measure of t in our equilibrium tariff equation. As can be clearly seen, for all single-year equations, α_L is very tightly estimated, in all cases significant at the 1% through 5% levels, except for 1984. As has been explained in section II, α_L is the proportion of the population that is politically organized. Barring 1984, our estimates of α_L lie in the range of 0.65 to 0.80, implying that 65% to 80% of the population was politically organized. Note that these estimates lie in the economically meaningful range (0, 1), although no such restrictions were placed during estimation. For 1984, we have a very low figure of 0.29, but it is just marginally significant. The 95% confidence interval permits a value of α_L up to 0.76, whereas the corresponding value with a 90% interval is 0.69. All these estimates of α_L are much lower than the 88% and 95% obtained, respectively, by Goldberg and Maggi (1999) and Gawande and Bandyopadhyay (2000) for the United States. Our estimates of a (the weight on welfare relative to contributions) for the single-year equations are fairly precise, although not as tight as those of α_L. These estimates for various years lie in the range 76 through 104. These figures look quite high, but they are comparable to those of Goldberg and Maggi (1999) for the United States and are far lower than those of Gawande and Bandyopadhyay (2000).[30] The high magnitude of the

---

[28] The expected protection on being organized and the protection on remaining unorganized are important determinants of whether members of a sector decide to get organized. (See Mitra (1999).) Holding all other characteristics constant, there should be a substantial difference between protection received by an organized sector and that received by an unorganized sector with the same set of other characteristics.

[29] It is interesting to note that across years almost all of the organized sectors were correctly classified, so that missclassification occurred almost exclusively in sectors that we characterized as unorganized.

[30] Goldberg and Maggi obtain a value of $\beta = a/(1 + a)$ that equals 0.986, which implies an estimated a equal to 70, whereas Gawande and Bandyopadhyay obtain an estimated a equal to 3,175. McCalman (2000) has estimates in the range of 41 to 47. Note that, for our results, the t-ratio associated with Goldberg and Maggi's β is given by $(1 + a)$ times the

Table 1.—Estimation Results for NRP/(1 + NRP) equation

			Single Year Results (NL2SLS)			
Year	c	α_L	a	D_{84}	D_{88}	D_{90}
1983	0.36***	0.65***	76.30*	n.a.	n.a.	n.a.
	(0.03)	(0.21)	(42.42)			
1984	0.36***	0.29*	92.43**	n.a.	n.a.	n.a.
	(0.03)	(0.24)	(43.13)			
1988	0.34***	0.67**	63.82*	n.a.	n.a.	n.a.
	(0.03)	(0.28)	(38.96)			
1990	0.24***	0.80***	104.35*	n.a.	n.a.	n.a.
	(0.04)	(0.29)	(58.17)			

			Panel Results			
	c	α_L	a	D_{84}	D_{88}	D_{90}
NL2SLS (DV)	0.36***	0.68**	85.11**	0.03*	−0.02	−0.14***
	(0.04)	(0.29)	(35.54)	(0.03)	(0.03)	(0.03)
NL2SLS (DV) (excl. 1983)	0.39***	0.67**	80.24**	n.a.	−0.05	−0.16***
	(0.04)	(0.34)	(40.94)	n.a.	(0.03)	(0.03)
	c_{83}	α_L	a	c_{84}	c_{88}	c_{90}
NL2SLS (FE-SI)	0.37***	0.76***	96.84***	0.39***	0.35***	0.23***
	(0.03)	(0.20)	(36.47)	(0.02)	(0.02)	(0.03)
NL2SLS (FE-SI) (excl. 1983)	0.38***	0.61**	85.35**	n.a.	0.34***	0.22***
	(0.03)	(0.26)	(35.34)	n.a.	(0.03)	(0.03)
GMM (FE-SI)	0.38***	0.88***	85.95***	0.39***	0.35***	0.24***
	(0.01)	(0.06)	(17.39)	(0.01)	(0.01)	(0.01)
GMM (FE-SI) (excl. 1983)	0.39***	0.91***	89.00***	n.a.	0.35***	0.24***
	(0.02)	(0.25)	(31.23)	n.a.	(0.02)	(0.02)

DV stands for regressions with dummy variables, FE for fixed effects, and SI for regressions with year-specific instruments.
Standard errors in parentheses. * represents absolute value of the *t*-ratio greater than 1, ** for an absolute value greater than 2, and *** for greater than 2.5.
Overidentifying restrictions accepted at the 5% level for all cases, except 1984 wherein they are accepted at the 4% level (test described in section III).

estimates of a and α_L (in this as well as previous studies) can arise from, among other things, inadequate disaggregation of the data as well as restriction of focus only on trade policy in the Grossman-Helpman model.[31]

The first year in our data set is 1983, which is the last year under dictatorship, following which democracy returned to Turkey. The estimated a and α_L for the year 1983 are 76.3 and 0.65, respectively. The estimated value of a is higher for all other years except 1988. From our single year results, the mean value of the estimated a for the democratic period is around 87 (higher than the estimate for the dictatorship year 1983), and the mean value of α_L for this period is 0.59.[32] Thus the average estimated proportion of the population organized was lower in the democratic regime. This is quite consistent with the predictions of Mitra (1999), which shows that an increase in a leads to a reduction in the equilibrium number of lobbies and thus in the proportion of

the population that is organized. This arises from the reduction in the incentives to lobbying and lobby formation (and possibly lobby maintenance) from the reduction in the government's affinity for political contributions as reflected in an increase in a. If we plug in the estimates of a and α_L into $(1 - \alpha_L)/(a + \alpha_L)$, which is the sum of the coefficients of z/e and Iz/e, we see that the values are roughly the same (around 0.45) for both 1983 and for the post-1983 period on the average, implying that, in an organized sector with the same characteristics, z and e would receive the same protection in 1983 as in the democratic period. This is the exit effect of the organized population: as the organized population shrinks in response to an increase in a, the remaining organized population faces less competition, a force on organized sector protection acting in a direction opposite to the direct effect of the reduction in a. However, we do observe lower rates of protection for both organized and unorganized sectors in the democratic period because this was the period in which trade reforms were undertaken. This is because z_i/e_i generally declined from a mean value of 8.55 to a mean value of 6.89. Further, the constant term is estimated to be lower in the post-1983 period.

We now look at the panel regressions. From our dummy-variable regressions with a common set of instruments across years, we estimate the value of a to be 85 for all years pooled, whereas it is 80 for all years pooled except 1983. Both estimates are very tight. Again, the values are higher

_t_-ratio of our estimated a. Thus, if we were to use β instead of a, we would obtain highly significant results for all cases examined.

[31] See a more detailed discussion in subsection VD.

[32] As can be seen from tables 1 and 3, dropping 1983 from our panel lowers the estimate of a. Two forces drive this result: one comes from the additional variation in the LHS and RHS variables across years (that is, as we move from other years to 1983 or vice versa), and the other comes from the possibility that these relative variations within 1983 might be different from those for all other years combined. It is the latter kind of variations that would exclusively focus on when we compare dictatorship (1983) with democracy (the post-1983 period). Thus, the appropriate way to do this comparison is to compare the single-year equation for 1983 with the panel regressions for all years other than 1983 pooled together.

"PROTECTION FOR SALE" IN A DEVELOPING COUNTRY: DEMOCRACY VS. DICTATORSHIP   505

TABLE 2.—TEST STATISTICS FOR NRP/(1 + NRP) EQUATION

	Single Year Results (NL2SLS)		
$H_0 \rightarrow$	$1/a = 0$	$\alpha_L/(a + \alpha_L) = 0$	$\alpha_L = 0, 1/a = 0$
$H_1 \rightarrow$	$1/a > 0$	$\alpha_L/(a + \alpha_L) > 0$	$\alpha_L > 0, 1/a > 0$
Year	t-ratio	t-ratio	F-test
1983	1.80	1.22	4.98
1984	2.15	0.92	2.39
1988	1.64	1.53	5.33
1990	1.79	1.31	4.12

	Panel Results		
$H_0 \rightarrow$	$1/a = 0$	$\alpha_L/(a + \alpha_L) = 0$	$\alpha_L = 0, 1/a = 0,$ $\delta = 0$
$H_1 \rightarrow$	$1/a > 0$	$\alpha_L/(a + \alpha_L) > 0$	$\alpha_L > 0, 1/a > 0,$ $\delta \neq 0$
Year	t-ratio	t-ratio	F-test
NL2SLS (DV)	2.40	1.60	5.05
NL2SLS (DV) (excl. 1983)	1.96	1.51	10.65
NL2SLS (FE-SI)	2.66	2.41	240.18
NL2SLS (FE-SI) (excl. 1983)	2.41	1.81	184.29
GMM (FE-SI)	4.95	4.70	1053.05
GMM (FE-SI) (excl. 1983)	2.85	3.81	786.57

Table entries are test statistic values.
All alternative hypotheses are one sided, and critical values should be used accordingly.

than for 1983 alone. When we look at the regressions with year-specific fixed-effects (equivalent to dummy variables) and year-specific instruments, a is tightly estimated and varies from 85 to 97, depending on the specification. In any event, these estimates are much higher than for the single-year equation for 1983 alone.

For our dummy-variable regressions with a common set of instruments across years, the estimated value of α_L (again highly significant) is 67% to 68%, roughly the same as that for 1983 alone. When we look at the regressions with year-specific fixed-effects (effectively equivalent to dummy variables) and year-specific instruments, the estimated α_L's are 0.76 and 0.88 with NL2SLS and GMM, respectively, and are significant at the 1% level. When we drop 1983, the estimates are 0.61 and 0.91, respectively, and again extremely tight. The GMM estimates seem to be unreasonably high for Turkey. However, they are close to those obtained in the studies for the United States.

Following estimation, we perform certain tests. As can be seen from table 2, the model is generally significant at the 1% through 5% levels except for the single-year equation for 1984, which is significant at roughly the 10% level.[33] Furthermore, we reject the null hypothesis that $1/a = 0$ (the government is an aggregate welfare maximizer) against the one-sided alternative that $1/a > 0$ at the 1% through 5%

[33] For our nonlinear estimation, the significance of our model is given by the rejection of the null hypothesis that both $1/a$ and α_L simultaneously equal zero against the alternative that they are both greater than zero. For the panel regressions, there is an additional component $\delta = (\neq)0$ in our null (alternative) hypothesis.

levels in all cases. This test here is also roughly equivalent to looking at the significance of the coefficient of z/e, which is $1/(a + \alpha_L)$. As we can see, positive estimates of a and α_L (as we have obtained) produce positive values of $1/(a + \alpha_L)$, which is consistent with the Grossman-Helpman prediction that the coefficient of z/e is positive. Another Grossman-Helpman prediction of course is that the coefficient of Iz/e is negative. This coefficient is $(-\alpha_L/(a + \alpha_L))$, which is negative for positive estimates of a and α_L. We, therefore, test the null hypothesis that $\alpha_L/(a + \alpha_L) = 0$ against the alternative that $\alpha_L/(a + \alpha_L) > 0$. We reject the null at the 1% through 10% levels of significance for all the regressions except those for the years 1983 and 1984, which are significant at the 12% and 18% levels, respectively.

Based on these estimates of a and α_L (and their standard errors), we have also computed the composite coefficients (the coefficients of z/e and Iz/e) of the NRP equation (and their standard errors by the delta method). $-\alpha_L/(a + \alpha_L)$ is the coefficient of z/e, and it (as predicted by the theory) has a negative sign. This coefficient estimate has a small magnitude (less than but close to 0.01 in most cases) due to the very high estimated values of a. Almost all the estimates (single year and panel) are fairly precise (mostly significant at the 1% to 10% levels). The other composite coefficient (of Iz/e), $1/(a + \alpha_L)$, is estimated with a positive sign as predicted by the theory, and it is as significant as the coefficient of z/e. Again, this coefficient estimate has a small magnitude (around 0.01 in most cases), again primarily due to the very high estimated values of a.

B. Results with ERP and NTB

Table 3 presents the highlights of our results with ERP/$(1 + ERP)$ and NTB/$(1 + NTB)$ as dependent variables. As the Grossman-Helpman model is about tariffs (NRPs), results with these alternative protection measures should be considered as nothing more than robustness checks (or sensitivity analysis).

With ERPs, α_L is again very tightly estimated (ranging from 0.58 through 0.99 across years and specifications), in all cases significant at the 1% through 5% levels, except for the 1984 single-year equation (which has a marginally significant estimate of 0.24). Our estimates of a are very precise for the fixed-effects regression with year-specific instrument sets. The other regressions for ERP do not yield estimates of a that are as tight, but they still have reasonable significance. All these estimates of a for various years and from the different panel specifications lie in the range 46 through 89.

The estimated a for the year 1983, which is 47.49, is lower than the mean value (of around 54) of single-year estimates of a for the democratic period as well as all other years separately except 1984 (which has almost the same value (45.83)). The value of a is estimated to be 51–89 for all years pooled, and it is 48–77 for all years pooled except 1983, which again is higher than the estimate for 1983 alone.

TABLE 3.—ESTIMATION RESULTS

	ERP/(1 + ERP) equation Single Year Results (NL2SLS)					
Year	c	α_L	a	D_{84}	D_{88}	D_{90}
1983	0.41***	0.58**	47.49*	n.a.	n.a.	n.a.
1984	0.41***	0.24*	45.83**	n.a.	n.a.	n.a.
1988	0.43***	0.66**	52.22*	n.a.	n.a.	n.a.
1990	0.37***	0.94***	62.66*	n.a.	n.a.	n.a.
	Panel Results					
	c	α_L	a	D_{84}	D_{88}	D_{90}
NL2SLS (DV)	0.44***	0.84**	80.49**	0.03	−0.01	−0.09**
NL2SLS (DV) (excl. 1983)	0.47***	0.81*	76.82*	n.a.	−0.04	0.12***
	c_{83}	α_L	a	c_{84}	c_{88}	c_{90}
NL2SLS (FE-SI)	0.46***	0.99***	80.83**	0.47***	0.45***	0.37***
NL2SLS (FE-SI) (excl. 1983)	0.46***	0.74**	62.04**	n.a.	0.43***	0.35***
GMM (FE-SI)	0.45***	0.92***	51.29***	0.46***	0.45***	0.36***
GMM (FE-SI) (excl. 1983)	0.45***	0.83***	47.94***	n.a.	0.44***	0.34***
	NTB/(1 + NTB) equation					
Year	c		α_L		a	
1984	0.29***		0.85*		66.19*	
1988	0.08***		0.89***		47.56*	

See notes of table 1.

We only have two years (1984 and 1988) of data for NTBs for which α_L is very tightly estimated at 0.85 and 0.89, respectively. Our estimates of a are not as tight and are 47 and 66, respectively. As explained earlier, consistent with the predictions of Mitra (1999), the year that has a higher a with NTBs is the year with the lower α_L.

Again, in the case of the ERP and NTB regressions, we test the same hypotheses as the ones for NRP. The results are qualitatively very similar. Furthermore, the estimates of the composite coefficients are small in size, have the correct signs, and exhibit a fair amount of precision.

C. Sensitivity Analysis

We experiment with a number of different specifications. Firstly, as explained in section II, to capture the "vote delivering ability" of the agricultural sectors we experiment with an alternative specification as given in equation (5). The additional term is the interaction of the agricultural dummy with z/e, whose estimated coefficient turns out to be statistically insignificant.

In our NTB equation, we also experiment with scaled NTBs. As in Goldberg and Maggi (1999), we use scaling factors of 2 and 3. These scaled-up NTBs provide estimates of α_L greater than 1, and therefore we do not present those results.

In our regressions, we treat both the import demand elasticities and the political organization dummy as endogenous variables. We experiment with regressions that treat both these variables as exogenous, one at a time as well as both together. The results remain qualitatively unchanged. In fact, results are less sensitive to treating elasticities as

exogenous than to treating the political organization dummy as exogenous.

We also experiment with some additional exogenous variables (the hourly wage, the degree of unionization, index of intra-industry trade, and the growth rate of imports) thrown onto the right side of our estimating equation. All these variables turn out to be individually and jointly insignificant in all our regressions.

The last set of sensitivity analysis checks was performed by reestimating all equations using two different political organization dummy variables: the first was obtained from the ex post classification results of our discriminant analysis, and the second was obtained from the probit regressions of the ex ante membership-based classification on trade-related variables, import penetration ratio, and the import demand elasticity. In general, the results are robust to alternative measures of political organization. In most of these regressions, a and α_L were significantly estimated (at 1%–5% levels), with estimates in the range 55–100 for the former and 0.6–0.9 for the latter.

D. A Broader Interpretation of Results

The estimates of a and α_L in our study as well as in other papers are very high.[34] Certain features are common to our paper and other papers in the literature that drive such results.

[34] If concentration ratios are high and large industries are organized, it is possible for a large proportion of the relevant (to the sample) population to be organized. We are grateful to an anonymous referee for having pointed this out to us.

Firstly, the degree of disaggregation of the data may not be high enough. At the low level of disaggregation, import demand elasticities are low. Additionally, within a sector, certain subcomponent sectors may be organized and others may be unorganized. Treating such whole sectors as organized is equivalent to treating a bigger proportion of the economy as organized. Also, the tariff rates of the subcomponent organized sectors may be much higher than those of the sectors at the more aggregated level. Following the tradition of economic theory, the Grossman-Helpman model focuses on only one type of policy. However, in the real world, the government provides to its favored sectors a wide variety of concessions and services, abstracting from which in empirical analysis may result in overestimates of a and α_L.

VI. Conclusions

The Grossman and Helpman (1994) "Protection for Sale" model theoretically analyzes the determinants of cross-industry protection. They use a "political contributions" approach within a multisectoral, small, open economy setting. Using three-digit, industry-level data from a "genuine" small, open economy (Turkey), we empirically investigate and find support for the fundamental predictions of the Grossman-Helpman model. Our data set for four different years in the period 1983–1990 spans both dictatorial and democratic regimes.

We look at three kinds of protection measures: nominal protection rates, effective protection rates, and NTB coverage ratios. Thus, unlike the two well-known studies for the United States, the set of protection measures we study includes tariffs (nominal protection rates), which is the policy instrument of focus in the Grossman-Helpman model. Further, we perform cross-sectional, single-year regressions as well as panel regressions (with the data pooled across all the available years), thereby checking robustness across years and political regimes.

Our paper also features a few methodological advances. We use classification methods based on discriminant analysis to statistically validate the division of industries into organized and unorganized. We put the estimation problem in its natural, nonlinear form and estimate the structural parameters (and their standard errors) directly. Our pooled equations are estimated both by nonlinear 2SLS and generalized methods of moments (GMM).

As in the previous studies, we find that the government attaches a weight on welfare that is several times the size of its weight on political contributions. Additionally, we find that the weight on welfare relative to contributions was higher in the democratic regime than for dictatorship. We think this result is potentially of importance to researchers in all areas of political economy, and particularly to those studying the relationship between democracy and development.

REFERENCES

Anderson, Theodore W., *An Introduction to Multivariate Statistical Analysis* (New York: John Wiley and Sons, 1984).
Baldwin, Robert E., *The Political Economy of U.S. Import Policy* (Cambridge, MA: The MIT Press, 1985).
Bernheim, B. Douglas, and Michael D. Whinston, "Menu Auctions, Resource Allocation and Economic Influence," *Quarterly Journal of Economics* 101:1 (1986), 1–31.
Davidson, Russel, and James McKinnon, *Estimation and Inference in Econometrics* (New York: Oxford University Press, 1993).
Dhrymes, Phoebus, *Topics in Advanced Econometrics vol II: Linear and Non-Linear Simultaneous Equations* (New York: Springer-Verlag, 1994).
Feenstra, Robert, and Jagdish N. Bhagwati, "Tariff Seeking and the Efficient Tariff" (pp. 245–258), in J. N. Bhagwati (Ed.), *Import Competition and Response* (Chicago: The University of Chicago Press, 1982).
Findlay, Ronald, and Stanislaw Wellisz, "Endogenous Tariffs: The Political Economy of Trade Restrictions and Welfare" (pp. 223–234), in J. N. Bhagwati (Ed.), *Import Competition and Response* (Chicago: The University of Chicago Press, 1982).
Gawande, Kishore, and Usree Bandyopadhyay, "Is Protection for Sale? A Test of the Grossman-Helpman Theory of Endogenous Protection," this REVIEW 82:1 (2000), 139–152.
Gawande, Kishore, "U.S. Nontariff Barriers as Privately Provided Public Goods," *Journal of Public Economics*, 64:1 (1997a), 61–81.
——— , "Comparing Theories of Endogenous Protection: Bayesian Comparison of Tobit Models Using Gibbs Sampling Output," this REVIEW 80:1 (1997b) 128–140.
——— , "Stigler-Olson Lobbying Behavior and Organization: Evidence from a Lobbying Power Function," *Journal of Economic Behavior and Organization*, 35:4 (1998) 477–499.
Goldberg, Penelope K., and Giovanni Maggi, "Protection for Sale: An Empirical Investigation," *American Economic Review* 89:5 (1999), 1135–1155.
Grossman, Gene M., and Elhanan Helpman, "Protection for Sale," *American Economic Review* 84:4 (1994), 833–850.
——— , "Trade Wars and Trade Talks," *Journal of Political Economy* 103:4 (1995a), 675–708.
——— , "The Politics of Free Trade Agreements," *American Economic Review* 85:4 (1995b), 667–690.
Helpman, Elhanan, "Politics and Trade Policy," Tel-Aviv University working paper no. 30-95 (September 1995).
Hillman, Arye L., *The Political Economy of Protection* (London: Harwood Academic, 1989).
Johnson, Richard A., and Dean W. Wichern, *Applied Multivariate Statistical Analysis*, 3rd ed. (Upper Saddle River, NJ: Prentice-Hall, 1998).
Krishna, Pravin, and Devashish Mitra, "Reciprocated Unilateralism: A Political Economy Approach," Brown University and Florida International University mimeograph (2000).
Magee, Steve P., William A. Brock, and Leslie Young, *Black Hole Tariffs and Endogenous Policy Theory* (Cambridge, MA: Cambridge University Press, 1989).
Maggi, Giovanni, and Andres Rodriguez-Clare, "The Value of Trade Agreements in the Presence of Political Pressures," *Journal of Political Economy* 106:3 (1998), 575–601.
Mayer, Wolfgang, "Endogenous Tariff Formation," *American Economic Review* 74:5 (1984) 970–985.
Mayer, Wolfgang, and Raymond Riezman, "Endogenous Choice of Trade Policy Instruments," *Journal of International Economics* 23 (1987), 377–381.
——— , "Tariff Formation in a Multidimensional Voting Model," *Economics and Politics* 1:1 (1989), 61–79.
——— , "Voter Preferences for Trade Policy Instruments," *Economics and Politics* 2:3 (1990), 259–273.
McCalman, Phillip, "Protection for Sale and Trade Liberalization: An Empirical Investigation," University of California at Santa Cruz mimeograph (2000).
Mitra, Devashish, "Endogenous Lobby Formation and Endogenous Protection: A Long Run Model of Trade Policy Determination," *American Economic Review* 89:5 (1999), 1116–1134.

OECD, *Industrial Structure Statistics* (Geneva: OECD, various issues 1982–1995).

Ray, Edward J., "Tariff and Nontariff Barriers to Trade in the United States and Abroad," this REVIEW 61 (1981), 161–168.

Rodrik, Dani, "Tariffs, Subsidies, and Welfare with Endogenous Policy," *Journal of International Economics* 21 (1986), 285–294.

Shiells, Clinton R., Robert F. Stern, and Alan V. Deardorff, "Estimates of the Elasticities of Substitution Between Imports and Home Goods for the United States," *Weltwirtschaftliches Archiv* 122 (1986), 497–519.

Togan, Subidey, *Foreign Trade Regime and Trade Liberalization in Turkey During the 1980s* (Aldershot, U.K.: Avebury, 1994).

Thomakos, Dimitrios D., and Mehmet A. Ulubaşoğlu, "The Impact of Trade Liberalization on Import Demand," Florida International University mimeograph (2000).

Trefler, Daniel, "Trade Liberalization and the Theory of Endogenous Protection," *Journal of Political Economy* 101:1 (1993), 138–160.

United Nations, *Monthly Bulletin of Statistics Yearbook* (New York: United Nations, various issues).

United Nations, *UN Industrial Statistics Yearbook* (New York: United Nations, various issues).

United Nations, *UN Statistical Yearbook* (New York: United Nations, various issues).

APPENDIX A: SUMMARY OF DISCRIMINANT ANALYSIS METHODOLOGY AND RESULTS

Here, we provide a brief summary of the discriminant analysis methodology we follow and some of its results. (See chapter 6 of Anderson (1984) and chapter 11 of Johnson and Wichern (1998) for details.)

Consider the measurement variables mentioned in the text: the protection rate, the inverse import penetration ratio, the (absolute value of the) import elasticities, and the four-firm concentration ratio. Let X denote the $(n \times 4)$ matrix of observations on these variables, and let x_i' denote the ith row of X, $i = 1, 2, \ldots, n$. Using our TUSIAD membership-based ex ante classification variable, n_1 ($=16$) and n_2 ($=n - n_1 = 21$) observations (rows) of X come from the organized sector population and unorganized sector population, respectively. Our objective is to try to validate ex post the initial classification using the observations of the measurement variables.

The prior probabilities of classification are estimated from the ex ante separation of sectors as $\pi_1 = n_1/n \approx 0.43$ and $\pi_2 = n_2/n \approx 0.57$. These estimated prior probabilities are taken as the "true" frequencies of organized and unorganized sectors in Turkey. We assume equal cost of missclasification for both organized and unorganized sectors. Let $f_i(x)$ denote the (multivariate) normal density for $i = 1, 2$. If the parameters of the densities are known it can be shown that the region defined by

$$\frac{f_1(x)}{f_2(x)} \geq \frac{\pi_2}{\pi_1}$$

minimizes the expected missclasification cost.

This rule can be applied to the observations of X by substituting estimates for the (true) means and variances of the two normal densities. In most practical applications, it is assumed that the two densities have the same covariance matrix. It can then be shown that the ex post classification rule reduces to "classify x_i to the population of organized sectors if"

$$(\bar{x}_1 - \bar{x}_2)' \hat{\Sigma}^{-1} x_i - \frac{1}{2} (\bar{x}_1 - \bar{x}_2)' \hat{\Sigma}^{-1} (\bar{x}_1 + \bar{x}_2) \geq \ln\left(\frac{\pi_2}{\pi_1}\right)$$

where $\bar{x}_i$ denotes the sample mean of the observations belonging to the ith population and $\hat{\Sigma}$ denotes the estimator of the common covariance matrix, the estimates being derived using our ex ante classification. Thus, from the preceding classification rule, a requirement for successful classification is a substantial difference between the means of the two normal distributions, thereby requiring a test for their equality. The p-values (averaging 0.117) from the tests of equality of means show evidence that the means are not the same in the populations of organized and unorganized sectors.

After the ex post classification, we can compute the posterior probabilities, $\hat{\pi}_1 = \hat{n}_1/n$ and $\hat{\pi}_2 = \hat{n}_2/n$, and compare them to the prior probabilities from the ex ante classification (where the "hat" represents ex post values arrived at using the preceding rule). One can also compute the ex post apparent error rate (AER) of missclassification given by the number of missclassified observations as a proportion of the sample size. The posterior probabilities (with an average value of 0.45 for the organized sectors compared to a prior of 0.43) track the (estimated) prior probabilities quite well. There is a tendency to assign unorganized sectors to organized ones, which inflates the posterior probabilities of the organized sectors. The ex post apparent error rates are relatively low, averaging 0.227 (0.21, 0, 17, 0.29, and 0.24 for the years 1983, 1984, 1988, and 1990, respectively). Because the samples used in the classification are quite small, we feel that the above results support our ex ante classification.

Chapter 10

Can we obtain realistic parameter estimates for the 'protection for sale' model?

Devashish Mitra   *Department of Economics, Syracuse University*
Dimitrios D. Thomakos   *University of Peloponnese, Greece*
Mehmet Ulubaşoğlu   *Deakin University, Australia*

Abstract. In the Grossman and Helpman (1994) model of endogenous trade protection, sectoral lobbies try to influence an incumbent government that maximizes a weighted sum of political contributions and aggregate welfare. We empirically investigate this model using U.S. and Turkish data. Our specification is more tightly tied to theory than those in existing studies. Additionally, we assume all specific-factor owners to be organized into different lobbies. These changes, validated by hypothesis tests, yield more realistic parameter estimates of the government's concern for aggregate welfare and of the fraction of population organized into lobbies.

Peut-on obtenir des calibrations réalistes des paramètres du modèle de «protection en vue d'augmenter les ventes»? Dans le modèle de protection commerciale endogène de Grossman & Helpman (1994), des lobbys sectoriels tentent d'influencer un gouverne-ment en place qui maximise une somme pondérée des contributions politiques et du bien-être collectif. Les auteurs utilisent ce modèle pour analyser les données pour les Etats-Unis et la Turquie. On spécifie le modèle d'une manière qui serre de plus près la théorie que ce qui a été le cas dans les études antérieures. De plus, on assume que tous les propriétaires de facteurs de production spécifiques sont organisés en lobbys différ-ents. Ces changements, validés par des tests d'hypothèses, engendrent des estimations plus réalistes des paramètres de la fonction d'intérêt du gouvernement pour le bien-être collectif et pour la fraction de la population organisée en lobbys.

Devashish Mitra is also affiliated with the NBER. We thank seminar participants at the Winter Econometric Society Meetings (Atlanta, January 2002) for useful discussions. We are especially indebted to Gene Grossman and Dani Rodrik for very useful comments and suggestions and to Kishore Gawande for providing us with some of the data used in this paper. The standard disclaimer applies. Email: dmitra@maxwell.syr.edu

Canadian Journal of Economics / Revue canadienne d'Economique, Vol. 39, No. 1
February / février 2006. Printed in Canada / Imprimé au Canada

0008-4085 / 06 / 187–210 / © Canadian Economics Association

188   D. Mitra, D.D. Thomakos, and M. Ulubaşoğlu

1. Introduction

In the Grossman-Helpman (1994) 'Protection for Sale' model, trade protection is endogenously determined through contributions offered by 'politically organized' sectors. A 'politically organized' sector, in turn, is one where the sector-specific factor owners have jointly invested in a lobby to establish access to incumbent politicians to communicate to them their offers contingent on policy announcements. In addition to the sector-specific factors of production, there is also unskilled labour that is mobile across sectors and is used in every sector. Individuals who do not own sector-specific factors in the form of physical assets or skills but own only unskilled labour are not allowed to organize in this model by assumption. The government's objective function is a weighted sum of political contributions and aggregate welfare.[1] Owing to its affinity for contributions, the government indirectly cares more about the welfare of politically organized people than about the well-being of others.[2] Thus, the proportion of the country's population that is politically organized will be a determinant of sectoral protection levels. The intuition is that protection increases producer surplus, but it reduces consumer surplus; that is, it hurts consumers. When a large proportion of the population is politically organized, a significant fraction of consumers falls into one lobby or another, and the government then is more careful about the costs of protection.[3] Similarly, sectoral protection levels will also depend on the relative weights the government attaches to contributions and aggregate welfare in its objective function. From the empirical angle, the main contribution of the Grossman-Helpman theory is that the level of protection is derived as an estimable function of industry characteristics, such as the import-demand elasticity and import penetration, and national characteristics, such as the fraction of the economy's population that is politically organized and the government's weight on aggregate welfare relative to contributions in its objective function.

Two recent empirical papers, (Goldberg and Maggi 1999; Gawande and Bandyopadhyay 2000), find support for and estimate the parameters of the Grossman and Helpman model using industry-level data from the United

---

1 Aggregate welfare is the sum of profits, consumer surplus, tariff revenue and wage income generated in the overall economy, while sectoral welfare refers to the same accruing to owners of specific factors within a sector.

2 Note that the welfare of a lobby is just the sum of the utility levels of all its members. Therefore, through its preferential treatment of organized groups or lobbies, the government is placing a greater weight on the total welfare of the organized population, which is nothing but sum of the utility levels of individuals who are members of one lobby or another in the economy. It also needs to be noted that an individual by himself or herself will not be able to offer contributions to politicians. Contribution schedules can only be presented by lobbies.

3 Note that every organized sector here is going to lobby for higher protection for itself but lower protection for other sectors, since every person in the economy consumes all the different goods produced.

States. The measure of protection they use is the non-tariff barrier (NTB) coverage ratio. Using both tariff rates and NTB coverage ratios, Mitra, Thomakos, and Ulubaşoğlu (2002) find support for the same theory for Turkey, which, unlike the United States, fits the small, open economy assumption made in the 'Protection for Sale' model. Since the Turkish data span both dictatorial and democratic regimes, Mitra, Thomakos, and Ulubaşoğlu can investigate the applicability of the model across political regimes. McCalman (2004) investigates and finds support for the 'Protection for Sale' model for Australia for two separate years (1968–9 and 1991–2). Unlike the two papers on the United States, McCalman's study focuses on tariffs. He finds that the Australian trade liberalization was caused by changes in the parameters of the Grossman-Helpman model as well as by changes in the theoretically predicted, industry-specific determinants of protection.[4]

Even though all these papers find support for the Grossman-Helpman model, their empirical findings look somewhat unrealistic. Additionally, each of these papers, in terms of their results, is internally contradictory. These empirical studies estimate the proportion of the population that is politically organized to be very large – ranging from 40% to 98%, while the weight attached by the government to aggregate welfare is estimated to be around 40 to a few thousand times that on contributions.[5] Such governments are statistically distinguishable but not different enough from welfare-maximizing ones in order for the theory to be of much practical interest. Also, the contradiction here is that it does not seem realistic to have such a high proportion of the population to have an incentive to organize in the presence of a government that does not seem to care much about contributions.[6]

In this paper, using U.S. and Turkish industry-level data, we focus on this problem of unrealistic parameter estimates in the existing empirical literature. We argue in this paper that using an empirical specification tied more tightly to the theoretical model and classifying all sectors as 'politically organized' can produce more sensible estimated parameter combinations. According to the theory, all organized sectors will be able to obtain positive protection, while the unorganized ones will be given negative protection. However, all sectors in the United States as well as the Turkish datasets have positive or at least non-negative protection. Besides, in the case of the United States, information on political contributions is available and all the sectors in the U.S. dataset

---

4 For an excellent survey of the empirical literature on the political economy of trade policy, see Gawande and Krishna (2003).
5 In this context, it may be useful to point out that a recent working paper by Gawande and Krishna (2002), which very elegantly incorporates the activity of foreign lobbies into the theoretical and empirical analysis of the Grossman and Helpman model, fails to obtain significantly lower estimates of the government's weight on welfare and of the proportion of population organized than in the existing literature.
6 See Mitra (Mitra 1999) on endogenous lobby formation.

190   D. Mitra, D.D. Thomakos, and M. Ulubaşoğlu

provide positive amounts of political contributions. So there is a strong possibility that all these sectors are politically organized. In fact, the theory tells us that, given the positive protection and/or contributions associated with all sectors, we should treat all of them as organized.[7] Given the above definition of political organization of sectors and the assumption that owners of mobile, raw labour are not allowed to organize in the model, we can still have a substantial proportion of the population be 'politically unorganized.'

Goldberg and Maggi (1999) argue that classifying all sectors as politically organized would be appropriate only if contributions were made exclusively to influence trade policies or if we knew for sure that a positive proportion of each sector's contributions was trade related. However, the counter-argument to this is that a sector that has at least one Political Action Committee (PAC) representing it and is making positive contributions has established the necessary links with politicians to communicate the collective offers of its members and has the machinery to politically coordinate factor owners within it. The idea of being separately organized for trade policy as opposed to other kinds of policies does not sound very realistic and plausible. We show in this paper that, in many other ways, the data are consistent with the theory when all sectors are taken as organized. We also perform a few simple statistical tests that raise questions about the partitioning of sectors into organized and unorganized in the earlier papers.

An alternative could be to just focus on the sectors classified as organized in the earlier literature. Both ways of looking at the data will prevent us from exactly identifying the two key parameters of the model, namely, the weight on aggregate welfare relative to political contributions in the government's objective function and the proportion of the population that is politically organized. However, we will be able to shed light on the possible combinations of the two parameters and see whether the earlier parameter estimates fall in this set.

Also, we experiment with the elimination of sectors that are primarily export industries, that is, we eliminate sectors whose exports exceed imports. Since the data are only on import protection and in the 'Protection for Sale' theory it is import-competing sectors that get import tariffs, serious testing of the theory calls for at least experimenting with regressions with the export-oriented sectors eliminated.[8]

In addition, while the data on import-demand elasticities are available only at the three-digit level for the United States and Turkey, the protection data used in Gawande and Bandyopadhyay (2000) are at the four-digit level. Thus, the estimated welfare costs of protection, using three-digit elasticities along with with four-digit tariffs, will be underestimates. We should expect import-demand elasticities to increase in magnitude with the degree of disaggregation

---

7 See the discussion in section 3.
8 In this context, it is important to note that in the Grossman-Helpman model there is no intra-industry trade.

of the data, since goods at more disaggregated levels will have more substitutes and will thus possess greater substitution possibilities.[9] Though we do not have data on import-demand elasticities at a greater degree of disaggregation than at the three-digit level, we can and do explore and discuss the implications for the estimation of parameter values of using more disaggregated elasticities. We do so by obtaining a set of alternative parameter estimates for the United States in the presence of doubled three-digit elasticities, which might be closer to the true elasticities at the four-digit level for the reasons discussed above. Note that this is just one of the several things we experiment with in this paper. We also would like to point out that we do present a set of very realistic parameter estimates for the United States that are obtained without the doubling of the estimated three-digit import-demand elasticities. Also, for the Turkish case, we do not double any of the import-demand elasticities, since both the elasticity estimation and the entire empirical analysis of Turkish protection in this paper are done at the three-digit level.

The different experiments described above give us results that look more plausible. When around 90% of the population is taken as organized as in Goldberg and Maggi (1999), the weight on welfare in the U.S. case can be as low as twice and as high as five times the weight on contributions. The government turns out to be a maximizer of pure contributions, if the assumed proportion of organized population is 94–98%, which is close to the estimate of the organized population in Gawande and Bandyopadhyay (2000). An assumption of 50% of the population being organized is consistent with this relative weight being as low as 7 but as high as 30, depending on the combinations of the above experiments. For Turkey, an assumed value of 55–66% for the proportion of population organized can in many cases yield a pure contributions-maximizing government. In fact, even assuming that the proportion of the population organized is 10%, we obtain a weight on aggregate welfare that is roughly equal to that on contributions.

We argue in this paper that it is clearly the treatment of all sectors as organized, along with having an estimating equation more tightly tied to theory, that gives us the more realistic parameter estimates. Restricting our sample to sectors classified as organized in the existing literature does not make any further difference. Furthermore, just focusing on the import-competing sectors by dropping the export-oriented sectors does not make much of a difference either. When we double import-demand elasticities, with all sectors treated as organized, we get a further reduction in our estimates of the government's relative weight on aggregate welfare for a given proportion of

---

9 For example, there are greater substitution possibilities for rice than for food in general. Similarly, there are greater substitution possibilities for a particular kind of rice, say, jasmine rice, than for rice as a complete product category. See Panagariya, Shah, and Mishra (2001) on how estimation of the elasticity of U.S. import demand for apparel made in Bangladesh, with data finely disaggregated by type of apparel, can lead to up to an eight-fold increase in estimated import-demand elasticities, compared with those estimated using more aggregate data.

192   D. Mitra, D.D. Thomakos, and M. Ulubaşoğlu

the population politically organized. On eliminating the export-oriented sectors from the sample in the presence of these doubled elasticities, however, we can get an even further reduction in the estimate of one parameter, given that of the other.

We believe that one of the merits of this paper is that our investigation uses estimation techniques and tests that are fairly straightforward. Yet we are able to obtain more realistic estimated parameter combinations for the Grossman-Helpman model than has been done in previous studies. Unlike the previous papers, what we find is that the protection levels are consistent with a fairly low concern for aggregate welfare on the part of the government and a small proportion of the population being organized at the same time.

We would like to note, however, that, owing to our inability to observe or infer the extent of contributions made to influence the government specifically on trade policy issues, it is not possible to be fully confident of any classification of sectors into organized and unorganized.[10] Therefore, it is important to subject the theory to as many classification possibilities as we can. Thus, in our minds the previous literature remains important. One possible view, of course, is that as long as sectors have PACs to make contributions to influence any kind of policy, they should be treated as organized for all purposes and this is what we have tried to incorporate into this paper. Even the mere possibility that the true parameter combinations can be more realistic than in previous papers gives greater credibility to the 'Protection for Sale' theory.

2. Theoretical framework

In this section we provide a short description of the 'Protection for Sale' model (Grossman and Helpman 1994).

Consider a small, open economy. Individuals are assumed to have identical preferences. Each individual possesses labour and, at most, one kind of specific factor of production. There are N non-numeraire goods, each requiring a different kind of factor of production specific to that good and labour. In addition, there is a numeraire good that is produced under constant returns to scale using only labour. Unlike other factors in the model, labour is assumed to be mobile across sectors. On the consumption side, the model assumes a quasi-linear utility function that is linear in numeraire good consumption, concave in the consumption of each non-numeraire good, and additively separable across all goods.

It is also assumed that the only policy instruments available to politicians are trade taxes and subsidies. Further, the government redistributes revenue uniformly to all its citizens.

10 The fact that Goldberg and Maggi (1999) and Gawande and Bandyopadhyay (2000) differ significantly in their classification of sectors for the United States exactly proves this point.

In sectors that are politically organized, the specific-factor owners are able to lobby the government for preferential treatment in the form of higher trade protection for their own sectors and lower protection for other sectors. The interaction between the government and the lobbies takes the form of a 'menu-auction.' Thus, we have the following two-stage game:

First stage: Lobbies provide the government with their contribution schedules taking into account the government's objective function as described below. The 'schedule' in question is the contribution a lobby will make for each configuration of prices. Each lobby takes the contribution schedules of other lobbies as given.

Second stage: In the second stage, taking into account the contribution or offer schedules from the previous stage, the government sets trade policy to maximize a weighted sum of political contributions and overall social welfare.

The government's objective function is the following:

$$\Omega_G(\mathbf{p}) = \sum_{j \in \Lambda} C_j(\mathbf{p}) + a\Omega_A(\mathbf{p}), \tag{1}$$

where Λ is the set of organized interest groups (lobbies), $\mathbf{p} \in \mathbf{P}$ is the domestic price vector, $\Omega_A(\mathbf{p})$ is aggregate social welfare, $C_j(\mathbf{p})$ is the contribution schedule of the jth lobby, and $\mathbf{P}$ is the set of domestic price vectors from which the government may choose.[11] The set $\mathbf{P}$ is bounded such that each domestic price lies between some minimum and some maximum value. Grossman and Helpman restrict attention to equilibria that lie in the interior of $\mathbf{P}$. The parameter a in (1) is the weight the government attaches to aggregate social welfare relative to political contributions. The higher is a, the lower is the government's affinity for political contributions and the higher is its concern for social welfare.

Grossman and Helpman show that, with contribution schedules that are continuous in the price vector in the neighbourhood of the equilibrium, the government's problem of choosing its most preferred tariff vector, on receiving all the contribution schedules, is equivalent to maximizing the following function with respect to the domestic price vector $\mathbf{p}$:

$$\sum_{j \in \Lambda} \Omega_j(\mathbf{p}) + a\Omega_A(\mathbf{p}), \tag{2}$$

---

11 Note that the world price vector is taken as given and cannot be affected by tariffs, owing to the small country assumption made in this model. The wedge between the domestic price vector and the exogenously fixed world price vector is the tariff vector. Thus, there is no difference between choosing the trade policy vector and choosing the domestic price vector in this model.

194   D. Mitra, D.D. Thomakos, and M. Ulubaşoğlu

where $\Omega_j(\mathbf{p})$ is welfare of sector j. This maximization yields trade taxes and subsidies that satisfy the following, familiar Grossman-Helpman modified 'Ramsey Rule':

$$\frac{t_i}{1+t_i} = \frac{I_i - \alpha_L}{a + \alpha_L} \cdot \frac{z_i}{e_i}, \tag{3}$$

where t_i is the ad valorem tariff rate, z_i is the ratio of domestic output to imports or exports (depending on whether the sector is an import-competing or an export-oriented one), and e_i is the absolute value of price elasticity of import demand or export supply. I_i is an indicator variable that takes a value 1 if the sector is politically organized and zero for an unorganized sector, and α_L is the proportion of the country's population that is organized. Following the terminology used by Grossman and Helpman, an organized sector is one where the owners of the sector-specific factor of production are politically organized. As mentioned earlier, in the Grossman-Helpman model, not all individuals in the economy own sector-specific factors of production. Some own just unskilled labour, which is the factor that is mobile across sectors and in that sense is not tied to any particular sector. In this model, pure labourers are not allowed to politically organize. Only workers tied to a sector through investment in sector-specific skills are allowed to organize. Therefore, even when all sectors in our dataset are assumed to be politically organized, the proportion of the population that is politically organized will be less than one.

As explained in the introduction, a higher proportion of the population being politically organized means lower protection to each politically organized sector. Similarly, how much protection each sector gets will depend on the relative weights the government attaches to contributions and aggregate welfare in its objective function.

The above tariff expression can be written as the following empirically estimable form:

$$\frac{t_i}{1+t_i} = \frac{1}{a + \alpha_L}\left[I_i \cdot \left(\frac{z_i}{e_i}\right)\right] - \frac{\alpha_L}{a + \alpha_L}\left(\frac{z_i}{e_i}\right). \tag{4}$$

Since $a \in [0, \infty]$ and $\alpha_L \in [0, 1]$, the coefficient of $[I_i \cdot (z_i/e_i)]$ should be positive and that of (z_i/e_i) should be negative. Also, the coefficient of the former is larger than the latter. This means that the protection received by an organized sector is increasing in (z_i/e_i), while it is decreasing in (z_i/e_i) in the case of an unorganized sector. In the theoretical model, organized sectors are given positive protection, while unorganized sectors are exploited through negative protection, which is usually modified in the empirical model through the use of a constant term. Thus, there is deviation from free trade in opposite directions for organized and unorganized sectors, and the size of this deviation is increasing in (z_i/e_i). The reasons are as follows: the deadweight costs of this deviation are increasing in the magnitude of the trade elasticities; the benefits to lobbies from protection are higher if their output levels are higher; and the costs of deviation from free trade are lower, the lower is the volume of actual and potential trade.

3. Econometric methodology

If we want to tie our empirical work tightly to the theory, we should not contaminate equation (4), derived directly within the Grossman-Helpman model, with other additional terms. Moreover, all sectors should be treated as organized, given that all of them receive positive protection and/or make positive contributions.[12] Goldberg and Maggi (1999) argue that treating all sectors making positive contributions as organized would be valid only if contributions were made exclusively to influence trade policies or if we knew for sure that a positive proportion of each sector's contributions was trade related. However, the counter-argument to this is that all the sectors in the U.S. dataset have PACs representing them through which they make positive contributions and have therefore established the necessary links with politicians to communicate their offers. Thus, they have the machinery to politically coordinate specific-factor owners within their respective sectors for any purpose. Therefore the idea of being separately organized for trade policy, as opposed to other kinds of policies, does not sound very realistic.

Let $y_i = t_i/(1 + t_i)$. We define $\beta = (1 - \alpha_L)/(a + \alpha_L)$, treat all sectors as organized and transfer (z_i/e_i) to the left-hand side to obtain our new estimable equation:

$$y_i \cdot \left(\frac{e_i}{z_i}\right) = \beta + u_i,$$ (5)

where $\{u_i\}_{i=1}^n$ is the regression error term, that captures possible measurement errors in the right-hand-side variables, as well as other factors (outside the theoretical model) that affect the determination of the right-hand-side variable.

The above equation conforms a priori to both the theory requirements and the available data. It makes each of the structural parameters (a and α_L), given the other, a non-linear function of β. Clearly, both a and α_L cannot be identified simultaneously. However, equation (5) affords a very flexible way of obtaining estimates of a from an estimate of β and a sequence of assumed values for α_L. Let $w_i = y_i(e_i/z_i)$. The β coefficient estimate, $\widehat{\beta}$ from the above OLS regression equation (5) equals the sample mean $\bar{w} = n^{-1}\Sigma_{i=1}^n w_i$, and, given an assumed value for $\alpha_L = \alpha_L^*$, an estimator for a is given by

---

12 Alternatively, we could use only those sectors that are determined as organized in previous studies. We pursue both alternatives in the empirical analysis. That is, we uniformly treat all sectors as organized but also select those sectors identified as organized by a couple of different indicator variables used in the previous papers.

196   D. Mitra, D.D. Thomakos, and M. Ulubaşoğlu

$$\hat{a} = \frac{1 - (1 + \hat{\beta})\alpha_L^*}{\hat{\beta}}. \tag{6}$$

After estimating the standard error for $\hat{\beta}$, which would equal the standard error of $\bar{w}$, by running the regression represented by equation (5), we can use that estimate as an input into the calculation of the standard error for $\hat{a}$ using the delta method.

It is important to note that for an unorganized sector, the theory predicts that $w_i = -\alpha_L/(a + \alpha_L)$. However, this variable is never observed to be negative. We thus perform some simple tests to allow for a weaker version of the Grossman-Helpman theory that would simply imply a higher value of the variable w_i for an organized sector, compared with an unorganized sector. A useful method in this respect and for empirically validating the above methodology is to consider the differences in the estimated β (same as the mean differences or distribution differences of the composite variable $w_i = [t_i/(1 + t_i)] \cdot (e_i/z_i)$) between sectors that have previously been classified as organized and unorganized. If our arguments are valid, we should not find any evidence supporting different means or distributions between the two sets of observations.[13] We perform standard t-tests for the mean differences between sectors and Kolmogorov-Smirnov (KS) goodness-of-fit tests for the sectors' distributional differences. The Kolmogorov-Smirnov test is non-parametric, in contrast to the t-test for the difference in the means. The KS test is appropriate in our context, since it looks for differences in the observed (i.e., empirical) distribution functions of the two samples. As such, it takes into account both the location and the shape of these distribution functions, while the t-test looks for differences in only one particular measure of location, that is, the mean. Thus, the KS test is more general than the t-test and it enhances our inference results. The actual KS statistic is based on the maximum absolute difference between the empirical distribution functions from the two samples. It is important to note here that the KS test is not affected by problems of heteroscedasticity, since it is a test based on the comparison of the complete empirical distributions and not just their means.

The estimating equation in Mitra, Thomakos, and Ulubaşoğlu (2002) was

$$y_i = c + \frac{1}{a + \alpha_L}\left[I_i \cdot \left(\frac{z_i}{e_i}\right)\right] - \frac{\alpha_L}{a + \alpha_L}\left(\frac{z_i}{e_i}\right) + u_i, \tag{7}$$

which is the Grossman-Helpman tariff equation plus a constant term. The estimating equation in Gawande and Bandyopadhyay (2000) the same as (7), but with an additional input protection term as well as more control variables.

---

13 In other words, if the theory is correct and all the sectors in our data set are, in fact, organized, the means and the distributions of the two subsets (organized and unorganized, as classified in the previous papers) of observations should not be different.

In Mitra, Thomakos, and Ulubaşoğlu, the above equation was estimated by non-linear, two-stage least squares. In that paper, organized sectors are identified from the overall pool of sectors based on manufacturers' and industrialists' association membership, newspaper reports, and statistical validation through discriminant analysis, a brief summary of which we provide in the appendix. The above estimating equation, in both Gawande and Bandyopadhyay and Mitra, Thomakos, and Ulubaşoğlu, has a constant term that, though not present in the theory, can reconcile the positive protection granted to all sectors, with some sectors being organized and others unorganized. Dropping the constant term results in negative expected protection for unorganized sectors, a feature that cannot be entertained, given the positively skewed distribution of the data. Both Gawande and Bandyopadhyay and Mitra, Thomakos, and Ulubaşoğlu accommodate positive protection for all sectors, both organized and unorganized, through the incorporation of the constant term. In addition, Gawande and Bandyopadhyay use other control variables on the right hand side. Goldberg and Maggi (1999) do not have a constant term in their estimating equation, but they formulate their protection equation as a censored regression (Tobit) model that accommodates negative protection through the use of a latent (unobservable) variable.

4. Data

The U.S. data on protection, import penetration, import demand elasticities, and the political organization indicator variable were kindly provided by Kishore Gawande and are from the dataset used in Gawande and Bandyopadhyay (2000). We refer the interested reader to the original paper for the detailed data description and sources. All U.S. data are for manufacturing only. The NTB data are those for 1983, while the tariff rates are the post-Tokyo round ad-valorem tariffs. The NTB data are only in terms of coverage ratios, not in terms of tariff equivalents, and hence they contain less information than tariffs. The import-penetration data are also for the year 1983. Gawande and Bandyopadhyay constructed their political organization variable based on the ratio of corporate political action spending (PACFIRM) to value added (VA) for the period 1977–84. To identify politically organized industries, they regressed PACFIRM/VA on bilateral import penetration for a given partner interacted with industry dummies. Those dummies with positive coefficients indicated political organization in the trade arena vis-à-vis that partner. This was repeated for the five biggest partners of the United States and the union taken to determine the overall political organization of a sector. Alternatively, we also use the political organization indicator data from Goldberg and Maggi (1999), which they constructed using a threshold three-digit contribution level of $100 million for 1981–2.

The Turkish data we use in this paper were also used in Mitra, Thomakos, and Ulubaşoğlu (2002). Import-penetration data are constructed using data on

198   D. Mitra, D.D. Thomakos, and M. Ulubaşoğlu

imports obtained from the *UN International Trade Statistics Yearbook* (various issues) and those on domestic output from the *UN Statistical Yearbook* (various issues), *Monthly Bulletin of Statistics* (various issues), UN Food and Agriculture Organization Web site (http://www.fao.org), *OECD Industrial Structure Statistics* (various issues), and *UN Industrial Statistics Yearbook* (various issues).[14] Import-demand elasticities for 13 of the 37 product categories in our study are directly obtained from Thomakos and Ulubaşoğlu (2002), who followed the methodology of Shiells, Stern, and Deardorff (1986). The remaining 24 elasticities were estimated for the Mitra, Thomakos, and Ulubaşoğlu study with the same techniques used in Thomakos and Ulubaşoğlu (2002). Data on protection are obtained from Togan (1994). Our data for Turkey are for 37 three-digit manufacturing as well as primary product sectors. Examples of primary products included are aluminum, coal, copper, crude oil, iron ore, rice, rubber, wheat, and so on, while manufacturing sectors include chemicals, fertilizers, petroleum products, engineering products, pharmaceuticals, various kinds of machinery, textiles, automobiles, auto parts, and so on. Our data are available for 1983, 1984, 1988, and 1990. However, since results for these four years are qualitatively quite similar, we present our results using the most recent Turkish data, namely, those for the year 1990.[15]

5. Results

5.1. Results with U.S. data

We use the four-digit industry level data provided by Gawande to run our regressions for the United States. Our estimating equation is equation (5).[16] We run this regression first only for those sectors that are labelled as organized in the Gawande-Bandyopadhyay data set. We then run the regression for all sectors, treating every sector as organized. The next regression is run only for all import-competing sectors, treating all of them as organized, and the last one is run for those import-competing sectors that are already labelled as organized. Each of tables 1 through 4 follows the above sequence. It should be noted that in this paper we define a sector as import competing if its imports exceed its exports. As the data on import-demand elasticities are at the three-digit level – applied uniformly across four-digit industries within a three-digit sector – while the data on all other variables is at the four-digit level, we also try experimenting with doubling these elasticities, which, as explained in the introduction, may take us closer to the true four-digit elasticities. All our

---

14 It is important to note here that we are covering 86.2% of all imports of 1990.
15 The results for the earlier three years can be obtained from the authors upon request.
16 Though equivalent to each other, it is easier to run a regression of w on a constant term and the political organization rather than calculate separate means of the variable w for the organized and unorganized subsamples and then perform an explicit test of the equality of means. With this regression, we would just be able to perform a t-test for the coefficient of the political organization dummy variable.

estimation is carried out for both tariffs and NTB coverage ratios. As discussed in the data section, the NTB data are only in terms of coverage ratios, not in terms of tariff equivalents, and hence contain less information than tariffs. Therefore, we have more faith in our tariff results.

In table 1, which shows our estimation results for tariffs, the values of the estimated β for the different regressions lie roughly in the range 0.016–0.03. All are significant at the 1% level, which means that our composite variable w_i has a very representative mean and all the observations are closely clustered around this mean, which is what one should expect if all the sectors in the data set are indeed organized. The implied estimated values of a are also measured with great precision, given the assumed values of α_L. When α_L is assumed to be 0.1, the implied estimate of a lies in the range 29–49 and all the estimates are significant at the 1% level. As we increase this assumed value of α_L, the estimate of a falls. In particular, when we assume $\alpha_L = 0.5$, the estimated a falls to the range 7–30, and steeply to 0.75–5 when $\alpha_L = 0.9$. Note that $\alpha_L = 0.9$ is an important assumed value, since it roughly equals the value estimated by Goldberg and Maggi, who estimated their a to be around 70. The estimated a falls to zero when the assumed $\alpha_L = 0.94$ in some cases and up to 0.98 in others. These assumed values of α_L are also important, since they are very close to those estimated by Gawande and Bandyopadhyay. However, in sharp contrast to their estimated a of 3175, we find that the government at that assumed value of α_L is a maximizer of pure political contributions ($a = 0$). Clearly, the treatment of all sectors as organized, along with having an estimating equation more tightly tied to theory, gives us the more realistic estimates of β and the resulting combinations of a and α_L. Restricting our sample to sectors classified as organized in Gawande and Bandyopadhyay (2000) does not make any substantial, further difference. Furthermore, just focusing on the import-competing sectors by dropping the export-oriented sectors makes little difference.

In table 2, which shows our estimation results for *NTB*s, the values of the estimated β for the different regressions lie in a very similar range 0.017–0.03. Again, all are significant at the 1% level. The estimated values of a, when α_L is assumed to be 0.1, lies in the range 29–53 and all the estimates are significant at the 1% level. Again, as we increase this assumed value of α_L, the estimate of a falls. For the important assumed value of $\alpha_L = 0.9$, as explained above, a is estimated to be in the range 2–5. The estimated a falls to zero when the assumed $\alpha_L = 0.97$ in some cases and 0.98 in others.

For the reasons discussed above, when we double import-demand elasticities, with all sectors treated as organized, we get a further change in our estimates. Table 3 shows these estimation results with doubled elasticities for tariffs, while table 4 shows similar estimation results for *NTB*s. These estimates look even more realistic in that the estimated value of a for given α_L is even lower. In the presence of doubled elasticities, we get a further change in the estimated parameter combinations, again in the direction of greater

TABLE 1
Estimation results for tariffs

	Only organized sectors									
$\widehat{\beta}$	0.0182									
s.e.	0.0036	$N = 165$								
α_L	0.1	0.2	0.3	0.4	0.5	0.6	0.7	0.8	0.90	0.98
a	49.26	43.67	38.09	32.51	26.92	21.34	15.75	10.17	4.58	0.00
s.e.	9.83	8.74	7.65	6.55	5.46	4.37	3.28	2.19	1.09	0.20
	All sectors treated as organized									
$\widehat{\beta}$	0.0164									
s.e.	0.0026	$N = 242$								
α_L	0.1	0.2	0.3	0.4	0.5	0.6	0.7	0.8	0.90	0.98
a	54.65	48.47	42.28	36.11	29.92	23.73	17.55	11.37	5.18	0.00
s.e.	8.71	7.74	6.77	5.80	4.88	3.87	2.90	1.94	0.97	0.16
	Only import-competing organized sectors									
$\widehat{\beta}$	0.0303									
s.e.	0.0066	$N = 87$								
α_L	0.1	0.2	0.3	0.4	0.5	0.6	0.7	0.8	0.90	0.97
a	29.57	26.17	22.77	19.38	15.98	12.58	9.19	5.79	2.40	0.00
s.e.	6.47	5.75	5.03	4.31	3.59	2.87	2.16	1.44	0.72	0.21
	All import-competing sectors treated as organized									
$\widehat{\beta}$	0.0263									
s.e.	0.0046	$N = 133$								
α_L	0.1	0.2	0.3	0.4	0.5	0.6	0.7	0.8	0.90	0.97
a	34.09	30.19	26.29	22.39	18.49	14.59	10.70	6.80	2.90	0.00
s.e.	5.92	5.26	4.61	3.95	3.29	2.63	1.97	1.32	0.66	0.17

realism, when we eliminate the export-oriented sectors. When α_L is assumed to be 0.1, the implied estimate of a lies in the range 14–27 in table 3 for tariffs and in a very similar range for *NTB*s in table 4.

In tables 5 and 6 we test the null hypothesis of β being equal for the subsamples previously classified in the literature as organized and unorganized, against the alternative that β is higher for the former than the latter. From t-tests shown in table 5, we see that we cannot reject, even at the 20% level, the null hypothesis that the means of the composite variable, w, are the same for the two subsamples. This exactly should be the case if the theory is correct and all the sectors in the data set are organized. Note here that, while

TABLE 2
Estimation results for NTBs

	Only organized sectors									
$\widehat{\beta}$	0.0169									
s.e.	0.0034	$N = 165$								
α_L	0.1	0.2	0.3	0.4	0.5	0.6	0.7	0.8	0.90	0.98
a	53.09	47.08	41.07	35.06	29.05	23.04	17.03	11.02	5.01	0.00
s.e.	10.82	9.62	8.42	7.22	6.01	4.81	3.61	2.41	1.20	0.20

	All sectors treated as organized									
$\widehat{\beta}$	0.0188									
s.e.	0.0033	$N = 242$								
α_L	0.1	0.2	0.3	0.4	0.5	0.6	0.7	0.8	0.90	0.98
a	47.67	42.26	36.85	31.45	26.04	20.63	15.22	9.82	4.41	0.00
s.e.	8.34	7.42	6.49	5.56	4.64	3.71	2.78	1.85	0.93	0.18

	Only import-competing organized sectors									
$\widehat{\beta}$	0.0272									
s.e.	0.0063	$N = 87$								
α_L	0.1	0.2	0.3	0.4	0.5	0.6	0.7	0.8	0.90	0.97
a	32.95	29.18	25.40	21.63	17.86	14.09	10.32	6.54	2.77	0.00
s.e.	7.60	6.76	5.91	5.07	4.22	3.38	2.53	1.69	0.84	0.23

	All import-competing sectors treated as organized									
$\widehat{\beta}$	0.0304									
s.e.	0.0058	$N = 133$								
α_L	0.1	0.2	0.3	0.4	0.5	0.6	0.7	0.8	0.90	0.97
a	29.56	26.16	22.77	19.37	15.98	12.58	9.19	5.79	2.40	0.00
s.e.	5.63	5.01	4.38	3.75	3.13	2.50	1.88	1.25	0.63	0.19

table 5 uses the Gawande-Bandyopadhyay classification, table 6 uses the Goldberg-Maggi classification to perform the various tests. We use the Kolmogorov-Smirnov (KS) goodness-of-fit test to test the null hypothesis that the empirical distributions of the composite variable w_i are the same in terms of shape and location for these two sets of sectors against the alternative that they are different. The KS test in table 5 shows that, for all four cases reported, we cannot, even at the 40% level, reject the null hypothesis that the two empirical distributions of the composite variable, from the two subsamples, are no different from each other. The KS test results in table 6 shows similar results for three out of the four cases reported, where the null

TABLE 3
Estimation results for tariffs with import demand elasticities doubled

				Only organized sectors					
$\widehat{\beta}$	0.0365								
s.e.	0.0073	$N = 165$							
α_L	0.1	0.2	0.3	0.4	0.5	0.6	0.7	0.8	0.90	0.97
a	24.58	21.74	18.91	16.05	13.21	10.37	7.53	4.68	1.84	0.00
s.e.	4.92	4.37	3.82	3.28	2.73	2.19	1.64	1.09	0.55	0.19

				All sectors treated as organized					
$\widehat{\beta}$	0.0329								
s.e.	0.0052	$N = 242$							
α_L	0.1	0.2	0.3	0.4	0.5	0.6	0.7	0.8	0.90	0.97
a	27.28	24.13	20.99	17.85	14.71	11.57	8.43	5.28	2.14	0.00
s.e.	4.35	3.87	3.39	2.90	2.42	1.94	1.45	0.97	0.48	0.16

				Only import-competing organized sectors					
$\widehat{\beta}$	0.0607								
s.e.	0.0132	$N = 87$							
α_L	0.1	0.2	0.3	0.4	0.5	0.6	0.7	0.8	0.90	0.94
a	14.73	12.99	11.24	9.49	7.74	5.99	4.24	2.50	0.75	0.00
s.e.	3.23	2.87	2.51	2.16	1.80	1.44	1.08	0.72	0.36	0.21

				All import-competing sectors treated as organized					
$\widehat{\beta}$	0.0526								
s.e.	0.0091	$N = 133$							
α_L	0.1	0.2	0.3	0.4	0.5	0.6	0.7	0.8	0.90	0.95
a	16.99	15.00	13.00	11.00	9.00	7.00	5.00	3.00	1.00	0.00
s.e.	0.16	0.14	0.12	0.11	0.09	0.07	0.05	0.04	0.02	0.01

hypothesis cannot be rejected at significance levels ranging from 20% to 60%.[17]

5.2. Results with Turkish data

In table 7, we present our results with the Turkish data. Again, we first present our regression results only for those sectors that are labelled as organized in

17 Goldberg and Maggi use a somewhat arbitrary cut-off amount of contributions in dollars to classify sectors as organized and unorganized. This approach ignores the size of a sector and the nature of the product it produces. Their approach certainly also does not address their own concern as to whether contributions are trade related or not. As argued before, we do not find convincing their approach to classifying sectors into organized and unorganized.

TABLE 4
Estimation results for *NTB*s with import demand elasticities doubled

		Only organized sectors							

$\widehat{\beta}$	0.0338									
s.e.	0.0069	$N = 165$								

α_L	0.1	0.2	0.3	0.4	0.5	0.6	0.7	0.8	0.90	0.97
a	26.49	23.44	20.38	17.33	14.27	11.22	8.16	5.11	2.05	0.00
s.e.	5.41	4.81	4.21	3.61	3.01	2.41	1.80	1.20	0.60	0.20

		All sectors treated as organized							

$\widehat{\beta}$	0.0377									
s.e.	0.0066	$N = 242$								

α_L	0.1	0.2	0.3	0.4	0.5	0.6	0.7	0.8	0.90	0.96
a	23.79	21.03	18.28	15.52	12.77	10.02	7.26	4.51	1.75	0.00
s.e.	4.17	3.71	3.25	2.78	2.32	1.85	1.39	0.93	0.46	0.17

		Only import-competing organized sectors							

$\widehat{\beta}$	0.0545									
s.e.	0.0125	$N = 87$								

α_L	0.1	0.2	0.3	0.4	0.5	0.6	0.7	0.8	0.90	0.95
a	16.42	14.49	12.55	10.62	8.68	6.74	4.81	2.87	0.94	0.00
s.e.	3.80	3.38	2.96	2.53	2.11	1.69	1.27	0.84	0.42	0.22

		All import-competing sectors treated as organized							

$\widehat{\beta}$	0.0607									
s.e.	0.0115	$N = 133$								

α_L	0.1	0.2	0.3	0.4	0.5	0.6	0.7	0.8	0.90	0.94
a	14.73	12.98	11.23	9.49	7.74	5.99	4.24	2.50	0.75	0.00
s.e.	0.17	0.15	0.13	0.11	0.10	0.08	0.06	0.04	0.02	0.01

our data set (Mitra, Thomakos, and Ulubaşoğlu 2002). We then present our regression results for all sectors, treating every sector as organized. The next regression is only for all import-competing sectors, with all of them treated as organized, and the last one is for those import-competing sectors that are already labelled as organized. The estimate of β lies in the range 0.23–0.30. We present the Turkish results only for tariffs, since NTB results are very similar. Thus, even when the proportion of population organized is taken as zero, the estimated implied *a* is never more than 4.2 but is not less than 3.3. It falls to 2.8–3.6 when we assume $\alpha_L = 0.1$, and it can go as low as 0.5 when $\alpha_L = 0.5$. It can fall to zero when the assumed value of α_L is between 0.7 and 0.8. Note that for Turkey we do not provide any parameter estimates using

204   D. Mitra, D.D. Thomakos, and M. Ulubaşoğlu

TABLE 5.1
Test for the equality of the means and distributions of w with tariffs with respect
to political organization, G-B dataset, all sectors

PoliticalOrg.	Count	Mean	St.Dev.
0	77	0.0126	0.0229
1	165	0.0182	0.0467
All	242	0.0164	0.0407
	t-test	KS-test	
	1.006	0.853	
	(0.316)	(0.461)	

TABLE 5.2
Test for the equality of the means and distributions of w with tariffs with respect to
political organization, G-B dataset, import-competing sectors

PoliticalOrg.	Count	Mean	St.Dev.
0	46	0.0187	0.0274
1	87	0.0303	0.0617
All	133	0.0263	0.0526
	t-test	KS-test	
	1.213	0.595	
	(0.227)	(0.871)	

TABLE 5.3
Test for the equality of the means and distributions of w with NTB with respect
to political organization, G-B dataset, all sectors

PoliticalOrg.	Count	Mean	St.Dev.
0	77	0.0230	0.0638
1	165	0.0169	0.0442
All	242	0.0188	0.0512
	t-test	KS-test	
	0.853	0.822	
	(0.395)	(0.509)	

TABLE 5.4
Test for the equality of the means and distributions of w with NTB with respect to
political organization, G-B dataset, import-competing sectors

PoliticalOrg.	Count	Mean	St.Dev.
0	46	0.0362	0.0798
1	87	0.0272	0.0584
All	133	0.0304	0.0665
	t-test	KS-test	
	0.742	0.551	
	(0.460)	(0.922)	

NOTE: P-values are shown in parentheses for the t- and KS-tests.

TABLE 6.1
Test for the equality of the means and distributions of w with tariffs with respect
to political organization, G-M dataset, all sectors

PoliticalOrg.	Count	Mean	St.Dev.
0	48	0.0308	0.0658
1	194	0.0129	0.0308
All	242	0.0164	0.0407
	t-test	KS-test	
	2.763***	1.560***	
	(0.006)	(0.015)	

TABLE 6.2
Test for the equality of the means and distributions of w with tariffs with respect
to political organization, G-M dataset, import-competing sectors

PoliticalOrg.	Count	Mean	St.Dev.
0	39	0.0370	0.0716
1	94	0.0219	0.0420
All	133	0.0263	0.0526
	t-test	KS-test	
	1.521	1.083	
	(0.131)	(0.192)	

TABLE 6.3
Test for the equality of the means and distributions of w with NTB with respect
to political organization, G-M dataset, all sectors

PoliticalOrg.	Count	Mean	St.Dev.
0	48	0.0329	0.0864
1	194	0.0154	0.0373
All	242	0.0188	0.0512
	t-test	KS-test	
	2.138**	0.550	
	(0.034)	(0.923)	

TABLE 6.4
Test for the equality of the means and distributions of w with NTB with respect
to political organization, G-M dataset, import-competing sectors

PoliticalOrg.	Count	Mean	St.Dev.
0	39	0.0399	0.0947
1	94	0.0264	0.0505
All	133	0.0304	0.0665
	t-test	KS-test	
	1.069	0.766	
	(0.287)	(0.600)	

NOTE: P-values are shown in parentheses for the t- and KS-tests.

206   D. Mitra, D.D. Thomakos, and M. Ulubaşoğlu

TABLE 7
Estimation results for Turkey, 1990

	Only organized sectors								
$\widehat{\beta}$	0.2384								
s.e.	0.1051	$N = 16$							
α_L	0.1	0.2	0.3	0.4	0.5	0.6	0.7	0.8	0.81
a	3.68	3.16	2.64	2.12	1.60	1.08	0.56	0.04	0.00
s.e.	1.67	1.48	1.30	1.11	0.93	0.74	0.56	0.37	0.36
	All sectors treated as organized								
$\widehat{\beta}$	0.2815								
s.e.	0.0841	$N = 37$							
α_L	0.1	0.2	0.3	0.4	0.5	0.6	0.7	0.78	
a	3.10	2.64	2.19	1.73	1.28	0.82	0.37	0.00	
s.e.	0.96	0.85	0.74	0.64	0.53	0.42	0.32	0.23	
	Only import-competing organized sectors								
$\widehat{\beta}$	0.2533								
s.e.	0.1113	$N = 15$							
α_L	0.1	0.2	0.3	0.4	0.5	0.6	0.7	0.8	
a	3.45	2.96	2.46	1.97	1.47	0.98	0.48	0.00	
s.e.	1.56	1.39	1.21	1.04	0.87	0.69	0.52	0.36	
	All import-competing sectors treated as organized								
$\widehat{\beta}$	0.3037								
s.e.	0.0906	$N = 34$							
α_L	0.1	0.2	0.3	0.4	0.5	0.6	0.7	0.77	
a	2.86	2.43	2.00	1.58	1.15	0.72	0.29	0.00	
s.e.	0.88	0.79	0.69	0.59	0.49	0.39	0.29	0.23	

doubled import-demand elasticities, since both the elasticity estimation as well as the empirical analysis in this paper are done at the three-digit level. Mitra, Thomakos, and Ulubaşoğlu (2002) obtained much higher estimates of a along with high estimates of α_L, when their three-digit sectors were classified as organized and unorganized based on association membership, newspaper reports, and validation through discriminant analysis, as explained in the data section and appendix.[18]

18 In that paper, as mentioned before, the inconsistency between the universal positivity of protection and the theoretical prediction of negative protection for unorganized sectors is resolved through a positive constant in addition to the Grossman-Helpman right-hand-side terms.

TABLE 8.1
Test for the equality of the means and distributions of w with tariffs with respect to political organization, all Sectors

PoliticalOrg.	Count	Mean	St.Dev.
0	21	0.3144	0.5797
1	16	0.2384	0.4205
All	37	0.2815	0.5117
	t-test	KS-test	
	0.4428	0.682	
	(0.661)	(0.742)	

TABLE 8.2
Test for the equality of the means and distributions of w with tariffs with respect to political organization, import-competing sectors

PoliticalOrg.	Count	Mean	St.Dev.
0	19	0.3436	0.6032
1	15	0.2533	0.4309
All	34	0.3037	0.5285
	t-test	KS-test	
	0.489	0.752	
	(0.628)	(0.624)	

NOTE: P-values are shown in parentheses for the t- and KS-tests.

Again, from table 8 we see that the t test, for mean differences, and the Kolmogorov-Smirnov test, for distributional differences, give similar results to those in the US case. While the null of no difference in means is not rejected even at 66%, that of no difference in distributions is not rejected even at 74%.

6. Conclusions

In this paper, we show that in estimating the parameters of the Grossman-Helpman model, tying the empirical specification more tightly to the theory and treating all sectors as organized can lead to more realistic and believable estimates of the government's weight on welfare relative to contributions and the proportion of the population that is politically organized. The previous papers in the literature showed that there was broad support for the predictions of the 'Protection for Sale' model in the data for countries of different levels of development and across political regimes. However, the results of the earlier studies indicated the need to further investigate the model empirically and focus on the possible values of the parameter estimates, since the long-run credibility of the model would crucially depend on those estimates.

We argue in this paper that it is clearly the treatment of all sectors as organized, along with having an estimating equation more tightly tied to theory, that can provide more realistic parameter estimates. Restricting our sample to sectors classified as organized in the existing literature does not make any further difference. Furthermore, just focusing on the import-competing sectors by dropping the export-oriented sectors makes little difference. When we double import-demand elasticities for the U.S. case, with all sectors treated as organized, we get a further reduction in our estimates of the government's relative weight on aggregate welfare for a given proportion of the population politically organized. On eliminating the export-oriented sectors from the sample in the presence of these doubled elasticities, however, we get a further reduction in the estimated parameter combinations.

We believe that one of the merits of this paper is that our investigation uses estimation techniques and tests that are fairly straightforward. Yet we are able to obtain more realistic estimated parameter combinations for the Grossman-Helpman model than has been done in previous studies. Unlike the previous papers, what we find is that the protection levels are not consistent with a very high concern for aggregate welfare on the part of the government and a large proportion of the population's being organized at the same time.

We find that when around 90% of the population is taken as organized, as estimated in Goldberg and Maggi (1999), the weight on welfare in the U.S. case can be as low as twice and as high as five times the weight on contributions. The government turns out to be a maximizer of pure contributions if the assumed proportion of organized population is 94–98%, close to the estimate of the organized proportion in Gawande and Bandyopadhyay (2000). An assumption of 50% of the population's being organized is consistent with this relative weight being as low as 7 but as high as 30. Thus, clearly, even if the U.S. government is not a maximizer of contributions, it does probably place a fairly high weight on it in its objective function.

For Turkey, an assumed value of 55–66% for the fraction of population organized can, in many cases, be consistent with a pure contributions-maximizing government. In fact, even assuming that the proportion of the population organized is 10%, we obtain a weight on aggregate welfare that is roughly equal to that on contributions. Thus, the Turkish government seems to put a higher relative weight on contributions than the U.S. government.

We end this paper with a note of caution. Owing to our inability to observe or infer the extent of contributions made to influence the government specifically on trade policy issues, it is not possible to be fully confident of any classification of sectors into organized and unorganized.[19] The fact that Goldberg and Maggi (1999) and Gawande and Bandyopadhyay (2000) differ

---

19 One view, of course, is that as long as sectors have PACs to make contributions to influence any kind of policy, they should be treated as organized for all purposes.

in their classification of sectors for the United States exactly proves this point. Therefore, it is important to subject the theory to as many classification possibilities as we can. Thus, in our minds the previous literature remains important. On the other hand, even the mere possibility, shown in this paper, that the true parameter combinations can be more realistic gives greater credibility to the 'Protection for Sale' theory.

Appendix: Discriminant analysis

A brief summary of the discriminant analysis procedure that is used is as follows. The overall set of all sectors is partitioned into two subsets, organized and unorganized, based on manufacturers' and industrialists' association membership data. There is a theoretical literature that deals with the measurable characteristics that are correlated with whether a sector is organized or unorganized. These characteristics are in most cases the determinants of protection, z and e, and protection itself. In addition, another measurable characteristic used is the four-firm concentration ratio, which determines the extent of ease or difficulty in organizing. Therefore, based on the sample means and correlations of all these characteristics of organized and unorganized subsets, respectively, the multivariate normal joint density functions are estimated separately for the organized population of sectors and for the unorganized population. For the initial classification/partitioning, which is based on manufacturers' and industrialists' association membership data, to be validated, the two joint density functions and their respective estimated parameter vectors should be significantly different. To compute the extent of error in the classification, a two-stage procedure is used: based on the two estimated density functions, first a new ex post classification is performed, and in the second stage, this is compared with an ex ante classification, whose percentage error in the margin is then calculated. In general, the discriminant analysis results support the initial classification.

References

Gawande, Kishore, and Usree Bandyopadhyay (2000) 'Is protection for sale? A test of the Grossman-Helpman theory of endogenous protection,' *Review of Economics and Statistics* 82, 139–52
Gawande, Kishore, and Pravin Krishna (2002) 'Foreign lobbies and US trade policy, mimeo, Brown University and Texas A & M University'
— (2003) 'The political economy of trade policy: empirical approaches,' in *Handbook of International Trade*, ed. James Harrigan and E. Kwan Choi (London: Basil Blackwell)
Goldberg, Penelope K., and Giovanni Maggi (1999) 'Protection for sale: an empirical investigation,' *American Economic Review* 89, 1135–55
Grossman, Gene M., and Elhanan Helpman (1994) 'Protection for sale,' *American Economic Review* 84, 833–50
McCalman, Phillip (2004) 'Protection for sale and trade liberalization: an empirical investigation,' *Review of International Economics* 12, 81–94

210   D. Mitra, D.D. Thomakos, and M. Ulubaşoğlu

Mitra, Devashish (1999) 'Endogenous lobby formation and endogenous protection: a long run model of trade policy determination,' *American Economic Review* 89, 1116–34

Mitra, D., Dimitrios D. Thomakos, and Mehmet Ulubaşoğlu (2002) 'Protection for sale in a developing country: democracy versus dictatorship,' *Review of Economics and Statistics* 84, 497–508

Monthly Bulletin of Statistics (New York: United Nations)

Panagariya, Arvind, Shekhar Shah, and Deepak Mishra (2001) 'Demand elasticities in international trade: are they really low?' *Journal of Development Economics* 64, 313–42

Shiells, Clinton R., Robert F. Stern, and Alan V. Deardorff (1986) 'Estimates of the elasticities of substitution between imports and home goods for the united states,' *Weltwirtschaftliches Archiv* 122, 497–519

Thomakos, Dimitrios D., and Mehmet Ulubaşoğlu (2002) 'The impact of trade liberalization on import demand,' *Journal of Economic and Social Research* 4, 1–26

Togan, Subidey (1994) *Foreign Trade Regime and Trade Liberalization in Turkey During the 1980s* (Aldershot, UK: Avebury)

UN Industrial Statistics Yearbook (New York: United Nations)

UN Statistical Yearbook (New York: United Nations)

Part IV

**Endogenous Choice of Policy Instruments:
Theory and Empirics**

Chapter 11

ON THE ENDOGENOUS CHOICE BETWEEN PROTECTION AND PROMOTION*

DEVASHISH MITRA[†]

In a model of strategic interaction between firms in lobbying activity, I show that capitalists might prefer tariffs (protection) to production subsidies (promotion). This is due to the congestion problem arising from the government's convex welfare costs of providing subsidies as opposed to both the free-rider problem and the congestion problem acting in opposite directions in the case of tariffs. If an industry association exists, coordination can be achieved when lobbying for tariffs, but not in the case of production subsidies.

1. INTRODUCTION

ONE OF the major propositions of the theory of domestic distortions and welfare, as developed by Bhagwati and Ramaswami (1963), Johnson (1965) and Bhagwati (1971), is that in the absence of directly trade-related distortions or policy goals, direct subsidies are superior to tariffs for achieving any economic or non-economic objective. Then, why do tariffs exist? It is the aim of this paper to provide an answer to this puzzle.

A few explanations for this puzzle exist in the literature. Broadly, these explanations can be categorized into those coming from the supply side and the ones coming from the demand side.[1] The simplest explanation is a supply-side one and is provided in the classic Bhagwati–Ramaswami (1963) paper itself. The argument there is that the supplier of protection, the government, prefers a tariff to a subsidy, since the latter costs revenues while the former generates them. Thus governments that place a higher weight on revenue than

*I am particularly indebted to Jagdish Bhagwati, John McLaren, Dani Rodrik and two anonymous referees for very useful comments on earlier versions of this paper. I would also like to thank Eric Bond, Ronald Findlay, Cem Karayalcin, Costas Syropoulos, Frank Westerman and seminar participants at FIU, the Midwest International Economics Conference (Spring, 1997) and the Southeastern International Trade Conference (Fall, 1997) for helpful discussions and suggestions. The standard disclaimer applies.

†Correspondence to: Devashish Mitra, Department of Economics, Florida International University, Miami, FL 33199, USA. E-mail: mitrad@fiu.edu

[1] I am indebted to Jagdish Bhagwati for having suggested to me this method of classification.

33

on other components of welfare in their objective functions may prefer tariffs to subsidies. On the other hand, a supply-side argument in the opposite direction can be made in a Bhagwati–Srinivasan (1980, 1982) framework of fully competitive revenue-seeking. If welfare again is the ranking criterion, subsidies are preferable as they are not subject to revenue seeking.[2]

Rodrik (1986) is the first paper that looks at this issue by endogenizing policy. This is done using a simplified version of the Findlay–Wellisz (1982) lobbying model. In this class of models, unlike the models mentioned above, the government has no "autonomy" or "ego" in determining the size of protection (tariff) or promotion (subsidy) and is just a "playground" or "clearing-house" for the lobbies.[3] Rodrik's argument is from the demand side. He argues that since tariffs are general to an industry and subsidies can, in principle, be firm specific, the free-rider problem in lobbying for (or demanding) tariffs may result in a much smaller level of endogenous tariffs than endogenous subsidies. This might reverse the conventional welfare ranking of tariffs and production subsidies.

The Rodrik result is important as empirical studies show that political economy considerations are significant determinants of policy outcomes. The importance of political contributions is shown indirectly by Pincus (1975), Saunders (1980), Marvel and Ray (1983), Godek (1985) and Trefler (1993) who find a positive empirical relationship between seller concentration in an industry and protection, possibly arising from free-rider problems in providing contributions to politicians. Similar results are also found with respect to geographical concentration of industries. Bandopadhyay and Gawande (1999) and Goldberg and Maggi (1999) show that a political contributions model such as Grossman and Helpman (1994) is quite good at predicting the pattern of protection across industries in the US.[4] Both these papers actually show that industries providing political contributions above a certain cutoff level are the ones that get higher levels of protection.

The choice between tariffs and subsidies has also been considered in a voting framework in a series of papers by Mayer and Riezman (1987, 1989

---

[2] There is, of course, the case where only part of the tariff revenue is subject to revenue seeking, while the rest is distributed through Meade-type lump-sum transfers. In this case, a reduction (due to revenue-seeking) in the factor inputs into production could lead to a welfare improvement in the presence of a price distortion like a tariff. Further, the welfare rankings could get reversed again. See Bhagwati et al. (1997) for a detailed discussion of DUP activities.

[3] See Bhagwati (1990) for a useful typology of governments in the political economy literature – the "puppet", "self-willed" and "clearing-house" governments.

[4] In this context, it is important to note that the Grossman–Helpman (1994) "Protection for Sale" paper also provides an argument for the presence of tariffs. They argue that the intensity of lobbying by the different organized industries could increase with the efficiency of the instrument being lobbied for. However, the effects of the increased lobbying efforts may get cancelled out in equilibrium.

and 1990). They show that tariffs can be chosen in equilibrium outcome when voters differ along dimensions other than factor endowments, such as tastes and preferences, treatment under income taxes, etc. Besides, income tax progressivity might mean that the cost of financing subsidies might be borne unevenly, which might lead some individuals to prefer tariffs whose costs are more evenly distributed. The Mayer–Riezman models again fall in the demand-side category since they focus on demand for redistribution through voting.[5]

The specific question I am trying to address in this paper is: Given that a tariff has to be general to an industry, while subsidies could be firm specific (as in Rodrik, 1986), under what conditions would capitalists prefer tariffs to production subsidies?[6] In Rodrik (1986), even though aggregate social welfare may be higher in the tariff regime than in the subsidy regime, capitalists are always better off in the subsidy regime than in the tariff regime.[7] If the capitalists can have control over the level of subsidies or tariffs through lobbying, there is no reason why they should not have a say when it comes to deciding on the actual mix of such instruments.

I argue in this paper that even though a production subsidy is a private good (as opposed to a tariff which is a public good), one must take into account the fact that all buyers of this private good go to the same market where they could act strategically. Stronger lobbying by a firm for a production subsidy requires other firms in that industry to lobby harder to get a given amount of promotion. This arises from the upward sloping supply function of the politicians' services to capitalists in turn arising from the convex total costs (increasing marginal costs) of providing such services.

The upward slope of the politicians' supply function and the convexity of their costs can be explained using arguments from Magee et al. (1989), also used by Baldwin (1988). First, the deadweight loss from a tariff or subsidy is proportional to its square, making incremental services on the part of politicians towards providing higher protection (or promotion) more costly in terms of social welfare losses. Second, the marginal return from advertising, through

---

[5] Staiger and Tabellini (1987), Magee et al. (1989), Wilson (1990), Feenstra and Lewis (1991a, 1991b) and Grossman and Helpman (1994) provide other useful explanations for this puzzle. For a detailed survey of the existing literature, see Rodrik (1995).

[6] The firm specificity of subsidies is an important aspect that needs to be taken into account. Studies such as Carlsson (1983), Martin and Page (1983) and others cited in Rodrik (1986) show that about 30 to 50 percent of all subsidies in Italy, Sweden and the UK are firm specific. There are other very close substitutes of firm-specific subsidies such as special loans and regional assistance. Furthermore, although a regime of firm-specific subsidies may be potentially partial, its actual operation may not be so because all firms will, in general, find it profitable to lobby and, therefore, will get some protection in equilibrium.

[7] Rodrik (1986) argues that the welfare ranking of the two regimes can determine the endogenous choice between regimes if everyone is under the "Rawlsian veil of ignorance" about one's identity (whether a capitalist or a worker) at the point this choice is made.

36   MITRA

campaign contributions in terms of the probability of winning for the incumbent party, is diminishing since this probability can asymptotically go only to unity. It could be further argued that small amounts of services provided by politicians to capitalists go unnoticed, while large amounts of these services become increasingly visible to the general public. Thus, every additional unit of service to the lobbies can be provided at higher and higher additional costs in terms of the likelihood of electoral success.

I present two models in this paper. Both these models have both the demand-side as well as the supply-side aspects to them. Also, the governments in both models have some degree of "autonomy" and so are "self-willed" to a certain extent. However, there are some elements of the "clearing-house" feature mentioned above.[8] In the first model (presented in section 2), I assume that each firm in the import competing industry lobbies through its own political action committee and there is no association at the industry level that coordinates the lobbying activities of individual firms in the industry. In the second model (presented in section 3), I allow the possibility of coordination through an industry-level association. Both cases are equally important in the US context.[9]

In the first model, lobbying for subsidies by an individual firm leads to a negative externality on other firms by raising their marginal cost of lobbying since this cost is increasing in aggregate industry lobbying and not just firm-level lobbying. Therefore, the perceived marginal cost of lobbying for a firm is less than the actual, which leads to excessive lobbying by all the firms in equilibrium (congestion problem). A tariff, on the other hand, is a public good for all the firms in the industry and, thus, gives rise to a free-rider problem, which is partially offset by the congestion problem.[10] This could make tariffs more attractive than production subsidies to the capitalists. It is worth noting that the difference between the actual and the perceived is arising from a strategic

---

[8] In the political economy literature on trade policy, the models that have all these features are Feenstra and Bhagwati (1982) and Grossman and Helpman (1994) and its extensions. Feenstra and Bhagwati have two layers of the government, one which has its own will and the other which is a clearing-house to lobbies. It is the interaction of the two layers that leads to the final tariff formation.

[9] Wilson (1981) writes that smaller firms dominate the running of the Chamber of Commerce. Large corporations are not prepared to entrust their political representation to the Chamber, so that they belong to the Chamber merely out of a limited sense of duty. Wilson also writes that though the "Business Roundtable" was later founded in 1972 as an association of large corporations, large corporations are still expanding their individual representation by establishing their own individual PACs. He has given examples of large individual corporations such as the American Shipbuilding Corporation, Gulf Oil, Minnesota Mining and Manufacturing Corporation, Northrop Aircraft, Gulf Oil, etc., which made large illegal campaign contributions during the Nixon regime. Therefore, an industry lobby as a coordinating mechanism may not exist or at least may not be operational in the case of a concentrated industry with large corporations. On the other hand, this coordinating mechanism may exist in the case of an industry with small firms.

[10] Buying protection by any firm for the whole industry will make the additional protection the other firms buy for the industry more expensive.

distortion much in the same way as in an oligopoly model (see, for example, Eaton and Grossman, 1986).[11]

In the second model, through the provision of an extremely valuable club good, an organized lobby at the industry level can be formed.[12] Individual firms are also given the option to lobby politicians over and above what is being done through the industry lobby.[13] In such a setup, it turns out that coordination can be achieved in lobbying for a tariff. On the other hand, in the case of production subsidies, since the Nash equilibrium level of lobbying exceeds the cooperative level, there is an incentive for each of the capitalists in the industry to lobby an extra amount on the side. In equilibrium, lobbying for subsidies is done only at the firm level, while lobbying for tariffs gets done only at the industry level.

2. A MODEL WITH STRATEGIC INTERACTION AMONG FIRMS IN LOBBYING ACTIVITY

There are two goods Y (import competing) and Z (exportable) being produced in a small open economy. Their outputs are given by the following CRS production functions:

$$Y = F(L_Y, K) \tag{1}$$
$$Z = L_Z \tag{2}$$

where L_Y and L_Z are the amounts of labor used in the Y and Z sectors respectively. K is the amount of capital in the economy and is only used in the production of Y. It is assumed that Z is the numeraire good, so that wage gets fixed at one. p^* is the world price ratio and p represents the domestic price.

[11] In a two-country, oligopolistic trade model, Eaton and Grossman (1986) show that the home firm's perceived marginal benefit will differ from the actual benefit of changing its output to the extent that the home firm's conjecture about the foreign firm's reaction to this change in output differs from its true reaction. This difference between the conjecture and the actual reaction leads to a strategic distortion from the point of view of the home firm. Under Cournot–Nash interaction, the conjectural variations parameter is zero (different from the foreign firm's actual reaction) and, therefore, such a strategic distortion would exist. Another strategic distortion would exist if there are a large number of home firms in Nash interaction with each other, since they impose pecuniary externalities on each other and produce too much, and therefore fail to exert their full monopoly power in the world market.

Brander (1995) argues that holding the conjectural variations parameter at zero is the "correct" conjectural variation for the Cournot model, since firms have to choose output levels simultaneously before observing the output of their rivals, i.e., commit to certain output levels and then allow the prices to adjust to clear the market. In other words, the output level chosen by each firm has to be a best response given the output levels of others. The same argument holds for the analysis of any Nash interaction including the lobbying interaction in this paper. Therefore, the correct conjectural variations parameter, measuring a capitalist's conjecture about the lobbying response of other capitalists in the industry to changes in her own lobbying intensity, is zero. Thus, we get distortions like the free-rider and congestion effects. For capitalists to receive collusive lobbying payoffs, they need to have non-zero conjectural variations which are inappropriate in a static game.

[12] This could be considered a formalization of Olson's "by-product" theory of group formation which says that a club good or a private good may be the main reason to form a group and the optimal provision of a public good may just be a "by-product".

[13] This is consistent with the fact that even smaller corporations have started establishing their own PACs, although they continue to be active members of the Chamber of Commerce (Wilson, 1981).

2.1 Production

There are n profit-maximizing capitalists each owning K/n units of capital. The total capital stock K is assumed to be fixed in the economy. For simplicity and mathematical tractability, it is also assumed that capitalists do not consume the Y good. Profit maximization implies that each capitalist earns a profit $\Pi(p)/n$, such that $\Pi' > 0$, $\Pi'' \geqslant 0$.

2.2 Lobbying

I assume that in order to get concessions from the government, capitalists provide contributions to politicians to buy their services such as the drafting of bills, their introduction in both houses, taking part in debates before voting on a bill, the actual voting on a bill, etc. The inverse supply function of politicians' services X is given by

$$p_X = p_X(X) \tag{3}$$

where $p_X'(X) > 0$.[14] This supply function can be thought of as being obtained from aggregating the supplies of services from individual price-taking politicians who maximize benefit from contributions net of some convex welfare costs.[15] The various possible reasons for the upward slope of the supply function and the convexity of the welfare costs of services have already been explained in section 1 in detail.[16]

A tariff regime is one where the government uses only tariff as a means of protection, while a subsidy regime is one where the government uses only production subsidy as a means of protection (or rather promotion). In a tariff–subsidy regime, lobbying can be done both for tariffs and subsidies.

The amount of protection received is a function of the amount of politicians' services bought by capitalists. Let X_i be the amount of politicians' services bought by the ith firm. The tariff level for the industry in the tariff regime and the firm-specific subsidy for the ith firm in the subsidy regime are given respectively by

[14] Although for firm-specific subsidies, any given firm may end up going only to one politician, that politician may have to lobby other politicians to mobilize their support for getting bills passed. Moreover, a capitalist always has the option of going to other politicians. Therefore, aggregating the supply of politicians' services to get their market supply is meaningful even in the subsidy regime.
[15] This supply function could also be considered to be the supply of protection if the tariff and subsidy formation functions in (4) are linear and pass through the origin at 45°.
[16] Alternatively, X could denote the services of price taking, profit maximizing lobbyists (professional lobby firms) who own a fixed amount of sector specific human capital (lobbying skills) which they combine with ordinary labor to produce these services, thereby giving rise to an upward sloping supply function of their services (assuming CRS with respect to human capital and labor). These services are in turn used in the tariff and subsidy formation functions in (4). Therefore, in the entire analysis in this paper, one could easily replace the politicians' services with lobbyists' services and obtain all the results.

$$T = g\left(\sum_{j=1}^{n} X_j \right) \text{ and } S_i = g(nX_i) \quad g' > 0, g'' \leqslant 0, g(0) = 0.^{17,18} \quad (4)$$

In the tariff regime, each capitalist earns a profit

$$\frac{\tilde{\Pi}(\Sigma X_j)}{n} = \frac{\Pi(p^*(1 + g(\Sigma X_j)))}{n}.$$

Similarly, in the subsidy regime, each capitalist earns a profit $\tilde{\Pi}(nX_i)/n$. In the appendix, I also look at a tariff–subsidy regime in which lobbying can be done simultaneously for a tariff as well as a production subsidy.

Cooperative Equilibrium in the Tariff Regime

The level of total politicians' services X bought by the industry is obtained by maximizing industry-level profits net of lobbying costs as follows:

$$\max_X \tilde{\Pi}(X) - Xp_X(X).$$

Equilibrium: $\tilde{\Pi}'(X) = \psi(X)$ where $\psi(X) = p_X(X) + Xp_X'(X)$. (5)

Non-Cooperative Equilibrium in the Tariff Regime

Each capitalist decides how much of the politicians' services to buy for every amount bought by other capitalists. Her optimization problem is as follows:

$$\max_{X_i} \frac{\tilde{\Pi}(\Sigma X_j)}{n} - X_i p_X(\Sigma X_j).$$

Equilibrium: $\frac{\tilde{\Pi}'(X)}{n} = \phi(X, n)$ where $\phi(X, n) = p_X(X) + \frac{X}{n}p_X'(X)$. (6)

[17] The reason for choosing these tariff and subsidy functions is that the cooperative equilibria of the two regimes coincide. The number of firms n is viewed as a fixed parameter by each firm. Due to the private good nature of subsidies, a firm's subsidy rate is made only to depend on the politicians' services bought by itself. Furthermore, since lobbying politicians by a firm is for firm specific benefits in a subsidy regime, the equivalence imposed implies that the politicians' input each firm buys is magnified by a factor that equals the inverse of its share in the industry. This ensures that with equal amounts of services bought by the industry as a whole in the presence of symmetric purchase of these services by different firms, both the tariff and subsidy functions will yield identical expressions. In practice, however, the outcomes will be different due to the varying degrees of receptivity politicians are likely to exhibit towards demands for protection of various kinds. In this model, I am simply ruling out these kinds of asymmetry, again so as to exclusively focus on the congestion and free rider externalities. It should be noted that the tariff and subsidy functions here are similar to the lobbying functions for tariffs and subsidies respectively in Rodrik (1986), the difference being that in his functions the argument was labor used for lobbying, while here the argument is politicians' services.

[18] One could analyze economies of scale here by alternatively assuming the tariff and subsidy functions in (4) to be convex. This would make the argument for the existence of tariffs even stronger since lobbying for tariffs in this model is being done at the industry level and the lobbying for subsidies at the firm level, thereby leading to a much larger scale of operation for the former.

40   MITRA

Cooperative Equilibrium in the Subsidy Regime

The cooperative equilibrium in the subsidy regime is the same as in the tariff regime.[19]

Non-Cooperative Equilibrium in the Subsidy Regime

Each capitalist's maximization problem is as follows

$$\max_{X_i} \frac{\tilde{\Pi}(nX_i)}{n} - X_i p_X(\Sigma X_j).$$

Equilibrium: $\tilde{\Pi}'(X) = \phi(X, n)$.   (7)

From now on in this paper, the "equilibrium" (level) will refer to the non-cooperative equilibrium (level), unless specified otherwise.

Proposition 1

(a) In the tariff regime, the equilibrium level of politicians' services X is less than the cooperative level, while in the subsidy regime it is higher than the cooperative level for $n > 1$.

(b) As the number of capitalists n increases, the equilibrium level of tariff in the tariff regime falls (below the cooperative level), while the level of subsidy in the subsidy regime rises (above the cooperative level).

Proof. For $n = 1$, there is no difference between the cooperative and non-cooperative levels. As n increases the cooperative level remains fixed. In the (non-cooperative) subsidy regime

$$\frac{dX}{dn} = \frac{\phi_2}{\tilde{\Pi}'' - \phi_1} > 0,$$

while in the (non-cooperative) tariff regime

$$\frac{dX}{dn} = \frac{\phi + n\phi_2}{\tilde{\Pi}'' - n\phi_1} < 0.\text{[20]}$$

This proves (a) and (b).

The cooperative level of X is determined by equating the actual marginal benefit $\tilde{\Pi}'$ to the actual marginal cost ψ. The divergence between perceived marginal benefit in the tariff regime $\tilde{\Pi}'/n$ and the actual marginal benefit $\tilde{\Pi}'$ represents the

---

[19] As mentioned earlier, though actually it should be more costly for politicians to work towards a tariff than a subsidy, I am abstracting from this difference to fully focus on the congestion and free rider problems.

[20] The denominator is negative for both the terms by the standard condition that the perceived marginal benefit is flatter than the perceived marginal cost curve. The numerator is negative in the first expression and can be shown to be positive in the case of the second expression.

free-rider effect which reduces lobbying, while the divergence between the perceived marginal cost ϕ and the actual ψ gives rise to the congestion problem which increases lobbying. In the subsidy regime, only the congestion problem is present.

One can now think of a two-stage game. In the first stage, the capitalists have to choose between the tariff and subsidy regimes. They then lobby for the size of protection or promotion (tariff or production subsidy) in the second stage, given the regime that was chosen in the first stage. In this kind of a game, there exists the possibility that the capitalists might actually prefer the tariff regime to the subsidy regime, if the congestion effect is strong relative to the free-rider effect.

Example. In order to show that there could be situations in which the tariff regime is more attractive to capitalists, I provide examples using functional forms. Let $Y = AK^{1/2}L^{1/2}$ and $Z = L$ be the production functions of the two goods in the model. $T = \Sigma_{j=1}^{n} X_j$ and $S_i = nX_i$ are the tariff and subsidy functions respectively and $p_X = BX$ is the inverse aggregate supply of politicians.[21]

It can be shown that for $n > 1$ and for all values of B for which the second-order conditions of both regimes are satisfied, $N\Pi_T^* > N\Pi_S^*$, i.e., the equilibrium net profits (i.e., profits net of lobbying costs) of firms under the tariff regime exceed those under the subsidy regime. Moreover, both the difference between net profits $N\Pi_T^* - N\Pi_S^*$ and the percentage difference between them $(N\Pi_T^* - N\Pi_S^*)/N\Pi_S^*$ go up as n increases. As n increases, both the congestion problem and the free-rider problem become more severe, partly offsetting each other in the tariff regime but making matters worse in the subsidy regime.

Using a more general Cobb–Douglas production function $Y = K^\alpha L^{1-\alpha}$ and the same tariff and subsidy functions and the politicians' supply function, simulation results show that the percentage difference between the net profits in the tariff and subsidy regimes keeps increasing as the share α of capital in the total output decreases. As the share of the fixed factor falls, both output and profits become more elastic with respect to price and so capitalists would highly value an increase in price. This makes the congestion problem much more severe relative to the free-rider problem and so the tariff regime becomes more preferable relative to the subsidy regime. Another factor driving the result here is that labor is available at a constant wage fixed by the Ricardian sector. A decrease in B makes lobbying for protection or promotion more attractive to capitalists and so the congestion problem is more severe relative to the free-rider problem, thereby increasing the relative profitability of the tariff regime.

3. ORGANIZATION OF INTERESTS UNDER TARIFF AND SUBSIDY REGIMES

Mancur Olson (1965) argued that collective action in large groups takes place through selective incentives, i.e., through the provision of a private good or a

---

[21] B is a parameter reflecting how much politicians in general care about the welfare of voters. It could also be considered to be an indicator of the political awareness of voters.

club good within the lobby along with the provision of the public good. According to Olson's "by-product" theory of group formation, a club good or a private good may be the main reason to form a group and the optimal provision of a public good may just be a "by-product" requiring an additional contribution that is small relative to the lobby's total dues. In other words, the optimum level of the public good can be provided by using the margin between the dues and the cost of club good provision. All of this is also confirmed by empirical studies by Moe (1980), Salisbury (1992) and Walker (1991). Their case studies have also shown the existence of political leaders/entrepreneurs who devise different coordination mechanisms.

So the question is: Given that there exists a potential political entrepreneur, would she find it optimal from the point of view of the group to actually get the group politically organized? In other words, would she collect extra dues to lobby politicians? The answer is that this would depend on whether the capitalists are lobbying for a tariff or a subsidy.

In order to make things clear, I construct a simple example.[22] It is assumed that in the import competing sector in addition to production costs, there are other costs, say, managerial costs. Let only labor be used in management in any firm and let it just be proportional to the capital stock owned by the firm, so that

$$L_{M_i} = \gamma K_i. \tag{8}$$

(If the production and management costs are combined, the production function can be written as $Y = F(L, \min(K, L_M/\gamma))$ which is also CRS. For an optimizing firm, it would always be the case that $K = L_M/\gamma$.) Let $d\gamma \in [0, d\bar{\gamma}]$ be the reduction in γ that can be brought about if a certain know-how is available. However, this technology may not yield a net benefit to a single capitalist if she buys it for herself. Sharing the cost of this technology makes it economically feasible. It is assumed that this technology can be shared at no extra cost. One of the capitalists is the leader who fixes the dues for the club members to have access to the cost-reducing technology (available only to club members).

The leader is assumed to operate under the constraint that this industry association is a non-profit organization. Therefore, the leader's benefits are maximized when the industry net benefits are maximized.

I assume that it costs $c \cdot d\gamma$ to get this technology. Suppose the leader (or the President of the club) sets individual dues at

$$d = \frac{c \cdot d\bar{\gamma}}{n} + \frac{E}{n}$$

where E/n is the per person lobbying expenditure by the industry-level lobby, n being the number of capitalists in the import competing sector. The political entrepreneur announces that if r people agree to join and pay the dues then $d\gamma = (r/n)d\bar{\gamma}$ and the industry association's lobbying expenditure is given by

---

[22] One could construct other examples with other kinds of club goods as well.

$LE = (r/n)E$ (so that when all n capitalists join, the expenditure on lobbying by the industry association is E). In the spirit of Olson's "by-product" theory, I assume that the lobbying expenditure is always a negligible proportion of the total dues which in turn is much smaller than the gains from the cost-reducing technology. Thus, given the dues set by the political entrepreneur, joining the club by all the members in the group becomes a "coalition-proof" Nash equilibrium.[23] However, the political entrepreneur has control over setting the level of E that is optimal for the industry.

I can now define a three-stage game as follows.[24]

First Stage

Capitalists choose between a tariff regime and a subsidy regime.

Second Stage

This stage can be divided into two sub-stages:

(a) The leader or the potential political entrepreneur comes in with the technology, sets dues (per member) which include the cost of the technology and lobbying expenditure.[25]

(b) Given the dues set in (a), capitalists decide whether or not to join the association. The dues are then collected from those who decide to join.

Third Stage

This is the stage in which the club good gets provided, the lobbying gets done and the tariff or the subsidy level gets set. In this stage, *I do not rule out the possibility that individual firms will directly lobby the politicians over and above what is being done through the industry lobby if they feel that it is in their interest to do so.*[26]

[23] Bernheim et al. (1987) look at an important class of "noncooperative" environments where players can freely discuss their strategies, but cannot make binding commitments. They introduce a refinement of the Nash set, the concept of Coalition-Proof Nash equilibrium. An agreement is coalition-proof if and only if it is Pareto efficient within the class of self-enforcing agreements. In turn an agreement is self-enforcing if and only if no proper subset (coalition) of players, taking the actions of its complement as fixed, *can agree to deviate* in a way that makes all its members better off.

[24] Changing the sequence of stages might lead to indeterminacy in the model, since ex post, firms should be indifferent between a tariff and an equivalent level of subsidies. Furthermore, since the paper is showing that making the government *precommit* to tariff protection is what the capitalists would like, the sequence used in this paper seems to be the most appropriate.

[25] The lobbying expenditure is determined by the leader such that the industry net profits are maximized, taking into account the response of capitalists in stage 3. If the optimal E is zero, then the association is only a club. If, on the other hand, the optimal level of E is positive, then it is also a political lobby.

[26] This is consistent with the fact that even smaller corporations have started establishing their own PACs even though they are active members of the Chamber of Commerce (Wilson, 1981).

Let X^* be the solution to the following problem:

$$\max \, \bar{\Pi}(X) - p_X(X)X.$$

Let $E^* = p_X(X^*)X^*.$[27]

Assuming that the total benefits from the club good (e.g., new technology) are great compared to the dues (so that everybody joins the association in the second stage), I look at the third stage.

Let X_i^E be the extra amount of politicians' services the ith capitalist wants to buy in the third stage. Each capitalist decides on this for a given decided (in the previous stage) amount E to be spent by the industry association and given other capitalists' decision on the extra amount of politicians' services they are buying. In other words, each capitalist treats her dues as a sunk cost. The tariff for the industry and the subsidy that the ith firm can obtain are given by

$$T = g\left(\frac{E}{p_X} + \sum_{j=1}^{n} X_j^E\right) \quad \text{and} \quad S_i = g\left(\frac{E}{p_X} + nX_i^E\right). \tag{9}$$

(It should be noted that the share in E of any firm is E/n and therefore, for the firm, the effect of politicians' services bought through the industry lobby in the subsidy regime is given by $n[(E/n)/p_X] = E/p_X$.)[28]

Let X^L be the amount of services bought by the industry association. I will use X^E to denote $\Sigma \, X_j^E$. The supply of politicians' services is $X(p_X)$, so that $p_X X(p_X) = p_X[X^L + X^E] = E + p_X X^E$ and hence, we can write

$$E + p_X X^E = h(p_X) \tag{10}$$

where $h(p_X) = p_X X(p_X)$. Holding X^E constant, differentiating both sides of (10) with respect to E and then suitably rearranging the terms yields

$$\frac{\partial p_X}{\partial E} = \frac{1}{X^L + p_X X'(p_X)} > 0. \tag{11}$$

Similarly, holding E constant and differentiating with respect to X^E (followed by suitable rearrangement of terms) gives

$$\frac{\partial p_X}{\partial X^E} = \frac{p_X}{X^L + p_X X'(p_X)} > 0. \tag{12}$$

Thus, from (11) and (12), the price p_X of the politicians' services can be written as an increasing function of the amount X^E of extra services bought by the

---

[27] One must note that the managerial costs do not need to be subtracted in any of the maximization problems here since the firm-level and industry-level capital stock are fixed and, therefore, the managerial costs are also fixed for a given management technology.

[28] Both the tariff and subsidy functions again have the property that they yield the same expressions for the same amount of the total politicians' services bought by the industry (assuming symmetric firms). Moreover, since the subsidy is firm specific in nature, the effect of a firm's purchase of politicians' services gets magnified by the inverse of its share in the industry.

capitalists in the third stage and expenditure E by the industry lobby and so we can write

$$p_X = \tilde{p}(\Sigma X_j^E, E) \quad \tilde{p}_1 > 0, \tilde{p}_2 > 0 \tag{13}$$

where the subscripts "1" and "2" denote partial derivatives with respect to the first and second arguments respectively.

Proposition 2. When an industry association is formed, coordination is possible with tariffs, but not with subsidies.

Proof. Subsidy regime: For a given E, each capitalist will solve the following problem in the third stage in the subsidy regime:

$$\max_{X_i^E} \frac{1}{n} \tilde{\Pi} \left(\frac{E}{\tilde{p}(\Sigma X_j^E, E)} + n X_i^E \right) - \tilde{p}(\Sigma X_j^E, E) X_i^E.$$

As shown above, the partial derivatives of $\tilde{p}(\Sigma X_j^E, E)$ with respect to both arguments are positive. X is the total amount of services bought by the capitalists (through the industry lobby as well as on their own on the side) and sold by the politicians. With the earlier linear supply function of politicians' services given by $X = p_X/B$, the first-order condition (which is with respect to X_i^E) for the above maximization problem translates in terms of X and E as follows:

$$\tilde{\Pi}'(X) = \left[\frac{\tilde{\Pi}'(X)E + BX(BX^2 - E)}{n(BX^2 + E)} \right] + BX. \tag{14}$$

Let us denote the right-hand side of the above equation as $l(X, E)$. For B large enough, $l_1 > 0$. Moreover, $l_2 < 0$ when $\tilde{\Pi}'(X) < 2BX$ (which is always true in the subsidy equilibrium for $n > 1$).

$$\frac{dX}{dE} = \frac{l_2}{\tilde{\Pi}'' - l_1} > 0.^{29}$$

At $E = 0$, the Nash level of X is the same as the subsidy regime in section 2, which is above the optimal level. Increasing E, then, keeps further reducing the net (of lobbying costs) profits of the capitalists.[30] Hence, *the political entrepreneur's best strategy is to set $E = 0$ in the second period. Therefore, the club just remains a club and does not get converted into a political lobby.*

---

[29] The denominator is negative by the standard condition that the marginal benefit curve is flatter than the marginal cost curve.

[30] The intuition here is that in the subsidy regime E cannot fully crowd out the lobbying expenditure by firms because each firm takes into account the effect of E only on its own marginal cost of lobbying and not on the marginal cost of the industry. This is done taking other capitalists' action as given. A sufficient condition here is that net profits are globally concave in X.

46   MITRA

Tariff Regime

For a given E, each capitalist solves the following problem:

$$\max_{X_i^E} \frac{1}{n} \tilde{\Pi}\left(\frac{E}{\bar{p}(\Sigma X_j^E, E)} + \Sigma X_j^E \right) - \bar{p}(\Sigma X_j^E, E) X_i^E.$$

The first-order condition gets translated into

$$\tilde{\Pi}'(X) \leqslant nl(X, E), \; [\tilde{\Pi}'(X) - nl(X, E)] X^E = 0.^{31} \tag{15}$$

At $E = E^*$ and $X^E = 0$, we have $\tilde{\Pi}'(X^*) < nl(X^*, E^*)$. Therefore, if E is set at E^*, each firm sets X_i^E to zero. *Hence, setting $E = E^*$ in the second stage is the optimal strategy for the political entrepreneur. Therefore, the group also gets organized for political purposes under a tariff regime. Hence, in the first stage capitalists will always choose the tariff regime.*

The intuition here is that the club can coordinate if non-cooperative lobbying is too little. The collection of dues that include the cooperative lobbying expenditure would leave no incentive to lobby on one's own on the side in the case of tariffs, since the perceived marginal net benefit of lobbying further is negative. This fixes the total amount of lobbying at the cooperative level. In the subsidy regime, there exists an incentive to lobby additionally on the side as in section 2 since the non-cooperative level exceeds the cooperative level. Therefore, the capitalists may want the government to precommit to the tariff regime.

4. CONCLUSION

This paper shows how, in a model of strategic interaction between large firms in lobbying activity, the Nash equilibrium in the tariff regime may be better for the capitalists than the one in the subsidy regime. This is due to the congestion problem arising from the government's convex welfare costs of protection when lobbying for subsidies as opposed to both the free-rider problem and the congestion problem acting in opposite directions in the case of tariffs. If an industry association exists, coordination can be done when lobbying for tariffs, but not for subsidies.

APPENDIX

Tariff–Subsidy Regime in the Absence of an Industry Association

The tariff–subsidy regime is one in which lobbying can be done for both tariffs and subsidies simultaneously. In the tariff–subsidy regime, two polar cases are analyzed. In the first case, which I call "joint protection", I assume that total protection to a firm is dependent on the sum of the average lobbying for tariff (as

---

[31] In this case, I write the full Kuhn–Tucker condition because, depending on the value of E, the non-negativity constraint on the choice variable may or may not be binding.

it is a public good) and the firm-specific lobbying for production subsidies so that we have

$$T + S_i = g(n(\bar{X}^T + X_i^S)) = g\left(\sum_{j=1}^n X_j^T + nX_i^S \right) \tag{A1}$$

where the superscripts T and S represent the services purchased for tariff and subsidy lobbying respectively. $\bar{X}^T$ is the average (across all firms in the industry) amount of politicians' services purchased to lobby for tariffs. The government can use some arbitrary rules to divide the total protection between tariffs and subsidies. For example, we can have

$$T = g\left(\sum_{j=1}^n X_j^T \right) \quad \text{and} \quad S_i = g\left(\sum_{j=1}^n X_j^T + nX_i^S \right) - g\left(\sum_{j=1}^n X_j^T \right).$$

In other words, the total industry lobbying for tariffs determines the level of the tariff and extra protection in the form of a subsidy is given to a firm depending on the firm's intensity of lobbying for it. Another possible division rule is $T/(T + \tilde{S}) = \bar{X}^T/(\bar{X}^T + \bar{X}^S)$ where the "bar" on top just represents the average level. There are several other possible division rules that can be used. However, it will be shown later that the division rule used is totally inconsequential to the Nash equilibrium outcome.

In the second case (of the tariff–subsidy regime) which I call "separable protection", we have

$$T = g\left(\sum_{j=1}^n X_j^T \right) \quad \text{and} \quad S_i = g(nX_i^S). \tag{A2}$$

In this case the tariff formation function and the subsidy formation function are totally independent of each other. The two cases analyzed under the tariff–subsidy regimes are polar opposites of each other. The real world could be considered to lie in between the two.

In the tariff–subsidy regime under the "joint protection" assumption, each capitalist earns

$$\frac{\tilde{\Pi}(\Sigma X_j^T + nX_i^S)}{n} = \frac{\Pi(p^*(1 + g(\Sigma X_j^T + nX_i^S)))}{n},$$

while under the "separable protection" case she earns

$$\frac{\hat{\Pi}(g(\Sigma X_j^T) + g(nX_i^S))}{n} = \frac{\Pi(p^*(1 + g(\Sigma X_j^T) + g(nX_i^S)))}{n}.$$

Cooperative Equilibrium

(a) "Joint protection" case: The industry-level purchase of politicians' services for tariff lobbying X^T and for subsidy lobbying X^S are obtained by solving the following maximization problem:

48   MITRA

$$\max_{X^T, X^S} \tilde{\Pi}(X^T + X^S) - (X^T + X^S)p_X(X^T + X^S).$$

Equilibrium: $\tilde{\Pi}'(X) = \psi(X)$ where $\psi(X) = p_X(X) + Xp'_X(X)$
$$\text{and } X = X^T + X^S \qquad \text{(A3)}$$

which implies that the total protection and, therefore, the level of net profits for the capitalists are the same as the cooperative equilibria in the previous two regimes.

(b) "Separable protection" case:

$$\max_{X^T, X^S} \hat{\Pi}(g(X^T) + g(X^S)) - (X^T + X^S)p_X(X^T + X^S).$$

Equilibrium: $\hat{\Pi}'g'(X/2) = \psi(X)$ where $X^T = X^S = X/2$. $\qquad$ (A4)

Here, $X^S = X^T$ since subsidy and tariff formation functions are independent and identical. However, the total amount of protection and the net profits are higher than in all the other cooperative equilibria that have been analyzed so far in this paper. Since there are diminishing returns to lobbying for each kind of protection and since the lobbying functions for the two instruments are independent of each other, these two instruments act like differentiated inputs in the profit function.

Non-Cooperative Equilibrium

(a) "Joint protection" case:

$$\max_{X^T_i, X^S_i} \frac{\tilde{\Pi}(\Sigma X^T_j + nX^S_i)}{n} - (X^T_i + X^S_i)p_X(\Sigma X^T_j + \Sigma X^S_j).$$

Equilibrium: $\tilde{\Pi}'(X^S) = \phi(X^S, n),\ \ X^T = 0,$ $\qquad$ (A5)

which means that *this coincides with the non-cooperative equilibrium of the subsidy regime*. The intuition here is that since the perceived marginal benefit of politicians' services in tariffs is an nth fraction of that in subsidies, while the marginal costs are the same, *all lobbying is done only for subsidies. These subsidies increase as n increases exactly in the same way as in the subsidy regime.*

(b) "Separable protection" case:

$$\max_{X^T_i, X^S_i} \frac{\tilde{\Pi}(g(\Sigma X^T_j) + g(nX^S_i))}{n} - (X^T_i + X^S_i)p_X(\Sigma X^T_i + \Sigma X^S_j).$$

Equilibrium: $\dfrac{\hat{\Pi}'g'(X^T)}{n} = \phi(X, n),\ \hat{\Pi}'g'(X^S) = \phi(X, n)$
where $X = X^T + X^S$. $\qquad$ (A6)

The above first-order conditions can be written as

$$X^T = \theta(X^S, n), \quad -1 < \theta_1 < 0, \theta_2 < 0 \quad \text{and} \quad X^S = \omega(X^T, n),$$
$$-1 < \omega_1 < 0, \omega_2 > 0.$$

Differentiating these two equations, we have

$$\frac{dX^S}{dn} = \frac{\omega_1\theta_2 + \omega_2}{1 - \omega_1\theta_1} > 0, \quad \frac{dX^T}{dn} = \frac{\omega_2\theta_1 + \theta_2}{1 - \omega_1\theta_1} < 0.$$

At $n = 1$, equal amounts of lobbying will be done for tariffs and subsidies. As n increases, tariff lobbying goes down and subsidy lobbying goes up, thereby converging to the pure subsidy regime as n goes up. Moreover, one should note that if $g'' = 0$, there is no difference between the joint and separable protection cases and so the tariff lobbying again becomes zero and only lobbying for subsidies is done.

Therefore, when we use the "joint protection" formulation, capitalists would prefer the tariff regime to the subsidy and the tariff–subsidy regimes if the congestion effect is strong relative to the free-rider effect. If we use the separable protection formulation, a strong congestion effect would still make the pure subsidy regime the worst of the three regimes from the point of view of the capitalists. In any case, with a strong enough congestion effect, we would see some tariffs in equilibrium.

In the example used in section 2, there is no difference between the "joint" and "separable" protection formulations, as the protection formation function is linear, passing through the origin. Therefore, in that example, even if the tariff–subsidy regime is added to the choice set of protection regimes, the capitalists would want the government to precommit to the pure tariff regime.

Tariff–Subsidy Regime in the Presence of an Industry Association

In this regime, again, lobbying will be done only for subsidies in the "joint protection" case and the political entrepreneur will set $E = 0$ and the payoff to the capitalists will be the same as in the subsidy regime. However, in the separable protection case, both instruments will exist in equilibrium, but coordination will not be achieved. However, the beneficial "differentiated inputs" effect will exist. In the tariff–subsidy regime, for the joint protection case, we have $T + S_i = g((E/p_X) + \Sigma X_j^{TE} + nX_i^{SE})$ and for the separable protection case we have $T = g((E^T/p_X) + \Sigma X_j^{TE})$, $S_i = g((E^S/p_X) + nX_i^{SE})$ where the SE and TE superscripts denote extra purchases of services at the firm level used for lobbying for subsidies and tariffs respectively. E^T and E^S are lobbying expenditures by the club for tariffs and subsidies respectively and $E = E^T + E^S$. For the joint protection case again, different division rules can be used. However, the Nash equilibrium outcome will not be affected by the particular division rule adopted.

DEVASHISH MITRA
Department of Economics,
Florida International University

50   MITRA

REFERENCES

Baldwin, R. E., 1988, The political economy of protectionism, in: R. E. Baldwin, ed., *Trade Policy in a Changing Economy* (University of Chicago Press, Chicago and London) 97–120.

Bandopadhyay, U. and K. Gawande, 1999, Is protection for sale? A test of the Grossman–Helpman theory of endogenous protection. *Review of Economics & Statistics*, forthcoming.

Bernheim, B. D., B. Peleg and M. D. Whinston, 1987, Coalition-proof Nash equilibria. *Journal of Economic Theory* 42(1), 1–12.

Bhagwati, J. N., 1971, The generalized theory of distortions and welfare, in: J. N. Bhagwati et al., eds., *Trade, Balance of Payments and Growth* (North-Holland, Amsterdam) 69–90.

——, 1990, The theory of political economy, economic policy and foreign investment, in M. Scott and D. Lal, eds., *Public Policy and Economic Development* (Clarendon Press, Oxford) 217–230.

—— and V. K. Ramaswami, 1963, Domestic distortions, tariffs and the theory of the optimum subsidy. *Journal of Political Economy* 71, 44–50.

—— and T. N. Srinivasan, 1980, Revenue seeking: a generalization of the theory of tariffs. *Journal of Political Economy* 88, 1069–1087.

—— and ——, 1982, The welfare consequences of directly unproductive profit-seeking (DUP) lobbying activities: price versus quantity distortions. *Journal of International Economics* 13, 33–44.

——, A. Panagariya, and T. N. Srinivasan, 1997, *Lectures in International Trade* (MIT Press, Cambridge, MA).

Brander, J. A. 1995, Strategic trade policy, in: G. Grossman and K. Rogoff, eds., *Handbook of International Economics*, vol. 3 (North-Holland, Amsterdam).

Carlsson, Bo, 1983, Industrial subsidies in Sweden: macroeconomic effects and an international comparison. *Journal of Industrial Economics* 32(1), 1–23.

Eaton, J. and G. M. Grossman, 1986, Optimal trade and industrial policy under oligopoly. *Quarterly Journal of Economics* 101, 383–406.

Feenstra, R. C. and J. N. Bhagwati, 1982, Tariff seeking and the efficient tariff, in: J. N. Bhagwati, ed., *Import Competition and Response* (University of Chicago Press, Chicago and London).

—— and T. R. Lewis, 1991a, Distributing the gains from trade with incomplete information. *Economics and Politics* 3(1), 21–40.

—— and ——, 1991b, Negotiated trade restrictions with political pressure. *Quarterly Journal of Economics* 106, 1287–1307.

Findlay, R. and S. Wellisz, 1982, Endogenous tariffs, the political economy of trade restrictions and welfare, in: J. N. Bhagwati, ed., *Import Competition and Response* (University of Chicago Press, Chicago and London) 223–234.

Godek, P. E., 1985, Industry structure and redistribution through trade restrictions. *Journal of Law and Economics* 28, 687–703.

Goldberg, P. K. and G. Maggi, 1999, Protection for sale: an empirical investigation. *American Economic Review*, forthcoming.

Grossman, G. M. and E. Helpman, 1994, Protection for sale. *American Economic Review* 84(4), 833–850.

Johnson, H. G., 1965, Optimal trade intervention in the presence of domestic distortions, in: R. E. Caves, H. G. Johnson, and P. B. Kenen, eds., *Trade, Growth and Balance of Payments* (North-Holland, Amsterdam) 3–34.

Magee, S. P., W. A. Brock, and L. Young, 1989, *Black Hole Tariffs and Endogenous Policy Theory* (Cambridge University Press, Cambridge and New York).

Martin, J. P. and J. M. Page, Jr., 1983, The impact of subsidies on x-efficiency in LDC industry: theory and empirical tests. *Review of Economics and Statistics* LXV(4), 608–617.

Marvel, H. P. and E. J. Ray, 1983, The Kennedy Round: evidence on the regulation of trade in the US. *American Economic Review* 73, 190–197.

Mayer, W. and R. Riezman, 1987, Endogenous choice of trade policy instruments. *Journal of International Economics* 23, 377–381.

——— and ———, 1989, Tariff formation in a multidimensional voting model. *Economics and Politics* 1(1), 61–79.

——— and ———, 1990, Voter preferences for trade policy instruments. *Economics and Politics* 2(3), 259–273.

Moe, T. M., 1980, *The Organization of Interests* (University of Chicago Press, Chicago and London).

Olson, M., 1965, *The Logic of Collective Action* (Harvard University Press, Cambridge, MA).

Pincus, J. J., 1975, Pressure groups and the pattern of tariffs. *Journal of Political Economy* 83, 757–778.

Rodrik, D., 1986, Tariffs, subsidies, and welfare with endogenous policy. *Journal of International Economics* 21, 285–296.

———, 1995, Political economy of trade policy, in: G. M. Grossman and K. Rogoff, eds., *Handbook of International Economics*, vol. 3 (North-Holland, Amsterdam) 1457–1494.

Salisbury, R. H., 1992, *Interests and Institutions* (University of Pittsburg Press, Pittsburg and London).

Saunders, R. S., 1980, The political economy of effective protection in Canada's manufacturing sector. *Canadian Journal of Economics* 13, 340–348.

Staiger, R. W. and G. Tabellini, 1987, Discretionary trade policy and excessive protection. *American Economic Review* 77(5), 823–837.

Trefler, D., 1993, Trade liberalization and the theory of endogenous protection. *Journal of Political Economy* 101, 138–160.

Walker, J. L., 1991, *Mobilizing Interest Groups in America* (University of Michigan Press, Ann Arbor, MI).

Wilson, J. D. 1990, Are efficiency improvements in government transfer policies self-defeating in equilibrium? *Economics and Politics* 2(3), 241–258.

Chapter 12

PROTECTION VERSUS PROMOTION: AN EMPIRICAL INVESTIGATION

DEVASHISH MITRA*, DIMITRIOS D. THOMAKOS,
and MEHMET A. ULUBAŞOĞLU

Using Turkish industry-level data from 1983 to 1990, we find that politically organized industries receive both higher protection and promotion than unorganized ones. Tariff rates are decreasing (increasing) in
the import-penetration ratio and the absolute value of the import-
demand elasticity for organized (unorganized) industries. Subsidy rates
are decreasing (increasing) in the output-supply elasticity for organized
(unorganized) industries. The results are consistent with the predictions
of the Grossman–Helpman model and its extension in this paper. The
mix of protection and promotion is inversely related to the ratio of their
respective marginal deadweight cost measures.

1. INTRODUCTION

IN THE absence of any trade-related distortions or policy goals, direct subsidies are superior to tariffs in that they achieve the desired objective with a
lower welfare loss. This is a major proposition of the theory of domestic
distortions and welfare, as developed by Bhagwati and Ramaswami (1963),
Johnson (1965), and Bhagwati (1971).

Endogenizing the levels of policy instruments, however, may not always
preserve the above welfare rankings.[1] Rodrik (1986) studies the welfare
rankings of policies by considering tariffs and subsidies as endogenously
determined through lobbying by capitalists. He recognizes the free-rider
problem associated with the lobbying for tariffs and the possible firm-specific
nature of subsidies. Under such conditions of endogenous determination of
tariffs and subsidies, Rodrik argues that the conventional welfare rankings
can get reversed. Mitra (2000) argues that even capitalists themselves may
prefer tariffs as the firm-specific nature of subsidies may result in costly
competition among producers within an industry, while the public good
nature of the tariff will prevent this from happening.

*Corresponding author: Department of Economics, Syracuse University, Eggers Hall, Syra-
cuse, NY 13244, USA. E-mail: dmitra@maxwell.syr.edu

[1]The existence of rent or revenue-seeking or directly unproductive, profit-seeking (DUP)
activities and their impact on welfare rankings of different types of policies have been studied by
Krueger (1974), Bhagwati and Srinivasan (1980), Anam (1982), and Bhagwati et al. (1984).

147

148   MITRA ET AL.

Grossman and Helpman (1994) also explain, how in the presence of lobbying, inefficient policy instruments may get chosen over more efficient means of transferring incomes to politically influential groups. Competition among lobbies can lead to excessive contributions when policies are very efficient. Thus lobbies may want to tie the hands of the government and constrain it to use relatively inefficient policies.

Another strand in the political-economy literature puts forth the idea that tariffs are informationally efficient. Magee et al. (1989), Austen-Smith (1991), and Coate and Morris (1995) model this idea in different ways.[2] Feenstra and Lewis (1991) model, under asymmetric information, a benevolent government that takes action to protect the losers from a world price shock. They show that import protection is more useful than promotion (subsidies) in this regard (see section 2 for details of the argument).

In this paper, we use Turkish industry-level data to empirically investigate the determinants of protection (tariffs) and promotion (subsidies) and of the relative mix of these two instruments. Even though there is now a fairly large empirical literature on the industry-level determinants of import protection,[3] to our knowledge, there has been no attempt so far to empirically analyze, using industry-level data, the cross-industry variation in production subsidies and its size relative to import-protection (the issue of the choice of instruments).[4] We use the Grossman–Helpman (1994) "Protection for sale" model to guide us in our empirical analysis. In this model, the government's objective function is a weighted sum of political contributions and aggregate welfare, while each lobby maximizes its welfare net of political contributions. Within such a framework, Grossman and Helpman derive the level of protection as an estimable function of industry characteristics and other political and economic factors. Protection to organized sectors is negatively related to import-penetration and to the (absolute value of) import-demand elasticity while protection to unorganized sectors is positively related to these two variables. Other things remaining equal, organized sectors receive higher protection than unorganized sectors.[5] We also use the same frame-

[2]See Rodrik (1995) for an in-depth survey of the theoretical literature on the choice of policy instruments.
[3]The well-known papers in this area are Trefler (1993), Goldberg and Maggi (1999), and Gawande and Bandypadhyay (2000).
[4]Recently, Ederington and Minier (2001) have used cross-country data on average tariffs, subsidies and other country characteristics such as per capita GDP, income taxes, budget deficit, literacy, democracy/dictatorship, availability of newspapers etc. to test at the aggregate level the various competing theoretical explanations for the preference of governments for tariffs as a means of redistribution. They find that the "revenue explanation" is the "most supported by the data," since the use of tariffs relative to subsidies is higher by countries that are more revenue-constrained (i.e. those that have relatively larger budget deficits).
[5]It needs to be noted here that we also empirically investigated the Grossman–Helpman model for "protection" (using the same dataset) in Mitra et al. (2002). The reason we present the results using the same model is to compare the results with those for "promotion" which also are based on an extension of the original Grossman–Helpman model. This, in turn, provides us with a better understanding of the protection–promotion mix.

work to derive the political-economy equilibrium level of production subsidies. Again the subsidy rate is higher for organized sectors than for unorganized sectors. The key variable in this case is *the output-supply elasticity in place of the import-demand elasticity*. While the subsidy rate is decreasing in this elasticity for organized sectors, it is increasing in it for unorganized sectors. While the import-penetration ratio and the import-demand elasticity together determine the deadweight costs associated with protection, the output-supply elasticity determines the excess burden on society associated with promotion. Therefore, we believe that the relative marginal costs (as a function of the above two elasticities and the import-penetration ratio) of these two instruments will determine relative levels of these two instruments used.

We use data for the years 1983, 1984, and 1990. Our measures of protection and promotion are the nominal rate of protection (NRP) and nominal subsidy rate (NSR), respectively. Our main right-hand-side variables are the import-penetration ratios, import-demand elasticities, output-supply elasticities and a dummy variable indicating whether the industry is politically organized or not. We use additional control variables such as four-firm industry concentration ratios, changes in world prices (as a proportion of initial world price), and geographical concentration.

We specifically look at Turkey for the following reasons. Detailed data on tariffs and subsidies are readily available for Turkey. Also, this is a "genuine" small, open economy and so terms-of-trade motivations, by interacting with other factors, will not complicate our analysis. Finally, it also allows us to see how some of the theories, written specifically in the context of developed countries, perform when taken to developing-country data.

Our empirical results are consistent with the theoretical results of the Grossman–Helpman model and of its extension using subsidies. The mix of policy instruments used also depends on the relative costs as suggested by the model. There is also some evidence that the mix is more in favor of protection relative to promotion for more concentrated industries. This may just be because the severity of the free-rider problem in tariffs is decreasing in industry concentration, while subsidies can in principle be firm-specific. We find some (even though somewhat weak) evidence for the negative (positive) impact of import price increases (decreases) on the protection–promotion ratio, as predicted by Feenstra and Lewis (1991).

Final remarks in this section have to do with the estimation methodology. We estimate our main equations using both (iterative) weighted least squares (WLS) as well as weighted two-stage least squares (W2SLS) (in order to account for any possible endogeneity and measurement error problems associated with our right-hand-side variables as well as any heteroskedasticity concerns that may arise from the panel nature of our dataset).

In section 2, we discuss the theory. We present the econometric specification in section 3 while section 4 explains the data. The results of our empirical analysis are given in section 5. Finally, in section 6 we provide some concluding remarks.

2. THEORY

In this section we first provide an abridged description of the "Protection for sale" model of Grossman and Helpman (1994).

Consider a small, open economy. Individuals are assumed to have identical preferences. Each individual possesses labor and at most one kind of specific factor of production. There are N non-numéraire goods, each requiring a different kind of factor of production specific to that good, and labor. In addition, there is a numéraire good which is produced under constant returns to scale using only labor. A quasi-linear utility function, that is linear in numéraire good consumption, concave in the consumption of each non-numéraire good, and additively separable across all goods, is assumed.

It is also assumed that the only policy instruments available to politicians are trade taxes and subsidies. Further, the government redistributes revenue uniformly to all its citizens.

In sectors that are politically organized, the specific factor owners are able to lobby the government for preferential treatment in the form of higher trade protection for their own sectors and lower protection for other sectors. The interaction between the government and the lobbies takes the form of a "menu-auction" as in Bernheim and Whinston (1986). Thus, we have the following two-stage game.

First stage. Lobbies provide the government with their contribution schedules taking into account the government's objective function (described below). Each lobby takes the contribution schedules of other lobbies as given.

Second stage. In the second stage, taking into account the contribution or offer schedules from the previous stage, the government sets trade policy to maximize a weighted sum of political contributions and overall social welfare.

The government's objective function is the following:

$$\Omega_G(\mathbf{p}) = \sum_{j \in \Lambda} C_j(\mathbf{p}) + a\Omega_A(\mathbf{p}), \tag{1}$$

where Λ is the set of organized interest groups (lobbies), $\mathbf{p} \in \mathbf{P}$ is the domestic price vector, $\Omega_A(\mathbf{p})$ is aggregate social welfare, $C_j(\mathbf{p})$ is the contribution schedule of the jth lobby and $\mathbf{P}$ is the set of domestic price vectors from which the government may choose.[6] The parameter a in (1) is the weight the

[6]The set $\mathbf{P}$ is bounded such that each domestic price lies between some minimum and some maximum value. Grossman and Helpman (1994) restrict attention to equilibria that lie in the interior of $\mathbf{P}$.

PROTECTION VERSUS PROMOTION   151

government attaches to aggregate social welfare relative to political contributions. The higher is a, the lower is the government's affinity for political contributions and the higher is its concern for social welfare.[7] The outcome of the game is a set of trade taxes and subsidies that satisfy the following, familiar Grossman–Helpman modified "Ramsey rule":

$$\frac{t_i}{1 + t_i} = \frac{I_i - \alpha_L}{a + \alpha_L} \cdot \frac{z_i}{e_i}, \tag{2}$$

where z_i is the ratio of domestic output to imports or exports (depending on whether the sector is import-competing or an exporting one) and e_i is the absolute value of price elasticity of import demand or export supply. I_i is an indicator variable that takes a value 1 if the sector is politically organized and is zero for an unorganized sector. α_L is the proportion of the country's population that is organized.

The intuition behind the above tariff equation is that deviations around free trade (positive for organized sectors and negative for unorganized sectors) are costly, the cost being increasing in the import-demand or export-supply elasticity and in the import-penetration ratio (decreasing in its inverse). A higher inverse import-penetration ratio also means higher political power (from the higher output relative to trade). Therefore, for sectors with high import-demand elasticities and import-penetration ratios, the deviations from free trade are smaller. A higher a (the weight on aggregate welfare relative to contributions) leads understandably to smaller deviations from free trade – both the size of the positive protection to organized sectors and the absolute value of the negative protection to unorganized sectors are lower. A high α_L means the proportion of the population politically organized is large and so there are more people claiming a share of the pie of rents. So each organized group will get a smaller slice, i.e. a smaller amount of protection. However, each remaining unorganized group is taxed more (provided higher negative protection) as there is a bigger organized population throwing its weight on a smaller unorganized population.

In place of trade taxes and subsidies, if the government had at its disposal production subsidies and taxes, it is very straightforward to show that the outcome of the game would be subsidy rates s_i that satisfy

$$\frac{s_i}{1 + s_i} = \frac{I_i - \alpha_L}{a + \alpha_L} \cdot \frac{1}{e_i^s}, \tag{3}$$

[7]Grossman and Helpman show that, with contribution schedules that are continuous in the price vector in the neighborhood of the equilibrium, the government's problem of choosing its most preferred tariff vector (on receiving all the contribution schedules) is equivalent to maximizing the function $\sum_{j \in \Lambda} \Omega_j(\mathbf{p}) + a\Omega_A(\mathbf{p})$ with respect to the domestic price vector $\mathbf{p}$ where $\Omega_j(\mathbf{p})$ is welfare of sector j. This new reduced-form maximand is an additively separable form of the more general Hillman (1989) political support function; i.e. Grossman and Helpman (1994) provide microfoundations for models that use the political–support function approach.

where e_i^s is the price elasticity of output supply.[8] Note that in the production subsidy regime, for every good, consumers face the world price while producers face a different price whose wedge with respect to the world price is determined by the production tax or subsidy. The intuition for everything is almost the same as in the case of trade taxes and subsidies, except that, since the subsidy or tax now is on the entire output, import-penetration and import-demand elasticities do not matter. The deadweight costs now are increasing in the output-supply elasticities instead for a given amount of intervention.

While introducing both trade taxes and subsidies and output taxes and subsidies in the same model can lead to a corner solution in which only one type of policy instrument is used, introducing additional (convex) costs of financing production subsidies or raising tariff revenues can, as shown by Ederington and Minier (2003), lead to a regime in which we have both kinds of instruments. Developing a model incorporating such additional costs is clearly beyond the scope of this paper which we view primarily as an empirical contribution to the literature. However, it is obvious that the relative marginal deadweight costs will be important in determining this policy mix and so the tariff equation divided by the subsidy equation will provide us with such a relationship:

$$\frac{t_i/(1 + t_i)}{s_i/(1 + s_i)} = \frac{z_i e_i^s}{e_i}, \tag{4}$$

where $[t_i/(1 + t_i)]/[s_i/(1 + s_i)]$ is a measure of the policy mix while $z_i e_i^s/e_i$ is a measure of the relative marginal deadweight costs. There are other relative costs in addition to the ones mentioned above. However, those costs are not expected to vary across industries and so will hopefully be captured by a constant term (see the next section).

We now discuss the theory behind some of the control variables we use in this paper:

1. *Four-firm concentration ratio.* Rodrik (1986) argues that when trade policies are endogenously determined by lobbying, the resultant free-rider problem due to the public-good nature of the tariffs reduces the incentives for lobbying since all firms will benefit from an imposition of a tariff, even when not every firm lobbies for it. As the number of firms in an industry increases, the aggregate incentive to devote resources at the industry level to the public good – lobbying expenditure – diminishes. The end result is less protection, meaning higher social welfare. Once a

---

[8]In this model, we assume that the subsidy is not firm-specific but is general to all firms in an industry. Therefore, in this respect our modeling here of production subsidies is different from Rodrik (1986) and Mitra (2000). We believe that production subsidies in the real world have firm-specific as well as general components. We try to take both these aspects into account in our empirical work on the protection–promotion mix in this paper.

threshold number of firms is reached, a tariff regime will become, from the aggregate welfare point of view, preferable to a subsidy regime. It needs to be noted here that subsidy levels are insensitive to the number of firms existing in the industry. Since each firm can individually lobby for "firm-specific" subsidies, their full costs as well as benefits are felt by individual firms. Thus, in equilibrium, there is no linkage between the number of firms in the industry and the subsidy rate.

2. *Percentage change in the world price.* Feenstra and Lewis (1991) model, under asymmetric information, a benevolent government that takes action to protect the losers from an import price shock. A tariff, as a protective instrument, is imposed to compensate domestic producers for their losses from world price shocks, ensuring that nobody is worse off with respect to the initial situation. As a result, this objective of the government implies a negative (positive) relationship between an increase (decrease) in world price and the level of protection. If the asset ownership of each individual producer is not known fully, it is much harder to achieve this objective through subsidies.

3. *Budget deficit.* Tariffs generate revenue while production subsidies cost revenues. Therefore, when the budget deficit is large, the mix of protection and promotion mix may switch towards protection.

4. *Geographical concentration.* Finally, geographical concentration can affect costs of organization and lobbying as well as the political clout of an industry.

3. ECONOMETRIC SPECIFICATION AND METHODOLOGY

From the theories above, we have the following estimating equations:

$$NRP_{it}/(1 + NRP_{it}) = \alpha_{0t} + \alpha_1 I_i z_{it}/e_{it} + \alpha_2 z_{it}/e_{it} + \varepsilon_{it} \tag{5}$$

$$NSR_{it}/(1 + NSR_{it}) = \beta_{0t} + \beta_1 I_i(1/e_{it}^s) + \beta_2(1/e_{it}^s) + u_{it} \tag{6}$$

$$[NRP_{it}/(1 + NRP_{it})]/[NSR_{it}/(1 + NSR_{it})] = \gamma_{0t} + \gamma_1(ze_{it}^s/e_{it}) + v_{it}, \tag{7}$$

where $i = 1, 2, \ldots, 37$ denotes the ith industry and $t = 1983, 1988, 1990$ denotes the relevant year. NRP stands for the nominal rate of protection, NSR is the nominal subsidy rate, $\alpha_{0t}, \beta_{0t},$ and γ_{0t} are the year-specific constants, z is the inverse import-penetration ratio, e is the absolute value of the import-demand elasticity, and e^s is the elasticity of output supply. Since in the data all sectors (irrespective of whether they are organized or unorganized) are provided positive protection and promotion, we add a constant term to the actual equations from the theory. We also run augmented regressions with controls. Our control variables are wp: the proportional change in the world

154   MITRA ET AL.

price of the product;[9] *GEO*: the geographical concentration dummy; *CR*4: the four-firm concentration ratio; and *BD*: the budget deficit.

We perform both (iterative) weighted least squares (WLS) as well as (iterative) weighted two-stage least squares (W2SLS). The former takes care of heteroskedasticity problems,[10] while the latter in addition takes care of our endogeneity and measurement error problems. The inverse import-penetration variable z and our import-demand elasticity variable e are endogenous to protection. Additionally, e is an estimated variable and so there is a measurement error problem associated with this variable. The extent of intra-industry trade, hourly wage, and unionization can affect these variables and so are used as instruments.[11]

4. DATA

In this section, we describe our data, their sources and methods followed in constructing new variables. Table 1 provides summary statistics of our left-hand-side variables and our main right-hand-side variables.

4.1 Nominal Rates of Protection

While most empirical studies, especially those on developed countries, use quota-coverage ratios as measures of protection, we have tariff (*NRP*) data available for Turkey. Tariffs are the protection measures looked at in most theoretical models. The relevant data for various sectors are obtained from Togan (1994).

4.2 Nominal Subsidy Rates

We also need data on promotion (subsidies). The related measure is the nominal subsidy rate (*NSR*) which, again, we obtain from Togan (1994). *NSR* incorporates subsidies provided through different kinds of credits, tax

---

[9]Note that what is important here is not the percentage change in the world price of the product, but the percentage change in this price relative to some average price level. Since the percentage change in the ratio of the world price of the product to the average price level equals the difference between the proportional changes in these two prices, the year-specific constant will capture the effect of the economy-wide average price level (common to all sectors). Thus, we can just use wp (the proportional change in the world price of the product) as an explanatory variable to empirically investigate the Feenstra–Lewis (1991) hypothesis.

[10]The weights used in W2SLS estimation are the reciprocals of the estimated residual variances from each yearly regression. Initial estimates for these variances are obtained from preliminary, unweighted, 2SLS estimation. Using the W2SLS estimates a new set of residual variance estimates is obtained and the process is iterated to convergence. Note that we do not need to use a system method of estimation like 3SLS as it is unlikely that there is correlation in the regression error terms across years (which is what 3SLS would correct for).

[11]As relationships between our right-hand-side endogenous variables and exogenous variables (inclusive of instruments) may be non-linear, we do not restrict ourselves to using just levels of these instrumental variables, but, as is well accepted in the literature, we also make use of their squares and cross-products.

PROTECTION VERSUS PROMOTION   155

TABLE 1   SUMMARY STATISTICS

	Min.	Max.	Mean	Std. dev.
NRP	0.065	3.728	0.511	0.453
NSR	−0.040	1.011	0.269	0.275
z	0.032	40.816	5.813	8.405
e	0.069	3.657	1.152	0.739
I	0	1	0.432	0.502
e^s	0.011	0.896	0.279	0.154

rebates, concessional purchases of intermediates, foreign exchange alloca-
tions, corporate tax concessions, incentives to freight, and through the
Support and Price Stabilization Fund and Resource Utilization Support
Fund, net of different taxes.

4.3   Political Organization

Since no data were available on political contributions, the political organization dummy variable is constructed by other means. Our approach involves two steps: in the first step, membership data for the Turkish
Industrialists and Businessmen Association (TUSIAD) are obtained[12] based
on which, as well as on newspaper reports, an initial determination of organized sectors is made; in the second step, we use discriminant analysis
methods to statistically validate the choice made in the first step.[13] Details of
the construction procedure and the discriminant analysis method used are
discussed in Mitra et al. (2002).

4.4   Import Penetration

The import data for each industry are obtained from the *UN International
Trade Statistics Yearbook* (various issues). Domestic output are from the
UN Food and Agriculture Organization website (http://www.fao.org), *UN
Statistical Yearbook* (various issues), *Monthly Bulletin of Statistics* (various
issues) and OECD *Industrial Structure Statistics* (various issues).

4.5   Import-Demand Elasticities

Data on import-demand elasticities for 13 product categories are from
Thomakos and Ulubaşoğlu (2002), who followed Shiells et al. (1986) in estimation. The other 24 elasticities are from Mitra et al. (2002), who estimated

[12]We are grateful to Mr. Abdullah Akyuz, Washington Representative of TUSIAD, for his
generosity in providing us with the list of TUSIAD members.
[13]TUSIAD is a private organization consisting of 470 individual members that hold business
positions in a variety of sectors. Large import-competing firms are heavily represented. The
organization is very active in Turkish public life and some of its members are household names.
It has representative offices in Washington and Brussels and publishes its own newsletter and
quarterly economic survey.

these elasticities with the same techniques used in Thomakos and Ulubaşoğlu (2002).

4.6 Output Supply Elasticities

Assuming Cobb–Douglas production functions (in sector-specific capital and the general factor, labor) for each of the non-numéraire sectors in the presence of a Ricardian numéraire sector as in the Grossman–Helpman model, we can derive our output supply elasticities as

$$e_{it}^s = \frac{\theta_{it}}{1 - \theta_{it}}, \tag{8}$$

where θ_{it} is the income share of labor.[14] The data on total wages and bills paid in each industry and value added are from the OECD *Industrial Structure Statistics*.

4.7 Industry Concentration

*CR*4 represents the proportion of output produced by the top-four firms in the industry. These concentration data were obtained from the Turkish State Institute of Statistics (SIS).[15]

4.8 World Price Changes

These are the percentage changes in import prices (exclusive of tariffs) charged on Turkish imports. The import prices are derived from import values and import quantities for each sector, the data on which are obtained from the *UN International Trade Statistics Yearbook* (various issues).

4.9 Geographical Concentration

Since there were no data available on the geographical concentration of Turkish industries, we constructed a new variable. This measure is a dummy variable which assigns a value 1 to a geographically concentrated industry and 0 to others. We assign 1 to a certain industry if the total number of firms in the Marmara district (the most populous and industrially developed district, containing the metropolitan area of Istanbul) is higher than the total number in the same sector in the rest of the six districts combined.

4.10 Instruments

Our instruments include unionization, hourly wage, and the index of intra-industry trade. Index of intra-industry trade data are from Togan (1994). We

---

[14]Going strictly by the model, output-supply elasticity is the share of labor divided by that of capital (in capital plus labor income). This is exactly what we have calculated.
[15]These data are available for Turkey only after 1985. Therefore, we used the 1985 data for 1983.

obtained the unionization data from the *Household Labor Force Survey* of SIS. The *Employment and Wage Structure Survey* of SIS provided the nominal hourly-wage data, but for 1994 only. Therefore, we calculated the nominal wages for other years with an adjustment of the data using the inflation rate that is based on the GDP deflator.

5. RESULTS

5.1 Protection

In Table 2, we present the results where the dependent variable is $NRP/(1 + NRP)$. Both with WLS and W2SLS, we obtain very similar results. The coefficients of both $I_i(z_{it}/e_{it})$ and (z_{it}/e_{it}) are statistically very significant. While the former is positive, the latter is negative but smaller in absolute value. Thus, organized industries get higher protection than unorganized ones. While protection to organized industries is decreasing in the absolute value of the import-demand elasticity and the import-penetration ratio (increasing in the inverse import-penetration ratio), unorganized sector protection is related to the same two variables in the opposite direction. The implied estimate of the government's weight "a" on aggregate welfare relative to contributions is 333 and that of "α_L," the proportion of the overall population that is organized is 0.60, very similar to the numbers found in the existing empirical literature: Goldberg and Maggi (1999), Gawande and Bandyopadhyay (2000), and Mitra et al. (2002).[16] Use of controls listed in the above section leads to statistically insignificant results for most controls except for the budget deficit whose coefficient is negative and significant. This negative sign of the coefficient of the budget deficit is not economically meaningful and we interpret it as spurious correlation. Therefore, we present only the results for *NRP* using the strict Grossman–Helpman specification.[17]

5.2 Promotion

In Table 3, we present the results where the dependent variable is $NSR/(1 + NSR)$. Both with WLS and W2SLS, we obtain very similar results. The coefficients of both I_i/e_{it}^s and $1/e_{it}^s$ are statistically very significant. While the former is positive, the latter is negative but smaller in absolute value. Thus,

---

[16]It needs to be noted here that these parameter estimates in this paper and in the entire empirical literature on the Grossman–Helpman model turn out to be exceedingly high. We leave this issue to future research.

[17]Detailed results using this specification and using alternative measures of import protection (*NRP*, *ERP*, and *NTB*) are discussed in Mitra et al. (2002). In that paper, the authors directly estimate the government's weight on aggregate welfare relative contributions as well as the fraction of the population that is organized. The results in that paper are qualitatively the same as in this current paper. The numbers, however, are not exactly the same because different econometric techniques have been used in the two papers. The choice of techniques in this paper has been partly driven by specific comments of referees. In any event, the qualitative similarity of results show their robustness to the use of alternative econometric techniques.

158   MITRA ET AL.

TABLE 2   SPECIFICATION: $NRP_{it}/(1 + NRP_{it}) = \alpha_{0t} + \alpha_1 I_i(z_{it}/e_{it}) + \alpha_2(z_{it}/e_{it}) + \varepsilon_{it}$

Weighted least squares

$\hat{\alpha}_{0,1983}$	$\hat{\alpha}_{0,1988}$	$\hat{\alpha}_{0,1990}$	$\hat{\alpha}_1$	$\hat{\alpha}_2$	$\chi^2(2)$	R^2
0.352***	0.325***	0.215***	0.003***	−0.002**	6.45**	0.30
(0.019)	(0.019)	(0.014)	(0.001)	(0.001)	(0.04)	

Weighted two-stage least squares

$\hat{\alpha}_{0,1983}$	$\hat{\alpha}_{0,1988}$	$\hat{\alpha}_{0,1990}$	$\hat{\alpha}_1$	$\hat{\alpha}_2$	$\chi^2(2)$	R^2
0.359***	0.324***	0.221***	0.003***	−0.002**	4.48*	0.30
(0.023)	(0.020)	(0.016)	(0.001)	(0.001)	(0.10)	

Notes: *** denotes significance at 1%, ** denotes significance at 5%, and * denotes significance at 10% level respectively, $\chi^2(2)$ denotes the Wald test for the joint significance of the slope coefficients (p-values in parentheses). R^2 is the square of the correlation coefficient between the actual and the fitted values.

TABLE 3   SPECIFICATION: $NSR_{it}/(1 + NSR_{it}) = \beta_{0t} + \beta_1 I_i(1/e_{it}^s) + \beta_2(1/e_{it}^s) + u_{it}$

Weighted least squares

$\hat{\beta}_{0,1983}$	$\hat{\beta}_{0,1988}$	$\hat{\beta}_{0,1990}$	$\hat{\beta}_1$	$\hat{\beta}_2$	$\chi^2(2)$	R^2
0.290***	0.209***	0.123***	0.006***	−0.005**	7.15**	0.48
(0.019)	(0.013)	(0.013)	(0.002)	(0.0025)	(0.03)	

Weighted two-stage least squares

$\hat{\beta}_{0,1983}$	$\hat{\beta}_{0,1988}$	$\hat{\beta}_{0,1990}$	$\hat{\beta}_1$	$\hat{\beta}_2$	$\chi^2(2)$	R^2
0.297***	0.207***	0.122***	0.005	−0.004	3.20	0.48
(0.020)	(0.017)	(0.013)	(0.004)	(0.004)	(0.20)	

Notes: *** denotes significance at 1%, ** denotes significance at 5%, and * denotes significance at 10% level respectively. $\chi^2(2)$ denotes the Wald test for the joint significance of the slope coefficients (p-values in parentheses). R^2 is the square of the correlation coefficient between the actual and the fitted values.

organized industries get higher subsidies than unorganized ones. While protection to organized industries is decreasing in the output elasticity, the unorganized sector subsidy is positively related to it. The implied estimate of the government's weight "a" on aggregate welfare relative to contributions is 175, and that of "α_L," the proportion of the overall population that is organized, is 0.92. Use of controls listed in the above section leads to statistically insignificant results for most controls except for the budget deficit whose coefficient is negative and significant. This negative sign of the coefficient of the budget deficit may imply that the government finds it difficult to finance subsidies when it faces budgetary problems. The four-firm concentration ratio is negative and significant. Since the controls are either statistically insignificant and in many cases lack economic meaning, we only present the results from the estimating equation without any controls. The virtue of this equation without controls is that it is derived from a theoretical model.

5.3 Protection–Promotion Mix

Tables 4 and 5 present results on the protection–promotion mix. The dependent variable here is the ratio of the above two dependent variables and is $[NRP_{it}/(1 + NRP_{it})]/[NSR_{it}/(1 + NSR_{it})]$. This ratio, which is a measure of the mix of protection and promotion, is inversely related to the ratio of a measure of marginal deadweight costs of protection to that of promotion. Thus, we see that $[NRP_{it}/(1 + NRP_{it})]/[NSR_{it}/(1 + NSR_{it})]$ is positively related to ze_{it}^s/e_{it} which is a measure of the deadweight costs of promotion relative to protection. The coefficient of ze_{it}^s/e_{it} is highly significant. When we use controls, we find that while the policy mix supporting a more concentrated industry is biased in favor of protection (the free-rider problem associated with protection is low) it turns out that budget deficits shift the policy mix away from protection.[18] Since there are only three observations on the budget deficit, we cannot read too much into this result. The coefficient of the *wp* variable shows that there is some weak evidence for negative world price shocks resulting in the mix moving more towards protection and away from promotion.

6. CONCLUSION

In this paper, we empirically investigate the factors that determine protection and promotion as well as the mix of these two instruments. Our investigation is guided by the theoretical literature in this area. Using Turkish industry-level data from 1983 to 1990, we find that politically organized industries receive both higher protection and promotion than unorganized ones. Tariff rates are decreasing in the import-penetration ratio and the absolute value of the import-demand elasticity for organized industries, while they are increasing in these variables for unorganized sectors. Subsidy rates are decreasing in the output-supply elasticity for organized industries and they are increasing in this elasticity for unorganized sectors. While the results for tariffs are consistent with the predictions of the Grossman–Helpman model, the results for subsidies are consistent with the predictions of a model that uses the Grossman–Helpman framework but replaces trade policy with output taxes and subsidies at the disposal of the government. The mix of protection and promotion is inversely related to the ratio of

---

[18]In this context, it must be noted that pioneering empirical work in political economy by Gawande (1997, 1998) provides evidence using US data for the existence of the free-rider problem in lobbying expenditures in general and in lobbying for non-tariff barriers in particular.

160   MITRA ET AL.

TABLE 4   SPECIFICATION: $[NRP_{it}/(1+NRP_{it})]/[NSR_{it}/(1+NSR_{it})] = \gamma_{0t} + \gamma_1(ze_{it}^s/e_{it}) + v_{it}$

Weighted least squares

$\hat{\gamma}_{0,1983}$	$\hat{\gamma}_{0,1988}$	$\hat{\gamma}_{0,1990}$	$\hat{\gamma}_1$	$\chi^2(1)$	R^2
1.199***	1.822***	1.652***	0.055***	5.61**	0.02
(0.152)	(0.0184)	(0.661)	(0.023)	(0.02)	

Weighted two-stage least squares

$\hat{\gamma}_{0,1983}$	$\hat{\gamma}_{0,1988}$	$\hat{\gamma}_{0,1990}$	$\hat{\gamma}_1$	$\chi^2(1)$	R^2
1.119***	1.720***	1.623***	0.071**	5.41**	0.02
(0.181)	(0.0179)	(0.684)	(0.031)	(0.02)	

Notes: *** denotes significance at 1%, ** denotes significance at 5%, and * denotes significance at 10% level respectively. $\chi^2(1)$ denotes the Wald test for the joint significance of the slope coefficients (*p*-values in parentheses). R^2 is the square of the correlation coefficient between the actual and the fitted values.

TABLE 5   SPECIFICATION: $[NRP_{it}/(1+NRP_{it})]/[NSR_{it}/(1+NSR_{it})] = \delta_0 + \delta_1(ze_{it}^s/e_{it}) + \delta_2 CR4_{it} + \delta_3 wp_{it} + \delta_4 BD_t + \delta_5 GEO + w_{it}$

Weighted least squares

$\hat{\delta}_0$	$\hat{\delta}_1$	$\hat{\delta}_2$	$\hat{\delta}_3$	$\hat{\delta}_4$	$\hat{\delta}_5$	$\chi^2(5)$	R^2
0.321	0.037	1.085**	−0.145	−0.049**	−0.422	17.76***	0.04
(0.575)	(0.024)	(0.517)	(0.093)	(0.022)	(0.270)	(0.00)	

Weighted two-stage least squares

$\hat{\delta}_0$	$\hat{\delta}_1$	$\hat{\delta}_2$	$\hat{\delta}_3$	$\hat{\delta}_4$	$\hat{\delta}_5$	$\chi^2(5)$	R^2
0.078	0.054**	1.243*	−0.147	−0.053**	−0.369	20.10***	0.04
(0.627)	(0.027)	(0.678)	(0.090)	(0.021)	(0.262)	(0.00)	

Notes: *** denotes significance at 1%, ** denotes significance at 5%, and * denotes significance at 10% level respectively. $\chi^2(5)$ denotes the Wald test for the joint significance of the slope coefficients (*p*-values in parentheses). R^2 is the square of the correlation coefficient between the actual and the fitted values.

measures of their respective marginal deadweight costs as derived using the Grossman–Helpman approach. Control variables turn out to be statistically insignificant in most cases and lack of economic meaning in some cases.

ACKNOWLEDGMENTS

We are grateful to John Boyd III, Josh Ederington, Cem Karayalcin, two anonymous referees for useful discussions and comments, and Giyas

Gokkent for assistance in putting together our data. The standard disclaimer applies.

DEVASHISH MITRA
Syracuse University and NBER

DIMITRIOS D. THOMAKOS
*Florida International University
and University of Peloponnese, Greece*

MEHMET A. ULUBAŞOĞLU
Deakin University, Australia

REFERENCES

Anam, M., 1982, Distortion-triggered lobbying and welfare: a contribution to the theory of directly-unproductive profit-seeking activities. *Journal of International Economics* 13, 15–32.

Austen-Smith, D., 1991, Rational consumers and irrational voters. *Economics and Politics* 3, 73–92.

Bernheim, B. D. and M. D. Whinston, 1986, Menu auctions, resource allocation and economic influence. *Quarterly Journal of Economics* 101(1), 1–31.

Bhagwati, J. N., 1971, The generalized theory of distortions and welfare, in: J. N. Bhagwati et al., eds., *Trade, Balance of Payments and Growth* (North-Holland, Amsterdam) 69–90.

—— and V. K. Ramaswami, 1963, Domestic distortions, tariffs and the theory of the optimum subsidy. *Journal of Political Economy* 71, 44–50.

—— and T. N. Srinivasan, 1980, Revenue seeking: a generalization of the theory of tariffs. *Journal of Political Economy* 88, 1069–1087.

——, R. A. Brecher, and T. N. Srinivasan, 1984, DUP activities and economic theory. *European Economic Review* 24, 291–307.

Coate, S. and S. Morris, 1995, On the form of transfers to special interests. *Journal of Political Economy* 103, 1210–1235.

Ederington, J. and J. Minier, 2001, The endogenous choice of tariffs and subsidies. Unpublished paper, University of Miami.

—— and ——, 2003, Reconsidering the empirical evidence on the Grossman–Helpman model of endogenous protection. Unpublished paper, University of Miami.

Feenstra, R. C. and T. R. Lewis, 1991, Distributing the gains from trade with incomplete information. *Economics and Politics* 3(1), 21–39.

Gawande, K., 1997, U.S. nontariff barriers as privately provided public goods. *Journal of Public Economics* 64, 61–81.

——, 1998, Stigler–Olson lobbying behavior and organization: evidence from a lobbying power function. *Journal of Economic Behavior and Organization* 35, 477–499.

—— and S. Bandopadhyay, 2000, Is protection for sale? A test of the Grossman–Helpman theory of endogenous protection. *Review of Economics and Statistics* 82(1), 139–152.

Goldberg, P. K. and G. Maggi, 1999, Protection for sale: an empirical investigation. *American Economic Review* 89(5), 1135–1155.

Grossman, G. M. and E. Helpman, 1994, Protection for sale. *American Economic Review* 84(4), 833–850.

Hillman, A. L., 1989, *The Political Economy of Protection* (Harwood Academic, New York).

162   MITRA ET AL.

Johnson, H. G., 1965, Optimal trade interventions in the presence of domestic dis-
tortions, in: R. Caves, H. G. Johnson, and P. Kenen, eds., *Trade Growth and
Balance of Payments* (North-Holland, Amsterdam) 3–34.
Krueger, A. O., 1974, The political economy of the rent-seeking society. *American
Economic Review* 64, 291–303.
Magee, S. P., W. A. Brock, and L. Young, 1989, *Black Hole Tariffs and Endogenous
Policy Theory* (Cambridge University Press, Cambridge, UK).
Mitra, D., 2000, On the endogenous choice between protection and promotion.
Economics and Politics 12, 33–51.
———, D. D. Thomakos, and M. A. Ulubaşoğlu, 2002, Protection for sale in a de-
veloping country: democracy vs. dictatorship. *Review of Economics and Statistics*
84(3), 497–508.
OECD, *Industrial Structure Statistics* (OECD, Geneva). Various issues.
Rodrik, D., 1986, Tariffs, subsidies, and welfare with endogenous policy. *Journal of
International Economics* 21, 285–294.
———, 1995, Political economy of trade policy, in: G. M. Grossman and K. Rogoff,
eds., *Handbook of International Economics*, Vol. 3 (North-Holland, Amsterdam)
1457–1494.
Shiells, C. R., R. F. Stern, and A. V. Deardorff, 1986, Estimates of the elasticities of
substitution between imports and home goods for the United States. *Welt-
wirtschaftliches Archiv* 122, 497–519.
———, D. D. Thomakos, and M. A. Ulubaşoğlu, 2002, The impact of trade liber-
alization on import demand. *Journal of Economic and Social Research* 4(1), 1–26.
Togan, S., 1994, *Foreign Trade Regime and Trade Liberalization in Turkey During the
1980s* (Avebury, Aldershot, UK).
Trefler, D., 1993, Trade liberalization and the theory of endogenous protection.
Journal of Political Economy 101, 138–160.
United Nations, *Monthly Bulletin of Statistics* (United Nations, New York). Various
issues.
———, *UN International Trade Statistics Yearbook* (United Nations, New York).
Various issues.
———, *UN Statistical Yearbook* (United Nations, New York). Various issues.

Part V

Political Economy of Trade Policy:
Surveys of the Literature with Applications

Chapter 13

Political Economy of Trade Policy*

Devashish Mitra

This area of research tries, through the introduction of politics in economic models, to explain the existence and the extent of anti-trade bias in trade policy. The two main approaches, namely, the median-voter approach and the special-interest approach are surveyed. Certain applications of these approaches to policy issues, such as trade agreements, the issue of reciprocity versus unilateralism in trade policy, regionalism versus multilateralism, hysteresis in trade policy and the choice of policy instruments, are discussed. Finally, the empirical literature on the political economy of trade policy is surveyed. The new literature that employs a more 'structural' approach is emphasized.

Keywords: congestion problem; Cournot oligopoly; customs unions; deadweight loss; free trade; free trade areas; free-rider problem; Heckscher–Ohlin trade theory; hysteresis in trade policy; intermediate goods; international trade; lobby formation; lobbying; majority rule; median voter model; monopolistic competition; multilateralism in trade policy; non-tariff barriers; optimal obfuscation principle; political competition; political economy; political support function; political-contributions model; progressive and regressive taxation; proportional representation; protection; reciprocity in trade policy; regional and preferential trade agreements; risk sharing; single-peaked preferences; special-interest politics; specific-factors trade theory; tariff-formation function; tariffs; tariffs vs. subsidies; terms of trade; trade agreements; trade policy, political economy of; trade-diverting vs. trade-creating bilateral agreements; unilateralism in trade policy; World Trade Organization; Back to top.

While economists clearly understand the benefits of free trade, they have always found it difficult to explain departures from it in the real world. Most of these departures are in the direction of limiting the volume of trade. In trying to explain the existence and the extent of this anti-trade bias in trade policy, trade economists have introduced politics in their economic models. Parts of this political-economy literature have also tried to explain

---

*This chapter has appeared previously as an entry in the second edition of the *New Palgrave Dictionary of Economics*.

why policy instruments that are more efficient than trade policy and can achieve the same political and economic objectives are not often used. An important empirical contribution of the political-economy literature has been to uncover the main determinants of cross-country and cross-industry variations in protection.

Modelling approaches

Median-voter approach

Political economy models of trade are of two main types. One of them adopts the majority voting approach. Such models are called 'median voter' models in the literature. Preferences are assumed to be 'single peaked' and conditions are imposed such that the most preferred policy of each individual is monotonic in a certain characteristic. Then, with other individual characteristics held constant across the population, the tariff chosen under two-candidate electoral competition is the median voter's most preferred tariff. The median voter here is the median individual in the economy when ranked according to the characteristic under consideration. Mayer (1984) applies this median-voter principle to the Heckscher–Ohlin and specific-factors trade models. In the Heckscher–Ohlin case, the political economy equilibrium tariff is the most-preferred tariff of the median individual in the economy-wide ranking of the ratio of capital to labour ownership. If this median individual's capital to labour ratio is less than the economy's overall capital to labour ratio — that is, if the asset distribution in the economy is unequal — the equilibrium trade policy is different from free trade and is one that redistributes income from capital to labour — pro-trade in a labour-abundant economy and anti-trade in a capital-abundant economy.

Special-interest politics

The other type of political economy model in the trade literature focuses on 'special-interest' politics. The first papers to model lobbying explicitly in the trade arena were by Findlay and Wellisz (1982) and Feenstra and Bhagwati (1982). The Findlay–Wellisz model is a two-sector model in which production in each sector is carried out using a factor of production specific to that sector — land for food production and capital for manufactures — and an economy-wide general factor, namely, labour. Both types of specific factor owners are fully organized politically and they lobby against each other. This simple model shows the existence of an equilibrium tariff determined through the Nash interaction between the two opposing groups.

The government is modelled very indirectly through a tariff formation function which is increasing in the amount of labour devoted to lobbying by the import-competing specific factor and decreasing in labour used in lobbying by the specific-factor owners in the export sector.

While only labour is used as an input in lobbying in the Findlay–Wellisz model, both capital and labour are used as inputs into lobbying in the Feenstra–Bhagwati model. However, only one sector is assumed to be politically active in the model. Unlike in the Findlay–Wellisz model, the government in the Feenstra–Bhagwati model is not a monolithic entity but has a two-layered structure. While one layer is a clearing house for lobbies, the other cares about social welfare. The tariff is determined through an interaction between the two layers.

Another approach to modelling 'special-interest' trade politics is the 'political support function' approach pioneered by Hillman (1989). (Some of the classification terminology here is borrowed from Rodrik, 1995, to which the interested reader is referred for a detailed typology of political-economy models. See also Helpman, 2002, for an analytical survey within a unified framework.) Under such an approach, the government's objective function, also called the political support function, incorporates its preferential treatment of each organized industry as well as the cost of protecting this industry given by the excess burden on society. Van Long and Vousden (1991) use a specific form of Hillman's political support function which is linear in the welfare levels of different types of specific-factor owners, with different weights being assigned to different factors.

Magee, Brock and Young (1989) explicitly model electoral competition. They use a two-sector, two-factor Heckscher–Ohlin set-up with two political parties — one pro-trade and another pro-protection — and two lobbies — one representing capital and the other labour. Lobbies contribute to their respective favoured political parties to maximize their chances of winning elections. Policy platforms here are chosen prior to decisions on campaign contributions.

The special-interest approach has evolved from the simple Findlay–Wellisz 'tariff-formation function' approach to the state-of-the-art Grossman and Helpman (1994) 'political-contributions' model. The latter is path-breaking for several reasons. First, it is multi-sectoral. Second, it provides micro-foundations for the behaviour of organized lobbies and politicians. A 'menu-auctions' approach is used in modelling policy bidding by interest groups. Multiple principals, namely, the various organized lobbies, try to influence the common agent, namely the government. The government's objective function is a weighted sum of political contributions and aggregate welfare, while each lobby maximizes its welfare net of political contributions. Most importantly, especially from the empirical angle, the level of protection for each industry is derived as an estimable function of industry characteristics and other political and economic factors. Protection to organized sectors is negatively related to import penetration and the (absolute value of) import demand elasticity, while protection to unorganized sectors is positively related to these two variables. With everything else held constant, organized sectors are granted higher protection than unorganized sectors.

While Grossman and Helpman in their models take the existence of organized lobbies as given, Mitra (1999) extends their framework to endogenize lobby formation. He shows that we are closest to free trade when the government cares too little or too much about aggregate welfare relative to political contributions. While the former leads to the formation of a large number of mutually opposing lobbies, the latter situation is one where hardly any lobbies get formed. Mitra also shows that a higher concentration of asset ownership in the economy leads to the formation of a larger number of organized lobbies representing sectors that are heavily protected. Magee (2002) analyses a single lobby's organization problem in the context of the collection of political contributions in a repeated game setting. (See also Pecorino, 1998, for an analysis of the same issue with a tariff-formation function approach.)

Theoretical applications

Trade agreements

The first important theoretical application we discuss is the issue of trade agreements. Using their political-contributions approach, Grossman and Helpman (1995a) analyse trade policy in a setting with two large countries, where they show an additional terms-of-trade component in the tariff expression in a non-cooperative setting. This component gets eliminated in a cooperative setting of international trade negotiations, and the relative size of protection in any sector in the two countries then depends on the relative political power of the same industry in the two countries. Thus there is a rationale for 'trade talks' as opposed to 'trade wars'. Using what is very close to a 'political-support' function approach, Bagwell and Staiger (1996; 1999) show that, even when political economy considerations are taken into account, the only rationale for (reciprocal) trade agreements is the elimination of terms-of-trade externalities. They use this approach to develop a rationale for the General Agreement on Tariffs and Trade (GATT)/World Trade Organization (WTO) and its different rules. (See Bagwell and Staiger, 2002, for an in-depth discussion.)

The next natural question then is whether free trade agreements are of any value to countries whose actions have no impact on the international terms of trade. Maggi and Rodriguez-Clare (1998) have a political economy explanation for the unilateral commitment to free trade agreements by small countries. Their setting is one in which owners of capital first decide in which sector to invest, and then those who invest in a particular sector (the import-competing sector) lobby the government for protection. The lobbying is modelled as a Nash bargaining game between the lobby and the government. While the lobby at least compensates the government for the deadweight losses generated in the second stage, it may not compensate the government for the welfare loss through the inter-sectoral misallocation of capital in the first stage in the expectation of protection in the second stage. In such a situation, it is possible that a government will commit to a free trade agreement in a prior stage 'zero'.

Mitra (2002) builds on the Maggi–Rodriguez-Clare version of the Grossman–Helpman framework, augmenting it with the decision to incur fixed costs (to build relationships with politicians in power and/or to form a lobby) prior to the actual lobbying, but, importantly, not providing room for any capital mobility. However, the main result of the Maggi–Rodriguez-Clare model goes through even in this newly modified set-up. This is the result that generally governments with low bargaining power with respect to domestic lobbies are the ones that precommit to free trade agreements.

Grossman and Helpman (1995b) have provided a detailed analysis of political-economy factors responsible for the emergence of free trade agreements. Using their 'political-contributions' approach, they show that such agreements between two countries are impossible if in every sector one country has a higher tariff than the other. These agreements might be politically feasible only when tariffs on some goods are higher in one country while other tariffs are higher in its partner country. The possibility of exclusion of certain sectors from the trade agreement also raises the chances that the agreement will be signed.

Reciprocity and unilateralism in trade policy

I now move to the issue of reciprocity and unilateralism in trade policy. Bagwell and Staiger (1996; 1999; 2002) have analysed the issue of reciprocal trade liberalization in considerable detail in both bilateral and multilateral settings (see also Hillman and Moser, 1996). In their models, reciprocity is a way of eliminating terms-of-trade externalities in the setting of trade policy. While considerable work has been done on the role of reciprocity in trade policy, the causal interaction between unilateral and reciprocal trade liberalization has been a somewhat neglected issue. Krishna and Mitra (2005) modify the Mitra (1999) lobby-formation framework to study exactly this link. (See Bhagwati, 1990, for an early informal discussion of this idea. See also Coates and Ludema, 2001, for an alternative channel based on risk sharing through which unilateralism induces reciprocity.) While reciprocal reduction in trade barriers can reasonably be expected to occur in contexts involving trade negotiations between countries, Krishna and Mitra examine instead the question of whether unilateral trade liberalization by one country can induce reciprocal liberalization by its partner *in the absence of any communication or negotiations* between the two countries. In this context, they show that unilateral liberalization by one country can affect the political economy equilibrium in the partner country through the formation of an export lobby there, in a manner that induces it to liberalize trade.

The political economy of regionalism versus multilateralism

An important question raised by Bhagwati (1993; 1994) in several of his writings is whether regionalism is a 'stumbling block' or a 'stepping stone' to multilateralism. (For a purely economic answer that relies on coordination failure based on sector-specific sunk costs and 'friction' in trade negotiation, see McLaren, 2002.) Levy (1997) uses a Heckscher–Ohlin set-up with monopolistic competition and a median-voter approach to address this issue. He finds that bilateral agreements between countries similar in factor endowments result in the subsequent blocking of multilateral trade agreements. He also finds that bilateral agreements can never increase the political support for multilateralism. Krishna (1998) addresses the same issue in a political economy set-up where profits get a much greater weight than other components of welfare in the government's objective function (political-support function approach). The set-up is one of Cournot oligopoly. He finds greater political support for trade-diverting bilateral agreements (regionalism) than for trade-creating ones. Such agreements can also make previously feasible multilateral agreements politically infeasible.

This effect turns out to be increasing in the magnitude of the trade diversion that takes place under bilateralism.

Free trade areas versus customs unions

Next I move to the determinants of the actual shape or form a preferential trading arrangement will take. Panagariya and Findlay (1996) study the choice between a customs union and a free-trade area in the context of how they affect lobbying activity and the structure of external tariffs. Using a tariff-formation function approach, they focus on the free-rider problem in lobbying in the case of customs union arising from the requirement of a common external tariff. Richardson (1994) is similar in spirit and finds the same free-rider effect under a customs union, due to which free-trade areas are preferred by import-competing producers.

McLaren (2004) takes a different approach to the choice between a free trade area and a customs union. He analyses what he calls the 'dynamics of political influence'. As the external tariff is common across members of a customs union, it has to be set jointly by all the members, which can be done only if an agreement is reached among them. This makes the external tariff relatively less reversible under a customs union than under a free-trade area. It is this relative irreversibility that McLaren focuses on, even though he abstracts from the uniformity aspect. Using a political contributions approach with Nash bargaining between the capitalists and the government, he finds that a customs union is more likely when the government has a short lifespan and firms have a long lifespan. This is because the more permanent nature of trade policy under a customs union requires the upfront payment of contributions, which is the government's share in the present value of the stream of surpluses generated over time.

The choice of policy instruments

The next important application concerns the choice of policy instruments. One of the major propositions of the theory of commercial policy is that, if distortions or policy goals are not directly trade-related, then direct subsidies are more efficient than tariffs (Bhagwati and Ramaswami, 1963; Johnson, 1965; Bhagwati, 1971). One simple explanation for the existence of tariffs despite their low efficiency is that they generate revenues while subsidies use them up (see for instance Bhagwati and Ramaswami, 1963).

However, in a Bhagwati and Srinivasan (1980; 1982) framework of fully competitive revenue seeking, subsidies can be preferable to tariffs as they are not subject to revenue seeking.

Rodrik (1986) is the first author to look at this issue by endogenizing policy. He does this by using a simplified version of the Findlay–Wellisz model. He argues that, since tariffs are general to an industry and subsidies can, in principle, be firm-specific, the free-rider problem in lobbying for tariffs may result in a smaller level of endogenous tariffs than endogenous subsidies, thereby possibly reversing the conventional welfare ranking of tariffs and subsidies. Mitra (2000) argues that, even from the point of view of the import-competing firms, tariffs may be preferable to subsidies since lobbying in the latter may face a congestion problem while in the former the free-rider problem may offset the congestion problem.

This issue of the choice of instruments is also addressed by Grossman and Helpman (1994). They argue that, when the policy instrument used for redistribution is more efficient, it creates greater competition among lobbies and thus results in a larger proportion of the surplus in the hands of the government. Therefore, lobbies themselves may want to tie the hands of the government to using relatively inefficient instruments. Wilson (1990) makes a similar argument in a model with electoral competition where he shows that a higher efficiency of redistributive instruments leads to more contributions and more transfers in equilibrium.

The choice between tariffs and subsidies has also been considered in a voting framework in a series of papers by Mayer and Riezman (1987; 1989; 1990). They show that tariffs can be chosen in equilibrium outcome when voters differ along dimensions other than factor endowments, such as tastes and preferences, treatment under income taxes, and so forth. Besides, income tax progressivity might mean that the cost of financing subsidies is borne unevenly, which might lead some individuals to prefer tariffs whose costs are more evenly distributed.

Feenstra and Lewis (1991) argue that tariffs are informationally more efficient than subsidies. When the world price of importables falls, a tariff equivalent to this decline will compensate the losers without making others worse off relative to the initial situation. This will be possible without any knowledge on the part of the government of individual production and consumption levels. Magee, Brock and Young (1989) propose another information-based explanation, which they call the principle of 'optimal obfuscation'. Indirect policies such as tariffs are less observable by those who bear its costs.

Staiger and Tabellini (1987) argue that, when governments provide surprise protection to those hurt by world price fluctuations, the time-inconsistency problem might be less severe with more inefficient policies.

Hysteresis in trade policy

A model that helps us understand status quo bias in trade policy is Fernandez and Rodrik (1991). They consider a two-sector economy that initially has a certain given tariff on its imports. Eliminating this tariff will result in a movement of workers from the import-competing sector to the export sector. What is *ex ante* unknown is which of the workers initially in the import-competing sector will be successful in moving to the export sector. All the workers who are in the export sector right from the beginning will gain, while those who are always in the import-competing sector and remain there after the reforms will lose. Another group that gains is the group of movers from the contracting import-competing sector to the expanding export sector. Suppose 30 per cent of the population is in the export sector and 70 per cent in the import-competing sector to start with. After the reforms, let us suppose that this split is 60 per cent and 40 per cent respectively. This means that 60 per cent of the population will gain *ex post* from the reform. While 30 per cent who are initially in the export sector know for sure *ex ante* they are going to benefit, the remaining 70 per cent do not know which 30 per cent out of them will lose and which 40 per cent will gain. If they know for sure that the loss incurred by the losing 40 per cent is greater than the gain to the remaining 30 per cent, then all the voters who are initially in the import-competing sector will vote against the reform. Due to the individual-specific uncertainty faced by workers in the import-competing sector, each of them will vote on the basis of an expected loss, arising from the fact that losers in this sector lose much more than gainers in that sector gain. Thus, even though *ex post* a majority gain from the reforms, *ex ante* a majority of the workers vote against the trade reforms. However, if a dictator or an international financial institution forces a reform upon these people, it will not be reversed since as we know in this case *ex post* there is going to be majority support for the reforms.

Beyond the monolithic government

In the existing political economy literature on trade policy determination, a single, monolithic policymaker is often assumed. Until very recently, the paper by Feenstra and Bhagwati (1982) was the only exception.

McLaren and Karabay (2004) make a departure from such a simple structure to study trade policy setting in the presence of parliamentary or congressional institutions. They also incorporate electoral competition between political parties and show that in their setting the equilibrium tariff is the optimum of the median voter in the median district. They find that the relationship between the likelihood of import protection and the geographical concentration of import-competing interests is non-monotonic, with a maximum occurring at moderate levels of concentration. Too much concentration leads to a control of too few seats, while too much dispersion leads to no control of any seats.

A paper by Grossman and Helpman (2005) allows actual policy formation to be the interplay between the policy platform announced by the party leadership and the actions of individual legislators who want to maximize political success. Maximization of political success involves resolving the trade-off between conforming to the party platform and making one's constituents happy, thereby resulting in a deviation of 'policy reality' from 'policy rhetoric'. The authors find a protectionist bias when the legislature operates under majority rule. This bias is increasing in the geographical concentration of assets and capital market imperfections, and is decreasing in party discipline.

Empirical evidence

The old empirical literature

The empirical literature in this area has evolved from being highly 'reduced form' and atheoretical to being fairly 'structural' and guided by tight theoretical models. Important papers in the earlier literature include Caves (1976), Saunders (1980), Ray (1981), Marvel and Ray (1983), Ray (1991) and Trefler (1993). (See Rodrik, 1995, for a detailed survey of this literature.) The main finding of this early empirical literature is that protection is higher for sectors that are labour-intensive, low-skill and low-wage, for consumer-goods industries, for industries facing high import penetration, where geographical concentration of production is high but that of consumers is low, and in sectors with low levels of intra-industry trade. (For an examination of the cross-national variation in average protection levels across industrialized countries, see Mansfield and Busch, 1995. They find that non-tariff barriers are increasing in country size, unemployment rate and number of parliamentary constituencies, and are higher for countries that use proportional representation as their electoral system.)

The new empirical literature

In the Heckscher–Ohlin version of the Mayer median-voter model, a simple comparative static exercise produces the result that a rise in asset inequality will make trade policy more pro-trade in a labour-abundant economy and more protectionist in a capital-abundant economy. Dutt and Mitra (2002) find strong support for this result using cross-country data on inequality, capital-abundance and diverse measures of protection. (In this context, it is also important to mention Milner and Kubota, 2005, who use a median-voter approach to empirically investigate the relationship between democratization and trade reforms in developing countries.)

Dutt and Mitra (2005) also perform a cross-country empirical investigation of the role of political ideology in trade policy determination. They use a political-support function approach within a two-sector, two-factor Heckscher–Ohlin model (see Milner and Judkins, 2004, on this issue. Hiscox (2001) studies six Western nations to look at how historically the nature and structure of partisanship on trade issues change over time and depend on the extent of inter-sectoral factor mobility. Hiscox (2002) looks at the same question exclusively for the United States, analysing major pieces of congressional trade legislation between 1824 and 1994.

Two empirical papers, Goldberg and Maggi (1999) and Gawande and Bandyopadhyay (2000), estimate the Grossman–Helpman 'Protection for Sale' tariff expressions using industry-level data from the United States. The two papers are similar in the questions they address, but are somewhat different in the details of their approaches. While Goldberg and Maggi restrict their focus to the protection expressions, Gawande and Bandyopad-hyay concentrate more on the lobbying aspects and the determinants of the magnitude of contributions. Goldberg and Maggi use the basic Grossman–Helpman framework, while Gawande and Bandyopadhyay introduce inter-mediate goods. The econometric specifications are therefore somewhat different in the two papers. However, the results in the two papers are very similar. Both confirm empirically the Grossman–Helpman prediction regarding the relationship of protection to import penetration and import-demand elasticity. With everything else held constant, organized sectors are granted higher protection than unorganized sectors. Both papers find that the weight on aggregate welfare in the government's objective function is several times higher than that on contributions. Also, the estimates of the proportion of the population organized are very high in both papers.

Mitra, Thomakos and Ulubasoglu (2002) and McCalman (2004) obtain similarly high parameter estimates of the Grossman–Helpman model for Turkey and Australia respectively. An interesting result that comes out of the empirical exercise by Mitra, Thomakos and Ulubasoglu is that the relative weight on aggregate welfare was higher in the democratic regimes than under the dictatorial regimes in Turkey.

Gawande, Krishna and Robbins (2006) empirically investigate 'the susceptibility of government policies to lobbying by foreigners'. Using a new data-set on foreign political activity in the United States, they investigate the empirical relationship between trade protection and lobbying activity. Their theoretical framework is an extension of the 'Protection for Sale' model to include foreign lobbies. They find that foreign lobbying activity has significantly affected US trade barriers in a negative direction, as predicted by their model. They conclude: 'If the policy outcome absent any lobbying by foreigners is characterized by welfare-reducing trade barriers, lobbying by foreigners may result in reductions in such barriers and raise consumer surplus (and possibly improve welfare).'

In another empirical application through an extension of the Grossman–Helpman model, Gawande and Krishna (2005) investigate the effects of lobbying competition between upstream and downstream producers for US trade policy. Their parameter estimates are a significant improvement over those in the earlier literature even though they do not completely resolve the puzzle.

Thus, we see that the political economy literature on trade policy has evolved a great deal on both the theoretical and the empirical sides, as well as in terms of the complexity of applications it can handle.

Bibliography

Bagwell, K. and Staiger, R. 1996. Reciprocal trade liberalization. Working Paper No. 5488. Cambridge, MA: NBER.

Bagwell, K. and Staiger, R. 1999. An economic theory of GATT. *American Economic Review* 89, 215–48.

Bagwell, K. and Staiger, R. 2002. *The Economics of the World Trading System.* Cambridge, MA, and London: MIT Press.

Bhagwati, J. 1971. The generalized theory of distortions and welfare. In *Trade, Balance of Payments and Growth*, eds. J. Bhagwati et al. Amsterdam: North-Holland.

Bhagwati, J. 1990. Aggressive unilateralism. In *Aggressive Unilateralism*, eds. J. Bhagwati and H. Patrick. Ann Arbor: University of Michigan Press.

Bhagwati, J. 1993. Regionalism and multilateralism: an overview. In *New Dimensions in Regional Integration*, eds. A. Panagariya and J. De Melo. Washington, DC: World Bank.

Bhagwati, J. 1994. Threats to the world trading system: income distribution and the selfish hegemon. *Journal of International Affairs* 48, 279–85.

Bhagwati, J. and Ramaswami, V. 1963. Domestic distortions, tariffs and the theory of the optimum subsidy. *Journal of Political Economy* 71, 44–50.

Bhagwati, J. and Srinivasan, T. 1980. Revenue seeking: a generalization of the theory of tariffs. *Journal of Political Economy* 88, 1069–87.

Bhagwati, J. and Srinivasan, T. 1982. The welfare consequences of directly unproductive profit-seeking (DUP) lobbying activities: price versus quantity distortions. *Journal of International Economics* 13, 33–44.

Caves, R. 1976. Economic models of political choice: Canada's tariff structure. *Canadian Journal of Economics* 9, 278–300.

Coates, D. and Ludema, R. 2001. A theory of trade policy leadership. *Journal of Development Economics* 65, 1–29.

Dutt, P. and Mitra, D. 2002. Endogenous trade policy through majority voting: an empirical investigation. *Journal of International Economics* 58, 107–33.

Dutt, P. and Mitra, D. 2005. Political ideology and endogenous trade policy: an empirical investigation. *Review of Economics and Statistics* 87, 59–72.

Feenstra, R. and Bhagwati, J. 1982. Tariff seeking and the efficient tariff. In *Import Competition and Response*, ed. J. Bhagwati. Chicago and London: University of Chicago Press.

Feenstra, R. and Lewis, T. 1991. Distributing the gains from trade with incomplete information. *Economics and Politics* 3, 29–40.

Fernandez, R. and Rodrik, D. 1991. Resistance to reform: status-quo bias in the presence of individual-specific uncertainty. *American Economic Review* 81, 1146–54.

Findlay, R. and Wellisz, S. 1982. Endogenous tariffs, the political economy of trade restrictions and welfare. In *Import Competition and Response*, ed. J. Bhagwati. Chicago and London: University of Chicago Press.

Gawande, K. and Bandyopadhyay, S. 2000. Is protection for sale? A test of the Grossman–Helpman theory of endogenous protection. *Review of Economics and Statistics* 82, 139–52.

Gawande, K. and Krishna, P. 2003. The political economy of trade policy: empirical approaches. In *Handbook of International Trade*, eds. J. Harrigan and E. Kwan Choi. Malden, MA: Basil Blackwell.

Gawande, K. and Krishna, P. 2005. Lobbying competition over US trade policy. Working Paper No. 11371. Cambridge, MA: NBER.

Gawande, K., Krishna, P. and Robbins, M. 2006. Foreign lobbies and US trade policy. *Review of Economics and Statistics* (forthcoming).

Goldberg, P. and Maggi, G. 1999. Protection for sale: an empirical investigation. *American Economic Review* 89, 1135–55.

Grossman, G. and Helpman, E. 1994. Protection for sale. *American Economic Review* 84, 833–50.

Grossman, G. and Helpman, E. 1995a. Trade wars and trade talks. *Journal of Political Economy* 103, 675–708.

Grossman, G. and Helpman, E. 1995b. The politics of free trade agreements. *American Economic Review* 85, 667–90.

Grossman, G. and Helpman, E. 2005. A protectionist bias in majoritarian politics. *Quarterly Journal of Economics* 120, 1239–82.

Helpman, E. 2002. Politics and trade policy. In *Interest Groups and Trade Policy*, eds. G. Grossman and E. Helpman. Princeton, NJ: Princeton University Press.

Hillman, A. 1989. *The Political Economy of Protection.* Chur: Harwood Academic Publishers.

Hillman, A. and Moser, P. 1996. Trade liberalization as politically optimal exchange of market access. In *The New Transatlantic Economy*, eds. M. Canzoneri, W. Ethier and V. Grilli. Cambridge: Cambridge University Press.

Hiscox, M. 2001. *International Trade and Political Conflict: Commerce, Coalitions and Mobility.* Princeton, NJ: Princeton University Press.

Hiscox, M. 2002. Commerce, coalitions, and factor mobility: evidence from congressional votes on trade legislation. *American Political Science Review* 96, 593–608.

Johnson, H. 1965. Optimal trade interventions in the presence of domestic distortions. In *Trade Growth and Balance of Payments*, eds. R. Caves, H. Johnson and P. Amsterdam: North-Holland.

Krishna, P. 1998. Regionalism and multilateralism: a political economy approach. *Quarterly Journal of Economics* 113, 227–51.

Krishna, P. and Mitra, D. 2005. Reciprocated unilateralism in trade policy. *Journal of International Economics* 65, 461–87.

Levy, P. 1997. A political-economic analysis of free-trade agreements. *American Economic Review* 87, 506–19.

Magee, C. 2002. Endogenous trade policy and lobby formation: an application to the free-rider problem. *Journal of International Economics* 57, 449–71.

Magee, S., Brock, W. and Young, L. 1989. *Black Hole Tariffs and Endogenous Policy Theory.* Cambridge and New York: Cambridge University Press.

Maggi, G. and Rodriguez-Clare, A. 1998. The value of trade agreements in the presence of political pressures. *Journal of Political Economy* 106, 574–601.

Mansfield, E. and Busch, M. 1995. The political economy of trade barriers: a cross-national analysis. *International Organization* 49, 723–49.

Marvel, H. and Ray, E. 1983. The Kennedy Round: evidence on the regulation of trade in the US. *American Economic Review* 73, 190–7.

Mayer, W. 1984. Endogenous tariff formation. *American Economic Review* 74, 970–85.

Mayer, W. and Riezman, R. 1987. Endogenous choice of trade policy instruments. *Journal of International Economics* 23, 377–81.

Mayer, W. and Riezman, R. 1989. Tariff formation in a multidimensional voting model. *Economics and Politics* 1, 61–79.

Mayer, W. and Riezman, R. 1990. Voter preferences for trade policy instruments. *Economics and Politics* 2, 259–73.

McCalman, P. 2004. Protection for sale and trade liberalization: an empirical investigation. *Review of International Economics* 12, 81–94.

McLaren, J. 2002. A theory of insidious regionalism. *Quarterly Journal of Economics* 117, 571–608.

McLaren, J. 2004. Free trade agreements, customs unions and the dynamics of political influence. Mimeo, University of Virginia.

McLaren, J. and Karabay, B. 2004. Trade policy making by an assembly. In *Political Economy of Trade, Aid and Foreign Investment Policies*, eds. D. Mitra and A. Panagariya. Amsterdam: Elsevier.

Milner, H. and Judkins, B. 2004. Partisanship, Trade policy, and globalization: is there a left–right divide on trade policy? *International Studies Quarterly* 48, 95–119.

Milner, H. and Kubota, K. 2005. Why the move to free trade? Democracy and trade policy in the developing countries. *International Organization* 59, 107–43.

Mitra, D. 1999. Endogenous lobby formation and endogenous protection: a long run model of trade policy determination. *American Economic Review* 89, 1116–34.

Mitra, D. 2000. On the endogenous choice between protection and promotion. *Economics and Politics* 12, 33–52.

Mitra, D. 2002. Endogenous political organization and the value of trade agreements. *Journal of International Economics* 57, 473–85.

Mitra, D., Thomakos, D. and Ulubasoglu, M. 2002. 'Protection for sale' in a developing country: democracy vs. dictatorship. *Review of Economics and Statistics* 84, 497–508.

Panagariya, A. and Findlay, R. 1996. A political-economy analysis of free trade areas and customs union. In *The Political Economy of Trade Reform: Essays in Honor of Jagdish Bhagwati*, eds. R. Feenstra, D. Irvin and G. Grossman. Cambridge, MA: MIT Press.

Pecorino, P. 1998. Is there a free-rider problem in lobbying? Endogenous tariffs, trigger strategies and the number of firms. *American Economic Review* 88, 652–60.

Ray, E. 1981. The determinants of tariff and non-tariff restriction in the United States. *Journal of Political Economy* 89, 105–21.

Ray, E. 1991. Protection of manufactures in the United States. In *Global Protectionism: Is The US Playing on a Level Field?*, ed. D. Greenaway. London: Macmillan.

Richardson, M. 1994. Why a free trade area? The tariff also rises. *Economics and Politics* 6, 79–96.

Rodrik, D. 1986. Tariffs, subsidies and welfare with endogenous policy. *Journal of International Economics* 21, 285–96.

Rodrik, D. 1995. Political economy of trade policy. In *Handbook of International Economics*, Vol. 3, eds. G. Grossman and K. Rogoff. Amsterdam: North-Holland.

Saunders, R. 1980. The political economy of effective protection in Canada's manufacturing sector. *Canadian Journal of Economics* 13, 340–8.

Staiger, R. and Tabellini, G. 1987. Discretionary trade policy and excessive protection. *American Economic Review* 77, 823–37.

Trefler, D. 1993. Trade liberalization and the theory of endogenous protection. *Journal of Political Economy* 101, 138–60.

Van Long, N. and Vousden, N. 1991. Protectionist responses and declining industries. *Journal of International Economics* 30, 87–103.

Wilson, J. 1990. Are efficiency improvements in government transfer policies self defeating in equilibrium? *Economics and Politics* 2, 241–58.

Chapter 14

Unilateralism in Trade Policy: A Survey of Alternative Political-Economy Approaches

PRAVIN KRISHNA[a] and DEVASHISH MITRA[b,*]

[a]*Department of Economics, Brown University, Box B, 64 Waterman Street, Providence, RI 02912, USA*
[b]*Department of Economics, The Maxwell School of Citizenship and Public Affairs, 133 Eggers Hall, Syracuse University, Syracuse, NY 13244, USA*

Abstract

While much of the literature has considered the merits of the two policy stances of unilateralism and reciprocity independently of each other, we focus on the possible causal connection between the two. Can unilateral trade liberalization by one country lead to reciprocal liberalization by its partner in the absence of negotiations between the two countries? In this survey paper, we consider this issue analytically in the context of different political economy approaches to trade policy determination.

Keywords: Trade policy, political economy, lobby formation, unilateralism, reciprocity

JEL classifications: F10, F13, F02

---

*Corresponding author.
  E-mail address:* dmitra@maxwell.syr.edu

198   *P. Krishna and D. Mitra*

9.1. INTRODUCTION

The relative merits of two alternative approaches to progressing towards free trade, unilateralism (I drop my trade barriers) and reciprocity (I drop my trade barriers if you drop your trade barriers), have long been debated in the theoretical literature on trade policy.

The arguments used to support these policy stances are well known. The argument for unilateral trade liberalization has relied on the demonstration that, in the absence of "distortions", free trade is welfare maximizing. Further, even in the presence of a very wide variety of distortions in the system, the merits of a policy of free trade (coupled usually with non-trade interventions) have been decisively established.[1] A policy stance of reciprocity, on the other hand, relies on the large country assumption that leads to directly trade-related distortions in the form of "terms-of-trade" effects with or without political-economy forces in the economy. Thus, for instance, Mayer (1981) shows that in the presence of terms-of-trade motivations for tariffs, international negotiations could lead to a better outcome than the non-cooperative Nash outcome derived earlier by Johnson (1953). Equally, political economy influences have been considered in models explaining agreed-upon reciprocal trade liberalization in the work of Mayer (1984a), Hillman and Moser (1996), and Bagwell and Staiger (1999), among others.[2]

While most of the literature has considered these two approaches to trade liberalization independent of each other, we have, in Krishna and Mitra (2003a,b), studied their possible causal interaction.[3] We have found that unilateral trade liberalization in one country can induce reciprocal liberalization by another country in the *absence of any communication or negotiations* between the two countries. This causal linkage between unilateralism and reciprocity is explored in these two papers in the context of two different models of trade policy determination. The first (the one in Krishna and Mitra (2003a)) is a framework in which trade policy changes are voted upon by voters and where outcomes are determined by the majority (as, for instance, in Fernandez and Rodrik (1991)).[4] In this context, we demonstrate that unilateral trade liberalization by a trading partner increases the electoral support for trade liberalization in the home country.

---

[1] See Johnson (1965) and the classic generalized treatment of Bhagwati (1971).

[2] In this context, see also Grossman and Helpman (1995), where they analyze the merits of "trade talks" over "trade wars" in a two-country, specific-factors setting with lobbying taking place within each country.

[3] See Bhagwati (1990) for an early informal discussion of this idea.

[4] See also Mayer (1984b) for the first median-voter model of trade policy determination, both in Heckscher–Ohlin and specific-factor contexts.

Unilateralism in Trade Policy 199

The second framework (Krishna and Mitra, 2003b) is the popular Grossman and Helpman (1994) model of trade policy determination in which the policy in the home country is assumed to be determined through the interaction between the government and organized lobbies representing economic interests. We augment this with the lobby formation framework of Mitra (1999). In this context too, we show that unilateral liberalization by one country can influence another country to liberalize its trade regime through the formation of an export lobby there.

Coates and Ludema (2001), in an important paper, study the impact of unilateral tariff reduction on negotiation outcomes (specifically the likelihood of success in reaching and ratifying bilateral agreements in the presence of the "political risk" of domestic opposition to trade agreements) and argue that unilateral trade liberalization may be the optimal policy for a large country. In their framework, "unilateral liberalization acts as insurance" by providing a "risk-sharing" role. Unilateral tariff reduction lowers the political stakes associated with trade liberalization in the foreign country, thereby lowering the overall political cost of reaching and implementing trade agreements and increasing the probability of successful agreements. While our own work in this area relies on perfectly non-cooperative interaction between trading partners, Coates and Ludema use a more cooperative setting where negotiations take place between countries.

Whatever the political-economy channel, the possibility that unilateral liberalization induces liberalization by the partner suggests a greater case for a policy stance of unilateralism than is traditionally recognized in the literature. We believe that this result carries important normative implications. Specifically, it challenges the frequently proposed strategy of the use (or the threat of the use) of raising one's trade barriers to remove those of others, for example, the United States' recent use of the "Super-301" provision to retaliate against "unreasonable" trade barriers by raising its own.[5]

The preceding discussion has focused on the possibility of unilateral liberalizations inducing reciprocity in a partner country. While countries may unilaterally liberalize with this end in mind, they may also do it for other reasons. We round out our discussion by briefly considering some political-economy models of endogenous unilateralism (Maggi and Rodriguez-Clare, 1998; Mitra, 2002). While these papers have not focused on the issue of reciprocity by partners,

---

[5] The policy recommendations that follow from this analysis of unilateralism and reciprocity have been elegantly summarized by Bhagwati (2002) as follows (1) "Go alone (that is, cut trade barriers unilaterally) if others will not go with you", (2) "If others go simultaneously with you (i.e., there is reciprocity in reducing trade barriers), that is still better", and finally (3) "If you must go alone, others may follow suit later: unilateralism then leads to sequential reciprocity".

reciprocity of the type we have discussed may follow even in the contexts that they analyze.

The rest of this chapter proceeds as follows. In Section 9.2 we present first a non-technical discussion of political-economy mechanisms driving what we call "reciprocated unilateralism" in trade policy. The first model is a median-voter model, while the second is a Grossman–Helpman lobbying model augmented with lobby formation. We end this section with a brief discussion of the Coates–Ludema model. We then discuss in Section 9.3 some political-economy models which have demonstrated the possibility of endogenous unilateralism. In Section 9.4 we present some concluding observations.

9.2. MODELS OF RECIPROCATED UNILATERALISM

9.2.1. A median-voter model

We, here, provide a very non-technical and abridged version of the analysis in Krishna and Mitra (2003a). Consider an economy with two sectors, M (import competing) and E (exportable). We assume that both goods in this economy are produced under constant-returns to scale using labor alone. However, different individuals have different levels of productivities in the production of the two goods. We assume that prior to the trade reform, there is a positive import tariff in place, which goes down to zero if and when the trade reform is implemented. We also assume that a person works in the sector that pays her a higher wage determined by her productivity. Thus, every individual in the economy has his or her comparative advantage in the production of the export good relative to producing the import-competing good, given by the ratio of the person's productivity in the export sector relative to that in the import-competing sector. This measure of comparative advantage needs to be greater than the relative price of the import-competing good for an individual to decide to work in the export sector. Thus given the relative price of the importable, we can determine who and what fractions of the people will work in the two sectors. In equilibrium, the marginal worker will be indifferent between working in the export and import sectors.

We are unambiguously able to show that individuals who were originally in the exportable sector will benefit from these reforms. All individuals who were originally in the M sector and remain there in the post reform equilibrium are clearly shown to be worse off. Finally, we look at the individuals who were in the import-competing sector prior to the reforms but are in the export sector in the post-reform equilibrium. In other words, these are individuals that end up moving to the relatively more lucrative sector for them after the reforms. Note that given

Unilateralism in Trade Policy   201

the post-reform relative prices, the export sector might be relatively more lucrative but some of these people may be worse off relative to their pre-reform situation in which the domestic relative price was different. After taking this into account, we see how the overall support (the number of people who were originally in the export sector plus the people changing their profession who benefit from these reforms) for reforms responds to the world relative price of imports and to the size of the original tariffs. Not surprisingly, the support for the reform is decreasing in the world relative price of imports as well as the initial tariff. This is intuitive since for given relative productivity and tariff, the potential relative wage of an individual in the import sector (relative to that in the export sector) is increasing in the world relative price of the importable. And so if majority voting is the mechanism through which decision on the reforms is made, it takes place when the world price is below a certain threshold price.

For a small country, the world price, though independent of its own tariff, can depend on and be increasing in the tariff of a large trading partner. Thus, if such a partner country reduces its tariff, the world price of the importable will go down (equivalent to the relative price of the exportable going up) and the support for a trade reform in this partner country will go up. The intuition is that with a lower world relative price of the importable, the relative wage advantage (disadvantage) from working in sector M is lower (higher) for any given initial tariff. This reduces (increases) the attractiveness of being in the import-competing sector without a trade reform.

We next consider the case of two large open economies trading with each other. In this case, the world price will be a function of the tariffs of the two countries, and therefore, a trade reform in the partner country raises support for reforms in the home country. If foreign tariff is very high, the support for reform at home is small and so there is no reform and this country is stuck at the intial tariff as reforms cannot take place. For a foreign tariff below a critical level, there is majority support for the reform and the home tariff goes down to zero. Analogously, for a home tariff below a critical level, there is majority foreign support for a reform in their country and the foreign tariff goes down to zero. Thus, there is the possibility of multiple equilibria—either both countries liberalize or both countries remain stuck at their respective initial tariffs. Therefore, a dictator or an international organization forcing reform in one country can, indirectly (through majority voting), bring about a reform in the partner country. This situation can then become a new equilibrium consistent with majority voting in both countries.

The above analysis is also generalizable to the case with endogenous tariff levels and to the introduction of individual-specific uncertainty of the type analyzed in Fernandez and Rodrik (1991). The results described above remain qualitatively unchanged.

202   *P. Krishna and D. Mitra*

9.2.2. A model with trade policy lobbying and endogenous lobby formation

The development here follows Krishna and Mitra (2003b) very closely but the presentation is much more non-technical. Consider a small open home economy, exactly as in Grossman and Helpman (1994), producing a numeraire good using labor with Ricardian technology and two non-numeraire goods (an import-competing and an exportable good), each requiring a different kind of factor of production specific to that good and labor for their production. Individuals in this economy are assumed to have identical preferences represented by utility functions linear in the consumption of the numeraire good, strictly concave in the consumption of each of the other two goods and additively separable in the consumption of all three goods.

First, we assume that each individual in the economy is endowed with exactly *l* units of labor. Further, we assume that each individual owns only *one* type of specific factor and that owners of any particular type of specific factor are symmetric (that is, they own identical amounts of that specific factor).

For given lobbies, the trade policy vector is exactly the same as in Grossman and Helpman (1994). When only the import-competing sector is organized, there is an import tariff in place for this sector and there is an export tax on the other non-numeraire sector. Given our assumptions above (in particular that the assumption that the fraction of the population owing either specific factor sums to one), it is well known that the Grossman–Helpman trade tax vector would equal the zero vector if *both* sectors were organized.

In what follows, we examine incentives for the export sector to get organized in the presence of an already organized import-competing sector—for such an outcome would take this economy from its initially distorted position to one of free trade. In this context, members of the exportable group decide whether to form a lobby or remain unorganized. To form the lobby, they face a fixed labor cost. Nash interaction among group members is assumed in their contribution decisions towards the provision of the fixed labor cost of lobby formation. However, once the lobby is formed, it is assumed here that the lobby machinery can enforce perfect coordination among the members of that group in the collection of political contributions, i.e., given the symmetry of capital ownership by members within a group, the lobby machinery can enforce collection of equal amounts of political contributions from each capitalist in the sector.

Now, depending upon the magnitude of the fixed costs relative to the benefits of lobby formation, there are three possibilities:

(1) The benefit to any one individual within the exportable lobby exceeds the cost of forming the lobby. Here, contributing to the full financing of the fixed

Unilateralism in Trade Policy 203

cost F is the only Nash equilibrium outcome among the group members, i.e., a lobby is always formed.

(2) Alternately, the cost of lobby formation exceeds the benefit to any one individual but is less than the total benefit to the lobby. In this situation, there are two possible Nash equilibrium outcomes—either there is no contribution to the provision of the lobby or the fixed cost is fully financed. We assume that pre-play communication can take place. For example, when capitalists in an industry feel that they are going to benefit from forming a lobby, they start communicating with each other—write letters, make phone calls, etc. Hence, one can use some popular communication based refinements here. The better equilibrium for the group (i.e., the lobby is formed) satisfies the conditions for the three popular communication based refinements—coalition-proof Nash, strong Nash and the Pareto-dominance refinement and hence, group coordination becomes the likely equilibrium outcome.

(3) The cost of forming the lobby exceeds the benefit of lobby formation to the group. Here, the Nash equilibrium outcome is obviously "not providing the lobby".

From the analysis of the above three cases, the conclusion that emerges is that a lobby is formed when the total benefit exceeds the total fixed costs. Having described the initial equilibrium that we focus on and having derived conditions under which an (initially non-existent) export lobby may be formed, we proceed to analyze the impact of unilateral trade reform on this initial equilibrium.

We are interested in how a unilateral tariff reduction by a large partner country (leading to an improvement in the export price faced by the "small" home country) may affect the initial equilibrium. In particular we are interested in how this may affect the equilibrium structure of lobbies and finally on the equilibrium structure of tariffs.

With truthful contributions, as in Grossman and Helpman (1994), any lobby when formed will have to pay the government an amount that makes it indifferent between treating that lobby as organized and treating it as unorganized, given the contribution schedules of the other lobbies. As argued in Krishna and Mitra (2003b), the export lobby should compensate the government for the reduction in the import lobby's welfare due to its entry and for changes in overall social welfare. Netting out these contributions in the calculation of the benefit from being organized, we are able to show that with a pre-existing import competing lobby, the net benefit to the exporting sector from the formation of an export lobby (gross of fixed costs) is proportional to the sum of the deadweight losses created (relative to the free trade level) in the importable and the exportable sectors by the equilibrium trade policies that result when only the import competing sector is organized. The constant of proportionality here is increasing in the government's weight on welfare.

Let us now analyze the effect of the large partner country's tariff liberalization, that raises the world price of home's exportable, on the structure of lobbies in the home country. It needs to be noted first that we are able to show that a higher world price of the exportable leads to a higher per unit (specific) export tax in equilibrium when only the import-competing sector is organized. This is because with a higher world price of the exportable, the gains from a given tax are higher to the import lobby as consumers of the export good and as recipients of a fixed share of the export tax revenues. Therefore, the first component of the effect of the partner's tariff liberalization is the change in the deadweight loss in the exportable sector due to an increase in the absolute value of the tax. It is straightforward to see that this effect is positive. The second component is the change in the absolute value of the export tax for a given change in international export prices. We know that this is positive as well. The first two effects are multiplicative, and therefore, the resultant is positive. As we show in Krishna and Mitra (2003b), the third component, which is just the effect of a higher world exportable price on the deadweight loss at a given per-unit export tax, is also positive under the most empirically plausible conditions on the curvature of the export supply function.

Thus, we establish our primary result that unilateral liberalization by a large partner country within this framework will induce reciprocal liberalization. Profiles of the net benefit from lobby formation and the per unit trade taxes as functions of the world exportable price p^* are illustrated in Figure 9.1. As can be easily seen, once we have $p^* \geq \bar{p}$, we have free trade. It is also useful to interpret the political-economy mechanism just stated in terms of how the welfare level of the exportable group varies with the world price of the exportable differently when this group is organized than when it is not. Figure 9.2 illustrates that an increase in the world price of the exportable increases welfare of the exportable group whether it is organized or unorganized. Thus, the welfare levels are shown with positive slopes. Note that the welfare level of the exportable group when organized (net of political contributions but gross of the fixed cost of lobby formation) is higher than when it is not organized. Note also that the net benefit NB (net of contributions but gross of fixed costs) from forming a lobby is increasing in p^* implies that the welfare locus when unorganized has flatter slope—implying, in turn, with large enough fixed costs, some point of intersection with the welfare locus when organized (net of both fixed costs and political contributions). The price at which this takes place is, again, $\bar{p}$. Beyond this price, the lobby is formed. Below it, it does not.

How might the large country benefit from such a political-economy dynamic? Clearly, the (induced) movement of any single small country to free trade does not

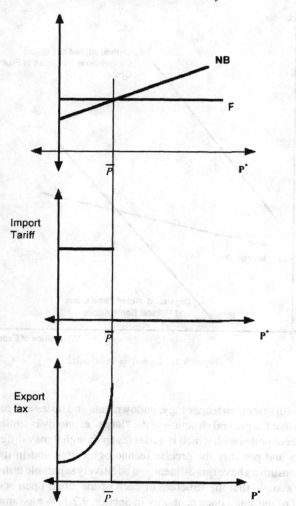

Figure 9.1:   Net benefits from lobby formation and trade taxes vs. world exportable price.

affect world prices and its liberalization of its trade regime is of little consequence to the large country. We, therefore, analyze here circumstances under which the large country may nevertheless benefit from the induced reciprocity in its small trading partners. Specifically, we now consider a large open economy trading with a continuum of small open economies. These small open economies are identical to

206   *P. Krishna and D. Mitra*

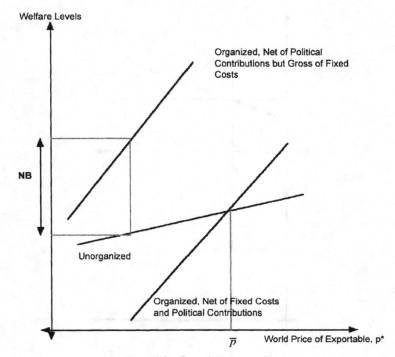

Figure 9.2:   Incentives to organize.

each other with respect to technology, endowments and tastes and preferences. We assume also that the general structure of the "large" economy is similar to that of the small open economies with which it trades (even though it may differ from them in endowments and possibly the precise technologies used and in its exact preferences): its consumers have quasi-linear and additively separable utility as described before. We assume that the structure of each of the small open economies is the same as that of the small open economy in Section 9.2.1. We assume that the large country exogenously cuts (sets) its import tariff and in each of the small open economies, trade policy is set using political economy considerations as in Grossman and Helpman (1994). From this analysis of a large country facing a large number of small countries, we obtain the following two main results:

(a) For large enough reductions in tariffs by the large country, reciprocal liberalization by the small open economies is likely.

(b) The large country's optimal (i.e., welfare-maximizing) tariff is smaller when it takes into account its effect on the incentives for lobby formation in its partner countries than when it takes the lobby structure in the partner countries as given.

Thus far, the argument has been developed in the context of a small trading partner whose trade policy has been distorted due the *exclusive* initial presence of an import-competing lobby. We next analyze the issue under other different initial conditions:

(1) No lobbies are present in the small country initially.
(2) An export lobby rather than an import lobby is initially present.

In fact, we endogenize the initial conditions to the initial fixed costs, factor endowments and world relative price. Therefore, at every point in time, which lobby (lobbies) is (are) organized will be determined completely endogenously.

From our simulations, we now describe our findings pertaining to two important cases. In our first case, for low values of the export price, we have a unique equilibrium with just the import-competing sector organized. As the export price rises, this initially continues to be the unique equilibrium. After p^* rises even further the export lobby gets formed and the unique equilibrium here involves the formation of both lobbies (with free trade as the equilibrium trade policy) since the net benefit from lobby formation make political organization feasible for both sectors, each taking the other as organized. This scenario is consistent with what we have focused on so far and illustrates our main argument. Note, however, that if fixed costs were a bit higher in the import-competing sector, at low values of p^*, the import-competing sector (as well as the exportable sector) would not be organized. If this were the initial condition, a reduction in tariffs by the large country would now induce the import-competing lobby to form first—a change in economic circumstances that would be welfare decreasing since agents in the small economy will have moved from an efficient trade regime (with free trade) to an inefficient one having incurred additionally the fixed costs of lobby formation. This may appear damaging to the argument regarding the use of unilateralism to induce reciprocity, but this is not the case since, of course, the argument is conditional on some tariffs being imposed by the partner country in the first place. Also, with further tariff reductions (i.e., increases in the world price, p^*), the export lobby gets formed and we have free trade. Thus, with high enough tariff reductions by the large country, free trade obtains in the partner country (even if the path to this is non-monotonic and fixed costs of lobby organization have been incurred along the way).

Next, fixed costs of lobby organization for the export sector are assumed to be lower than that in the importable sector. At low levels of p^*, it is now the export lobby that is organized while the import lobby is not. Trade policy is initially distorted with export and import subsidies, an empirically nearly irrelevant case but a clear theoretical possibility. Here, too, a high enough increase in the world price of the exportable results in the formation of the import lobby with free trade emerging as the policy outcome. While such an outcome would benefit the small country (if the welfare gain from the move to the undistorted policy regime outweighed the fixed costs of lobby formation), the large country would be faced with a policy regime less favorable to it.

9.2.3. A model of leadership in trade policy negotiations

Almost every model of endogenous protection, while trying to incorporate certain aspects of reality abstracts from others. Coates and Ludema argue that firstly, "the trade policy process involves many political actors, none of whom completely controls the outcome". Secondly, they believe that "actions taken by political actors inside a country may be unobservable to outsiders." Incorporating these "real-world complications", while taking a black-box approach to lobbying (relative to the Grossman–Helpman framework), they look at a set up where one large country (the leader) proposes to its partner a pair of tariffs (its own and its partner's). The partner then decides whether to accept or reject the proposal. If the proposal is rejected by the partner, the two countries go back to their initial tariffs. If the proposal is accepted by the partner country, it is sent for political ratification within the country. The import competing sector in the partner country can lobby to reduce the likelihood of ratification. If the ratification does not take place, the large country unilaterally sets its tariff and negotiations start once again.

Coates and Ludema show that lowering this unilateral tariff makes the proposal of a given reciprocal tariff reduction more attractive to the partner country and at the same time increases the probability of ratification. The higher attractiveness of the proposal to the partner country government comes from the lower risk associated with ratification success or failure in the sense that with a low tariff set unilaterally by the large country the worse of the two outcomes is also not that bad. This, effectively, is a situation of risk sharing between the two countries. The lower probability of ratification failure arises from the fact that a lower unilateral tariff by the large country means a lower relative price for the import-competing good (a higher relative price for the exportable good) of the partner country for any given tariff set by it, thereby making the protection situation relatively less attractive to the import-competing lobby than before. In turn this will lead to less intense lobbying by it against ratification.

Unilateralism in Trade Policy   209

Thus, the equilibrium outcome in this model is one in which the large country unilaterally liberalizes to increase the probability of reciprocation by its partner.

9.3. MODELS OF ENDOGENOUS UNILATERALISM

9.3.1. Unilateral commitment to free trade as a means of preventing capital misallocation

Maggi and Rodriguez-Clare (1998) have an elegant and interesting political economy explanation for the unilateral commitment to free trade agreements by small countries. They formalize the frequently heard argument that free trade agreements "provide a way for the government to credibly distance itself from the domestic special-interest groups that lobby for protection". More specifically, "the idea is that, by committing to free trade, a government may be able to foreclose political pressures at home".

The setting in Maggi and Rodriguez-Clare is one in which owners of capital first decide in which sector to invest and then those who invest in a particular sector (the import-competing sector) lobby the government for protection. The lobbying is modeled as a Nash bargaining game between the import-competing lobby and the government over tariffs and political contributions. The lobby ends up at least compensating the government for the deadweight losses purely generated in the second stage. However, it may not compensate the government for the welfare loss through the intersectoral misallocation of capital in the first stage in the expectation of protection in the second stage. In such a situation, it is possible that a government may exercise its option, if available, of committing to a free trade agreement in a prior (to stage one) stage zero. Such a situation is one in which, in the absence of the agreement, the welfare loss from the resource misallocation in the first stage is valued more by the government than its gain from sharing the redistributed surplus in the second stage.

9.3.2. Unilateral commitment to free trade as a means of preventing wasteful political (organizational) activity

The Maggi–Rodriguez-Clare framework demands a government with a long enough horizon as intersectoral capital mobility is a fairly long-run phenomenon. Such an assumption is perfectly valid when the focus is on developed countries that have stable governments. However, in the recent past, quite a few developing countries have joined or have expressed a desire to join the GATT/WTO. In such countries, governments are generally weak and often do not last long. In such

The Political Economy of Trade Policy

P. Krishna and D. Mitra

situations, they could hardly be expected to care about long-term problems such as capital misallocation and thus capital mobility may not be an aspect one would like to focus on. With the frequent entry and exit of parties into and from power, lobbies need to constantly incur costs build new relationships.

In this context, Mitra (2002) builds on the Maggi–Rodriguez-Clare version of the Grossman–Helpman framework, augmenting it with the decision to incur fixed costs (build relationships with politicians in power and/or to form a lobby) prior to the actual lobbying, but, importantly, not providing room for any capital-mobility. However, the main result of the Maggi–Rodriguez-Clare model goes through even in this newly modified set up. This is the result that generally governments with low bargaining power with respect to domestic lobbies are the ones that want to precommit to free trade agreements.

Thus, there is a general point to be made here, which is that the precommitment to a free trade agreement does not have to be driven specifically by the possibility of capital misallocation alone (or solely by the possible incurring of organizational costs) arising in the expectation of protection. It is applicable to any kind of resource costs (including, for example, costs of political organization) incurred prior to lobbying through actions taken in the expectation of successful lobbying in the next stage. In this respect, the paper by Mitra and the one by Maggi and Rodriguez-Clare are complementary.

9.4. CONCLUDING REMARKS: THE CURRENT STATE OF THE LITERATURE AND ISSUES FOR FUTURE RESEARCH

The debate over the merits of unilateralism versus reciprocity is a long standing one. Of special interest to us is the role of unilateralism in trade policy in inducing reciprocity from trading partners. While much of the literature has considered the merits of the two policy stances of unilateralism and reciprocity independently of each other, we focus on the possible *causal* connection between the two. Can unilateral trade liberalization by one country lead to reciprocal liberalization by its partner in the absence of negotiations between the two countries? Krishna and Mitra (2003a,b) have considered this issue analytically in the context of *two* separate political economy models of trade policy determination. While one is based on majority voting, the other is based on lobbying through political contributions to the incumbent government when the formation of lobbies is endogenous. In this survey chapter, we provide a non-technical, descriptive and intuitive treatment of these two models.

While the aspects of voting and lobbying are rigorously modeled with full microfoundations in our two papers, Coates and Ludema, by usefully abstracting

Unilateralism in Trade Policy 211

from the microfoundations of lobbying, focus on other real-world complications of the political process. They incorporate aspects like leadership in negotiations, domestic political ratification of international agreements and the imperfect observability of the political process in foreign countries into their analysis. They also predict a "reciprocated unilateralism" in their setting which is considerably more "cooperative" than those we considered. Given that the real world is a combination of cooperative and non-cooperative interactions, we believe that our research and that of Coates and Ludema are complementary.

In addition to examining the scope for unilateral policies to induce reciprocity in partner countries, we have also covered briefly the analysis provided in the literature (by Maggi and Rodriguez-Clare (1998) and then by Mitra (2002)) of other contexts in which unilateral trade liberalization may be undertaken. It goes without saying that reciprocity by partners of the sort we have discussed may follow even in these contexts.

Finally, given the current state of the literature on unilateral trade liberalization, what do we think are the open questions and issues for future research in this area? In our work in Krishna and Mitra (2003b) as well as in Coates and Ludema, the political economy of the unilaterally liberalizing country has not been rigorously modeled. What is fully modeled is the political economy response of the reciprocating country. The final step in understanding "reciprocated unilateralism" has to be the construction of a completely closed model with the full modeling of political economy forces in both countries. In fact, our median-voter model in Krishna and Mitra (2003a) is completely closed and free of black boxes, even though some would consider a majority-voting-based story to be less realistic than one based on lobbying.

The focus of this chapter has been on unilateralism. We look at what the trade literature, especially the strand that employs political economy models, has to say about the desirability and feasibility of unilateral trade liberalization. While classical trade theory clearly has a lot to say about desirability, the feasibility issue has been studied in some detail by Maggi and Rodriguez-Clare (1998) and then by Mitra (2002).

Another issue for future research are the reasons behind the recent unilateral trade reforms by many countries. While there is a large and sophisticated literature trying to explain the existence of protection, there is no satisfactory work on why it is disappearing. Models need to map the actual changing conditions in liberalizing countries to key assumptions in models to generate an equilibrium outcome of trade liberalization.

Finally, we also need to investigate why unilateral reforms take place in stages and why there are so many rounds of tariff cuts. A model of learning in which information gets uncovered over time might be promising. Also, reforms in stages might be a way of working around domestic political constraints.

212   P. Krishna and D. Mitra

REFERENCES

Bagwell, K. and Staiger, R. (1999). An economic theory of GATT. *American Economic Review*, 89, 215–248.

Bhagwati, J. (1971). "The generalized theory of distortions and welfare," in *Trade Balance of Payments and Growth: Papers in International Economics in Honor of Charles Kindleberger*, J. N. Bhagwati, R. W. Jones, R. A. Mundell and J. Vanek (eds.), Amsterdam: North-Holland.

Bhagwati, J. (1990). "Aggressive unilateralism," in *Aggressive Unilateralism*, J. Bhagwati and H. Patrick (eds.), Ann Arbor, MI: University of Michigan Press.

Bhagwati, J. (2002). *Free Trade Today*, Princeton, NJ: Princeton University Press.

Coates, D. and Ludema, R. (2001). A theory of trade policy leadership. *Journal of Development Economics*, 65(1), 1–29.

Fernandez, R. and Rodrik, D. (1991). Resistance to reform: status-quo bias in the presence of individual-specific uncertainty. *American Economic Review*, 81(5), 1146–1154.

Grossman, G. and Helpman, E. (1994). Protection for sale. *American Economic Review*, 84, 833–850.

Grossman, G. and Helpman, E. (1995). Trade wars and trade talks. *Journal of Political Economy*, 103, 675–708.

Hillman, A. and Moser, P. (1996). "Trade liberalization as politically optimal exchange of market access," in *The New Transatlantic Economy*, M. B. Canzoneri, V. Grilli and W. J. Ethier (eds.), Cambridge, UK: Cambridge University Press, 295–316.

Johnson, H. (1953). Optimum tariffs and retaliation. *Review of Economic Studies*, 21, 142–153.

Johnson, H. G. (1965). "Optimal trade intervention in the presence of domestic distortions," in *Trade, Growth and the Balance of Payments*, Caves, Johnson and Kenen (eds.).

Krishna, P. and Mitra, D. (2003a). Reciprocated unilateralism: a median-voter approach, mimeo, Brown University and Syracuse University.

Krishna, P. and Mitra, D. (2003b). Reciprocated unilateralism in trade policy. *Journal of International Economics*, in preparation.

Maggi, G. and Rodriguez-Clare, A. (1998). The value of trade agreements in the presence of political pressures. *Journal of Political Economy*, 106(3), 574–601.

Mayer, W. (1981). Theoretical considerations on negotiated tariff adjustments. *Oxford Economic Papers*, 33, 135–143.

Mayer, W. (1984a). The political economy of tariff agreements. *Schriften des Vereins fur Socialpolitik*, 148, 423–437.

Mayer, W. (1984b). Endogenous tariff formation. *American Economic Review*.

Mitra, D. (1999). Endogenous lobby formation and endogenous protection: a long run model of trade policy determination. *American Economic Review*.

Mitra, D. (2002). Endogenous political organization and the value of trade agreements. *Journal of International Economics*, 57, 473–485.

Index

Note: Pages numbers followed by "n" refer to notes.

271

Printed in the United States
By Bookmasters